CONTROL AND DYNAMIC SYSTEMS

Advances in Theory and Applications

Volume 20

CONTRIBUTORS TO THIS VOLUME

EDWARD M. DUIVEN
BERNARD FRIEDLAND
VOLKMAR HELD
JAMES R. HUDDLE
JOSEPH F. KASPER, JR.
W. LECHNER
DAVID F. LIANG
PETER S. MAYBECK
CHARLES L. MEDLER

CONTROL AND DYNAMIC SYSTEMS

ADVANCES IN THEORY AND APPLICATIONS

Edited by
C. T. LEONDES

School of Engineering and Applied Science
University of California
Los Angeles, California

VOLUME 20: NONLINEAR AND KALMAN FILTERING TECHNIQUES
Part 2 of 3

1983

ACADEMIC PRESS
A Subsidiary of Harcourt Brace Jovanovich, Publishers

New York London
Paris San Diego San Francisco São Paulo Sydney Tokyo Toronto

ACADEMIC PRESS RAPID MANUSCRIPT REPRODUCTION

ACADEMIC PRESS, INC.
111 Fifth Avenue, New York, New York 10003

United Kingdom Edition published by
ACADEMIC PRESS, INC. (LONDON) LTD.
24/28 Oval Road, London NW1 7DX

LIBRARY OF CONGRESS CATALOG CARD NUMBER: 64-8027

ISBN 0-12-012720-2

PRINTED IN THE UNITED STATES OF AMERICA

83 84 85 86 9 8 7 6 5 4 3 2 1

CONTENTS

Advanced Applications of Kalman Filters and Nonlinear Estimators in Aerospace Systems

Peter S. Maybeck

Application of Model Switching and Adaptive Kalman Filtering for Aided Strapdown Navigation Systems

W. Lechner

Use of Filtering and Smoothing Algorithms in the Analysis of Missile-System Test Data

Edward M. Duiven, Charles L. Medler, and Joseph F. Kasper, Jr.

Inertial Navigation System Error Model Considerations in Kalman Filter Applications

James R. Huddle

Comparisons of Nonlinear Recursive Filters for Systems with Nonnegligible Nonlinearities

David F. Liang

CONTRIBUTORS

Numbers in parentheses indicate the pages on which the authors' contributions begin.

Edward M. Duiven (185), *The Analytic Sciences Corporation, One Jacob Way, Reading, Massachusetts 01867*

Bernard Friedland (1), *Singer Aerospace and Marine Systems, Kearfott Division, Little Falls, New Jersey 07424*

Volkmar Held (47), *Elektronik-System-Gesellschaft mbH, 8000 Munchen 80, West Germany*

James R. Huddle (293), *Litton Guidance and Control Systems, Woodland Hills, California 91365*

Joseph F. Kasper, Jr. (185), *The Analytic Sciences Corporation, One Jacob Way, Reading, Massachusetts 01867*

W. Lechner (155), *DFVLR, Institut für Flugführung, 3300 Braunschweig, West Germany*

David F. Liang (341), *Defence Research Establishment Ottawa, Department of National Defence, Shirley's Bay, Ottawa, Canada*

Peter S. Maybeck (67), *Department of Electrical Engineering, Air Force Institute of Technology, Wright-Patterson AFB, Ohio 45433*

Charles L. Medler (185), *The Analytic Sciences Corporation, One Jacob Way, Reading, Massachusetts 01867*

PREFACE

In the series *Control and Dynamic Systems* this is the second volume of a trilogy whose theme is advances in the techniques and technology of the application of nonlinear filters and Kalman filters. These three volumes comprise a modern and rather extensive treatment of the basic theoretical techniques, a unique treatment of the computational issues, and a selection of substantive examples of the techniques and technology of the application of nonlinear filters and Kalman filters.

In this volume the first two chapters complete the second part on issues in computational techniques and the remaining five chapters deal with very substantial examples of applications of these filters. A volume devoted to a number of additional applications completes the trilogy.

The first contribution in this volume, ''Separated-Bias Estimation and Some Applications,'' by Bernard Friedland, the man perhaps most notably identified with this area, develops the techniques in this area of major applied importance and its numerous significant applications, not the least of which is failure detection and estimation. In preparing this chapter Friedland solicited the assistance of many of the leading contributors in this area on the international scene. The next chapter, by Volkmar Held, is a rather comprehensive treatment of techniques for determining the descriptive parameters of the stochastic inputs to filters. This is an absolutely essential starting point for the development of filters and yet is taken for granted or glossed over in many treatments of the subject. Held has done a superb job of treating many techniques and issues in this area. This chapter on computational techniques and issues completes the second part of the trilogy.

The next chapter in this volume on techniques and issues in applications begins the third part of the trilogy. This chapter, by Peter Maybeck, one of the leading figures on the international scene in this area, presents a number of significant issues in advanced applications in aerospace systems.

Aided strapdown navigation systems are a relatively recent and most important technology development. Hence it is essential to have such a contribution in this trilogy, and W. Lechner has provided an excellent treatment of the techniques and issues in this area.

It is also essential in a unique trilogy such as this to examine the techniques and analysis of filtering of systems test data. E. M. Duiven, C. L. Medler, and J. F. Kasper, Jr., do this in the next chapter.

In the next chapter, by J. R. Huddle, one of the first major application areas of Kalman filters in the mid 1960s was to inertial navigation systems; and Huddle has provided a modern and comprehensive treatment of this major application area.

The volume concludes with a unique chapter by Liang comparing various non-linear filters.

The excellent contributions to this volume make it a uniquely valuable source reference, which practitioners will find useful for years to come.

CONTENTS OF PREVIOUS VOLUMES

Volume 4

Volume 5

Volume 6

Volume 16

Volume 17

Volume 18

Separated-Bias Estimation and Some Applications

BERNARD FRIEDLAND

The Singer Company, Kearfott Division
Little Falls, New Jersey

I. INTRODUCTION

The recursive filtering theory of Kalman and Bucy [1,2] has greatly influenced system science since World War II. The theoretical significance and practical utility of this work became widely recognized within a few short years of its advent in the early 1960s. Dozens of papers soon appeared which presented alternative derivations and interpretations

ISBN 0-12-012720-2

and demonstrated potential applications in various fields -- most notably aerospace but also in industrial process control and even in the field of econometrics.

All this activity quickly made the benefits of Kalman-Bucy filtering evident to a wide audience, and it exposed some of the limitations not at first obvious. One such limitation was the tendency of the calculated quantities (particularly the "covariance matrix") to become ill-conditioned, with the elapse of time, in processes of large dimension. (Considerable research has been devoted to general methods of improving the numerical conditioning of the required calculations, and although it continues to the present, this general subject is beyond the scope of this article.)

Even when ill-conditioning did not cause serious problems, the implementation of the Kalman filter in many instances created a severe burden for the typical airborne computer of the early 1960s and motivated a quest for ways of reducing the computational requirements, even at the expense of a sacrifice in the theoretically attainable performance.

The problems of computer loading and prospective ill-conditioning had to be faced in one of the early proposed applications of Kalman filtering: mixing navigational aid data in aided-inertial navigation systems. In this application [3], most of the variables to be estimated are constants (biases, drift rates, scale-factor errors, misalignment angles, etc.). The customary treatment of these unknown constants as state variables results in state vectors of large dimension. To reduce the complexity of the filter, and thereby to alleviate the computational burden and to minimize the possibility of ill-conditioning, around 1969 we reasoned that it should be possible to exploit the fact that many, if not most, of the state variables are constants. We initiated an analysis which culminated in our paper [4] in which the estimation of the constant or "bias" parameters was separated from the estimation of the dynamic state variables.

We showed that it is possible to obtain an optimum estimate $\hat{x}$ of the dynamic state by using a filter having the structure shown in Fig. 1 and consisting of a bias-free state estimator, a bias estimator, and a bias-correction matrix V. Mathematically, the optimum state estimate $\hat{x}$ is the sum of the bias-free state estimate $\bar{x}$ and a correction term $V\hat{b}$, where $\hat{b}$ is the optimum estimate of the bias, i.e.,

$$\hat{x} = \bar{x} + V\hat{b}. \tag{1}$$

The bias-free state estimate $\bar{x}$ is obtained by processing the observations in a Kalman filter designed under the assumption that the bias vector b is identically zero. In the standard implementation of the bias-free filter, the difference

$$\bar{r} = y - \bar{y} \tag{2}$$

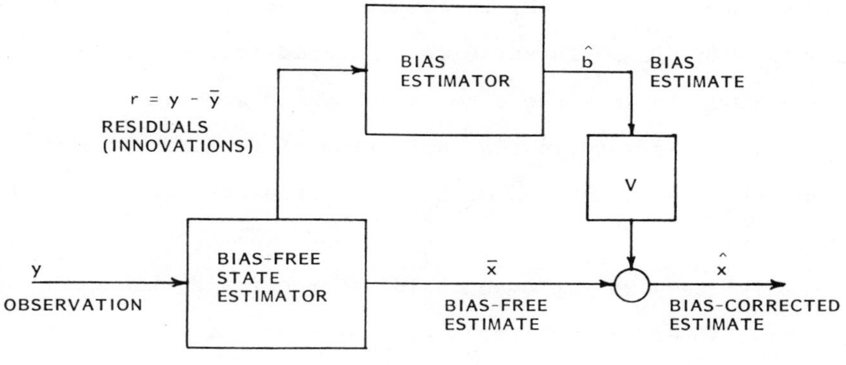

Fig. 1. Schematic representation of separated-bias estimation.

between the actual observation and the estimate thereof is produced. This difference signal known as the "residual" or nowadays by the more popular term "innovation" is the input to a second filter which can be called the "bias estimator" because its output is the optimum estimate $\hat{b}$ of the unknown bias vector b. The bias estimate $\hat{b}$ multiplied by the correction matrix V is finally added to $\bar{x}$ in accordance with Eq. (1) to yield the desired optimum state estimate.

We anticipated that the bias-separated filter implementation would require fewer numerical operations than the augmented-state implementation. This was theoretically verified in general by Samant and Sorenson [5] and in a specific application by Duffy [6,7].

Another advantage of the bias-separated implementation is to avoid numerical ill-conditioning when caused by state vectors of large dimension. In the augmented-state implementation the overall process is of the order N + K, where N is the number of dynamic state variables (i.e., the dimension of x), K the number of biases (the dimension of b), and the N + K variables are all coupled, in the filter and in the covariance matrix propagation. In the bias-separated implementation, the maximum dimension one needs to be concerned with is the larger of N or K, and errors in the estimation of the bias do not contaminate the estimation of the bias-free estimate $\bar{x}$ of the dynamic state.

The strategy we employed in 1969 for deriving the bias-separated filter was motivated by a similar strategy we had then been using in our study of quasi-optimum control. Investigators unfamiliar with that technique found that the results lacked motivation. Several authors (Agee and Turner [8], Mendel and Washburn [9,10], and Bierman [11]) have contributed to the correction of this deficiency by providing alternative derivations and interpretations.

The bias-free residuals (or innovations) occurred naturally in the derivation of [4], but their significance was not fully appreciated at the time: the interpretations resulting from the work of Kailath and Frost [12,13] exemplify one of the applications that can be made of the residuals of a Kalman filter. Failure detection and diagnosis [14] exemplify another application that can be made of the residuals. We shall subsequently return to this application.

II. REVIEW OF THEORY

It was stated earlier that the bias-separated structure of Fig. 1 can be derived in a number of different ways. Since new methods of derivation can afford new insights, we offer here still another derivation based on the theory of linear observers. Since the latter theory does not depend on properties of stochastic processes, the derivation shows that the structural properties of the separated-bias estimation algorithm transcends the stochastic process underpinnings. This derivation is similar to one used by Earhart and Cavin [15] in 1972, in connection with observers for systems in tandem.

For simplicity we consider only a continuous-time process

$$\dot{x} = Ax + Bb + u, \tag{3}$$

with observations given by

$$y = Cx + Db + v, \tag{4}$$

where b is a constant (but unknown) vector (called the "bias") and u and v are white-noise processes having known spectral density matrices Q and R, respectively. The matrices in Eqs. (3) and (4) and the spectral density matrices may all be functions of time with no loss in generality. In the following development, however, we assume that these matrices are constant.

In accordance with well-known theory [16], an observer for the process of Eqs. (3) and (4) is defined by

$$\dot{\hat{x}} = A\hat{x} + B\hat{b} + K_x(y - C\hat{x} - D\hat{b}), \tag{5}$$

$$\dot{\hat{b}} = K_b(y - C\hat{x} - D\hat{b}). \tag{6}$$

These relations are depicted in Fig. 2a. The gain matrix

$$K = \begin{bmatrix} K_x \\ K_b \end{bmatrix} \tag{7}$$

is chosen to make the observer asymptotically stable. If the gain matrix is chosen optimally, the observer [Eqs. (5) and (6)] is the Kalman filter; otherwise the observer has only the property that the error

$$e = \begin{bmatrix} x - \hat{x} \\ b - \hat{b} \end{bmatrix}$$

tends asymptotically to zero.

Now consider the possibility of expressing the observer [Eqs. (5) and (6)] in the bias-separated form shown in Fig. 2b, i.e.,

$$\hat{x} = \bar{x} + V\hat{b}, \tag{8}$$

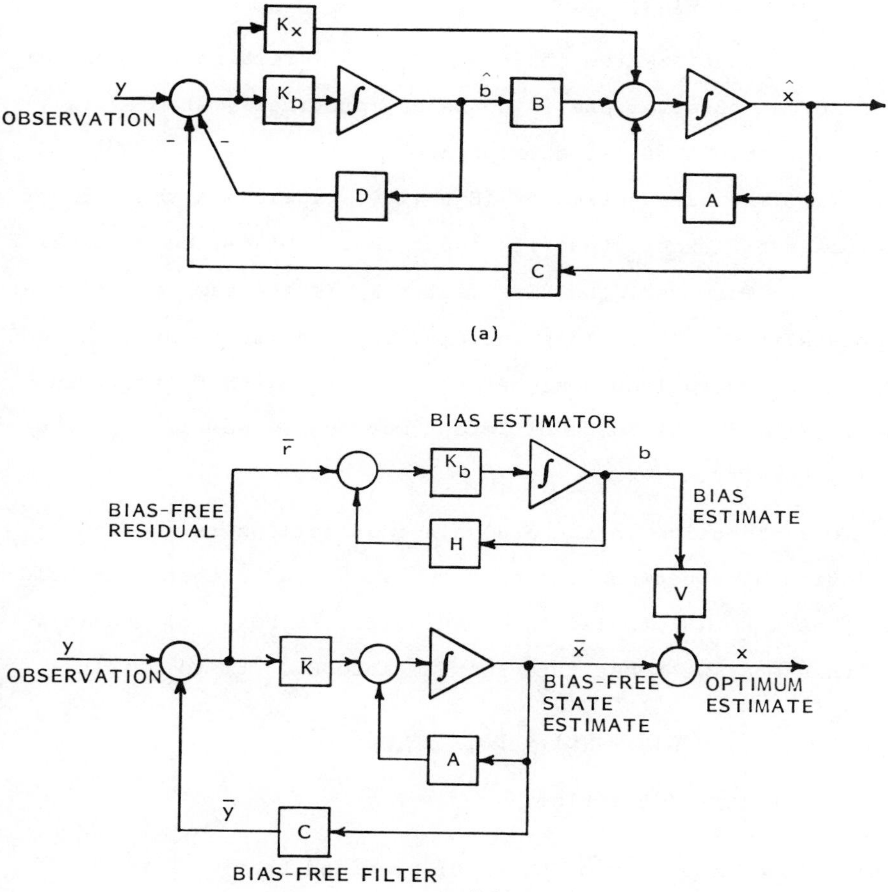

Fig. 2. Two forms of observers for linear systems with bias: (a) augmented-state filter; (b) bias-separated filter.

where $\bar{x}$ is the state of the bias-free observer given by

$$\dot{\bar{x}} = A\bar{x} + K\bar{r}, \tag{9}$$

and $\hat{b}$ is the bias estimate given by

$$\dot{\hat{b}} = K_b(\bar{r} - H\hat{b}), \tag{10}$$

where $\bar{r}$ is the bias-free residual given by

$$\bar{r} = y - C\bar{x}. \tag{11}$$

Note the following:

(1) The bias-free observer [Eq. (9)] retains the general form of an observer and is hence asymptotically stable if $\bar{K}$, as yet unspecified, is appropriately chosen.

(2) The bias estimator [Eq. (10)] is also in the form of an observer, except that its input is the bias-free residual $\bar{r}$ (not y). Moreover, the bias filter K_b is the same matrix that appears in Eq. (6). In principle, the results to be obtained could be generalized somewhat by permitting the K_b terms in Eqs. (6) and (10) to be different matrices. We shall not do this, however.

Our objective in the analysis that follows is to find relationships between the matrices V, $\bar{K}$, and H that must hold so that Eqs. (8) to (11) are equivalent to Eqs. (5) and (6). To this end, we substitute Eq. (8) into Eq. (6) to obtain

$$\begin{aligned}\dot{\hat{b}} &= K_b[y - C(\bar{x} + V\hat{b}) - D\hat{b}] \\ &= K_b[\bar{r} - (CV + D)\hat{b}],\end{aligned}$$

which is of the form of Eq. (10) provided that

$$H = CV + D. \tag{12}$$

This is one of the relations we are seeking.

We substitute Eq. (8) into Eq. (5) to obtain

$$\begin{aligned}\dot{\bar{x}} + V\dot{\hat{b}} + \dot{V}\hat{b} &= A(\bar{r} + V\hat{b}) + B\hat{b} + K_x(\bar{r} - H\hat{b}) \\ &= A\bar{x} + K_x\bar{r} + (B + AV - K_xH)\hat{b}.\end{aligned} \tag{13}$$

But, from Eqs. (9) and (10), the left-hand side of Eq. (13) is

$$\dot{\bar{x}} + V\dot{\hat{b}} + \dot{V}\hat{b} = A\bar{x} + \bar{K}\bar{r} + VK_b(\bar{r} - H\hat{b}) + \dot{V}\hat{b}.$$

The Ax term cancels on both sides of the result, leaving

$$(\bar{K} + VK_b)\bar{r} + \dot{V} - VK_bH)\hat{b} = K_x\bar{r} + (B + AV - K_xH)\hat{b}$$

Thus Eq. (5) is satisfied for all $\bar{r}$ and $\hat{b}$ provided that

$$\bar{K} = K_x - VK_b, \tag{14}$$

$$\dot{V} = AV + VK_bH + B - K_xH = (A - \bar{K}C)V + B - \bar{K}D. \tag{15}$$

Thus the augmented-state observer of Fig. 2a, with gain matrices K_x and K_b obtained by any method whatsoever, can be transformed into the bias-separated form of Fig. 2b, provided that the matrices H, V, and $\bar{K}$ satisfy the two algebraic equations (12) and (14) and the matrix differential equation (15), which becomes the matrix Riccati equation

$$\dot{V} = (A - K_xC)V + VK_bD + VK_bCV + B - K_xD \tag{16}$$

upon substitution of Eq. (14).

This derivation is strictly algebraic and does not require that any significance be attached to the matrices that appear in the respective relations, but only that a matrix V satisfying Eq. (16) be found. [The general conditions on A, B, C, D, K_x, and K_b that guarantee the existence of a solution to Eq. (16), to our knowledge, have not been explored.] In particular, there is no requirement that K_x and K_b be optimal for the noise u and v. And, regardless of the optimality of these gains, the steady-state errors in the estimation of x and b will tend to zero if these gains result in a stable observer. An alternative demonstration of this property was given in [17].

If the observer gains K_x and K_b are optimal for the noises u and v in Eqs. (3) and (4), however, then the bias-separated filter is also optimum, and it is then possible to provide interpretations of the matrices $\bar{K}$ and V. In particular, as shown in [4], $\bar{K}$ is the optimal gain for the bias-free filter, i.e., for estimating the state x when b is known to be identically zero:

$$\bar{K} = \bar{P}C'R^{-1}, \tag{17}$$

where

$$\dot{\bar{P}} = A\bar{P} + \bar{P}A' - \bar{P}C'R^{-1}C\bar{P} + Q, \tag{18}$$

with Q and R the spectral density matrices of u and v, respectively. Moreover, the matrix V can be interpreted as the ratio of the cross-covariance matrix of x and b to the covariance matrix of b. Specifically, if

$$\begin{aligned} P_{xb} &= E[(x - \hat{x})(b - \hat{b})'], \\ P_b &= E[(b - \hat{b})(b - \hat{b})'], \end{aligned} \tag{19}$$

then, as shown in [4],

$$V = P_{xb}P_b^{-1}. \tag{20}$$

This helps provide an intuitive interpretation of the bias-correction equation (8), in which V is seen to be the gain matrix for correcting the bias. By Eq. (20) this matrix is proportional to the cross correlation between the error in estimating the state and the error in estimating the bias. If the influence of the latter on the former is relatively weak, as measured by a small cross-correlation matrix P_{xb}, it is only reasonable to expect that correction of the bias-free estimate $\overline{x}$, when knowledge of b is obtained, would likewise be small. Also, if the cross correlation between the bias and state estimates is strong, we should expect a large bias correction. In addition, we should expect the magnitude of the bias correction to be inversely proportional to the uncertainty in the estimate, and this would explain the presence of P_b^{-1} in Eq. (20).

Another useful relationship involving V, as given in [4], is

$$\hat{P} = \overline{P} + VP_bV' \tag{21}$$

where $\hat{P}$ is the covariance matrix of the estimate of x in the presence of bias, and $\overline{P}$ is the covariance in the absence of bias. Since VMV' is a positive-(semi-)definite matrix, it is clear that $\hat{P}$ is larger than $\overline{P}$, which is of course to be expected; Eq. (21), however, quantifies the difference between $\hat{P}$ and $\overline{P}$. In particular, if VP_bV' is small relative to P, then the increase in error due to b is correspondingly small and b is not significant in the estimation of x. Since it is possible to include all the bias variables except one, say, b_i in the state x and to apply the result of Eq. (21) to b_i alone, this provides a way of assessing the effect of each component b_i of the bias vector b on the estimate of x. Those components that do not contribute significantly to the increase in $\hat{P}$ over $\overline{P}$ are candidates for omission in a suboptimal implementation.

A useful interpretation of the bias-estimation equation (10) can be had by considering the problem of estimating an unknown constant b observed through noise, i.e.,

$$b = 0, \tag{22}$$

with observation $\bar{r}$ given by

$$\bar{r} = Hb + \xi \tag{23}$$

where ξ is white noise having a spectral density matrix R. Direct application of basic Kalman filter theory shows that the optimum estimator has exactly the form of Eq. (10) with the gain matrix K_b given by

$$K_b = P_b H' R^{-1}, \tag{24}$$

with P_b being the solution of the variance equation

$$\dot{P}_b = -P_b H' R^{-1} H P_b. \tag{25}$$

It is shown in [4] that these are precisely the relations that are satisfied by K_b and P_b. Hence the operation of the bias estimator [Eq. (10)] can be interpreted as the extraction of a constant observed in white noise, with the residual vector $\bar{r}$ being the observation. If the bias b is known to be zero, then by Eq. (23) $\bar{r}$ is zero-mean white noise with the same spectral density as the original observation noise. This confirms a well-known property of the residuals in a bias-free filter. But Eq. (23) also explains the effect of a nonzero bias b in the original dynamic equations on the residual of a Kalman filter designed for zero bias. In particular, the residual $\bar{r}$ is not a zero-mean process but rather has a mean given by Hb with the "equivalent observation" matrix H given by Eq. (12). As one might have expected, the observation bias matrix D appears directly in H, but the dynamic bias matrix B appears in H only through its influence on V. Moreover, since D also appears in the equation for V, it is not entirely accounted for by the D term in Eq. (12).

The interpretation of Eq. (10) as the extraction of a constant observed in white noise was first advanced by Mendel and Washburn [9,10] (see also [17]). This interpretation is particularly useful in failure-detection applications, to be discussed.

For simplicity, the previous review was given in terms of a continuous-time process. There are exactly analogous results for discrete-time systems, and these are presented in summary form in the Appendix. A more efficient version of the discrete-time algorithm was developed by Duffy in 1975 [6,7].

III. EXTENSIONS OF THEORY

A. *ALTERNATIVE DERIVATIONS*

As often happens with theoretical results, not everyone was pleased with the method used to derive the bias-separated filter, and several investigators contributed alternate derivations which may provide added insight or suggest further extensions.

In 1971, Lin and Sage [18] reported on their approach to bias estimation using maximum-likelihood methods and entailing solution of a two-point boundary-value problem. They obtained results which were subsequently shown by Godbole [19] to be identical to the original results in [4]. As Godbole pointed out, this fact was hardly surprising since it had been known for several years that the Kalman filter is a recursive implementation of the solution of the two-point boundary-value problem (see Section IV).

In 1972, Agee and Turner [8] derived equations for the (discrete-time) bias-separated filter by starting with the correction equation of the form $\hat{x} = \overline{x} + V\hat{b}$, and by a method somewhat similar to the method used in Section II determined the conditions under which the decoupling was possible. One of their conclusions is that the partitioning is only possible when the bias is not a random process. In other words, although the bias need not be a constant, but may rather be given by

$$\dot{b} = Zb, \tag{26}$$

it would not be permissible to include a noise input on the right-hand side of Eq. (26). Hence any attempt at extending the result to the case in which the bias is a random process must of necessity lead to a suboptimum filter. It is noted, however, that the derivation in Section II is independent of the manner in which the gains K_x and K_b are obtained for the augmented-state filter. The augmented-state filter (Fig. 2a) and the corresponding gains K_x and K_b can generally be found even if the bias b is a random process. Thus it would seem that the restriction that b not be a random process is somehow superfluous. The Agee and Turner result of [8] thus suggests either that the bias-free filter Fig. 2b that produces $\bar{x}$ is not the optimum filter for the process with $b \equiv 0$, or that a solution to Eq. (16) for the correction matrix V annot be found. It is interesting, but of not real importance, that $\bar{x}$ is the estimate of x in the absence of bias. If this were not the case, and if we could solve for V, K, and H, then the bias-separated structure of Fig. 2b could still be used.

Also in 1972, Earhart and Cavin [15] considered the design of a Luenberger observer [16] for a system comprising two systems connected in tandem: a plant defined by

$$\dot{x} = Ax + Bd \tag{27}$$

and an "input system" (which could be an actuator, for example) governed by

$$\dot{d} = Dd + B_1 u_1, \tag{28}$$

where D_1 is the control input. The observation equation they used was

$$y = Cx + D_1 u_1, \tag{29}$$

which is a less general form than Eq. (4), but their analysis would apply to the more general case as demonstrated in Section II.

Earhart and Cavin used a deterministic approach similar to that of Section II and calculations typical of the theory of observers [16] and obtained a deterministic version of the basic result given by Eqs. (8) to (11). Owing to the presence of the matrix D in Eq. (28), their results actually represent a generalization. Tacker *et al.* [20] in studying control of interconnected energy systems (apparently independently) discovered the bias-separation result within the framework of linear optimum control theory.

In the early 1970s, the square root method of implementing the optimum recursive filter had been gaining in popularity as another method of overcoming problems of numerical conditioning. In 1975, Bierman [11], an active investigator in this field, suggested that "the [square root information filter] SRIF is a natural method of dealing with biases," and developed a derivation using this methodology. In the course of this development, several additional results and interpretations emerged. He showed the relationship between the correction matrix V and the "estimation sensitivity" and "consider covariance" matrices of importance in orbit determination. He also pointed out how the bias-separation method could be used to compute smoothing solutions.

A very rigorous development of the results of [4] for both continuous- and discrete-time systems was published in 1978 by Mendel and Washburn [9,10] based on Washburn's doctoral dissertation. The development assumed the bias-separated form of Eq. (8) and, like Agee and Turner, found the conditions under which Eq. (8) is valid. In the course of this development they demonstrated that the estimation of the bias using the residuals (innovations) of the bias-free filter is equivalent to extraction of a constant observed in white noise, and they used this property to apply well-known algorithms in which the bias vector changes dimension with time.

B. EXTENSION TO TIME-VARYING BIAS

The original development of the bias-separated algorithm, as given in [4], was confined to a constant bias, i.e., $b = 0$, but it was remarked at that time that the extension to a time-varying bias would be fairly simple. The explicit extension was first presented by Tacker and Lee [21] in 1972. Bierman [22] subsequently pointed out that the results of Tacker and Lee could be obtained more directly by noting that if $\dot{b} = Zb$, then $b(t) = \Phi(t, 0)b_0$ where $\Phi(t, 0)$ is the state transition matrix corresponding to Z and hence the time-varying bias-estimation problem could be replaced by the problem of estimating the initial state b_0 of $b(t)$.

C. EXTENSION TO NONLINEAR SYSTEMS

Few dynamic systems of practical interest are linear; nevertheless, Kalman-Bucy filtering is often used to estimate the state of such nonlinear systems. The standard technique used for nonlinear systems is the extended Kalman filter (EKF) in which the actual nonlinear equations are used in computing the residuals and for the dynamic model, but in which the correction due to the residual is linear. Specifically, for a continuous-time process

$$\dot{z} = f(z) + u, \tag{30}$$

with observations given by

$$y = g(z) + v, \tag{31}$$

in which u and v are white-noise processes, and the EKF equations are

$$\dot{\hat{z}} = f(\hat{z}) + Kr, \tag{32}$$

with

$$\hat{r} = y - g(\hat{z}). \tag{33}$$

The gain matrix K is computed from the covariance matrix $\hat{P}$, i.e.,

$$K = \hat{P}G'R^{-1} \tag{34}$$

with

$$\dot{\hat{P}} = F\hat{P} + \hat{P}F' - \hat{P}G'R^{-1}G\hat{P} + Q \tag{35}$$

in which F and G are Jacobian matrices of f and g, respectively. evaluated along the estimated trajectory, i.e.,

$$F = \left[\frac{\partial f}{\partial z}\right]_{z=\hat{z}} \quad \text{and} \quad G = \left[\frac{\partial g}{\partial z}\right]_{z=\hat{z}}.$$

The covariance matrix $\hat{P}$ is computed, along with $\hat{z}$, as part of the EKF algorithm.

In many practical applications, the EKF algorithm outlined above works quite well. In these applications it would be worthwhile to develop a bias-separated form of the EKF for the case in which the state z includes dynamic variables and biases, i.e., in systems in which the state vector z can be partioned into a dynamic state x and a bias b:

$$z = \left[\frac{x}{b}\right], \tag{36}$$

and hence $f(z) = f(x, b)$ and $g(z) = g(x, b)$.

The direct extension of the separated-bias form to the EKF is not as obvious as it might appear at first glance, owing to the nonlinear nature of f( ) and g( ). In particular, the Jacobian matrices that enter into the covariance matrix $\hat{P}$ of the Eq. (35) are evaluated at the optimum estimate of x and b, so that the representation of the variance equation in the manner of Eq. (21), which leads to the separated-bias form, may not be valid, and this leads to some difficulty in determining the gains $\bar{K}$ and K_b to be used in the bias-separated form. It may be argued, with Agee and Turner [8], that the EKF is not optimal anyway, and hence any reasonable choice of gains might be acceptable. Adopting this viewpoint, however, does not end the matter. In the bias-separated structure, for example, the bias-free residual is $\bar{r} = y - C\bar{x}$. The counterpart of this in the nonlinear equation is $\bar{r} = y - g(\bar{x}, 0)$. In other words, the state used to compute the expected observation is $\bar{x}$, not $\hat{x}$. This is counter to the spirit of the EKF in which the linearization is always made about the complete state estimate. If the effect of the bias on the estimated state is small, it may not matter too much whether the linearization is about $\hat{x}$ or about $\bar{x}$. When the bias is significant, however, the difference between $\hat{x}$ and $\bar{x}$ may be enough to affect the results significantly.

The generalization of the bias-separation algorithm to nonlinear dynamics was considered by Sinha and Mahalanabis [23] in 1972. They applied the results of [4] to partitioning the dynamic state and bias-estimation equations. They considered both the discrete- and the continuous-time cases, but did not elucidate the problem of where to evaluate the requisite partial derivatives.

The special case in which the bias b enters linearly into the dynamics and observations was studied carefully by Mendel [24] in 1976. Considering only the discrete-time problem, he showed that the separated-bias algorithm fits into the EKF algorithm, except that the matrix V in the correction equation must be recomputed after the bias-free state update in order to implement the EKF algorithm exactly. He does not address the issue of whether the additional computer time needed to compute V twice per time-update step is justifiable in view of the likelihood that the EKF is not optimal.

A method of possibly overcoming any problems that might arise because of nonlinear effects on the difference between $\hat{x}$ and $\bar{x}$ is to reset the bias computation from time to time, i.e., by setting $\bar{x}$ to $\hat{x}$ and, simultaneously, $\hat{b}$ to zero. This operation merely resets the means. It would be improper to reset the covariance matrices, since the uncertainty in the bias is not changed by resetting the mean. The resetting operation can be performed whenever a suitable (ad hoc) test reveals that the difference between $\hat{x}$ and $\bar{x}$ has a significant *nonlinear* effect.

There are certain situations in which the EKF can be improved upon by using second-order terms in the filter. In the case of a continuous-time process with discrete-time observations, the state estimate between observations is determined by

$$\dot{\hat{z}} = f(\hat{z}) + \frac{1}{2}(\partial f/\partial z)'P, \tag{37}$$

where

$$(\partial f/\partial \hat{z})'P = [\mathrm{tr}(\partial f_1/\partial \hat{z})'P \cdots \mathrm{tr}(\partial f_n/\partial \hat{z})'P]',$$

where P is the covariance matrix. The state estimate is updated at instants t_i of observation using

$$\hat{z}(t_i) = \tilde{z}(t_i) + K[y(t_i) - g(\tilde{z}(t_i))], \tag{38}$$

where $\tilde{x}(t_i)$ is the optimum estimate of the state just prior to the observation, obtained by integrating Eq. (37) over the interval $[t_i, t_{i-1}]$ starting with $\hat{z}(t_{i-1})$. The presence of the term $\frac{1}{2}(\partial f/\partial \hat{z})'P$ in Eq. (37) distinguishes the second-order filter from the EKF.

In 1974, Shreve and Hedrick [25] showed that the covariance matrix could be propagated in the separated form, as given in the Appendix, but the fundamental state separation equation [Eq. (1)] does not generally apply unless the observation equations are linear.

Caglayan and Lancraft [26] have considered the nonlinear bias-estimation problem using the EKF approach. Their discussion includes some of the questions mentioned earlier.

D. EXTENSION TO NOISE ON BIAS

By the manner in which the basic theory was developed in [4], it was apparent that it would be difficult to extend the bias-separation result to the case in which b is a random process, i.e., $\dot{b} = \xi$, where ξ is white noise. The difficulty was confirmed by the aforementioned 1972 analysis of Agee and Turner [8].

Since an absolutely constant bias is a mathematical idealization (no physical bias is perfectly constant for all time), an extension of the bias-separation algorithm, even as an approximation, would be highly desirable. The need for such an extension was recognized by Tanaka [27] who in 1975 developed an algorithm for discrete-time systems which retains some of the features of the original algorithm but does not completely decouple the bias calculations from the calculation of the dynamic state. The possibility of dropping terms in Tanaka's algorithm when the noise on the bias is small might merit attention, but it does not seem to have been explored.

More recently, Washburn and Mendel [28] have generalized the results [4] in several directions. They considered the general process

$$\dot{x} = Ax + \epsilon Bz + u, \quad \dot{z} = Cz + \epsilon Dx + w, \tag{39}$$

with $y = Hx + \epsilon Mz + v$, which, as $\epsilon \to 0$, reduces to two uncoupled systems in which the substate z is not observed. They treated this problem by assuming the desired optimum estimate $\hat{x}$ to be of the form

$$\hat{x} = G\tilde{x} + V\hat{z} + \hat{\xi}. \tag{40}$$

This is a generalization of the basic separated-estimation formula [Eq. (1)] owing to the appearance of the matrix G and the correction term $\hat{\xi}$. For the general case of Eq. (39), the generalized separated-bias estimation formula has scarcely any advantage over the augmented-state form that would arise directly from Eq. (39). When ϵ is small, however, they show by using perturbation methods that a suboptimal estimator of the form of Eq. (1) (i.e., with $G = 1$ and $\xi = 0$) can be found. These results are illustrated [28] by a simple example which is not very convincing, however; perhaps it does not show the results to their best advantage. Another shortcoming of the Washburn-Mendel analysis is that too many terms are deleted when $\epsilon \to 0$. There is no need to include ϵ in front of B and M in Eq. (39) since existing theory already permits the treatment of these terms without the need for approximation. Nevertheless, this analysis suggests the possibility of using perturbation methods as a general method of extending the results of the separated-bias estimation algorithm.

IV. FIXED-INTERVAL SMOOTHING

From the earliest years of Kalman filtering theory, it has been known that the filter output $\hat{z}(t)$ is an optimum estimate of the state $z(t)$, given the observations up to time t, i.e., $\{y(\tau)$ for $\tau \leq t\}$. There are many applications which require obtaining a best estimated trajectory given data over a finite time interval, say, $[0, T]$. Of course, $\hat{z}(T)$ is the optimum estimate of $z(T)$ at the end of the finite interval, but the values of $\hat{z}(t)$ for $t < T$ are not necessarily optimum estimates. The difference between $\hat{z}(t)$ and the true optimum (i.e., "smoothed") estimate $\hat{z}_s(t)$ is frequently large enough to justify correcting the former.

The problem of obtaining the smoothed state estimate for continuous-time processes was first treated by Bryson and Frazier [29] using variational calculus. Shortly thereafter, Rauch, Tung, and Streibel [30] used a different approach to obtain equivalent results for discrete-time systems. The general idea of these smoothing algorithms was to first obtain the Kalman-filter estimate $\hat{z}(T)$ and the corresponding covariance matrix $\hat{P}(T)$. These are used to integrate a set of linear differential (or difference) equations backward from the terminal time T to obtain the optimum smoothed estimate $\hat{z}_s(t)$ and the corresponding covariance matrix $\hat{P}_s(t)$. In addition to $\hat{z}(T)$ and $\hat{P}(T)$, the Bryson-Frazier (BF) algorithm requires storage of only the observation sequence $\{y(t), 0 \leq t \leq T\}$; all other quantities are calculated in the "backward sweep." The Rauch-Tung-Streibel (RTS) algorithm, on the other hand, does not require the storage of $\{y(t), 0 \leq t \leq T\}$, but it does require the storage of the Kalman filter output $\{\hat{z}(t), 0 \leq t \leq T\}$ and the covariance matrix $\{\hat{P}(t), 0 < t < T\}$. The BF algorithm clearly entails less storage but, in general, more computation than the RTS algorithm. In a nonlinear system, however, the backward pass uses a set of linearized equations for which a reference trajectory is needed. This is generally the trajectory $\hat{z}(t)$ obtained as the output of an extended Kalman filter. In any case, since $\hat{z}(t)$ must be stored for this purpose in nonlinear systems, it would appear that the RTS algorithm is preferable with regard to storage requirements. The computation requirements of the smoothing algorithm in either case have motivated further investigation. Various improvements to the two basic algorithms have been proposed over the years. (See [31] for an up-to-date list of references for these algorithms.) These improvements notwithstanding, the computational burden is still heavy. In the interest of reducing this burden, Duffy [6,7] in 1975 and (apparently independently) Melzer [32] in 1978 considered the separation of the dynamic state smoothed estimate $\hat{x}_s(t)$ from the smoothed estimate $\hat{b}_s(t)$ of the bias. Not surprisingly, they found that the smoothed estimate of the bias $\hat{b}_s(t)$ is the optimum estimate $\hat{b}(T)$ obtained on the "forward pass" through the data. In addition, Melzer [32] showed that the smoothed estimate $\hat{x}_s(t)$, for $t < T$, of the dynamic state vector can be expressed as the sum of the bias-free smoothed state estimate $\bar{x}_s(t)$ and a correction due to the presence of the bias estimate $\hat{b}(T)$ already determined, i.e.,

$$\hat{x}_s(t) = \bar{x}_s(t) + L(t, T)\hat{b}(T), \quad 0 < t < T, \tag{41}$$

where $\bar{x}_s(t)$ is the smoothed estimate of $x(t)$ calculated as if there were no bias present. Thus it is only necessary to calculate the correction matrix $L(t, T)$ $(0 \leq t \leq T)$ in order to correct the bias-free smoothed estimate for the bias. The algorithm developed by Duffy [6,7] organizes the calculations differently from Eq. (41) but achieves an equivalent computational simplification.

In order to appreciate how this separation comes about, consider the nth-order dynamic process

$$\dot{z} = Fz + Gu, \tag{42}$$

with observations given by

$$y = Hz + v, \tag{43}$$

where u is white noise with spectral density matrix Q, and v is white noise with spectral density matrix R. Bryson and

Frazier [29] showed that the smoothed estimate $\hat{z}_s(t)$ and the corresponding covariance matrix $\hat{P}_s(t)$ are solutions to the following two-point boundary-value problems:

(1) For the smoothed state estimate,

$$\begin{bmatrix} \dot{\hat{z}}_s \\ \hline \dot{\lambda} \end{bmatrix} = \mathscr{S} \begin{bmatrix} \hat{z}_s \\ \hline \lambda \end{bmatrix} - \begin{bmatrix} 0 \\ \hline H'R^{-1} \end{bmatrix} y, \qquad 0 \le t \le T, \tag{44}$$

with

$$\hat{z}_s(0) = \hat{z}(0) \quad \text{(a priori estimate)}, \qquad \lambda(T) = 0 \tag{45}$$

where $\mathscr{S}$ is a "Hamiltonian" $2n \times 2n$ matrix given by

$$\mathscr{S} = \left[\begin{array}{c|c} F & GQG' \\ \hline H'R^{-1}H & -F' \end{array}\right]. \tag{46}$$

(2) For the covariance matrix,

$$\begin{bmatrix} \dot{P}_s & \dot{P}_{s\lambda} \\ \dot{P}'_{s\lambda} & \dot{P}_\lambda \end{bmatrix} = \mathscr{S} \begin{bmatrix} P_s & P_{s\lambda} \\ P'_{s\lambda} & P_\lambda \end{bmatrix} + \begin{bmatrix} P_s & P_{s\lambda} \\ P'_{s\lambda} & P_\lambda \end{bmatrix} \mathscr{S}'$$
$$+ \begin{bmatrix} GQG' & 0 \\ 0 & H'R^{-1}H \end{bmatrix}, \quad 0 \le t \le T, \tag{47}$$

with

$$P_s(0) = \hat{P}(0) \quad \text{(a priori covariance)},$$
$$P_{s\lambda}(T) = 0, \qquad P_\lambda(T) = 0. \tag{48}$$

[The vector λ in Eq. (44) is the Lagrange multiplier or "costate" variable that arises out of the variational formulation.]

It is well known that Eqs. (44) and (47) are satisfied by the Kalman filter solution at (and only at) $t = T$, i.e.,

$$\hat{z}_s(T) = z(T), \tag{49}$$

$$\hat{P}_s(T) = P(T), \tag{50}$$

where

$$\dot{\hat{z}} = F\hat{z} + K(y - H\hat{z}), \tag{51}$$

$$K = \hat{P}H'R^{-1}$$

$$\dot{P} = FP + PF' - PH'R^{-1}HP + GQG'. \tag{52}$$

Having thus obtained $\hat{z}_s(T)$ and $\hat{P}_s(T)$ on the forward pass defined by Eqs. (51) and (52), Eqs. (44) and (47) become initial value problems in that they can be integrated backward to yield $\hat{z}_s(t)$ and $\hat{P}_s(t)$ for $t < T$.

Let the state transition matrix corresponding to $\mathscr{S}$ be

$$\Phi(t, \tau) = \left[\begin{array}{c|c} \Phi_{11}(t, \tau) & \Phi_{12}(t, \tau) \\ \hline \Phi_{21}(t, \tau) & \Phi_{22}(t, \tau) \end{array}\right], \tag{53}$$

with arbitrary t and τ. Using this transition matrix and the boundary conditions Eqs. (45) and (48)-(50) with the general theory of linear systems, it follows that

$$\hat{z}_s(t) = \Phi_{11}(t, T)\hat{z}(T) + \int_T^t \Phi_{12}(t, \tau)H'R^{-1}y(\tau)\,d\tau \tag{54}$$

$$\hat{P}_s(t) = \Phi_{11}(t, T)\hat{P}(T)\Phi'_{11}(t, T) + \int_T^t \Big[\Phi_{11}(t, \tau)GQG'\Phi'_{11}(t, \tau) + \Phi_{12}(t, \tau)H'R^{-1}H\Phi'_{12}(t, \tau)\Big]\,d\tau. \tag{55}$$

These results apply to a general dynamic system of the form of Eqs. (42) and (43). In our case, however, z is given by Eq. (36). Correspondingly,

$$F = \left[\begin{array}{c|c} A & B \\ \hline 0 & 0 \end{array}\right], \qquad G = \left[\begin{array}{c} I \\ \hline 0 \end{array}\right], \qquad H = [C \mid D]. \tag{56}$$

The presence of the zero elements in F and G imply that the submatrices Φ_{11} and Φ_{12} of the state transition matrix have the following form:

$$\Phi_{11}(t, \tau) = \left[\begin{array}{c|c} \bar{\Phi}_{11}(t, \tau) & J(t, \tau) \\ \hline 0 & I \end{array}\right] \tag{57}$$

$$\Phi_{12}(t, \tau) = \left[\begin{array}{c|c} \bar{\Phi}_{12}(t, \tau) & 0 \\ \hline 0 & 0 \end{array}\right], \tag{58}$$

where

$$\bar{\Phi}(t, \tau) = \left[\begin{array}{c|c} \bar{\Phi}_{11}(t, \tau) & \bar{\Phi}_{12}(t, \tau) \\ \hline \bar{\Phi}_{21}(t, \tau) & \bar{\Phi}_{22}(t, \tau) \end{array}\right] \tag{59}$$

is the state transition matrix for the bias-free process, i.e., corresponding to the Hamiltonian matrix

$$\mathscr{S} = \left[\begin{array}{c|c} A & Q \\ \hline CR^{-1}C' & -A' \end{array}\right], \tag{60}$$

$$J(t, \tau) = \int_{\tau}^{t} \left[\bar{\Phi}_{11}(t, \xi)B + \Phi_{12}(t, \xi)C'R^{-1}D\right] d\xi. \tag{61}$$

As a result of Eq. (57) we find that

$$\hat{x}_s(t) = \bar{\Phi}_{11}(t, T)\hat{x}(T) + \int_{T}^{t} \bar{\Phi}_{12}(t, \tau)C'R^{-1}y(\tau)\, d\tau + J(t, T)\hat{b}(T). \tag{62}$$

However, $\hat{x}(T) = \bar{x}(T) + V(T)\hat{b}(T)$, so Eq. (62) becomes

$$\hat{x}(t) = \bar{\Phi}_{11}(t, T)\bar{x}(t) + \int_T^t \Phi_{12}(t, \tau)C'R^{-1}y(\tau)\, d\tau$$
$$+ [\bar{\Phi}_{11}(t, T)V(t) + J(t, T)]\hat{b}(T). \tag{63}$$

The first two terms on the right-hand side of Eq. (63) are recognized as $\bar{x}_s(t)$, the bias-free smoothed estimate. Thus Eq. (63) is the same as Eq. (41) with

$$L(t, T) = \Phi_{11}(t, T)V(T) + J(t, T). \tag{64}$$

A similar analysis on Eq. (55) yields

$$\hat{P}_{xs}(t) = \bar{\Phi}_{11}(t, T)\bar{P}_x(T)\bar{\Phi}'_{11}(t, T)$$
$$+ L(t, T)P_b(T)L'(t, T). \tag{65}$$

The first term on the right-hand side of Eq. (65) is recognized as $\bar{P}_x(t)$, the bias-free smoothed covariance matrix. The second term of Eq. (65) gives the correction due to the bias. Thus the matrix L(t, T), which can be obtained from the state transition matrix of the bias-free system, is the matrix needed to correct both the smoothed state estimate, via Eq. (41), and the covariance matrix, via Eq. (65). For the discrete-time version of these results, the reader should consult [6], [31], and [32].

V. FAILURE DETECTION AND ESTIMATION

The difference between the actual observation and its optimum estimate, known as the residual (r) or innovation process, has known statistical properties, namely,

(1) $E[r] = 0$,

(2) $E[r(t)r'(\tau)] = W\delta(t - \tau)$ (white noise of spectral density W).

Deviations of the empirical statistics of the process, such as those obtained from operating data, may serve as indicators that the actual process is not the same as the process for which the optimum filter was designed. If such deviations start small but suddenly become large, this might be evidence that a change (i.e., a failure) has taken place in the system. The general use of residuals for fault detection and isolation was suggested in 1971 by Mehra and Peschon [14]. A number of investigators subsequently took this suggestion and developed techniques for estimating changes in bias, and hence for detecting and correcting system failures that may be attributed to such changes.

In the context of failure detection, it is useful to draw a distinction between determining whether or not a bias is present and estimating its size (i.e., magnitude and direction), given (or assuming) that it is present. Since an estimated bias $\hat{b}$ of zero is equivalent to no bias, it is reasonable to believe that the separated-bias estimation algorithm can be used to advantage for failure detection and estimation. In 1977, Bellingham and Lees [34] reported using essentially this procedure for detection of malfunctions in chemical process control systems. The basic technique and some simulation results are given in [34] and some experimental results are presented in [35].

A significant limitation of the separated-bias algorithm, as developed in [4], is that it rests on the assumption that the bias is constant from the start of estimation and forever after. The consequence of this assumption is that the bias-estimator gain matrix tends to zero (as 1/t) and hence the capability of the estimator to track a bias change that occurs after the estimator is turned on diminishes with time. Since the theory was developed on the assumption that the bias does not change, there is no reason to expect the bias estimator to have such a capability, but it does impose a practical limitation upon using the basic algorithm without modification. One obvious ad hoc modification would be simply to prevent the bias-estimator gain from going to zero by assuming, for example, that the uncertainty in the bias cannot be reduced beyond an arbitrarily specified level. This assumption prevents the bias-estimator gain from being reduced to zero. As has been shown in [17] and [36], constant bias is estimated with zero steady-state error. This means that even if the bias changes after the estimator is turned on, if it remains constant after the change, it will be estimated without error. In fact, if the bias is piecewise constant, but the intervals between transitions are widely spaced in time, the bias filter will track the piecewise-constant bias moderately well. However, preventing the bias-estimator gain from going to zero is an ad hoc remedy, and it ought to be possible to achieve better performance by using more sophisticated statistical procedures.

One procedure for failure detection which has been receiving a great deal of attention is the generalized likelihood ratio (GLR) technique, developed over the past two decades on the basis of the pioneering work of Abraham Wald on sequential estimation. The direct application of the GLR technique for estimating jumps (including, in principle, but not limited to, changes in bias) in dynamic systems was proposed by

Willsky and Jones [37] in 1976. They showed that the residual in case of bias change can be expressed as

$$r = G\nu + w, \tag{66}$$

where ν is the bias change to be estimated, w the zero-mean white noise, and G a matrix calculated in the GLR algorithm. Reasoning from Eq. (66), they established a recursive correction equation of the form

$$\hat{x} = \bar{x} + (\Phi - F)\hat{\nu}, \tag{67}$$

where $\bar{x}$ is the estimate of x under the hypothesis of no failure, $\hat{\nu}$ the GLR estimate of x, and Φ and F are matrices defined by the GLR algorithm. The GLR estimate of ν is obtained by processing the sequence of residuals, as explained in [37].

These results were apparently obtained independently of the prior results on bias estimation. It became clear subsequently, however, that the matrix G in Eq. (66) is equivalent to H in Eq. (23) given earlier, and Φ - F is equivalent to V in Eq. (1). Hence a close relationship between the GLR method and the earlier bias-estimation method can be seen: both methods use the residuals of the bias-free filter to obtain an estimate of the bias ($\hat{b}$ or $\hat{\nu}$), and both use the resulting estimate to correct the bias-free estimate. The procedures used to obtain the estimate $\hat{b}$ or $\hat{\nu}$ are different, of course. Owing to the assumption that b is a constant for all time, the estimation equation for $\hat{b}$ is linear and fairly simple, whereas the GLR algorithm for obtaining $\hat{\nu}$ is nonlinear and quite complex. In circles in which the GLR algorithm is popular, it is generally felt that the added complexity of the algorithm gives it advantages in terms of superior performance.

Later in 1976, Chien and Adams [38] published another failure-detection method which also used the residuals of the bias-free estimator. This technique employs the sequential probability ratio test (SPRT), which also derives from the original work of Wald but differs in some of its details from the GLR method of Willsky and Jones. Chien and Adams observed one deficiency of the SPRT, namely, that the latter does not account for a transition from a normal to a failure mode. Consequently, if a failure were to occur, it would be detected with an undesirable extra time delay. They proposed a resetting correction to the SPRT to overcome this deficiency and demonstrated the applicability of the method to an inertial navigation system.

In 1979, Chang and Dunn [39] returned to the GLR approach of Willsky and Jones. They presented a more computationally stable recursive algorithm for implementing the GLR calculations and showed that this algorithm could be interpreted as being that of a Kalman filter for estimating a constant bias, starting at the time of occurrence of the jump. The relationship between the bias-separation method and the GLR approach was thus made quite explicit. (This relationship has been considered further by Caglayan [40].)

Another approach to the problem of detecting and estimating the occurrence and magnitudes of transitions in a piecewise-constant signal was introduced by Friedland in 1979 [41,42]. The underlying idea is to model changes in the bias as the result of a highly non-Gaussian noise input, i.e., $b_{n+1} = b_n + v_n$, where v_n has a probability density function that includes a delta function at the origin to account for the finite probability that no transition in b takes place at any given instant. Using available theory for the maximum-likelihood estimation with non-Gaussian noise, Friedland developed an approximate recursive algorithm for obtaining a maximum-likelihood estimate of b_n. Then, assuming that the interpretation of Eq. (23) (i.e., that bias estimation is equivalent to extraction of a constant buried in white noise) remains valid when the bias is not constant but only piecewise constant, Friedland and Grabousky [33] developed a recursive algorithm for detection of failures in dynamic systems. This algorithm seems computationally comparable to the Chang-Dunn recursive implementation of the GLR algorithm, but a detailed comparison of the two, which would reveal any significant differences, remains to be performed.

VI. ADDITIONAL APPLICATIONS

A. *TRAJECTORY ESTIMATION*

Our work on separated-bias estimation was motivated by our observation that there are many problems in which there are relatively few dynamic state variables but a large number of parameters to be estimated and that separation of the parameter estimation from the estimation of the dynamic state variables would be computationally advantageous. This was borne out by the experience of Agee and Turner [8] who used the method in the program they developed for their best estimate of trajectory (BET) computer program. They found, for example, that although there might be only 9 dynamic state variables, there might be as many as 66 constant parameters in an accurate model of the sensors used on the White Sands Missile Range where the program would be employed. They examined several other techniques but discarded them because of numerical difficulties or because they did not produce satisfactory estimates of the bias. They reported using the algorithm, with the modifications discussed earlier, with both simulated and actual trajectory data.

We used the bias-separation technique in our own work on orbit and satellite-mass determination [43], which was reported in 1970. Although there were not a large number of parameters to be estimated, the method was beneficial because our program was to be developed by modifying an existing program in which no provision was made for estimating these parameters, and which was written in a manner that did not readily lend itself to increasing the dimension of the state vector to accommodate the additional state variables. However, it was fairly easy to add the bias-estimation capability to the existing program.

B. ADDED-INERTAIL NAVIGATION

When the Kalman filtering technique is applied to mixing inertial data with other navigation data, it is found that many of the variables to be estimated are actually biases. These include gyro and accelerometer bias ("drift rates") scale-factor uncertainties, misalignment angles, and uncertain parameters in the navigation aid such as Doppler scale-factor and bore-sight errors. The bias-separation technique described herein would be appropriate for this application. Its use in this context is suggested by Farrell [44] and alluded to by Nash *et al.* [45] in connection with testing of inertial navigation systems and components.

Duffy [6,7] reported the application of the separate-bias algorithm and the smoothing algorithms to a reentry-vehicle trajectory-estimation problem having 10 dynamic state variables and 47 biases to be estimated. The biases included parameters of an inertial platform on the reentry vehicle and biases on the range, azimuth, and elevation of the ground-based radar trackers. Extremely good performance was observed with both simulated and real flight-test data.

C. CALIBRATION

Also in connection with inertial navigation, as well as in other applications, it is necessary to determine the bias vector b in a system defined by Eqs. (3) and (4). An optimum estimate of the state x is often not required in such cases. It is clear that the structure of Fig. 1 can be used to obtain an optimum estimate $\hat{b}$, and the correction term $V\hat{b}$ can be omitted if $\hat{x}$ is not required. This application was described by Friedland [46] in 1977 in which the method was illustrated by an example of the calibration (i.e., determination of drift rates and g-dependent error coefficients) of a two-axis gyro.

A by-product of the analysis of [46] was an alternative representation of the bias-estimation equation [Eq. (10)]. It was shown that the bias b can be expressed as the product of the bias covariance matrix P_b as obtained in Eq. (25) with a vector q, which is obtained by integrating the weighted residuals. In mathematical terms, it was shown that

$$\hat{b} = P_b q, \tag{68}$$

where

$$\dot{q} = H'R^{-1}r. \tag{69}$$

This form of the bias-estimation equation is readily verified by substituting the expression for $\hat{b}$ and its derivative into Eq. (10), taking into account that $\dot{P}_b$ is given by Eq. (25).

This form of the calibration equation is advantageous when an estimate of b is needed only at the end of a fixed calibration interval. In this case it is necessary only to determine the vector q by numerical integration of the weighted residual $H'R^{-1}\bar{r}$. Then, at the end of the predetermined calibration time T_c, the estimate is obtined by multiplying $q(T_c)$ by the covariance matrix $P_b(T_c)$. It is thus not necessary to store P_b for other instants of time. This results in a considerable reduction in computer storage requirements over what might be required to compute $\hat{b}$ using Eq. (10).

From Eq. (25) it is readily determined that

$$P_b(t) = \left[P_b^{-1}(0) + L(t)\right]^{-1} ,$$

where

$$L(t) = \int_0^t H'(\tau)R^{-1}H(\tau)\, d\tau .$$

In the absence of a priori information on b, $P_b^{-1}(0) = 0$ and $P_b(t) = K^{-1}(t)$. Hence L must have an inverse for some value of t in order that b can be determined. In most cases it is necessary to introduce motion into the dynamic system, i.e., to make C(t) and D(t) time varying so as to produce a matrix H(t), defined by Eq. (12), which results in a nonsingular L matrix for some value of time. It is argued in [46] that an optimal choice of H would be such that L(t) is a diagonal matrix, which is a generalized orthogonality requirement on the elements of the matrix H.

The problem of combined state and parameter estimation is a more general version of the calibration problem. By use of the extended Kalman filter (EKF) approach, it becomes a nonlinear problem of the type discussed in Section III. Hence, subject to the reservations of that section, the bias-separation technique can be applied to this problem. The application of the method to helicopters has been reported by Hall *et al.* [47].

D. SATELLITE-ATTITUDE ESTIMATION

Melzer [32] considered the application of the bias-separation technique to satellite-attitude estimation using gyros and strapdown star sensors as the on-board instrumentation. The dynamic state variables in this application are the three attitude errors (defined as the differences between the quantities indicated by the gyros and the corresponding true quantities). The biases include the gyro-drift rates, misalignments, and scale-factor errors; and the star-sensor errors. Good results were reported, and the bias-separated algorithm was recommended as being preferable to state augmentation.

E. PROCESS CONTROL

It is often necessary to deal with biases in closed-loop systems. Fortunately, the bias-separation technique is applicable to closed-loop systems as well as to open-loop systems. This was demonstrated by Tacker *et al.* [20,21] in 1972 in connection with their studies of interconnected electric power systems. Another use of the separated-bias estimation technique in connection with decentralized control of power systems was reported by Venkateswarlu and Mahalanabis [48] in 1977. The use of this technique by Bellingham and Lees [34,35] in connection with closed-loop control of chemical processes has been discussed.

VII. CONCLUSIONS

The pervasiveness of Kalman-Bucy filtering theory in so many aspects of modern control and estimation has motivated a great deal of research toward making the theory easier to use. The bias-separation method reviewed in this article is a result of this type of research. We hope that this and other research in the same spirit will enhance the practical utility of the basic theory.

The bias-separation technique, originally presented in 1969 and subsequently extended in various directions, has a variety of practical applications, some of which were described here; however, a number of issues regarding this technique remain and merit further investigation. We have already remarked that the question of how the theory may be extended to cover the case in which the bias is not deterministic is not completely settled; the negative result of Agee and Turner counters the formal separation property used in the derivation presented in Section II of this article. Another issue that is not fully resolved is the proper extension to nonlinear systems.

Another area of investigation that might merit further attention is the relationship between the bias-separation method discussed here to other methods of simplifying the Kalman filter calculations. Some work in this direction has already been done. In 1974, Samant and Sorenson [5] compared the bias-separation method of this article with an order-reduction method in which only a portion of the state vector is optimally estimated. Both the Samant and Sorenson algorithm and the bias-separation algorithms are optimum under the same set of assumptions and hence ought to give the same results; however, there are differences in computational efficiency, as measured in storage and number of operations. Samant and Sorenson conclude that their algorithm requires a larger number of operations and is thus less efficient in terms of speed, but that it may be more efficient in terms of storage. In 1977, Chang and Dunn [49] studied the errors caused by omitting some state variables from the model used in the design of the estimator. If the states omitted are biases, then by virtue of Eq. (1), the error is given by $e = \hat{x} - \overline{x} = V\hat{b}$. Since V and the statistics of $\hat{b}$ are known, the statistical properties of the error due to omission of b can readily be determined. Chang and Dunn [49], however, consider a more general case than that represented by our model given by Eq. (3). Additional studies of these approximation methods might be worth while.

Another investigation that might be pursued is the determination of the implications of the dual of the bias-separation algorithm with regard to deterministic optimum control. The mathematical duality between deterministic (linear, quadratic) optimum control and Kalman-Bucy filtering is well known. Hence the bias-separation method ought to have a dual in optimum control, and this dual might have interesting properties with practical applications.

APPENDIX. BIAS-SEPARATION THEORY FOR DISCRETE-TIME SYSTEMS

Process and Observation Models

$$x(n + 1) = \Phi(n)x(n) + B(n)b + u(n),$$

$$y(n) = C(n)x(n) + D(n)b + v(n),$$

where b is a constant to be determined;

$$E[u(n)u'(k)] = Q(n)\delta_{nk}, \quad E[v(n)v'(k)] = R_n\delta_{nk},$$

$$E[u(n)v'(k)] = 0$$

in which E denotes mathematical expectation.

Bias-Separated Filter

$\hat{x}(n) = \bar{x}(n) + V(n)\hat{b}(n)$, where [after processing observation $y(n)$], $\hat{x}(n)$ is the optimum estimate corrected for bias, $\bar{x}(n)$ is the bias-free estimate, and $\hat{b}(n)$ is the optimum estimate of bias.

Bias-Free Filter

$\bar{x}(n) = \tilde{x}(n) + \bar{K}(n)\bar{r}(n)$, where $\tilde{x}(n) = \Phi(n - 1)\bar{x}(n - 1)$ is the predicted state of bias-free filter, $\bar{r}(n) = y(n) - C(n)\tilde{x}(n)$ is the bias-free residual, and $\bar{K}(n)$ is the bias-free filter gain matrix.

Bias Estimator

$$\hat{b}(n) = \hat{b}(n - 1) + K_b(n)[\bar{r}(n) - H(n)\hat{b}(n - 1)]$$

where $H(n) = C(n)U(n) + D(n)$, and $K_b(n)$ is the bias-estimator gain matrix.

Matrix-Propagation Equations

bias-free gain $\qquad \bar{K}(n) = \tilde{P}(n)C(n)[C(n)\bar{P}(n)C(n) + R(n)]^{-1}$

prior covariance $\qquad \tilde{P}(n + 1) = \Phi(n)\tilde{P}(n)\Phi'(n) + Q(n)$

posterior covariance $\qquad \bar{P}(n) = [I - \bar{K}(n)C(n)]\tilde{P}(n)$

bias gain $\qquad K_b(n) = M(n + 1)H(n)R^{-1}(n)$

bias covariance $\qquad M^{-1}(n + 1) = M^{-1}(n) + H'(n)[C(n)\tilde{P}(n)C'(n) + R(n)]^{-1}$

$$U(n + 1) = \Phi(n)V(n) + B(n)$$

$$V(n) = U(n) - \bar{K}(n)H(n)$$

ACKNOWLEDGMENTS

The author is indebted to a number of individuals who provided beneficial comments on an earlier draft of this article and who brought his attention to additional work of which he was not previously aware. In particular, he wishes to express his gratitude to the following: Gerald J. Bierman, Alper K. Caglayan, T.-T. Chien, James L. Farrell, Joseph F. Kasper, Jr., Stuart M. Melzer, Jerry M. Mendel, and Richard V. Spencer.

REFERENCES

1. R. E. KALMAN, "A New Approach to Linear Filtering and Prediction Problems," *J. Basic Engr. 82*, 34-45 (1960).

2. R. E. KALMAN and R. S. BUCY, "New Results in Linear Filtering and Prediction Theory," *J. Basic Engr. 83*, 95-108 (1961).

3. J. RICHMAN and B. FRIEDLAND, "Design of Optimum Mixer-Filter for Aircraft Navigation Systems," *Proc. Nat. Aerospace Electron. Conf.*, Dayton, Ohio, 429-438, May 1967.

4. B. FRIEDLAND, "Treatment of Bias in Recursive Filtering," *IEEE Trans. Autom. Control AC-14*, 359-367 (1969).

5. V. S. SAMANT and H. W. SORENSON, "On Reducing Computational Burden in the Kalman Filter," *Automatica 10*, 61-68 (1974).

6. T. J. DUFFY, "Decoupled State and Bias Estimation Applied to Trajectory Reconstruction," Ph.D. Dissertation, University of Pensylvania, Philadelphia, Pennsylvania, August, 1975.

7. T. J. Duffy, "Decoupled Estimation Techniques Applied to Trajectory Reconstruction," AIAA/AAS Astrodynamics Confer., Paper No. 76-820, San Diego, California, 18-20, August 1976.

8. W. S. AGEE and R. H. TURNER, "Optimal Estimation of Measurement Bias," Technical Rept. NO. 41 (AD 753961), Mathematical Services Branch, Analysis and Computation Division, National Range Operations Directorate, White Sands Missile Range, New Mexico, December 1972.

9. J. M. MENDEL and H. D. WASHBURN, "Multistage Estimate of Bias States," *Proc. 1976 IEEE Conf. Decision and Control*, Clearwater, Florida 629-630 (1976).

10. J. M. MENDEL and H. D. WASHBURN, "Multistage Estimation of Bias States in Linear Systems," *Int. J. Control 28*, No. 4, 511-524 (1978).

11. G. J. BIERMAN, "The Treatment of Bias in the Square-Root Information Filter/Smoother," *J. Optim. Theory and Appl. 16*, 165-178 (1975).

12. T. KAILATH, "An Innovations Approach to Least-Squares Estimation--I: Linear Filtering in Additive White Noise," *IEEE Trans. Autom. Control AC-13*, No. 6, 646-655 (1968).

13. T. KAILATH and P. FROST, "Innovations Approach to Least-Squares Estimation--II: Linear Smoothing in Additive White Noise," *IEEE Trans. Autom. Control AC-13*, No. 6, 655-660 (1968).

14. R. K. MEHRA and J. PESCHON, "An Innovations Approach to Fault Detection and Diagnosis in Dynamic Systems," *Automatica 7*, 637-640 (1971).

15. R. J. EARHART and R. K. CAVIN, III, "The Serial Design of Tandem System Observers," *Automatica 8*, 641-646 (1972).

16. D. G. Luenberger, "An Introduction to Observers," *IEEE Trans. Autom. Control AC-16*, No. 6, 596-602 (1971).

17. B. FRIEDLAND, "Notes on Separate-Bias Estimation," *IEEE Trans. Autom. Control AC-23*, No. 4, 735-738 (1978).

18. J. L. LIN and A. P. SAGE, "Algorithms for Discrete Sequential Maximum Likelihood Bias Estimation and Associated Error Analysis," *IEEE Trans. Systems, Man, and Cybernetics SMC-1*, No. 4, 314-324 (1971).

19. S. S. GODBOLE, "Comparison of Friedland's and Lin-Sage's Bias Estimation Algorithms," *IEEE Trans. Autom. Control AC-19*, No. 2, 143-145 (1974).

20. E. C. TACKER, C. C. LEE, T. W. REDDOCH, T. O. TAN, and P. M. JULICH, "Optimal Control of Interconnected Electric Energy Systems--A New Formulation," *Proc. IEEE 60*, 1239-1241 (1972).

21. E. C. TACKER and C. C. LEE, "Linear Filtering in the Presence of Time-Varying Bias," *IEEE Trans. Autom. Control AC-17*, No. 6, 828-829 (1972).

22. G. J. BIERMAN, "Comments on 'Linear Filtering in the Presence of Time-Varying Bias,' " *IEEE Trans. Autom. Control AC-18*, No. 4, 412 (1973).

23. A. K. SINHA and A. K. MAHALANABIS, "Modeling Error Compensation in Nonlinear Estimation Problems," *IEEE Trans. Systems, Man, and Cybernetics SMC-3*, No. 6, 632-636 (1973).

24. J. M. MENDEL, "Extension of Friedland's Bias Filtering Technique to a Class of Nonlinear Systems," *IEEE Trans. Autom. Control AC-21*, No. 2, 296-298 (1976).

25. R. L. SHREVE and W. R. HEDRICK, "Separating Bias and State Estimates in a Recursive Second-Order Filter," (Tech. Corresp.) *IEEE Trans. Autom. Control AC-19*, No. 5, 585-586 (1974).

26. A. K. CAGLAYAN and R. E. LANCRAFT, "A Bias Identification and State Estimation Methodology for Nonlinear Systems," Sixth IFAC Symposium on Identification and System Parameter Estimation, Washington, D.C., June 7-11, 1982.

27. A. TANAKA, "Parallel Computation in Linear Discrete Filtering," *IEEE Trans. Autom. Control AC-20*, No. 4, 573-575 (1975).

28. H. D. WASHBURN and J. M. MENDEL, "Multistage Estimation of Dynamical and Weakly Coupled States in Continuous-Time Linear Systems," *IEEE Trans. Autom. Control AC-25*, No. 1, 71-76 (1980).

29. A. E. BRYSON and M. FRAZIER, "Smoothing for Linear and Nonlinear Dynamic Systems," presented at Optimum Systems Synthesis Conference, Wright-Patterson Air Force Base, Ohio, Rept. ASD-TDR-63-119, September 11-13, 1962.

30. H. E. RAUCH, F. TUNG, and C. T. STRIEBEL, "Maximum Likelihood Estimates of Linear Dynamic Systems," *AIAA J. 3*, No. 8, 1445-1450 (1965).

31. G. J. BIERMAN, "A New Computationally Efficient Fixed-Interval, Discrete-Time Smoother," *Proc. 20th IEEE Conf. on Decision and Control 3*, San Diego, California, 1054-1060 (1981).

32. S. M. MELZER, "The Extension of Friedland's Technique for Decoupling State and Bias Estimates to Fixed Interval Smoothing," The Aerospace Corporation, Technical Memorandum ATM 78(3901-03)-16, May 1978.

33. B. FRIEDLAND and S. M. GRABOUSKY, "Estimating Sudden Changes of Biases in Linear Dynamic Systems," *IEEE Trans. Autom. Control AC-27*, No. 1 (1982).

34. B. BELLINGHAM and F. P. LEES, "Practical State and Bias Estimation of Process Systems with Initial Information Uncertainty," *Int. J. Systems Sci. 8*, No. 7, 813-840 (1977).

35. B. BELLINGHAM and F. P. LEES, "The Detection of Malfunction Using a Process Control Computer: A Kalman Filtering Technique for General Control Loops," *Chem. Eng. Prog. 55*, 253-265 (1977).

36. B. FRIEDLAND, "Recursive Filtering in the Presence of Biases with Irreducible Uncertainty," *IEEE Trans. Autom. Control AC-21*, No. 5, 789-790 (1976).

37. A. S. WILLSKY and H. L. JONES, "A Generalized Likelihood Ratio Approach to the Detection and Estimation of Jumps in Linear Systems," *IEEE Trans. Autom. Control AC-21*, No. 1, 108-112 (1976).

38. T.-T. CHIEN and M. B. ADAMS, "A Sequential Failure Detection Technique and Its Application," *IEEE Trans. Autom. Control AC-21*, No. 5, 750-757 (1976).

39. C. B. CHANG and K. P. DUNN, "On GLR Detection and Estimation of Unexpected Inputs in Linear Discrete Systems," *IEEE Trans. Autom. Control AC-24*, No. 3, 499-501 (1979).

40. A. K. CAGLAYAN, "Simultaneous Failure Detection and Estimation in Linear Systems," *Proc. 19th IEEE Conf. Decision and Control 2*, Albuquerque, New Mexico, 1038-1041 (1980).

41. B. FRIEDLAND, "Maximum-Likelihood Estimation of a Process with Random Transitions (Failures)," *IEEE Trans. Autom. Control AC-24*, No. 6, 932-937 (1979).

42. B. FRIEDLAND, "Multidimensional Maximum Likelihood Failure Detection and Estimation," *IEEE Trans. Autom. Control AC-26*, No. 2, 567-570 (1981).

43. B. FRIEDLAND, M. HUTTON, and J. RICHMAN, "Satellite Mass Determination Using Live Data," RADC-TR-69-375, Rome Air Development Center, Griffiss Air Force Base, New York, January 1970.

44. J. L. FARRELL, "Integrated Aircraft Navigation," Academic Press, New York, p. 183, 1974.

45. R. A. NASH, JR., J. F. KASPER, JR., B. S. CRAWFORD, and S. A. LEVINE, "Application of Optimal Smoothing to Testing and Evaluation of Inertial Navigation Systems and Components," *IEEE Trans. Autom. Control AC-16*, No. 6, 806-816 (1971).

46. B. FRIEDLAND, "On the Calibration Problem," *IEEE Trans. Autom. Control AC-22*, No. 6, 889-905 (1977).

47. W. E. HALL, J. BOHN, and J. VINCENT, "Development of Advanced Techniques for Rotorcraft State Estimation and Parameter Identification," Systems Control, Inc., NASA Contractor Rept. CR-159297, August 1980.

48. B. E. VENKATESWARLU and A. K. MAHALANABIS, "Design of Decentralized Load-Frequency Regulators," *Proc. IEE* (England) *124*, No. 9, 817-820 (1977).

49. C. B. CHANG and K.-P. DUNN, "Kalman Filter Compensation for a Special Class of Systems," *IEEE Trans. Aerospace Electron. Syst. AES-13*, No. 6, 700-706 (1977).

Techniques and Methodologies for the Estimation of Covariances, Power Spectra, and Filter-State Augmentation

VOLKMAR HELD
Elektronik-System-Gesellschaft mbH
Munich, Federal Republic of Germany

I. INTRODUCTION

For the design of optimal filters, the dynamic model of the system and information about the expected stochastic system disturbances and measurement errors are required [1]. The dynamic system model is generally derived without major problems from knowledge of the physical background of the system or from measurement of the system transfer function. Much more difficult is the determination of the system disturbances and measurement errors, here called system and measurement noise. They must be provided for the filter algorithms in the form of stochastic parameters: covariances

ISBN 0-12-012720-2

and power spectral densities. The estimation of these parameters requires theoretically an infinite number of measurements of a stationary stochastic noise process. In reality, only time-limited measurements exist, which are not exactly stationary and contain additional deterministic variables. The results of parameter estimation are approximations that are usually sufficient so long as some limiting conditions (controllability and observability of the system and stability of the designed filter [2]) are guaranteed.

Another problem is the requirement of Gaussian-distributed and uncorrelated (white) noise for the Kalman filter formulation. In reality, white noise does not exist. Real noise (for example, gyro drift or wind speed) is correlated, has a limited frequency band, and is called colored noise. Solution of this problem is possible by the so-called state vector augmentation [3]. Colored Gaussian noise can be generated by a linear shaping filter from Gaussian white noise (Fig. 1). The shaping filter, usually a first- or second-order linear filter, is added to the system model, and the state vector of the system is augmented by the order of the shaping filter. Although this procedure is applicable to system noise without problems, treatment of measurement noise is difficult, at least in theory. If measurement noise if integrated into the system by a shaping filter, the measurements are error free, which results in a loss of stochastic observability and filter

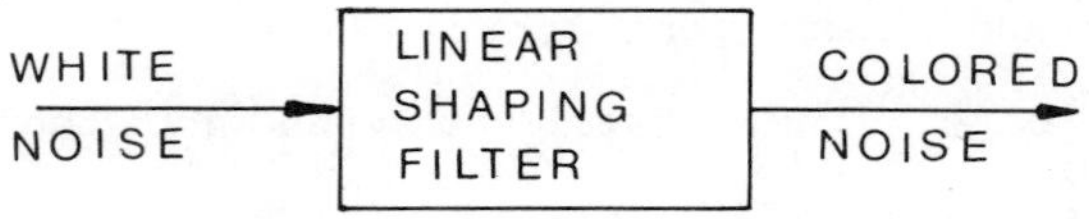

Fig. 1. Shaping filter.

stability. (Exact but relatively difficult solutions for colored noise are given in [4,2].) In reality, this is no problem. Colored measurement noise usually contains an additional part of high bandwidth that is approximately white and that can be separated from the colored part. Although the colored part is modeled by a shaping filter, the approximately white part serves in the filter algorithm as the required measurement noise. So, the application of colored system and measurement noise in a Kalman filter is possible.

In the following sections, techniques for estimating the noise parameters from real measurement for application in a Kalman filter are described. In particular, evaluations of the covariance, power spectrum (for continuous filters), and shaping filters are treated. These methods are based on the conventional mathematical realtions for linear stochastic processes [2,5].

II. DETERMINATION OF STATIONARY MEASUREMENTS

The large number of measurements required for the determination of stochastic parameters (e.g., variance or power spectral density) is generally not derived from an ensemble of measurements at a fixed time. The time-variable measurements of one ensemble member are usually applied. This is correct, if the ergodic hypothesis is valid, which means that this member is representative for the desired stationary stochastic noise process.

Unfortunately, such representative measurements are rarely available in practice. In most cases, nonobservable deterministic signals or measurement errors (trends) are superimposed on the stochastic noise. For example, the signal of a Doppler radar contains the deterministic aircraft velocity as well as the stochastic measurement-error noise. If no redundant measurements are available, a separation of the two variables is possible only by their frequency differences. The resonance frequency or the bandwidth of the observed system is approximately known from its physical background (e.g., phugoid of an aircraft). Usually, this frequency lies below the frequency band of the measurement noise so that a separation by a filter or smoothing procedure is possible. A smoothing procedure is described in the next paragraph that gives an excellent frequency separation.

Smoothing procedures have the property to provide off-line a smoothed value at time t_i from measurements before and after t_i. If the procedure is repeated for varying t_i, the result is a smoothed variable which consists of the lower frequency parts of the measurements. The smoothing procedure is characterized by the following steps:

(1) From the measurements $y(t_i + \nu)$, the data within a data window of length $2\nu_{max}$ (Fig. 2) are selected.

(2) The measurements are approximated by a second-order polynomial

$$\hat{y}(t_i + \nu) = a_0(t_i) + a_1(t_1)\nu + a_2(t_i)\nu^2/2. \tag{1}$$

(3) The differences

$$\hat{y}(t_i + \nu) - y(t_i + \nu) = \Delta y(t_i + \nu) \tag{2}$$

are weighted with a weighting function $g(|\nu|)$ that is symmetrical to t_i (Fig. 2).

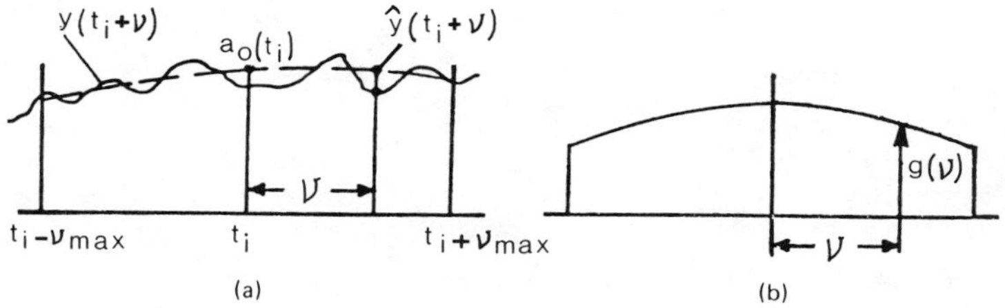

Fig. 2. (a) Measurement y (solid curve) and approximation y (dashed curve); (b) weighting function $g(|\nu|)$.

(4) The constants $a_0(t_i)$, $a_1(t_i)$, and $a_2(t_i)$ are estimated by the method of least squares.

(5) As shown later, the cutoff frequency of the smoothing procedure is defined by the length of the data window $2\nu_{max}$ and its transfer function by the weighting function $g(|\nu|)$.

(6) If the data window is shifted along the time scale, the smoothed data are given by $a_0(t_i)$ with variable i.

In detail, the evaluation of the polynomial coefficients and of the transfer function runs as follows. The differences, Eq. (2) are weighted, squared, and integrated from $-\nu_{max}$ to $+\nu_{max}$:

$$J = \int_{-\nu_{max}}^{+\nu_{max}} g(\nu)^2 (\hat{y}(t_i + \nu) - y(t_i + \nu))^2 \, d\nu. \tag{3}$$

With Eq. (1), differenting J and setting the differential to 0 for the minimum of J results in

$$\partial J/\partial a_k = 2\int_{-\nu_{max}}^{+\nu_{max}} g(\nu)^2 (\hat{y}(t_i + \nu) - y(t_i + \nu)) \times (\nu^k/k!) \, d\nu = 0, \tag{4}$$

where k = 0, 1, 2.

With Eq. (1) this yields

$$\int_{-\nu_{max}}^{+\nu_{max}} g(\nu)^2 \nu^k y(t_i + \nu)\, d\nu$$

$$= \int_{-\nu_{max}}^{+\nu_{max}} g(\nu)^2 \Big(a_0(t_i)\nu^k + a_1(t_i)\nu^{1+k} + a_2(t_i)\tfrac{1}{2}\nu^{2+k} \Big)\, d\nu. \qquad (5)$$

Uneven powers of ν disappear on the right-hand side of Eq. (5) during integration, and the following relation remains:

$$\int_{-\nu_{max}}^{+\nu_{max}} g(\nu)^2 \begin{bmatrix} y(t_i + \nu) \\ \nu y(t_i + \nu) \\ \nu^2 y(t_i + \nu) \end{bmatrix} d\nu$$

$$= \int_{-\nu_{max}}^{+\nu_{max}} g(\nu)^2 \begin{bmatrix} 1 & 0 & \frac{1}{2}\nu^2 \\ 0 & \nu & 0 \\ \nu^2 & 0 & \frac{1}{2}\nu^4 \end{bmatrix} d\nu \begin{bmatrix} a_0(t_i) \\ a_1(t_i) \\ a_2(t_i) \end{bmatrix}. \qquad (6)$$

The matrix on the right-hand side is nonsingular and can be inverted for the estimation of $a_k(t_i)$. Usually, only $a_0(t_i)$ is of interest; sometimes the first (a_1) or second (a_2) derivative is also required.

For the determination of the cutoff frequency ω_g and the transfer function $F(i\omega)$ of the smoothing procedure, Eq. (6) is Fourier transformed. The convolution of the left-hand side of Eq. (6) changes into the product of two Fourier-transformed integrals. The matrix of the right-hand side consists of constants which remain unchanged during the Fourier transform.

The result is Eq. (7):

$$\phi \begin{bmatrix} g(\nu)^2 \\ g(\nu)^2\nu \\ g(\nu)^2\nu^2 \end{bmatrix} \phi y(t_i) = \int_{-\nu_{max}}^{+\nu_{max}} g(\nu)^2 \begin{bmatrix} 1 & 0 & \frac{1}{2}\nu^2 \\ 0 & \nu & 0 \\ \nu^2 & 0 & \frac{1}{2}\nu^4 \end{bmatrix} d\nu \, \phi \begin{bmatrix} a_0(t_i) \\ a_1(t_i) \\ a_2(t_i) \end{bmatrix}. \tag{7}$$

Where ϕ is the Fourier transform with

$$\phi \begin{bmatrix} g(\nu)^2 \\ g(\nu)^2\nu \\ g(\nu)^2\nu^2 \end{bmatrix} = \int_{-\nu_{max}}^{+\nu_{max}} \begin{bmatrix} \cos \omega\nu g(\nu)^2 \\ -\sin \omega\nu g(\nu)^2\nu \\ \cos \omega\nu g(\nu)^2\nu^2 \end{bmatrix} d\nu. \tag{8}$$

The desired transfer functions

$$F(i\omega)_{a_0} = \frac{\phi a_0(t_i)}{\phi y(t_i)}, \qquad F(i\omega)_{a_1} = \frac{\phi a_1(t_i)}{\phi y(t_i)},$$

$$F(i\omega)_{a_2} = \frac{\phi a_2(t_i)}{\phi y(t_i)} \tag{9}$$

are determined by solution of Eq. (7).

The transfer functions depend exclusively on the weighting function $g(\nu)^2$ that must be chosen such that the smoothing procedure approximates an ideal low pass as closely as possible. Therefore, in Section III, different weighting functions are examined.

III. WEIGHTING FUNCTIONS

The simplest weighting function is a rectangular function $g_0(\nu) = 1$. The measurements within a data window are weighted equally (Fig. 3).

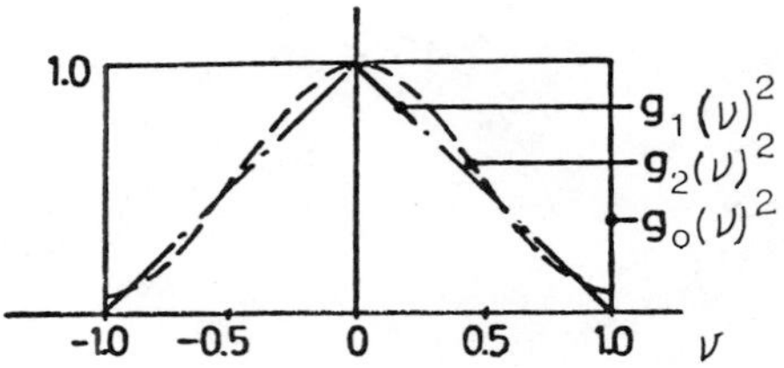

Fig. 3. Weighting functions $g_1(\nu)^2$ and $g_2(\nu)^2$.

The value of the corresponding transfer function $F_0(i\omega)a_0$ from Eq. (9) is shown in Fig. 4. The function decreases down to a frequency of $0.5/\nu_{max}$ very rapidly, which results in a sharp frequency cutoff. For increasing frequencies the function oscillates, which means that the smoothed signal still contains parts of higher frequencies. To eliminate this disadvantage, two different weighting functions are tested. These functions are used in [6] for the smoothing of power spectral densities:

$$g_1(\nu)^2 = 1 - (|\nu|/\nu_{max}), \tag{10}$$

$$g_2(\nu)^2 = 0.54 + 0.46\cos(\pi\nu/\nu_{max}). \tag{11}$$

The values of the corresponding transfer functions $F_1(i\omega)a_0$ and $F_2(i\omega)a_0$ [Eqs. (10) and (11)] are shown in Fig. 4; F is displayed, dependent on the relative frequency $f\nu_{max}$ where $2\nu_{max}$ is the width of the smoothing function. The decrease of F_2 and F_3 is slighter than of F_1, but the oscillations are much smaller, especially for the weighting function $g_2(\nu)$.

In the logarithmic diagrams of Fig. 5 these properties are more distinctively shown. For comparison, low-pass filters of first and second order are also displayed. Only with the weighting function $g_2(\nu)$ does the smoothing procedure yield a much better frequency separation than a second-order bandpass

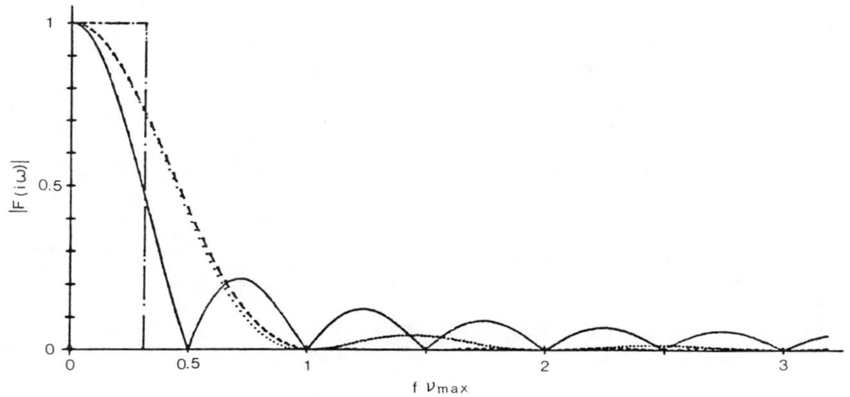

Fig. 4. Amount of transfer functions for different weighting functions: F_0 (solid curve); F_1 (dotted curve); F_2 (dashed curve); ideal low pass (dot-dash curve).

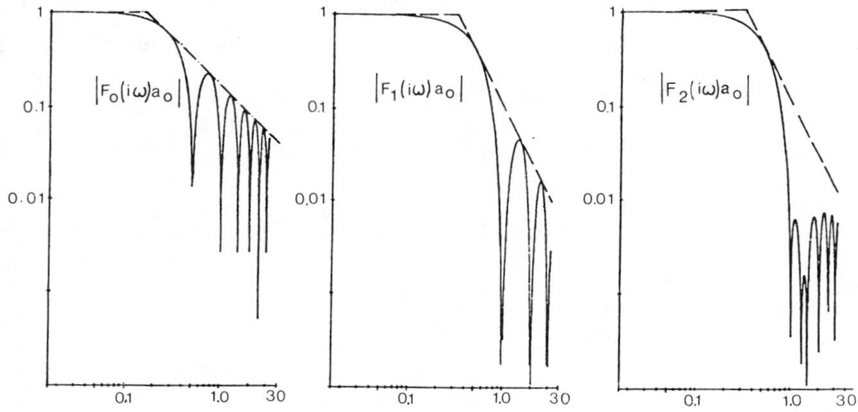

Fig. 5. Amount of transfer functions: low pass, first order (dot-dash line). Low pass, second order (dashed line).

filter. In this case it is a good approximation of an ideal low pass. Therefore, the weighting function $g_2(\nu)$ is recommended for application in the described smoothing procedure. The cutoff frequency is $f = 1/\nu_{max}$ (Fig. 5). The smoothing procedure now separates deterministic or stochastic signals $\hat{y}(t_i) = a_0(t_i)$ from stochastic noise, $\Delta y(t_i)$, which is approximately stationary.

IV. TEST OF GAUSSIAN DISTRIBUTION

Prior to the estimation of stochastic parameters from stochastic noise, a Gaussian probability-distribution test is performed to prove the stochastic behavior of the noise. Figure 6 and Table I show an example of this test (probability distribution of stochastic gyrodrift data that result from in-flight measurements). The criterion is a χ^2 test and a straight line in the Gaussian probability-distribution paper

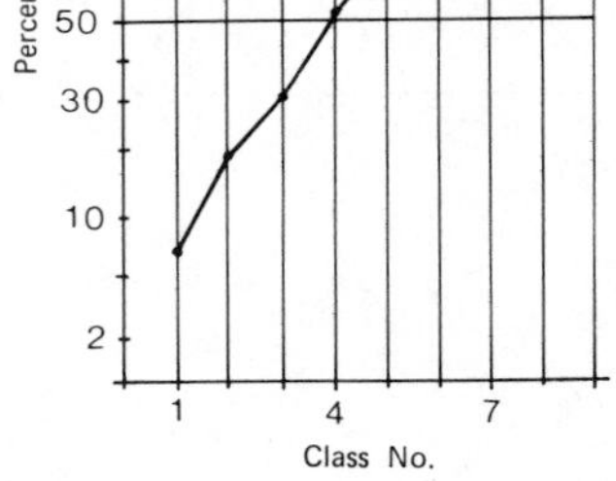

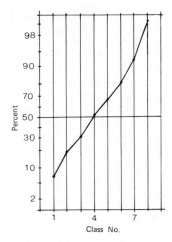

Fig. 6. Probability distribution of 133 gyrodrift measurements; χ^2 test and Gaussian probability distribution paper test.

Table I. Probability Distribution of Stochastic Gyrodrift Data which Result from In-Flight Measurements ($\chi^2 = 7.68$).

CLASS No.	RANGE FROM	RANGE TO	NUMBER OF MEASUREMENTS		DISTRIBUTION
0		-11.75	0	0	
1	-11.75	- 8.81	9	9	////X////
2	- 8.81	- 5.87	16	25	////X////X////X/
3	- 5.87	- 2.94	17	42	////X////X////X//
4	- 2.94	0	28	70	////X////X////X////X////X///
5	0	2.94	19	89	////X////X////X////
6	2.94	5.87	19	108	////X////X////X////
7	5.87	8.81	15	123	////X////X////X
8	8.81	11.75	9	132	////X////
9	11.75		1	133	/

test. The result of the χ^2 test ($7.68 < 9.24$) as well as the approximately straight line shows that the distribution of the gyrodrift is Gaussian.

V. ESTIMATION OF COVARIANCES AND POWER SPECTRA

In Sections II to IV a technique was devised for extracting stationary stochastic system, or measurement-noise, data from measurements which contain system signals, deterministic errors, or trends. The stochastic parameters (covariances and power spectral densities), which are required for the Kalman filter, can now be estimated. Because the smoothing procedure runs in a digital computer, the noise output is a discrete-time series. Therefore the following equations are also given in discrete formulation.

A. *CORRELATION FUNCTIONS*

For two discrete stochastic series $y_1(t_j)$ and $y_2(t_j + m\,\Delta T)$ with $j = 0, 1, \ldots, l - k$; $m = 0, 1, \ldots, k$; mean value 0; and constant ΔT, the correlation function is

$$R^*_{y_1, y_2}(m\,\Delta T) = (l - k)^{-1} \sum_{j=0}^{l-k} y_1(t_j)\,y_2(t_j + m\,\Delta T), \quad (12)$$

where $y_1 = y_2$ is the autocorrelation, and $y_1 \neq Y_2$ is the cross correlation. For negative m,

$$R^*y_1, y_2(-m\,\Delta T) = R^*y_2, y_1(m\,\Delta T). \tag{13}$$

The covariance is given by $R^*y_1, y_2(0)$.

B. POWER SPECTRAL DENSITY

In the frequency domain the stochastic functions y_1, y_2 are described by the power spectral density (signal power per Hertz at a frequency of $n\,\Delta f$). The power spectral density is determined by the discrete Fourier transform of the correlation function:

$$\begin{aligned} S^*y_1, y_2(n\,\Delta f) &= \phi\{Ry_1, y_2(m\,\Delta T)\} \\ &= \Delta T\Bigg[R^*y_1, y_2(0) + \sum_{m=1}^{k-1}\Big(R^*y_1, y_2(m\,\Delta T) \\ &\quad + R^*y_2, y_1(m\,\Delta T)\Big)\cos\pi(nm\,\Delta f/f_g) \\ &\quad + \frac{1}{2}\Big(R^*y_1, y_2(k\,\Delta T) + R^*y_2, y_1(k\,\Delta T)\Big) \\ &\quad \times \cos\pi(nk\,\Delta f/f_g\Bigg] - i\,\Delta T \\ &\quad \times\Bigg[\sum_{m=1}^{k-1}\Big(R^*y_1, y_2(m\,\Delta T) - R^*y_2, y_1(m\,\Delta T)\Big) \\ &\quad \times \sin\pi(nm\,\Delta f/f_g + \frac{1}{2} \\ &\quad \times \Big(R^*y_1, y_2(k\,\Delta T) - R^*y_2, y_1(k\,\Delta T)\Big) \\ &\quad \times \sin\pi(nk\,\Delta f/f_g)\Bigg], \end{aligned} \tag{14}$$

with $\underline{n} = 0, 1, 2, \ldots, k$; $\Delta f = \frac{1}{2}k\,\Delta T$ frequency resolution; $f_g = \frac{1}{2}\Delta T$ cutoff frequency [5]; and $i = \sqrt{-1}$. $y_1 \neq y_2$ has an imaginary part that disappears for $y_1 = y_2$.

For the enhancement of the statistic certainty of the power spectral density [Eq. (14)], the correlation function [Eq. (12)] can be multiplied by a weighting function $g(m\,\Delta T)$:

$$R_{y_1,\,y_2}(m\,\Delta T) = g(m\,\Delta T)R^*_{y_1,\,y_2}(m\,\Delta T). \tag{15}$$

The weighting function has a length of $2k\,\Delta T$. Multiplication in the time domain yields a convolution in the frequency domain:

$$\phi\{R_{y_1,\,y_2}(m\,\Delta T)\} = \phi\{g(m\,\Delta T)\} * \phi\left\{R^*_{y_1,\,y_2}(m\,\Delta T)\right\}. \tag{16}$$

It has been shown [6] that the weighting function $g_2(m\,\Delta T) = 0.54 + 0.46\cos(\pi m/k)$ smooths the spectral density and enhances the statistic certainty by 2.3. The convolution is very simple because $\phi\{g_2(m\,\Delta T)\}$ consists only of three values. The result is given by

$$\begin{aligned}
S_{y_1,\,y_2}(0) &= 0.54S^*_{y_1,\,y_2}(0) + 0.46S^*_{y_1,\,y_2}(\Delta f),\\
S_{y_1,\,y_2}(n\,\Delta f) &= 0.23S^*_{y_1,\,y_2}((n-1)\,\Delta f)\\
&\quad + S^*_{y_1,\,y_2}(n\,\Delta f) + 0.23S_{y_1,\,y_2}((n+1)\,\Delta f),\\
S_{y_1,\,y_2}(k\,\Delta f) &= 0.46S^*_{y_1,\,y_2}((k-1)\,\Delta f)\\
&\quad + 0.54S^*_{y_1,\,y_2}(k\,\Delta f),
\end{aligned} \tag{17}$$

For the gyro-drift data of Fig. 6 and Table I, the correlation function, the power spectral density, and the weighted spectral density are evaluated and displayed in Table II as an example. The frequency steps are $0.0159/\text{sec}^{-1}$, and the validity of the relation $\int S\,df = R(0)$ is checked. Table II shows a much smoother weighted spectral density **S** than the unweighted S^*.

Table II. Evaluation of Correlation Function, Power Spectral Density, and Convoluted Power Spectral Density[a]

TIME/FREQUENCY INCREMENTS	CORRELATION FUNCTION	SPECTRAL DENSITY	SPECTRAL DENSITY(CONV.)
0	34.2	894.8	747.5
1	31.7	574.5	510.4
2	27.6	-24.6	127.6
3	23.9	38.3	16.8
4	20.4	7.8	18.9
5	15.3	26.2	14.9
6	9.6	-4.3	5.5
7	4.5	8.1	2.2
8	0.1	-4.8	0.9
9	-3.8	7.1	2.0
10	-7.5	-3.1	1.6

[a]*Time increments, 3 sec; frequency increments, 0.0159* sec^{-1}*; integral Sdf, 34.3.*

VI. ESTIMATION OF LINEAR SHAPING FILTERS

One goal of the analysis of correlated stochastic noise data is the determination of linear shaping filters which generate colored noise from white noise. If the spectral density [Eq. (17)] is known, the following relation is valid [2]:

$$S_{y_1,\, y_1}(\omega) = |F(i\omega)|^2 S_0, \tag{18}$$

where S_0 is the power spectral density of white noise (constant); $S_{y_1,\, y_1}(\omega)$ the power spectral density of colored noise; and $F(i\omega)$ the transfer function of the shaping filter. From this the amount of the shaping-filter transfer function follows:

$$|F(i\omega)| = [S_{y_1,\, y_1}(\omega)/S_0]^{1/2}. \tag{19}$$

From the empirical spectral density $S_{y_1,\, y_1}(\omega)$, only the amount of the shaping-filter transfer function can be determined but not the phase. Therefore, all shaping filters can theoretically be used for the generation of colored noise, which fulfills Eq. (19) approximately. In reality, the simplest of all possible shaping filters is always used because the phase is of no interest in determining the noise.

A linear shaping filter is defined by its structure (differential equation) and its parameters (time constants, resonance frequencies, and damping ratios). Selection of the structure and estimation of the parameters are feasible by the following method: The amount of the transfer function [Eq. (19)] is drawn in double-logarithmic scale. Two examples, those of gyro drift and velocity-measurement error are shown in Fig. 7.

For a skilled person it is relatively easy to determine the structure of a linear filter which is a good approximation of the empirical value. For the examples of Fig. 7 the appropriate shaping-filter structures are given by the transfer functions (20) and (21) in the frequency domain

$$\mathbf{F}(i\omega) = \left[-\left(\omega^2/\omega_r^2\right) + i2\xi(\omega/\omega_r) + 1\right]^{-1}, \tag{20}$$

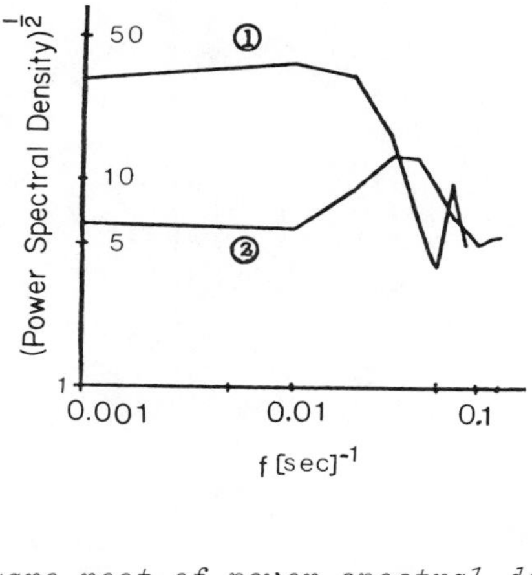

Fig. 7. Square root of power spectral density of (1) gyrodrift and (2) velocity-measurement error.

$$\mathbf{F}(i\omega) = \frac{iT\omega + 1}{-\left(\omega^2/\omega_r^2\right) + i2\xi(\omega/\omega_r) + 1} \tag{21}$$

where ω_r is the resonance frequency, ξ the damping constant, and T the time constant. Now the parameters α of the shaping filter (for example T, ξ, ω_r, and $\mathbf{S}_0$) have to be identified so that the empirical value $[\mathbf{S}y_1, y_1(\omega)]^{1/2}$ is optimally approximated. This is obtained by minimizing

$$\mathbf{J}(\alpha) = \sum_{\omega=0}^{\omega_g} \left\{[\mathbf{S}y_1, y_1(\omega)]^{1/2} - |\mathbf{F}(i\omega, \alpha)|\mathbf{S}_0^{1/2}\right\}^2 = \text{min.} \tag{22}$$

Equation (22) is nonlinear with reference to α. One possible solution is the development of $\mathbf{J}(\alpha)$ in a Taylor series [7]. The Taylor series is developed for $\alpha = \alpha^0$ (first approximation) and has three terms. For the scalar case (one parameter), this yields

$$\begin{aligned}\mathbf{J}(\alpha) &= \mathbf{J}(\alpha)\big|_{\alpha=\alpha^0} + (\partial\mathbf{J}/\partial\alpha)\big|_{\alpha=\alpha^0}(\alpha - \alpha^0) \\ &\quad + (\partial^2\mathbf{J}/\partial\alpha^2)\big|_{\alpha=\alpha^0}\tfrac{1}{2}(\alpha - \alpha^0)^2 = \text{min.}\end{aligned} \tag{23}$$

The minimum of α is given by

$$\begin{aligned}\partial\mathbf{J}(\alpha)/\partial\alpha &= 0 + (\partial\mathbf{J}/\partial\alpha)\big|_{\alpha=\alpha^0} + (\partial^2\mathbf{J}/\partial\alpha^2)\big|_{\alpha=\alpha^0}(\alpha - \alpha^0) \\ &= 0.\end{aligned} \tag{24}$$

For several parameters, a vector $\underline{\alpha} = (\alpha_1, \alpha_2, \ldots)^T$ is introduced. Instead of Eq. (24), the following equation is valid:

$$\underbrace{\begin{bmatrix} \partial \mathbf{J}/\partial\alpha_1 \\ \partial \mathbf{J}/\partial\alpha_2 \\ \vdots \end{bmatrix}_{\underline{\alpha}=\underline{\alpha}^0}}_{\underline{\Delta}} + \underbrace{\begin{bmatrix} \partial^2\mathbf{J}/\partial\alpha_1^2 & \partial^2\mathbf{J}/\partial\alpha_1\,\partial\alpha_2 & \cdots \\ \partial^2\mathbf{J}/(\partial\alpha_2\,\partial\alpha_1) & \partial^2\mathbf{J}/\partial\alpha_2^2 & \cdots \\ \vdots & \vdots & \end{bmatrix}_{\underline{\alpha}=\underline{\alpha}^0}}_{H}$$

$$\times \underbrace{\begin{bmatrix} \alpha_1 - \alpha_1^0 \\ \alpha_2 - \alpha_2^0 \\ \vdots \end{bmatrix}}_{\underline{\alpha} - \underline{\alpha}^0} = 0. \qquad (25)$$

The first step is to determine the differentials $\underline{\Delta}$ and H. This is not difficult, but it is tedious and is therefore omitted here. Roughly estimated parameters $\underline{\alpha}^0$ are then introduced into Eq. (25), and because H is usually nonsingular, improved parameters $\underline{\alpha}$ can be determined by

$$\underline{\alpha} - \underline{\alpha}^0 = -H^{-1}\big|_{\alpha=\alpha^0}\,\underline{\Delta}\big|_{\alpha=\alpha^0}. \qquad (26)$$

These parameters are inserted as $\underline{\alpha}^0$ in Eq. (22) in a second step, and an iteration can be started provided that the evaluated parameters converge toward the optimal parameters. In this case, $\mathbf{J}(\alpha)$ [Eq. (23)] is reduced from one iteration step to the next.

Unfortunately, practical applications have shown that this method very often does not converge because of too large steps of $\underline{\alpha}$ which overshoot the optimal parameters. This difficulty can be removed by a combination of Eq. (26) with a direct search method. After the determination of $\underline{\alpha} - \underline{\alpha}^0$ [Eq. (26)], $[(\underline{\alpha}^0 + n/10(\underline{\alpha} - \underline{\alpha}^0)), n = 1, 2, \ldots, 10]$ is evaluated. The parameter increment $n/10(\underline{\alpha} - \underline{\alpha}^0)$ which gives the smallest value of J is used for the next iteration step. With this combined technique fast convergence can be obtained in most cases. The example in Table III shows the iteration results of the velocity-measurement errors [Fig. 7 and Eq. (21)]. The four parameters are identified in four iteration steps. Remarkable is the reduction of J down to 2% of the initial value.

In Fig. 8 the transfer functions of the models with the optimal identified parameters are compared with the empirical values of Fig. 7. The fitting of the shaping filter is relatively good in the lower frequency range. A refinement of the model for higher frequencies is not worthwhile because of the small amounts in that region. If the curve fitting does not improve by an increasing number of iterations, the structure of the shaping filter should be altered.

The determination of the shaping-filter structure and parameters concludes the analysis of the stochastic system and measurement noise. The transformation of the shaping filter from the frequency domain into the time domain by Laplace or Fourier tables is now required. The resulting differential equation is included in the Kalman filter model, and the filter state vector is augmented by the order of the shaping filter.

Table III. Evaluation of Shaping-Filter Parameters for the Velocity-Measurement Errors

Parameter	S_0	T	ω_r	ξ	J
Initial Value	0.060	12.0	0.35	0.5	0.0732
1. Iteration	0.054	10.516	0.317	0.518	0.0103
2. Iteration	0.051	9.839	0.301	0.555	0.0019
3. Iteration	0.052	9.767	0.295	0.596	0.0015
4. Iteration	0.052	9.767	0.295	0.596	0.0015

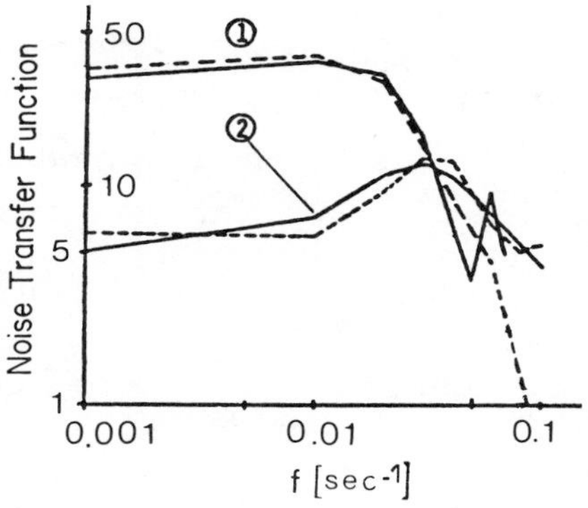

Fig. 8. Amount of transfer function of real colored noise (empirical values, solid curve) and its model with optimally identified parameters (dashed curve): (1) gyrodrift; (2) velocity-measurement errors.

VII. CONCLUSION

In the preceding sections, methods and techniques for the estimation of stochastic parameters have been derived from conventional stochastic operations and have proved to be remarkably effective in many applications [8]. The parameters are evaluated off-line with a digital computer from measurements which should be stationary with respect to the system and measurement noise. If considerable changes of the noise parameters independent of deterministic parameters (e.g., aircraft velocity or weather conditions) exist, this effect can also be modeled by the introduction of time-variable noise and shaping-filter parameters.

REFERENCES

1. R. E. KALMAN, "A New Approach to Linear Filtering and Prediction Problems," *J. Basic Engr. 83*, 35-45 (1960).

2. A. GELB, (ed.), "Applied Optimal Estimation," MIT Press, Cambridge, Massachusetts (1974).

3. H. W. SORENSEN and A. R. STUBBERND, "Linear Estimation Theory, Theory and Applications of Kalman-Filtering," *AGARDOGRAPH 139*, 1-42 (1970).

4. A. E. BRYSON and D. E. JOHANSEN, "Linear Filtering for Time-Varying Systems Using Measurements Containing Colored Noise," *IEEE Trans. Autom. Control AC-10*, 4-10 (1965).

5. W. GILOI, "Simulation and Analyse Stochastischer Vorgänge," R. Oldenbourg, München-Wien, 1967.

6. R. B. BLACKMAN and J. W. TUKEY, "Linear Data-Smoothing and Prediction in Theory and Practice," Addison-Wesley, Reading, Massachusetts, 1965.

7. G. A. BEKEY, "System Identification — an Introduction and a Survey," *Simulation*, 151-166 (1970).

8. V. HELD, "Die Bestimmung der wahren Lotrichtung im Flug," Ph.D. Dissertation, Universität Stuttgard, Stuttgart, 1976.

Advanced Applications of Kalman Filters and Nonlinear Estimators in Aerospace Systems

PETER S. MAYBECK

Department of Electrical Engineering
Air Force Institute of Technology
Wright-Patterson Air Force Base, Ohio

I. INTRODUCTION

A Kalman filter is a recursive data-processing algorithm that accepts incomplete noise-corrupted measurements from sensors to provide an estimate of the state variables that

ISBN 0-12-012720-2

describe the behavior of a dynamic system. It combines this real-time data with the results of stochastic modeling efforts, namely, (1) mathematical models of system dynamics and measurement device characteristics; (2) the statistical description of the system noises and disturbances, measurement errors, and uncertainties and/or inadequacies in the mathematical models themselves; and (3) any available a priori statistical information about the system states, to generate the desired state estimate. Under the assumptions that an adequate system model can be expressed in the form of a *linear* system driven by *white Gaussian* noise, its estimate can be shown to be optimal with respect to essentially any useful criterion of optimality: it is the minimum mean square error estimate, the generalized least squares estimate, the minimizer of any symmetric cost criterion, the maximum a posteriori estimate, the orthogonal projection of the true state onto the span of the measurements, the maximum likelihood estimate if there is no a priori state information (and superior to the maximum likelihood estimate if a priori statistics are available!), and, perhaps most important, its output *totally* defines the entire Gaussian conditional density function for the system state vector conditioned on the entire history of measurements that have been processed [1].

These optimality claims are impressive, but they are totally dependent upon the modeling assumptions. Mathematical models of both the system structure (state dynamics and measurement relations) and the uncertainties are inherently embodied in the Kalman filter structure, and the fidelity of these models dictates the performance of the filter in actual application. *Attaining an adequate mathematical model upon which to base the filter is the crux of the design problem.* Thus, despite the mathematical formalism of the Kalman filter approach, a substantial amount of engineering insight, fundamental modeling capability, and experience are required to develop an effective operational filter algorithm.

If the system model is nonlinear rather than linear, one generally cannot generate a finite-dimensional filter that is optimal with respect to all, or even any, of the previously mentioned criteria. Instead, *approximate* conditional moment estimators can be developed in the form of extended Kalman filters, second-order filters, and so forth, by truncating appropriate Taylor series expressions at different orders. Simultaneous adaptive estimation of uncertain parameters may well be warranted in practice, further compounding the nonlinearity of the estimation problem. Although there are additional complexities beyond those encountered in linear filtering, it is still true that attaining an adequate model for the basis of the filter algorithm is of paramount importance to the design of an implementable filter with acceptable performance.

Moreover, the designer typically does not have the luxury of implementing the filter based upon the best descriptive and most complete and complex model, often termed the "truth model." The final filter algorithm must meet the constraints of on-line computer time, memory, and wordlength, and these considerations dictate using as simple a filter as possible that also meets performance specifications. Consequently, the designer must be able to exploit basic modeling alternatives to achieve a simple but adequate filter, adding to or deleting from the model complexity according to performance needs and the requirements of practical constraints. The result is that he often generates not one, but several proposed filters of varying degrees of sophistication and performance potential, and a tradeoff analysis is conducted.

Evaluation of the *true* performance capabilities of simplified, reduced-order filters is thus of critical importance in the design procedure. Although a Kalman filter computes an error covariance matrix internally, this is a valid depiction of the true errors committed by the filter only to the extent that the filter's own system model adequately portrays true system behavior. It is very possible for the filter not to perform as well as it "thinks" it does. If the computed error covariance is inappropriately "small" (in norm, magnitude of individual eigenvalues, etc.), so is the computed filter gain: the filter discounts the data from the "real world" too much and weights its internal system model too heavily. Such a condition leads to filter state estimates not corresponding to true system behavior, with a simultaneous indication by the filter-computed covariance that the estimates are precise: filter divergence is exhibited. One significant task in the overall design process is the tuning of each proposed filter, iteratively choosing the design parameters (covariance matrix entries describing the statistics of uncertainties associated with the filter's dynamics and measurement models) that yield the best true estimation performance possible from that particular filter structure. This, in fact, is accomplished by choosing the design parameters so that the filter-computed mean squared errors *are* a good representation of the true mean squared errors.

The design of an effective operational Kalman filter entails an iterative process of proposing alternative designs through physical insights, tuning each, and trading-off performance capabilities and computer loading. Section II discusses the development of numerous proposed filters for a given application. Section III then develops the ability to analyze the performance capability of any Kalman filter configuration operating in the real-world environment. With such performance analysis available, Section IV presents a systematic design procedure, and Sections V and VI provide examples of exploiting these results.

II. PROSPECTIVE FILTER DESIGNS

Any prospective Kalman filter is based upon a design model of state dynamics and measurement characteristics. The design model dynamics equation for a *standard (linear) Kalman filter* is a linear stochastic differential equation for the n-dimensional state vector $\underline{x}(t)$:

$$\underline{dx}(t) = \underline{F}(t)\underline{x}(t)\,dt + \underline{B}(t)\underline{u}(t)\,dt + \underline{G}(t)\,\underline{d\beta}(t), \tag{1}$$

where $\underline{u}(t)$ is an r vector of deterministic control inputs and $\underline{\beta}(t)$ is an s-dimensional Brownian motion of diffusion $\underline{Q}(t)$ for all time t of interest, with statistical description given by

$$E\{\underline{\beta}(t)\} = \underline{0}, \tag{2a}$$

$$E\{[\underline{\beta}(t) - \underline{\beta}(t')][\underline{\beta}(t) - \underline{\beta}(t')]^T\} = \int_{t'}^{t} \underline{Q}(\tau)\,d\tau, \tag{2b}$$

where E{ } denotes expectation. The a priori information about the initial state $\underline{x}(t_0)$ is provided in the form of a Gaussian density specified by mean $\hat{\underline{x}}_0$ and covariance $\underline{P}_0$:

$$E\{\underline{x}(t_0)\} = \hat{\underline{x}}_0, \tag{3a}$$

$$E\{[\underline{x}(t_0) - \hat{\underline{x}}_0][\underline{x}(t_0) - \hat{\underline{x}}_0]^T\} = \underline{P}_0. \tag{3b}$$

Equation (1) is often written less rigorously as

$$\dot{\underline{x}}(t) = \underline{F}(t)\underline{x}(t) + \underline{B}(t)\underline{u}(t) + \underline{G}(t)\underline{w}(t), \tag{4}$$

by heuristically dividing through by dt, where $\underline{w}(t)$ is zero-mean white Gaussian noise [the hypothetical derivative of Brownian motion $\underline{\beta}(t)$] of strength $\underline{Q}(t)$:

$$E\{\underline{w}(t)\} = \underline{0}, \tag{5a}$$

$$E\{\underline{w}(t)\underline{w}^T(t + \tau)\} = \underline{Q}(t)\delta(\tau), \tag{5b}$$

where $\delta(\tau)$ is the Dirac delta function.

At each sample time t_i, an m-dimensional vector of measurements $\underline{z}(t_i)$ becomes available, modeled as a linear combination of the states plus additive noise:

$$\underline{z}(t_i) = \underline{H}(t_i)\underline{x}(t_i) + \underline{v}(t_i), \tag{6}$$

where $\underline{v}(t_i)$ is zero-mean white Gaussian discrete-time noise with covariance $\underline{R}(t_i)$:

$$E\{\underline{v}(t_i)\} = \underline{0}, \tag{7a}$$

$$E\{\underline{v}(t_i)\underline{v}^T(t_j)\} = \underline{R}(t_i)\delta_{ij}, \tag{7b}$$

where δ_{ij} is the Kronecker delta ($\delta_{ij} = 1$ if $i = j$; $\delta_{ij} = 0$ if $i \neq j$). The measurement corruption noise $\underline{v}(t_i)$ is usually assumed independent of the dynamics driving noise $\underline{w}(t)$ for all times t and t_i (although this is readily generalized [1]).

Once the system model has been defined by the structural parameters, i.e., the time histories of $\{\underline{F}, \underline{B}, \underline{G}, \underline{H}\}$, and the statistics of uncertainties, i.e., the $\{\hat{\underline{x}}_0, \underline{P}_0\}$ values and $\{\underline{Q}, \underline{R}\}$ time histories, the *Kalman filter algorithm* can be specified. Namely, the state estimate and error covariance are *propagated* from sample time t_{i-1} to the next sample time t_i by means of integrating

$$\dot{\hat{\underline{x}}}(t/t_{i-1}) = \underline{F}(t)\hat{\underline{x}}(t/t_{i-1}) + \underline{B}(t)\underline{u}(t), \tag{8}$$

$$\dot{\underline{P}}(t/t_{i-1}) = \underline{F}(t)\underline{P}(t/t_{i-1}) + \underline{P}(t/t_{i-1})\underline{F}^T(t) + \underline{G}(t)\underline{Q}(t)\underline{G}^T(t), \tag{9}$$

where the notation $\hat{\underline{x}}(t/t_{i-1})$ corresponds to the estimate (conditional mean) of $\underline{x}$ at time t, conditioned on measurements taken through sample time t_{i-1}, and $\underline{P}(t/t_{i-1})$ is the corresponding conditional state (and error) covariance. These are propagated from the initial conditions

$$\hat{\underline{x}}(t_{i-1}/t_{i-1}) = \hat{\underline{x}}(t_{i-1}^+), \quad \underline{P}(t_{i-1}/t_{i-1}) = \underline{P}(t_{i-1}^+), \tag{10}$$

using the results of the measurement update at time t_{i-1}, where the superscript + denotes "after measurement incorporation." Integration of Eqs. (8) and (9) yields the best prediction of $\underline{x}(t_i)$ before the measurement at t_i is incorporated, denoted as $\hat{\underline{x}}(t_i^-)$, and the associated error covariance $\underline{P}(t_i^-)$:

$$\hat{\underline{x}}(t_i^-) = \hat{\underline{x}}(t_i/t_{i-1}), \quad \underline{P}(t_i^-) = \underline{P}(t_i/t_{i-1}). \tag{11}$$

In fact, the solution to Eqs. (8) and (9) can be written explicitly as

$$\underline{\hat{x}}(t_i^-) = \underline{\Phi}(t_i, t_{i-1})\underline{\hat{x}}(t_{i-1}^+) + \int_{t_{i-1}}^{t_i} \underline{\Phi}(t_i, \tau)\underline{B}(\tau)\underline{u}(\tau)\, d\tau, \tag{12}$$

$$\underline{P}(t_i^-) = \underline{\Phi}(t_i, t_{i-1})\underline{P}(t_{i-1}^+)\underline{\Phi}^T(t_i, t_{i-1}) + \int_{t_{i-1}}^{t_i} \underline{\Phi}(t_i, \tau)\underline{G}(\tau)\underline{Q}(\tau)\underline{G}^T(\tau)\underline{\Phi}^T(t_i, \tau)\, d\tau, \tag{13}$$

in terms of the state transition matrix $\underline{\Phi}$ associated with $\underline{F}(t)$ in Eq. (1) or (4), i.e., the solution to $\dot{\underline{\Phi}}(t, t_0) = \underline{F}(t)\underline{\Phi}(t, t_0)$ and $\underline{\Phi}(t_0, t_0) = \underline{I}$. This form of propagation relation is especially useful for filter applications involving time-invariant system models, stationary noises, and fixed sampling periods, as a replacement for direct numerical integration of Eqs. (8) and (9). At sample time t_i, the measurement $\underline{z}(t_i)$ is incorporated into the estimate according to the *update relations*

$$\underline{K}(t_i) = \underline{P}(t_i^-)\underline{H}^T(t_i)\left[\underline{H}(t_i)\underline{P}(t_i^-)\underline{H}^T(t_i) + \underline{R}(t_i)\right]^{-1}, \tag{14}$$

$$\underline{\hat{x}}(t_i^+) = \underline{\hat{x}}(t_i^-) + \underline{K}(t_i)[\underline{z}(t_i) - \underline{H}(t_i)\underline{\hat{x}}(t_i^-)], \tag{15}$$

$$\underline{P}(t_i^+) = \underline{P}(t_i^-) - \underline{K}(t_i)\underline{H}(t_i)\underline{P}(t_i^-). \tag{16}$$

Starting from the initial conditions of $\underline{\hat{x}}_0$ and $\underline{P}_0$ given by Eq. (3), this algorithm recursively processes time propagations and measurement updates. The propagations between measurement sample times inherently use the system dynamics model [Eqs. (1) to (5)] to provide the predicted state and error covariance.

Through use of the measurement model [Eqs. (6) and (7)], it also generates the best estimate of what the next measurement will be before it actually arrives. The measuring devices are then sampled, the residual is computed as the difference between these measurements and their predicted values, and, finally, the filter gain [itself dependent on the structural and statistical models of Eqs. (1) to (7)] optimally weights this residual to produce the updated state estimate. Because these models are embedded in the structure of the filter algorithm, the performance potential of any Kalman filter is directly a function of the adequacy of its assumed models.

A systematic design procedure will encompass the generation of alternative filter designs, each based on a particular set of models, and an evaluation of realistic performance capabilities and computer loading for each one. It is possible to devise filters based on very extensive models, and, in fact, it is useful to investigate the performance of the filter based on the most complete model, known as a *truth model*, to establish a baseline of performance to which to compare others. However, such a filter is typically more sophisticated than required to meet performance specifications, and it is prohibitive computationally. The designer must seek simplified filter design models that retain the dominant features of the original system characteristics and provide adequate estimate precision. This is probably the most difficult aspect of designing a filter, and it requires substantial understanding of the real-world system and of stochastic modeling, as well as competence in filtering theory.

Suppose a large-dimensioned, complex system model existed upon which a filter could be based that far exceeded performance requirements. Since the number of multiplications (time-consuming on a computer) and additions required by the filter algorithm is proportional to n^3 and the number of storage locations is proportional to n^2, where n is the state dimension, one significant means of decreasing the computer burden is to *reduce the order by deleting and/or combining (or "aggregating") states* [1-10]. There is often considerable physical insight into the relative significance of various states upon overall estimation precision that suggests which states might be removed. States with consistently small rms values, such as those corresponding to higher order and/or higher frequency system modes, which typically have lower energy associated with them, especially warrant inspection for possible removal. Other noncritical system modes might also be discarded, especially if they are only weakly observable or controllable [11,12]. An error-budget performance analysis of the most complete filter (discussed in Section III) is an invaluable aid to this state dimension reduction.

In many applications, system models are in the form of the fundamental descriptive equations of some physical system, driven by time-correlated stochastic processes whose characteristics match those of physical phenomena such as noises and disturbances. These, in turn, are modeled as the outputs of linear "shaping filters" [1] driven by white Gaussian noise, with dimension and defining parameters chosen such that these model outputs have statistical properties that replicate or closely approximate empirically observed means, autocorrelation functions, power spectral densities, etc., of the actual physical phenomena. In these shaping filters particularly are substantial order-reduction efforts usually made. Often a high-dimensioned shaping filter in the overall truth model is replaced by a very low-order shaping filter, such as a first-order lag driven by zero-mean white Gaussian noise:

$$\dot{x}(t) = -[1/T]x(t) + w(t), \tag{17}$$

where the strength Q of the white noise w is $2\sigma^2/T$, so that the x process in steady state has mean of zero, mean squared value and variance of σ^2, an autocorrelation function of $E\{x(t)x(t + \tau)\} = \sigma^2 \exp\{-|\tau|/T\}$, so that T is the correlation time, and a power spectral density function $[2\sigma^2/T]/[\omega^2 + (1/T)^2]$, so that the bandwidth of x is (1/T). The values σ^2 and T are treated as design parameters to match the empirically observed mean squared value with σ^2 (or low-frequency power spectral density value with $2\sigma^2 T$) and bandwidth with (1/T), ignoring less predominant characteristics. In fact, if the bandwidth is wide compared to the bandpass of the system driven by this noise, a zero-state trivial shaping filter might be proposed: white Gaussian noise of strength to match the low-frequency power spectral density characteristics.

It must be emphasized that deleting states and combining many states into fewer "equivalent" states must be evaluated in terms of the resulting filter performance, as described in Section III. Experience has shown that reductions motivated by even the best of physical insight can sometimes degrade estimation accuracy unacceptably. Furthermore, an inappropriately reduced filter of state dimension n can often be outperformed by a filter involving fewer than n, differently chosen, states. The extreme case of this would be an unstable higher dimensioned filter being based upon an unobservable system model in which, for instance, two states correspond to different physical variables but are indistinguishable in their effect on the model outputs, whereas the lower dimensioned filter model combined states to achieve observability.

Simplification of system model matrices for a given dimension state model is also possible. *Dominated terms* in a single matrix element can be *neglected*, as in the replacement of the state transition matrix $\underline{\Phi}$ by $[\underline{I} + \underline{F}\ \Delta t]$ in a time-invariant or slowly varying model, with higher order terms ignored in each element. Moreover, *entire weak coupling terms can be removed*, producing matrix elements of zero, and thus fewer required multiplications. Such removal sometimes allows *decoupling* the filter: a decentralized design achieved through nonsingular perturbations [13]. In numerous applications, the terms that can be ignored comprise the time-varying nature of the model description, or at least the most rapid variations, so that a *time-invariant model* (or at least one that admits quasi-static coefficients) can be used for the basis of a computationally advantageous filter. Furthermore, a given problem can often be decomposed via *singular perturbations* [13-19] into a number of *simpler nested problems*, with "inner loops" operating at fast sample rates to estimate (and control) "high-frequency" dynamics states (assuming that slower states are random constants), and "outer loops" operating at longer sample periods to estimate (and control) slower dynamics (designed assuming that "faster" states have reached steady-state conditions).

The number of multiplications and additions required by a filter algorithm can be minimized by *transforming into a canonical state space representation*, since the resulting system matrices embody a high density of zeros. Obviously, one might also attempt to reduce the computational burden by *increasing the sample period* of the filter, if performance allows this option.

The methods discussed up to this point have involved the generation of a simplified model, with subsequent filter construction. It is also advantageous to consider *approximating the filter structure itself*. Because of the separability of the conditional mean and covariance equations in the filter, it is possible to precompute and store the filter gains rather than calculate them on-line. This *precomputed filter-gain history* can often be *approximated closely by curve-fitted simple functions*, such as piecewise constant functions, piecewise linear functions, and weighted exponentials. Thus, the filter covariance and gain calculations, which comprise the majority of the computer burden, are replaced by a minimal amount of required computation and storage. On-line practicality can be enhanced still further in the case of a filter based on a time-invariant system model driven by stationary noises. In many such applications, a short initial transient is followed by a long period of essentially steady-state constant gain, and the approximation of using these *constant gains for all time* may be entirely adequate for desired performance. Of course, there are some drawbacks to using stored gain profiles. Future gains do not change appropriately when scheduled measurements are not made, due to data gaps or measurement rejection by reasonableness tests on the residuals [1]. Nor can the prestored gains adapt on-line to compensate for filter divergence or a system environment that is different from that anticipated during the design phase. Finally, lengthy simulations are usually required to determine a single gain history that will perform adequately under all possible conditions for an actual application.

In many aerospace applications, the appropriate system model is not entirely linear as in Eqs. (1), (4), and (6), but admits nonlinearities in dynamics and/or measurement relationships, as

$$\underline{dx}(t) = \underline{f}[\underline{x}(t), \underline{u}(t), t]\, dt + \underline{G}(t)\, \underline{d\beta}(t), \tag{18a}$$

$$\dot{\underline{x}}(t) = \underline{f}[\underline{x}(t), \underline{u}(t), t] + \underline{G}(t)\underline{w}(t), \tag{18b}$$

$$\underline{z}(t_i) = \underline{h}[\underline{x}(t_i), t_i] + \underline{v}(t_i). \tag{19}$$

Here $\underline{f}$ and $\underline{h}$ are known functions of their arguments, with sufficient continuity assumptions on $\underline{f}$ to assure the existence of solutions to Eqs. (18a,b) and enough differentiability assumptions to be able to invoke Taylor series representations in the desired filters. The noises still enter the relations in a linear fashion and have the same statistics as in Eqs. (2), (5), and (7), and the initial statistics are as in Eq. (3). More extensive models can be exploited, such as allowing $\underline{G}$ in Eq. (18) to be a function of $\underline{x}(t)$ as well as t to yield Itô stochastic differential equation models for Markov state processes [1,20-22], or relaxing the differentiability assumptions on $\underline{f}$ and $\underline{h}$ [21], but these generalizations are often not required.

In some cases, it is sufficient to generate a *linearized Kalman filter*, linearized about an a priori nominal, i.e., the solution to $\dot{\underline{x}}_{nom}(t) = \underline{f}[\underline{x}_{nom}(t), \underline{u}_{nom}(t), t]$, to estimate deviations $\underline{\delta x}(t_i)$ from that nominal. Its structure is given by Eqs. (8) to (16), with $\underline{F}(t)$, $\underline{B}(t)$, and $\underline{H}(t)$ being, respectively, $\underline{\partial f}/\underline{\partial x}$, $\underline{\partial f}/\underline{\partial u}$, and $\underline{\partial h}/\underline{\partial x}$ evaluated along the nominal. It accepts perturbation measurements $\{\underline{z}(t_i) - \underline{h}[\underline{x}_{nom}(t_i), t_i]\}$ and produces estimates $\widehat{\underline{\delta x}}(t_i^+)$ with which total state estimates can be formed as $[\underline{x}_{nom}(t_i) + \widehat{\underline{\delta x}}(t_i^+)]$.

If a single a priori nominal cannot be declared with confidence, relinearizations can be exploited through the *extended Kalman filter* [1,20-22]:

$$\dot{\hat{\underline{x}}}(t/t_{i-1}) = \underline{f}[\hat{\underline{x}}(t/t_{i-1}), \underline{u}(t), t], \tag{20}$$

$$\hat{\underline{x}}(t_i^+) = \hat{\underline{x}}(t_i^-) + \underline{K}(t_i)\{\underline{z}(t_i) - \underline{h}[\hat{\underline{x}}(t_i^-), t_i]\}, \tag{21}$$

replacing Eqs. (8) and (15), respectively, and Eqs. (9), (14), and (16) calculated with $\underline{F}(t)$ and $\underline{H}(t_i)$ being replaced by $\underline{\partial f}/\underline{\partial x}$ and $\underline{\partial h}/\underline{\partial x}$ evaluated along the current state estimate. Here, the covariance and gain calculations are dependent on the state estimate itself and are not precomputable off-line. *Precomputed-gain extended Kalman filters* are similarly based on Eqs. (20) and (21), but with a gain such as that computed for the associated linearized Kalman filter, based on a given nominal. *Constant-gain extended Kalman filters* are a special case in which the steady-state constant gain of a fixed sample-rate linearized filter for time-invariant system models and stationary noises is used for all time as the precomputed gain. Although these simplifications may not yield the same estimation precision of the full-scale extended Kalman filter, they do have computational advantages and robustness properties that often warrant their consideration, especially if feedback control is applied so as to drive the system continually toward the nominal solution [21,23].

Extended Kalman filters are sometimes plagued by biased estimates caused by neglecting higher order terms in the Taylor series expansions for $\underline{f}$ and $\underline{h}$. This can be counteracted to some degree by *inclusion of bias correction terms* derived from second-order filters and replacement of Eqs. (20) and (21) with

$$\dot{\hat{\underline{x}}}(t/t_{i-1}) = \underline{f}[\hat{\underline{x}}(t/t_{i-1}), \underline{u}(t), t] + \hat{\underline{b}}_p(t/t_{i-1}), \tag{22}$$

$$\hat{\underline{x}}(t_i^+) = \hat{\underline{x}}(t_i^-) + \underline{K}(t_i)\{\underline{z}(t_i) - \underline{h}[\hat{\underline{x}}(t_i^-), t_i] - \hat{\underline{b}}_m(t_i^-)\}, \tag{23}$$

where the bias correction term $\hat{\underline{b}}_p(t/t_{i-1})$ is the n vector with kth component

$$\hat{b}_{pk}(t/t_{i-1}) = \frac{1}{2}\,\mathrm{tr}\left\{\frac{\partial^2 f_k[\hat{\underline{x}}(t/t_{i-1}), \underline{u}(t), t]}{\partial \underline{x}^2}\,\underline{P}(t/t_{i-1})\right\}, \tag{24}$$

and $\hat{\underline{b}}_m(t_i^-)$ is the m vector with kth component

$$\hat{b}_{mk}(t_i^-) = \frac{1}{2}\,\mathrm{tr}\left(\left\{\partial^2 h_k[\hat{\underline{x}}(t_i^-), t_i]/\partial \underline{x}^2\right\}\underline{P}(t_i^-)\right), \tag{25}$$

where tr( ) denotes trace [20,21,24]. Such first-order filters with bias correction terms often exhibit estimation performance comparable to that of second-order filters, but with considerably less computational expense. For instance, a *modified Gaussian second-order filter* would be composed of the same algorithm as that just described, except that the gain would be calculated as

$$\underline{K}'(t_i) = \underline{P}(t_i^-)\underline{H}^T(t_i) \cdot \left[\underline{H}(t_i)\underline{P}(t_i^-)\underline{H}^T(t_i) + \underline{R}(t_i) + \hat{\underline{B}}_m(t_i^-)\right]^{-1}, \quad (26)$$

where $\underline{H}(t_i)$ is again $\partial \underline{h}/\partial \underline{x}$ evaluated at the current estimate $\hat{\underline{x}}(t_i^-)$, but in which the new term $\hat{\underline{B}}_m(t_i^-)$ now appears, defined as an m × m matrix with $k\ell$ element as

$$\hat{B}_{mk\ell}(t_i^-) = \frac{1}{2}\,\mathrm{tr}\left(\left\{\partial^2 h_k[\hat{\underline{x}}(t_i^-),\ t_i]/\partial \underline{x}^2\right\} \cdot \underline{P}(t_i^-)\left\{\partial^2 h_\ell[\hat{\underline{x}}(t_i^-),\ t_i]/\partial \underline{x}^2\right\}\underline{P}(t_i^-)\right). \quad (27)$$

If a first-order filter does not provide acceptable performance, it is possible to employ this or other higher order filters or even nonlinear filters that do not explicitly depend on a Taylor series (such as assumed density filters and statistically linearized filters [21,25]). However, it is often preferable to seek a *better model* upon which to base an extended Kalman filter or a first-order filter with bias correction terms.

III. PERFORMANCE ANALYSIS

Throughout Section II, the critical significance of an *"adequate" system model within the filter structure* was stressed. To assess the capabilities of various filter designs relative to each other and to a set of performance specifications, one must have at his disposal a means of producing an accurate *statistical portrayal of estimation errors committed by each filter in the "real-world" environment*, without actually building and testing each in the real world. A

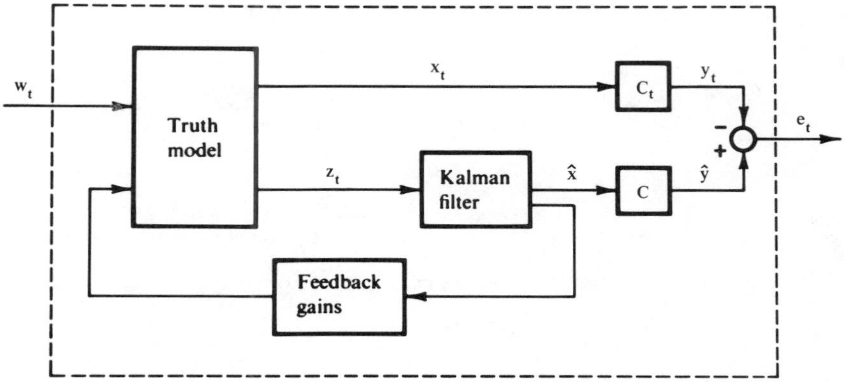

Fig. 1. Performance evaluation of a Kalman filter design. (From Ref. [1], by permission.)

performance analysis as depicted in Fig. 1 fulfills this objective by replacing the real-world measurement generation with the output of the best, most complete mathematical model that can be developed, called a truth model or reference model [1,25-28]. Extensive data analysis and shaping filter design and validation are expended to ensure that this provides a very accurate representation of the real world, since the ensuing performance evaluations and systematic design procedure are totally dependent upon this fidelity. For example, a very good generic model of the errors in an inertial navigation system (INS) has been constructed in the form of a linear model of about 70 states driven by white Gaussian noise [1,6,26,29-33]; thorough laboratory and flight testing of a particular INS allows complete specification of the model parameters to yield the truth model for that particular system. On the other hand, the design models used for the basis of operational aided-INS Kalman filters often represent these same characteristics with 15 or fewer states with less but acceptable fidelity.

The truth model is composed of a stochastic differential equation for the n_t dimensional state process $\underline{x}_t(t)$, where the subscript t denotes truth model, and an associated output equation to generate the true sampled-data measurements $\underline{z}_t(t_i)$ in Fig. 1. If the truth model itself is a linear model, then it can be expressed by equations of the form of Eqs. (1) to (7), but with subscript t added to all variables:

$$\dot{\underline{x}}_t(t) = \underline{F}_t(t)\underline{x}_t(t) + \underline{B}_t(t)\underline{u}(t) + \underline{G}_t(t)\underline{w}_t(t), \tag{28}$$

$$\underline{z}_t(t_i) = \underline{H}_t(t_i)\underline{x}_t(t_i) + \underline{v}_t(t_i), \tag{29}$$

where $\underline{w}_t(t)$ is zero-mean white Gaussian noise of strength $\underline{Q}_t(t)$ and $\underline{v}_t(t_i)$ is discrete-time zero-mean white Gaussian noise of covariance $\underline{R}_t(t_i)$ and independent of $\underline{w}_t(t)$; $\underline{x}_t(t_0)$ is described as Gaussian, of mean $\hat{\underline{x}}_{t_0}$ and covariance $\underline{P}_{t_0}$. These relations do not yet account for the feedback from the Kalman filter as depicted in Fig. 1; the required modifications shall be described to simulate such feedback of filter outputs to the real world for control purposes. It is also possible to consider a nonlinear truth model as

$$\dot{\underline{x}}_t(t) = \underline{f}_t[\underline{x}_t(t), \underline{u}(t), t] + \underline{G}_t(t)\underline{w}_t(t), \tag{30}$$

$$\underline{z}_t(t_i) = \underline{h}_t[\underline{x}_t(t_i), t_i] + \underline{v}_t(t_i), \tag{31}$$

with the statistical description of uncertainties given by $\{\hat{\underline{x}}_{t_0}, \underline{P}_{t_0}, \underline{Q}_t, \underline{R}_t\}$ as before. In fact, even more general Itô state stochastic differential equations can be used, such as allowing $\underline{G}_t$ to be a function of $\underline{x}_t$ as well as t, to produce useful Markov state processes [1,20-22].

We wish to achieve a meaningful comparison of filters that may differ substantially in state dimension and internal model specification when each is subjected to the realistic measurement environment generated by the truth model. However, for any given application, there are certain *variables of critical interest* no matter which filter is under consideration, and every proposed filter must be able to provide estimates of these quantities or variables functionally related to them. For instance, in aided-INS applications, position, velocity, and often attitude variables are paramount, and any additional states in a particular design are of secondary importance. These p critical variables, denoted here as the stochastic process $\underline{y}(t)$, shall serve as the basis of the performance analysis. They are assumed to be related to the filter states through a linear transformation so that

$$\hat{\underline{y}}(t/t_{i-1}) = \underline{C}(t)\hat{\underline{x}}(t/t_{i-1}), \tag{32a}$$

is the estimate of $\underline{y}(t)$ for any $t\epsilon(t_{i-1}, t_i)$ [using Eq. (8)], and

$$\hat{\underline{y}}(t_i^-) = \underline{C}(t_i)\hat{\underline{x}}(t_i^-), \tag{32b}$$

$$\hat{\underline{y}}(t_i^+) = \underline{C}(t_i)\hat{\underline{x}}(t_i^+), \tag{32c}$$

are the estimates of $\underline{y}(t_i)$ before and after incorporation of the measurement $\underline{z}_t(t_i)$. Often, $\underline{C}$ is time invariant, and if its structure is $[\underline{I} \vdots \underline{0}]$, then $\underline{y}$ is simply the first p of the n filter states.

As shown in Fig. 1, the truth model state process $\underline{x}_t(t)$ can also be used to generate something generally unavailable from the real world: the *true value of the quantities of interest* at any time t as

$$\underline{y}_t(t) = \underline{C}_t(t)\underline{x}_t(t), \tag{33}$$

again in terms of a linear transformation represented by a $p \times n$ matrix $\underline{C}_t(t)$. Of course, Eqs. (32) and (33) can be extended to nonlinear rather than linear functions, but the linear function case is being emphasized here. Having access to the true values $\underline{y}_t(t)$, we can represent the *true error committed by the particular Kalman filter in attempting to estimate the quantities of interest, when subjected to realistic measurements*, as

$$\underline{e}_t(t) = \hat{\underline{y}}(t/t_{i-1}) - \underline{y}_t(t), \tag{34a}$$

$$\underline{e}_t(t_i^-) = \hat{\underline{y}}(t_i^-) - \underline{y}_t(t_i), \tag{34b}$$

$$\underline{e}_t(t_i^+) = \hat{\underline{y}}(t_i^+) - \underline{y}_t(t_i), \tag{34c}$$

over the sample period before sample time t_i, and just before and after measurement incorporation at time t_i, respectively. If impulsive feedback control from the filter into the real-world system is admitted [1,6,25-27,31], then another error, corresponding to after both measurement updating and impulsive control application, is also of interest:

$$\underline{e}_t(t_i^{+c}) = \hat{\underline{y}}(t_i^{+c}) - \underline{y}_t(t_i^c), \tag{34d}$$

where the superscript c denotes the application of control. *The objective of a performance analysis is to characterize the true error process [Eq. (34)] statistically.* In a *Monte Carlo analysis* [1,28], many samples of the error stochastic process are produced by simulation, and the sample statistics are then computed directly. If the truth model itself is totally linear as in Eqs. (28) and (29), and if strictly linear output relations (32) and (33) and only linear feedback are used, then the time histories of the statistics themselves can be computed directly in *mean and covariance analyses* [1,26,27]. The relations for conducting either analysis are developed subsequent to a more precise definition of the feedback gains block of Fig. 1.

One type of *feedback* is impulsive control, or discrete-time reset, in which quantities in the real world can be changed instantaneously based upon the estimate $\hat{\underline{x}}(t_i^+)$. For example, in aided-INS Kalman filters, estimates of the position errors and velocity errors of the INS are fed back to the INS for correction by resetting the contents of computer memory locations. Once $\hat{\underline{x}}(t_i^+)$ is computed, the reset control is calculated as a function (assumed linear) of it, $[\underline{D}_t(t_i)\hat{\underline{x}}(t_i^+)]$, and after the control is applied, the truth-model state becomes

$$\underline{x}_t(t_i^c) = \underline{x}_t(t_i) - \underline{D}_t(t_i)\hat{\underline{x}}(t_i^+). \tag{35}$$

The filter should be "told" that this feedback to the system has occurred, so its state estimate is modified as

$$\hat{\underline{x}}(t_i^{+c}) = \hat{\underline{x}}(t_i^+) - \underline{D}(t_i)\hat{\underline{x}}(t_i^+) = [\underline{I} - \underline{D}(t_i)]\hat{\underline{x}}(t_i^+), \tag{36}$$

where the $n \times n$ $\underline{D}(t_i)$ models the effect of feedback through the actual $n_t \times n$ gains $\underline{D}_t(t_i)$ into the system. This $\hat{\underline{x}}(t_i^{+c})$ replaces $\hat{\underline{x}}(t_i^+)$ as the initial condition for the next time propagation. Some true system variables are controlled over the entire sample period rather than impulsively, which can be expressed by modifying Eq. (28) to

$$\dot{\underline{x}}_t(t) = \underline{F}_t(t)\underline{x}_t(t) - \underline{X}_t(t)\hat{\underline{x}}(t/t_{i-1}) + \underline{B}_t(t)\underline{u}(t) + \underline{G}_t(t)\underline{w}_t(t). \tag{37}$$

Again, the filter should be informed of such feedback, so Eq. (8) is changed to

$$\begin{aligned}\dot{\hat{\underline{x}}}(t/t_{i-1}) &= \underline{F}(t)\hat{\underline{x}}(t/t_{i-1}) - \underline{X}(t)\hat{\underline{x}}(t/t_{i-1}) + \underline{B}(t)\underline{u}(t) \\ &= [\underline{F}(t) - \underline{X}(t)]\hat{\underline{x}}(t/t_{i-1}) + \underline{B}(t)\underline{u}(t).\end{aligned} \tag{38}$$

Now, consider Fig. 1 again: if the truth model is linear, then the entire system enclosed by the dashed lines is itself a linear system driven by white Gaussian noises. To characterize the output process $\underline{e}_t(t)$ from such a system model, one first characterizes the Gauss-Markov state process for the overall system--the *augmented state process* $\underline{x}_a(t)$ composed of both truth model and filter states:

$$\underline{x}_a(t) \triangleq \begin{bmatrix} \underline{x}_t(t) \\ \hat{\underline{x}}(t/t_{i-1}) \end{bmatrix}. \tag{39}$$

From Eqs. (37) and (38), the augmented state process time-propagation relation is

$$\dot{\underline{x}}_a(t) = \underline{F}_a(t)\underline{x}_a(t) + \underline{B}_a(t)\underline{u}(t) + \underline{G}_a(t)\underline{w}_t(t), \tag{40}$$

where

$$\underline{F}_a(t) = \begin{bmatrix} \underline{F}_t(t) & -\underline{X}_t(t) \\ \underline{0} & [\underline{F}(t) - \underline{X}(t)] \end{bmatrix}, \quad \underline{B}_a(t) = \begin{bmatrix} \underline{B}_t(t) \\ \underline{B}(t) \end{bmatrix},$$
$$\underline{G}_a(t) = \begin{bmatrix} \underline{G}_t(t) \\ \underline{0} \end{bmatrix}, \tag{41}$$

as solved forward from time t_{i-1} with the initial conditions

$$\underline{x}_a(t_{i-1}^{+c}) = \begin{bmatrix} \underline{x}_t(t_{i-1}^{c}) \\ \hat{\underline{x}}(t_{i-1}^{+c}) \end{bmatrix}. \tag{42}$$

Measurement update relations are obtained by realizing that the truth model state is unaltered by a measurement

$$\underline{x}_t(t_i^{+}) = \underline{x}_t(t_i^{-}), \tag{43}$$

and that the filter update can be written as

$$\begin{aligned} \hat{\underline{x}}(t_i^{+}) &= \hat{\underline{x}}(t_i^{-}) + \underline{K}(t_i)[\underline{z}_t(t_i) - \underline{H}(t_i)\hat{\underline{x}}(t_i^{-})] \\ &= [\underline{I} - \underline{K}(t_i)\underline{H}(t_i)]\hat{\underline{x}}(t_i^{-}) \\ &\quad + \underline{K}(t_i)\underline{H}_t(t_i)\underline{x}_t(t_i) + \underline{K}(t_i)\underline{v}_t(t_i). \end{aligned} \tag{44}$$

Putting these into augmented form yields

$$\underline{x}_a(t_i^{+}) = \underline{A}_a(t_i)\underline{x}_a(t_i^{-}) + \underline{K}_a(t_i)\underline{v}_t(t_i), \tag{45}$$

where

$$\underline{A}_a(t_i) = \begin{bmatrix} \underline{I} & \underline{0} \\ \underline{K}(t_i)\underline{H}_t(t_i) & [\underline{I} - \underline{K}(t_i)\underline{H}(t_i)] \end{bmatrix},$$

$$\underline{K}_a(t_i) = \begin{bmatrix} \underline{0} \\ \underline{K}(t_i) \end{bmatrix}. \tag{46}$$

Similarly, using Eqs. (35) and (36), the impulsive control update can be represented by

$$\underline{x}_a(t_i^{+c}) = \underline{D}_a(t_i)\underline{x}_a(t_i^{+}), \tag{47}$$

$$\underline{D}_a(t_i) = \begin{bmatrix} \underline{I} & -\underline{D}_t(t_i) \\ \underline{0} & [I - \underline{D}(t_i)] \end{bmatrix}. \tag{48}$$

If feedback is not employed, $\underline{D}_a(t_i)$ is simply an $(n_t + n) \times (n_t + n)$ identity matrix, so that $\underline{x}_a(t_i^{+c}) = \underline{x}_a(t_i^+)$.

Finally, the true error committed by the filter can be expressed in terms of the augmented state vector as

$$\underline{e}_t(t) = \underline{C}_a(t)\underline{x}_a(t), \tag{49}$$

for any time t of interest where, from Eqs. (32) to (34),

$$\underline{C}_a(t) = [-\underline{C}_t(t) \quad \underline{C}(t)]. \tag{50}$$

Equations (39) to (42) and (45) to (50) are the *basis of a Monte Carlo analysis*, allowing simulation of many individual samples of the true error stochastic process. By taking appropriate expectations of these results, *mean and covariance analyses relations* can also be produced. For simplicity, we assume that all quantities are zero mean, and we concentrate our attention on the covariance analysis results (these are readily generalized to the case of nonzero $\hat{\underline{x}}_0$ and $\underline{u}$). The time history of the error covariance

$$\underline{P}_e(t) = E\left\{\underline{e}_t(t)\underline{e}_t^T(t)\right\} \tag{51}$$

is then the desired output, and

$$\underline{P}_a(t) = E\left\{\underline{x}_a(t)\underline{x}_a^T(t)\right\} \tag{52}$$

is first computed as a means of obtaining this result. The appropriate initial conditions are

$$\underline{P}_a(t_0) = \begin{bmatrix} \underline{P}_{t0} & \underline{0} \\ \underline{0} & \underline{0} \end{bmatrix}. \tag{53}$$

Propagating from sample time t_{i-1} to t_i is accomplished by integrating

$$\dot{\underline{P}}_a(t) = \underline{F}_a(t)\underline{P}_a(t) + \underline{P}_a(t)\underline{F}_a^T(t) + \underline{G}_a(t)\underline{Q}_t(t)\underline{G}_a^T(t) \tag{54}$$

forward from the initial condition $\underline{P}_a(t_{i-1}^{+c})$, as seen from Eqs. (40) to (42). The measurement update relation derived from Eqs. (45) and (46) is

$$\underline{P}_a(t_i^+) = \underline{A}_a(t_i)\underline{P}_a(t_i^-)\underline{A}_a^T(t_i) + \underline{K}_a(t_i)\underline{R}_t(t_i)\underline{K}_a^T(t_i). \tag{55}$$

From Eqs. (47) and (48), the impulsive control update is

$$\underline{P}_a(t_i^{+c}) = \underline{D}_a(t_i)\underline{P}_a(t_i^+)\underline{D}_a^T(t_i). \tag{56}$$

As the time history of $\underline{P}_a$ is generated recursively using Eqs. (54) to (56), the desired true error covariance can be obtained simultaneously via

$$\underline{P}_e(t) = \underline{C}_a(t)\underline{P}_a(t)\underline{C}_a^T(t), \tag{57}$$

as derived from Eqs. (49) and (50). Because the augmented-state system model is a linear system driven by white Gaussian noise, the covariance relations are not coupled to the actual measurement history realizations, so it is possible to perform this covariance analysis a priori, without resorting to explicit simulation of measurement process samples.

Although a covariance analysis is computationally more efficient than a Monte Carlo study and should thus be exploited for the case of linear or linearized Kalman filters and truth models, especially in initial design phases, there are advantages to using the Monte Carlo approach in addition. First, a Monte Carlo study encompasses a system simulation in which the actual, entire filter algorithm is embedded. As such, portions of the simulation can be replaced by actual data or hardware as it becomes available in the system evolution. Moreover, sign errors in the filter algorithm that may not be readily apparent in a covariance analysis due to squaring effects become evident from Monte Carlo and covariance analyses based on the same models disagreeing with each other. Finally, effects of nonlinearities such as device saturation or neglected terms in attaining linear perturbation equations cannot be evaluated by a covariance analysis except in an approximate manner based on describing functions [25], and a full investigation requires a Monte Carlo analysis.

Monte Carlo analyses are readily generalized to the evaluation of extended Kalman or other nonlinear filters subjected to a nonlinear truth model environment and possibly nonlinear output and feedback relations replacing Eqs. (32) to (36) [21,28]. Direct statistical computation such as in Eqs. (51) to (57) is generally not feasible without significant approximations, although covariance analyses of associated linearized Kalman filters are often conducted as small-scale perturbation analyses and preliminary tuning aids for extended Kalman filter designs.

IV. USE OF PERFORMANCE ANALYSIS IN DESIGN

Once a performance analysis capability is established, a systematic iterative design and tradeoff of proposed filters can be conducted. First of all, performance analysis allows proper *filter tuning* [1,6,20,25-28,31,34,37]. The basic objective of tuning is to achieve the best possible estimation accuracy from a proposed filter by selection of filter design parameters of $\underline{P}_0$ and the time histories of $\underline{Q}$ and $\underline{R}$ [see Eqs. (3), (5), and (7)]. Basically, $\underline{P}_0$ is the determining factor in the initial transient performance of the filter, whereas the $\underline{Q}$ and $\underline{R}$ histories dictate the longer term or steady-state performance and time duration of transients. These covariances not only account for actual noises and disturbances in the physical system, but are also a means of declaring how adequately the filter-assumed model represents the real-world system. Therefore, the simpler and less accurate the model, the stronger should the noise strengths be set (through addition of "pseudonoise" to the noises associated with true physical disturbance phenomena). However, it is difficult if not impossible to declare best parameter values a priori, and the specification is usually the result of an iterative search employing performance analyses.

When tuning a filter, it is useful to compare the actual estimation error statistics, as provided by $\underline{P}_e(t)$ or the sample statistics from a Monte Carlo evaluation, to the filter's own representation of its error statistics through its internally computed covariance matrix given by Eqs. (9), (13), (14), and (16). Superimposed plots of true and filter-computed rms errors in estimating individual quantities of interest, as depicted in Fig. 2, are an invaluable aid to tuning and are often provided interactively by performance analysis software [27,28]. If, due to mistuned noise parameters such as attributing inappropriately small uncertainty to the internal dynamics model, the filter underestimates its own errors as in Fig. 2a, the filter "believes" its model output too much and does not weight the measurement information heavily enough.

This can cause filter divergence [1,21,25,38-40] if the discrepancy is significant enough. On the other hand, if inappropriately small uncertainty and noise corruption are

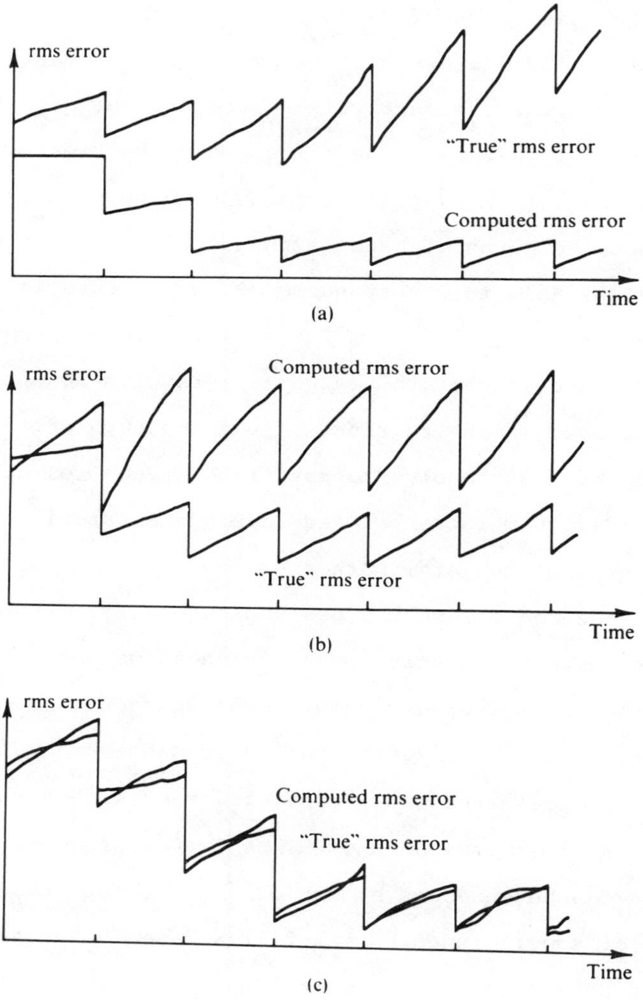

Fig. 2. Filter tuning through performance analysis: (a) filter underestimates its own errors (divergence); (b) filter overestimates its own errors (tracking of measurement noise); (c) well-tuned filter. (From Ref. [1], by permission.)

associated with the measurements, the filter overestimates its own errors and weights the measurements too heavily, expending too much effort tracking the noisy data and not exploiting the benefits of its internal model enough, as in Fig. 2b. By choosing the noise parameters so that the overall time histories of actual and filter-computed rms errors match well, the actual rms errors are effectively reduced at the same time, as seen in Fig. 2c. Allowing the filter to overestimate its own errors slightly, thereby guarding against divergence, is a commonly adopted means of generating a "conservative" or robust filter design, able to withstand modeling inaccuracies without becoming divergent [23]. Game theoretic minimax approaches [41] have also been used to design filters with acceptable performance over an entire range of uncertain parameter values. Filters are also purposely "robustified" in control applications in order to maintain closed-loop system stability despite large variations in system parameters or operating conditions from those assumed during the design phase [42]. Another more formal result than iterative pseudonoise adjustment is provided by the concept of a minimum-variance reduced-order estimator [43,44], but, again, the performance analysis should be used to indicate the true capabilities of such a tuning approach. Furthermore, both off-line tuning and on-line adaptation can be enhanced by exploiting the fact that the residuals of a well-tuned Kalman filter based on an adequate model should be a zero-mean, white Gaussian discrete-time process with covariance of $\left[\underline{H}(t_i)\underline{P}(t_i^-)\underline{H}^T(t_i) + \underline{R}(t_i)\right]$ as computed in the filter in Eq. (14) [1,21,25].

Once a particular filter has been tuned, an *error budget* [1,21,25,35-37] can be established. This is a depiction of the contributions of individual error sources to overall estimation errors, consisting of repeated performance analyses in which single or small groups of error sources in the truth model are "turned on" individually. If the filter under test were based upon the full-scale truth model, such an error budget would suggest potential choices of states to neglect in a reduced-order design (increasing the strength of appropriate noises to account for such deletion) that would yield the least performance degradation. On the other hand, if the filter under test were a proposed practical design and tuned properly, this error budget would indicate dominant sources of error, which may warrant either better models for error compensation within the filter or better system hardware (i.e., changes in the truth model) if better performance is sought. *Sensitivity* of estimation precision to *parameter variations* in the filter or system hardware can be obtained in a straightforward manner by repeated performance analyses embodying the parameter changes, or adjoint methods [45] can be used to describe local sensitivity to small variations in many parameters simultaneously.

A *systematic design procedure* would first entail developing a truth model to portray actual system behavior very accurately, as validated with laboratory and operational test data; if it is nonlinear, it should be linearized about an appropriate nominal for later covariance analyses. The filter based upon the truth model is generated as a benchmark of performance; for this filter there is no "tuning" to be accomplished and the filter-computed covariance is the desired true error covariance if all models are linear. Simplified, reduced-order system models are then proposed by deleting and combining states associated with nondominant effects, removing weak coupling terms, employing approximations such as constant gains, and the like (this part of the design effort requires substantial physical insights into the problem at hand). A performance analysis of each proposed filter is then conducted; as an iteration within this step, each filter is tuned to provide the best possible performance from each. A performance/computer-loading tradeoff analysis is generated to select a final design. This chosen design is then implemented on the on-line computer to be used in the actual system; for numerical stability and numerical precision of the on-line filter at modest wordlength, this implementation is best accomplished in square root or U-D covariance factorization form (expressing a covariance $\underline{P}$ as $\underline{SS}^T$ in terms of square root matrix $\underline{S}$, or as $\underline{UDU}^T$ in terms of unitary, upper triangular matrix $\underline{U}$ and diagonal matrix $\underline{D}$) [1,44,46-48]. Finally, checkout, any required final tuning, and operational test of the filter are performed. Even in this last phase, performance analyses can be used to investigate and extend the results observed in on-line filter operation [49]. Through such a design procedure, a logical decision process based on sufficient empirical data is incorporated into the filter implementation.

V. EXAMPLE OF REDUCED-ORDER LINEAR KALMAN FILTER DESIGN

A. *INTRODUCTION*

The U.S. Air Force is currently developing tactical weapon systems that will afford precision standoff delivery of ordnance. One such system is a glide vehicle with midcourse and terminal navigation and guidance accomplished through use of a strapdown INS aided by a radiometric area correlator (RAC).

Two different low-cost strapdown INSs are competing for implementation. Although both use conventional accelerometers to measure specific force, one INS employs laser gyroscopes to measure angular rates, whereas the other uses conventional dry gyros. This difference will be seen to have a significant impact on the error characteristics of the two systems and on Kalman filter performance capabilities.

As the glide vehicle flies a desired trajectory, the RAC provides a number of accurate position fixes by correlating a radiometric "picture" of the terrain immediately below the vehicle with a prestored reference map of that region. The number of such fixes is limited by the amount of computer memory allotted for the reference maps, five or six being a practical upper bound.

A Kalman filter was designed [50] to combine the information received from the INS and RAC, to estimate the errors being committed by the INS, and to feed back corrective signals to remove these estimated errors. Because of the restricted amount of computer memory allocated to the Kalman filter (less than 1000 words), the proposed design was very simple--two decoupled three-state filters. However, the adequacy of such a simple design to meet performance specifications was subject to significant question, so a covariance analysis was conducted to determine estimation precision capabilities in a realistic environment [51].

Certain aspects of this study, such as RAC performance characteristics and a detailed portrayal of the glide-vehicle trajectory (basically a nonmaneuvering glide with terminal pitchover and descent), are not available for public release at this time. For this reason, the analysis results are presented in the form of percentages or unscaled graphs.

B. *KALMAN FILTER DESIGN*

The proposed design is actually composed of two decoupled, three-state Kalman filters, each maintaining estimates of the INS position, velocity, and attitude-angle error states along a single coordinate direction (east and north are the chosen axes). Thus, the six state variables being estimated are δx_e and δx_n, the east and north components of the error in the INS-indicated position; δv_e and δv_n, errors in INS-indicated velocity; and ϕ_e and ϕ_n, the errors in INS-indicated attitude (tilts).

The dynamics model upon which the filters are based is

$$\begin{bmatrix} \dot{\delta x}_e \\ \dot{\delta v}_e \\ \dot{\phi}_n \end{bmatrix} = \begin{bmatrix} 0 & 1 & 0 \\ 0 & 0 & -g \\ 0 & 1/R_0 & 0 \end{bmatrix} \begin{bmatrix} \delta x_e \\ \delta v_e \\ \phi_n \end{bmatrix} + \begin{bmatrix} 0 & 0 \\ 1 & 0 \\ 0 & 1 \end{bmatrix} \begin{bmatrix} w_{e1} \\ w_{e2} \end{bmatrix}, \tag{58}$$

and a similar model for δx_n, δv_n, and ϕ_e. In Eq. (58), g is the magnitude of gravity and R_0 is the equatorial radius of the Earth. The driving term w_{e1} is a white Gaussian noise to model acceleration-level errors, and w_{e2} is an independent Gaussian noise to model errors associated with attitude-error angular rates. Equation (58) is in the form of Eq. (4) with constant $\underline{F}$ and $\underline{G}$ and $\underline{B} = \underline{0}$, i.e., a linear, constant coefficient, stochastic differential equation driven by stationary zero-mean white Gaussian noise with constant strength $\underline{Q}$ in Eq. (5b).

The sampled-data measurements made available to the filter algorithms are generated by differencing INS-indicated and RAC-indicated positions. For instance, the INS-indicated east position would be the true position plus the error state δx_e:

$$x_{e-INS} = x_{e-TRUE} + \delta x_e, \tag{59}$$

whereas the RAC-indicated east position would be modeled as the true position corrupted by white Gaussian noise v:

$$x_{e-RAC} = x_{e-TRUE} - v. \tag{60}$$

Differencing Eqs. (59) and (60) at sample time t_i yields

$$z(t_i) = x_{e-INS}(t_i) - x_{e-RAC}(t_i) = \delta x_e(t_i) + v(t_i)$$

$$= [1 \quad 0 \quad 0] \begin{bmatrix} \delta x_e(t_i) \\ \delta v_e(t_i) \\ \phi_n(t_i) \end{bmatrix} + v(t_i). \tag{61}$$

Equation (61) and the corresponding result for the difference of north position indications are of the form of Eq. (6) with $\underline{H}$ constant and v a scalar discrete-time zero-mean white Gaussian noise with time-varying autocorrelation as in Eq. (7).

Formulation of a viable system representation as a pair of independent three-state models depends upon insights and assumptions closely tied to the structure of both the full-scale INS error model and the measurement error model. First, the generally accepted nine-state model of INS error characteristics in which position, velocity, and attitude errors about three coordinate directions (east, north, up) are totally intercoupled [29-33], can be partitioned according to the state subsets $(\delta x_e, \delta v_e, \phi_n)$, $(\delta x_n, \delta v_n, \phi_e)$, ϕ_u, and $(\delta x_u, \delta v_u)$. The last set is only weakly coupled to the first seven states and is, in fact, totally decoupled from them if the vehicle is at rest and the Earth were nonrotating. Moreover, the errors in this vertical channel are kept suitably small with altimeter aiding external to the filter, so these two states are ignored.

Under the same assumption of the vehicle at rest on a nonrotating Earth, the first three sets of states also decouple, the first two being characterized by Schuler oscillations and depicted as in Eq. (58). When the vehicle-centered east-north-up frame moves over a rotating Earth, response mode modification and intercoupling occur. But the error oscillations are still Schuler dominated, since the Schuler angular rate $(g/R_0)^{1/2}$ is significantly greater than coupling terms on the order of Earth rate Ω relative to inertial space and vehicle position angular rate relative to the Earth (i.e., the velocity component divided by R_0); and the Schuler rate squared dominates vehicle position angular accelerations. Cross coupling occurs among the three attitude error states predominantly due to nonzero Earth rate and vehicle velocity, and the rate of change of velocity error states couple into these attitude errors through a nonzero specific force. For instance, terms to be added to the right-hand side of Eq. (58) include

$$\begin{bmatrix} 0 & 0 & 0 \\ 0 & -(f_u - g) & f_n \\ -\omega_u & 0 & \omega_e \end{bmatrix} \begin{bmatrix} \phi_e \\ \phi_n \\ \phi_u \end{bmatrix}$$

where f_u and f_n are specific force components, and ω_u and ω_e are components of the angular rate of the east-north-up frame with respect to inertial space; additional cross-coupling effects also develop among the nine error states. The uncertainties w_{e1} and w_{e2} in Eq. (58) partially account for these neglected terms, though in a rather crude manner. Were it not for the severe computer memory restriction, more explicit incorporation of these effects and inclusion of the azimuth-error state ϕ_u would warrant attention as a means of enhancing performance. Especially for the application envisioned here, in which flight is along a rather benign glide trajectory, the simplistic model given in Eq. (58) might well suffice.

Decoupling into two separate filters also requires that the measurements introduce no nonnegligible cross coupling. In fact, the measurement gradient matrix $\underline{H}$ associated with the full-scale INS error model does not intercouple the two horizontal channels with each other or the vertical channel. Moreover, if $v_1(t_i)$ and $v_2(t_i)$ are the measurement noises associated with east and north position differences, as in Eqs. (61) and (7), then the equiprobability ellipsoids for the vector $[v_1(t_i), v_2(t_i)]^T$ must either have their principal axes aligned with the reference coordinate directions or be (nearly) circular, so that there is no cross correlation to intercouple the two horizontal channels. This poses no difficulty for this particular problem.

The Kalman filter based upon a model described by Eqs. (58) to (61) is given by Eqs. (8) to (16). To specify the filter algorithm completely, the dynamic noise strength $\underline{Q}$ in Eqs. (5), (9), and (13), the measurement noise strength time history

$R(t_i)$ in Eqs. (7) and (14), and the initial state covariance $\underline{P}_0$ in Eq. (3) must be established for both filters. Finding the best such values iteratively through a process of filter tuning is discussed subsequently.

C. TRUTH MODEL DEVELOPMENT

In actual operation, the filter (the two three-state filters can be viewed as a single decoupled six-state filter) is driven by measurements $\underline{z}(t_i)$ from INS and RAC hardware, and provides estimates of the states $\hat{\underline{x}}(t_i^+)$ which are used as corrective feedback to the INS. For purposes of analysis, the real-world environment is replaced by a truth model as shown in Fig. 1, and the quantities of interest $\underline{y}$ are the six states being estimated.

The truth model required in the performance analysis can be described by Eqs. (28) and (29) with $\underline{B}_t = \underline{0}$, $\underline{G}_t = \underline{I}$, and $\underline{H}_t$ constant. Table I presents the 46 states of the truth model for the laser gyro system [33,51-53] and the 61 states corresponding to the conventional gyro system [33,51]. Associated with each state are its initial variance (appropriate $\underline{P}_{t0}$ diagonal term) and white driving noise strength ($\underline{Q}_t$ diagonal term); both $\underline{P}_{t0}$ and $\underline{Q}_t$ are assumed to be diagonal. For states that are modeled as random bias processes (the outputs of undriven integrator shaping filters), the appropriate $\underline{P}_{t0}$ term is given, and the $\underline{Q}_t$ term is given as zero. For states that are modeled as first-order Markov processes (outputs of first-order lags driven by white noise), the $\underline{Q}_t$ term is described in terms of the $\underline{P}_{t0}$ term and correlation time T in such a manner as to yield stationary processes.

The first nine states are the variables used to describe the error characteristics of an INS. Although each INS under consideration is a strapdown system, this error model can be expressed conveniently with respect to an east-north-up

Table I. Truth Model State Description[a]

State	Laser gyro INS system		Conventional gyro INS system	
	P_{i0} term	Q_i term	P_{i0} term	Q_i term
Basic INS:				
Position errors (3)	(1500 ft)^2	0	(1500 ft)^2	0
Velocity errors (3)	(2 ft/s)^2	0	(2 ft/s)^2	0
Attitude errors (3)	(0.5 millirad)^2	$7.6 \times 10^{\;11}$ rad^2/s	(0.5 millirad)^2	0
Accelerometers:				
Accelerometer biases (3) (day-to-day nonrepeatability)	$(250\mu g)^2$	0	$(200\mu g)^2$	0
Accelerometer scale factor errors (3)	(500 ppm)^2	0	(405.6 ppm)^2	0
Accelerometer input axis misalignments (6)	(10 arc-s)^2	0	(30 arc-s)^2	0
Accelerometer biases (3) (T_1 = 60 min)	$(40\mu g)^2$	$2P_{i0}/T_1$	$(60\mu g)^2$	$2P_{i0}/T_1$
Accelerometer biases (3) (T_2 = 15 min)	$(20\mu g)^2$	$2P_{i0}/T_2$	$(30\mu g)^2$	$2P_{i0}/T_2$
Gravity knowledge:				
Gravity deflections (2) (d_1 = 10 n. mi.)	$(26\mu g)^2$(east) $(17\mu g)^2$(north)	$2P_{i0}v/d_1$	$(26\mu g)^2$(east) $(17\mu g)^2$(north)	$2P_{i0}v/d_1$
Gravity anomaly (1) (d_2 = 60 n. mi.)	$(35\mu g)^2$	$2P_{i0}v/d_2$	$(35\mu g)^2$	$2P_{i0}v/d_2$
Gyros:				
Gyro drift rate biases (3)	(0.09 deg/h)^2	$1.47 \times 10^{\;18}$ rad^2/s^3	(2.0 deg/h)^2(roll axis) (1.33 deg/h)^2(other two)	0
Gyro scale factor errors (3)	(100 ppm)^2	0	(500 ppm)^2	0
Gyro input axis misalignments (6)	(6 arc-s)^2	0	(30 arc-s)^2	0
Gyro drift rate (3) (T_1 = 60 min)	. . .	. . .	(0.4 deg/h)^2(*oav*)[b] (0.6 deg/h)^2(*iav*)[c]	$2P_{i0}/T_1$
Gyro drift rate (3) (T_2 = 15 min)	. . .	. . .	(0.2 deg/h)^2 (*oav*) (0.3 deg/h)^2 (*iav*)	$2P_{i0}/T_1$
g-sensitive drift coefficients (6)	. . .	. . .	(2.0 deg/h/g)^2	0
g^2-sensitive drift coefficients (3)	. . .	. . .	(0.1 deg/h/g^2)^2	0
RAC:				
RAC biases (2)	P_{ba}(along-track) P_{bc}(cross-track)	0	P_{ba}(along-track) P_{bc} (cross-track)	0
Altimeter:				
Altimeter bias (1) (d = 250 n. mi.)	(500 ft)^2	$2P_{i0}v/d$	(500 ft)^2	$2P_{i0}v/d$
Altimeter scale factor error (1)	(0.03)^2	0	(0.03)^2	0

[a] *From [51], used with permission.*
[b] *oav, output axis vertical.*
[c] *iav, input axis vertical.*

coordinate frame [29,33]. The $\underline{Q}_t$ terms associated with attitude errors are due to gyro drift and shall be discussed subsequently.

Accelerometer errors are described by means of a day-to-day nonrepeatability bias, scale-factor error, two input-axis misalignments, and two first-order Markov process states for each accelerometer. Uncertainty in the knowledge of gravity also enters the truth model state equations at the acceleration level. The errors between the true geoid and the assumed ellipsoid for INS navigation computations have been described by means of first-order Markov process models [33], with mean-square values and correlation distances as described in Table I. If a correlation distance is denoted as d and the vehicle velocity magnitude as v, a corresponding correlation time is generated as T = d/v, thereby yielding the $\underline{Q}_t$ expression in Table I.

Gyro errors are depicted by a drift-rate bias state (or Brownian motion state for the laser gyro; i.e., the output of an integrator driven by white Gaussian noise), scale-factor error, two input-axis misalignments, two first-order Markov process states, two g-sensitive drift coefficients (spin and input axes), and one g^2-sensitive drift coefficient (major spin-input coefficient) for each gyro. For the laser gyros, only the first four of these nine states are included, since the others are essentially nonexistent. Another marked difference from conventional gyros is embodied in the drift-rate model. A typical gyro drift-rate model is composed of the sum of first-order Gauss-Markov components with an additive white Gaussian noise. In conventional gyros, the time-correlated contributions dominate the very wide-band (white) component, and the latter is often neglected. However, for laser gyros, the wide-band (modeled as white) component predominates; its noise strength is given by the $\underline{Q}_t$ terms driving INS attitude errors in Table I. A final difference between the two gyro types is the set of multiple table entries for certain conventional gyro states. For the Markov process states, *oav* denotes output axis vertical, whereas *iav* means input axis vertical. The roll axis gyro drift-rate bias entry is higher than the others because a different gyro design is employed to withstand and indicate the larger range of rates that can occur about this axis. In the laser-gyro INS, the gyro sensitive axes are canted off from the vehicle body axes to distribute high roll rates among three identical gyros.

Although Table I shows accelerometer errors to be very similar in the two inertial systems, the gyro characteristics are significantly worse in the conventional gyro INS. The low-frequency power spectral density value of the Gauss-Markov drift-rate components in the conventional gyro is three orders of magnitude worse than the laser gyro white noise component. Moreover, drift-rate biases, scale-factor errors, and misalignments are considerably greater; and the g and g^2 errors have no counterpart in the laser-gyro system.

The errors in the RAC data are modeled as corruptive white Gaussian noise plus bias. This is a necessarily unsophisticated model of RAC error characteristics, since only sparse and incomplete performance data were available at time of truth model development. Nevertheless, these data were sufficient to estimate appropriate noise strengths and to indicate that bias effects were nonnegligible. The strength of the two-dimensional white noise, $\underline{v}_t$ in Eq. (29), was found to be well modeled as

$$\underline{R}_t(t_i) = [\theta h(t_i)]^2 \underline{I}, \tag{62}$$

where $h(t_i)$ is the vehicle altitude and θ is a parameter with a classified numerical value. Each bias was modeled as a random constant with mean zero and variance as shown in Table I and again the numerical values are classified. Although physical reasoning could lead to altitude-dependent variances on the bias states as well, the available data were neither consistent nor complete enough to warrant this formulation. Because high statistical confidence could not be placed in this model, a study of performance sensitivity to bias model parameter variations was deemed essential; this is discussed further in the analysis presentation.

Finally, the altimeter errors are described in terms of a first-order Markov process noise plus a scale-factor error. The altimeter is used to damp out the inherently unstable vertical errors in the INS, and so its errors drive certain INS error states in the truth model.

D. ANALYSIS RESULTS

The covariance analysis technique was first used to tune the proposed filter for use in each of the two INS/RAC system configurations [51]. The $\underline{P}_0$ and the time histories of $\underline{Q}$ and $\underline{R}$ of the filter were iteratively modified to yield minimum rms values of the estimation error $\underline{e}_t$ components for all times of interest. For this application, terminal position errors are especially important, but the entire history of all errors must be considered to preclude being outside the bounds of a prestored RAC map at an update time and to ensure sending proper corrective control commands during the terminal phase of flight.

Figure 3 plots the rms error (in log scale) in the east position estimate provided by the filter tuned to the laser gyro system. To aid the tuning process, these "actual" rms errors were compared with the filter's own representation of its errors -- its own computed covariance $\underline{P}$. Despite the simple filter form and the fact that a constant $\underline{Q}$ is used for all time, the filter-computed rms error history essentially duplicates the results shown in Fig. 3. Moreover, this

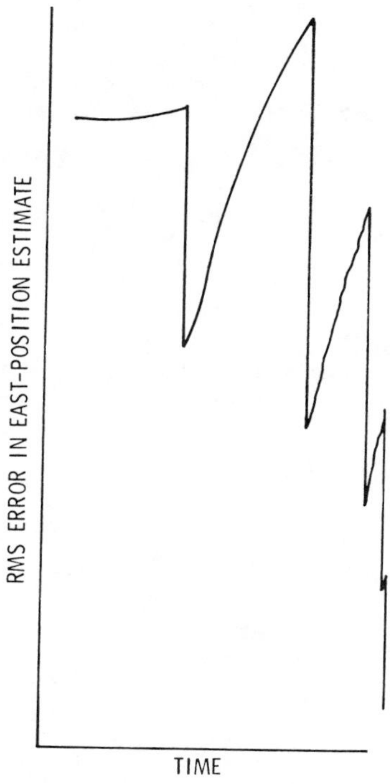

Fig. 3. rms error in east position estimate. (From Ref. [51], by permission.)

condition does effectively yield the best estimate precision. The results for the other five filter states and those for the conventional gyro system are very similar.

For computational simplicity, it was proposed to approximate the integral term in Eq. (13) by a diagonal matrix [50]. The original design was found to be severely out of tune, and even the best tuning achievable with a diagonal matrix form yielded a noticeably degraded performance. The degradation was naturally least in the channels for which direct measurements were available, i.e., position errors, and these are the estimates of primary interest for this application. However, the computation of three off-diagonal terms in a symmetric 3×3 matrix is not burdensome. Moreover, a follow-up study has indicated a substantial increase in the importance of these off-diagonal terms for obtaining good performance along more highly dynamic trajectories with optimized measurement sample times. Therefore, weapon system development and testing was pursued with the design changed to incorporate these terms.

An error budget was generated to depict the contributions of individual error sources to the rms errors throughout the vehicle flight. Once the filter was tuned, repeated covariance analyses were conducted, each with a single error source removed. Table II presents the results for rms position errors at the terminal time. From Table II, it is evident that the RAC errors have the greatest influence on estimate precision at the terminal time. This is caused by the extreme accuracy of low-altitude RAC position fixes and the fact that the last two fixes are taken shortly before the end of flight to maximize the benefit of the limited number of updates. Error

Table II. Error Budget [a]

Error source removed	% of terminal rms nav. errors	
	Laser gyro INS	Conventional INS
None (baseline)	100	100 (= 107.5% of laser error)
Accel. errors	100	99.9
Gyro errors	100	98.1
Initial condition	100	100.0
RAC bias	95	96
All RAC errors	9	11

[a] *From [51], used with permission.*

budgets for estimation errors earlier in the flight reveal an increased importance of INS sensor errors.

Table II also reveals that the laser gyro INS configuration outperforms the conventional gyro system, as would be predictable from the relative precision of instruments as described in Table I. Also, the white noise gyro drift-rate model in the filters is appropriate for a laser gyro, whereas a first-order Markov process model, requiring an additional state per filter, would be a significantly better model for a conventional gyro. Table II also shows that the gyro errors in the conventional INS system play a more dominant relative role in degrading performance than do the same errors in the laser gyro INS. These trends are accentuated at earlier times in the flight, especially in the case of dynamic trajectories.

Because of the significance of RAC errors and the sparse amount of test data concerning bias errors in this device, the sensitivity of estimation accuracy to varying bias levels was analyzed. Table III demonstrates the effect of varying the RAC bias variance from zero to four times the value listed in

Table III. Sensitivity to RAC Bias[a]

RAC bias model standard deviation	% of terminal rms nav. errors: Laser gyro INS	Conventional INS
0	95	96
standard	100	100
2 × standard	113	119

[a] *From [51], used with permission.*

Table I. These results and those depicted in Table II reveal that, if performance requirements are not met, seeking a better RAC system would be more beneficial than improving the INS precision. Similarly, if the filter complexity could be increased, it would be most advantageous to incorporate a better model for the errors in the RAC system position data.

Direct estimation of RAC biases by adding a fourth state to each filter is not feasible: adding the model $\dot{b} = w_3$ to Eq. (58), and modifying Eq. (61) to let z be $(\delta x_e + b + v)$, yields an unobservable system model. Basically, the filter would not be able to provide valid estimates of δx_e and b separately. Improved estimation performance can be achieved by replacing Eq. (62) with

$$\underline{R}(t_i) = \left\{[\theta h(t_i)]^2 + R_b(t_i)\right\}\underline{I} \tag{63}$$

in the filter formulation, where R_b scales with the variance of the RAC bias in the truth model. Although bias errors are not directly compensated, the better model for rms measurement errors yields more proper weighting of update information and thus enhanced performance. However, these conclusions are based upon the adequacy of the truth model depiction of RAC errors. Once enough performance data can be analyzed to have statistical confidence in the RAC error model, the preceding modification and other means of enhancement can be fully exploited in the operational filter.

Thus, because of severe restrictions on computer time and memory allotted, a very simple Kalman filter was designed to update a strapdown inertial system with position fixes from a radiometric area correlator. Nevertheless, its performance has been analyzed and found to meet specifications.

VI. AN ADAPTIVE EXTENDED KALMAN FILTER FOR TARGET-IMAGE TRACKING

A. *INTRODUCTION*

Current research and development efforts are examining several methods of tracking a target for the purpose of depositing high-power laser energy on that target in the presence of several disturbances. These disturbances include any effect that can cause relative motion between the beam and target, such as target motion, atmospheric jitter, vibration in optics mirrors, and sensor measurement errors.

One tracking method under investigation employs a forward-looking infrared (FLIR) sensor, together with a correlation algorithm to provide relative target position information to the laser-pointing system. The FLIR sensor generates averaged outputs of an array of IR detectors as they are mechanically scanned through a limited field of view. The digitized outputs can be either stored or displayed on a cathode ray tube (CRT) in real time, each output corresponding to the average intensity over one picture element (pixel). The horizontal and vertical scanning of the detectors through the FLIR field of view results in an array of pixels called a frame of data, with normal frame rates on the order of 30 Hz. Because of this rapid measurement rate, attention can be confined to a pixel array smaller than the entire frame for tracking purposes: an 8×8 array is a typical tracking window, yielding a tolerable amount of computer storage and loading.

The correlation algorithm [54-57] first stores a complete set of intensity data from the FLIR outputs and then correlates those data with the new information at a later time. In this manner, it estimates the two-dimensional position offset from one set of data to the next, which can be used to generate commands to keep the system centered on the target. This type of tracker needs no prior information about the type of target to perform the tracking function, and so it is well suited to many general applications.

In many practical tracking problems, however, the type of target being tracked will be known, if only in a very general sense. This implies that certain target parameters such as shape, size, and motion characteristics will be known or could be estimated. Moreover, the statistical effects of atmospheric disturbances on radiated wave fronts are known and could supply information to a tracker that would aid in separating the true target motion from the apparent motion (jitter) due to these disturbances. This separation is important since the wave front of the high-energy laser will not undergo the same distortion in the atmosphere as the IR wave fronts emanating from the target.

The purpose of this effort is to exploit the knowledge of potential target characteristics and atmospheric jitter in the design of an extended Kalman filter to replace the current correlation algorithm in the tracking loop. Initially, a simple extended Kalman filter algorithm is designed to track a point-source (distant) target with rather benign dynamics, based on FLIR measurements assumed to be corrupted by temporally and spatially uncorrelated noises, and assuming that all system-defining parameters have known nominal values [58,59]. Section VI,B establishes the required mathematical models and the basic filter, and Section VI,C analyzes its performance capabilities in a realistic environment via Monte Carlo analysis [58,59]. It consistently outperforms the correlation tracker under nominally assumed conditions, employing knowledge unused by that tracker to yield the enhanced capability. Robustness studies are conducted in Section VI,D to indicate how much the filter performance degrades when an accurate portrayal of the tracking problem differs from that assumed in the filter design [60,61]. Of specific interest are variations in (1) the height, spread, shape, and orientation of the target intensity pattern in the FLIR image plane; (2) target motion characteristics; and (3) background noise rms value and both spatial and temporal correlations. This investigation provides insights into a prioritized list of design modifications and on-line adaptation capabilities required to allow this type of filter to track highly maneuverable targets, with spatially distributed and changing image intensity profiles, against background clutter. The subsequent sections delineate specific modeling and adaptation methods to yield a filter capable of accurately tracking an air-to-air missile at close range, with performance evaluations of proposed designs achieved by Monte Carlo simulations [61,62].

B. MODELS AND FILTER FOR BENIGN TRACKING TASK

As originally conceived, the problem of interest was the accurate tracking of a point-source target based on FLIR measurements, to provide appropriate inputs to a pointing controller [58,59]. In essence, this involves determining the pointing errors in two dimensions from the center of the FLIR field of view, given measurements of average intensity levels over each of 64 pixels in an 8 × 8 "tracking window" array provided by the FLIR at a 30-Hz rate. Many applications for which this system is being considered do in fact require the acquisition and tracking of targets at long ranges. Because of these distances, even very large targets appear as point sources of IR radiation and can be accurately modeled as such. Due to the physics of wave propagation and optics, the resulting intensity pattern on the FLIR image plane can be modeled as a bivariate Gaussian function with circular equal-intensity contours. This is a special case of elliptical contours, as depicted in Fig. 4, in which $\sigma_{g1} = \sigma_{g2} = \sigma_g$. Letting $[x_{peak}(t), y_{peak}(t)]$ locate the center of the pattern relative to the center of the 8 × 8 pixel array, the apparent target-intensity model for circular equal-intensity contours is

$$
\begin{aligned}
I_{target}(\xi_x, \xi_y, t) &= I_{max} \exp\left[-\left(2\sigma_g^2\right)^{-1}\left\{[\xi_x - x_{peak}(t)]^2\right.\right. \\
&\qquad \left.\left. + [\xi_y - y_{peak}(t)]^2\right\}\right], \qquad (64)
\end{aligned}
$$

where the peak intensity value I_{max} and glint dispersion σ_g were originally assumed to be known. The apparent location of the target is actually the sum of effects due to true target dynamics, atmospheric disturbances, and vibrations (denoted, respectively, by subscripts d, a, and v):

$$x_{peak}(t) = x_d(t) + x_a(t) + x_v(t), \tag{65a}$$

$$y_{peak}(t) = y_d(t) + y_a(t) + y_v(t). \tag{65b}$$

The objective of the tracker is to estimate $x_d(t)$ and $y_d(t)$ so that they can be regulated by closed-loop control.

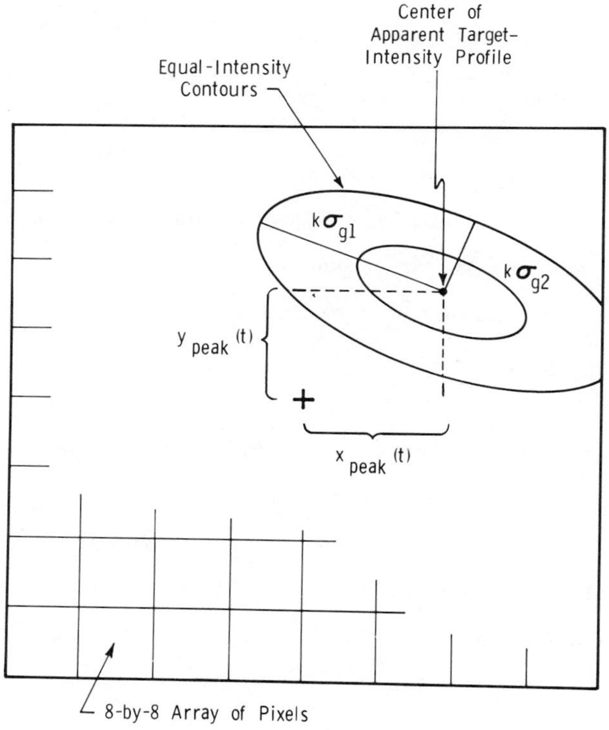

Fig. 4. Apparent target-intensity pattern on image plane. (From Ref. [62], by permission; ©1981 IEEE.)

A generally applicable model for benign target dynamics is desired, one that is simple and yet accounts for the time-correlated behavior of realistic targets. To fulfill these objective, an independent first-order Gauss-Markov model in each direction was chosen, as produced by

$$\dot{x}_d(t) = -[1/T_d]x_d(t) + w_{dx}(t), \tag{66}$$

where T_d is the characteristic correlation time of the target and w_{dx} is a zero-mean white Gaussian noise with autocorrelation function

$$E\{w_{dx}(t)w_{dx}(t + \tau)\} = [2\sigma_d^2/T_d]\,\delta(\tau), \tag{67}$$

so that σ_d is the rms value of $x_d(t)$, and similarly for $y_d(t)$. By a suitable choice of σ_d and T_d, samples from these processes can be made to exhibit amplitude and rate-of-change characteristics appropriate to a variety of long-range targets as seen in the image plane. Again, these two parameters were originally assumed to be known.

Atmospheric disturbance causes an apparent offset of the location of the intensity pattern known as jitter. Through spectral analysis of this phenomenon, it has been shown [63,64] that $x_a(t)$ and $y_a(t)$ can each be adequately modeled as the output of a third-order linear shaping filter [1] with transfer function $\left[K\omega_1\omega_2(s + \omega_1)^{-1}(s + \omega_2)^{-2}\right]$, driven by unit-strength white Gaussian noise. Here, $\omega_1 \cong 14$ rad/sec and $\omega_2 \cong 660$ rad/sec, and K can be adjusted to obtain the desired rms jitter characteristic on the output and was assumed to be known.

Vibrations of the FLIR system can also cause relative pointing errors. For this study, however, it is assumed to be on a ground-based stable platform, so that vibration effects are neglected. For airborne applications and other scenarios, vibration-induced effects may warrant considerably more attention.

Thus, the target-intensity pattern given by Eq. (64) has been fully described. However, this pattern is not directly available for observation: it is corrupted by background noise and inherent FLIR errors first. There are various forms of background noise ranging from night-sky background to clutter, i.e., from zero to high time and spatial correlations. FLIR errors such as thermal noise and dark-current effects can be modeled as temporally and spatially uncorrelated noise. Letting $z_{jk}(t_i)$ denote the measurement available at time t_i of the average intensity over the pixel in the jth row and kth column of the 8 × 8 array, then

$$z_{jk}(t_i) = A_p^{-1} \iint_{\substack{\text{region of} \\ \text{jkth pixel}}} I_{\text{target}}(\xi_x, \xi_y, t_i)\, d\xi_x d\xi_y + n_{jk}(t_i) + b_{jk}(t_i), \tag{68}$$

where A_p is the area of 1 pixel, $n_{jk}(t_i)$ models the FLIR noise effects, and $b_{jk}(t_i)$ models the background effects on the jkth pixel. Arraying the 64 scalar equations (68) in a single measurement vector yields a measurement model of the form

$$\underline{z}(t_i) = \underline{h}[\underline{x}(t_i), t_i] + \underline{n}(t_i) + \underline{b}(t_i), \tag{69}$$

where $\underline{x}$ is the output of an eight-state linear dynamics system model [one state equation as given by Eq. (66) and three coupled linear equations to generate x_a, and similarly for the y axis], and the other vectors are of dimension 64. From Eqs. (68) and (69) it can be seen that $\underline{h}$ represents the effect of the point-spread function given in Eq. (64). Note that, in such a formulation, the spatial correlation of background noise is readily represented by the off-diagonal elements of the 64 × 64 matrix $E\{\underline{b}(t_i)\underline{b}^T(t_i)\}$.

The model just developed accounts for time-correlated dynamics, bandwidth effects of jitter, and other pertinent characteristics. An extended Kalman filter could be based on this model to perform the desired tracking task.

First, to enhance computational feasibility, the model can be simplified to some degree. In view of the discrepancy between the two break frequencies of the atmospheric disturbance shaping filter and the greater importance of the lower frequency characteristics, atmospheric disturbance effects x_a and y_a were approximated as the outputs of first-order systems with break frequency ω_1 (thus preserving proper spectral shape at the significant frequencies below ω_2). This yielded a four-state linear time-invariant model of the form of Eq. (4) with $\underline{B} \equiv \underline{0}$ (until feedback control is added), constant diagonal $\underline{F}$, $\underline{G} \equiv \underline{I}$ and stationary white Gaussian input $\underline{w}(t)$. Thus, the filter equations for propagating the state estimate $\hat{\underline{x}}$ and error covariance $\underline{P}$ are given by Eqs. (12) and (13) where the state transition matrix $\underline{\Phi}$ (also diagonal) and input-noise covariance of Eq. (13),

$$\underline{Q}_d = \int_{t_{i-1}}^{t_i} \underline{\Phi}(t_i - \tau)\underline{G}\underline{Q}\underline{G}^T\underline{\Phi}^T(t_i - \tau)\, d\tau \qquad (70)$$

are constant and readily calculated once off-line. Because of the low state dimensionality, linearity, and time invariance of the dynamics model, these filter time propagations are especially simple.

Furthermore, each measurement equation [Eq. (68)] is simplified as well. First, the two-dimensional integral term is replaced by $I_{target}(x_{ck}, y_{cj}, t_i)$ where (x_{ck}, y_{cj}) is the location of the center of the jkth pixel. Second, the combined effects of $\underline{n}$ and $\underline{b}$ in Eq. (69) are represented by a single vector $\underline{v}$, assumed to have spatially and temporally uncorrelated components of constant and equal variance:

$$E\left\{\underline{v}(t_i)\underline{v}^T(t_j)\right\} = \begin{cases} R\underline{I}, & t_i = t_j, \\ \underline{0}, & t_i \neq t_j. \end{cases} \tag{71}$$

These simplifications are made to reduce complexity substantially, but are subject to reevaluation if performance capabilities are inadequate.

The large number of measurements causes a computational loading problem in the normal extended Kalman filter formulation of the measurement update [Eqs. (14), (16), and (21)] where $\underline{h}$ is defined in Eq. (69) and approximated componentwise by I_{target} evaluated at the center of each pixel, rather than its spatial average over the entire pixel; and $\underline{H}(t_i)$ is the partial of $\underline{h}$ with respect to $\underline{x}$, evaluated at $\hat{\underline{x}}(t_i^-)$. The gain calculation in Eq. (14) requires inversion of a 64 × 64 matrix. To circumvent this burden, Eqs. (14) and (16) are replaced by the equivalent inverse-covariance form [1,21]:

$$\underline{P}^{-1}(t_i^+) = \underline{P}^{-1}(t_i^-) + \underline{H}^T(t_i)\underline{R}^{-1}(t_i)\underline{H}(t_i), \tag{72}$$

$$\underline{P}(t_i^+) = \left[\underline{P}^{-1}(t_i^+)\right]^{-1}, \tag{73}$$

$$\underline{K}(t_i) = \underline{P}(t_i^+)\underline{H}^T(t_i)\underline{R}^{-1}(t_i). \tag{74}$$

This form only requires two 4 × 4 matrix inversions on-line; $\underline{R}^{-1}(t_i)$ is constant and is generated once off-line [it is also diagonal if Eq. (71) is used].

C. *PERFORMANCE ANALYSIS UNDER NOMINAL CONDITIONS*

The performance capabilities of the extended Kalman filter were evaluated and compared to those of the correlator algorithm by means of a Monte Carlo analysis [58,59]. In this analysis, the full-scale model developed in Section VI,B was used to generate sample-by-sample simulations, differing in particular realizations drawn from random-noise sources. Sample statistics of the tracking errors committed by each algorithm were computed on the basis of 20 simulation runs (chosen by observing the convergence of computed statistics to consistent values as the number of runs was increased).

This analysis was directed at four areas of primary interest:

(1) Performance as a function of signal-to-noise ratio (S/N) defined here as

$$S/N = I_{max}/(\text{rms value of background noise}); \tag{75}$$

ratios of 20, 10, and 1 were investigated.

(2) Performance as a function of intensity-pattern size (spot size on the image plane) relative to pixel size; Gaussian beam dispersion σ_g was set to 1 and 3 pixels.

(3) Performance as a function of the ratio of rms target motion to rms atmospheric jitter; (σ_d/σ_a) values of 5, 1, and 0.2 were considered.

(4) Performance as a function of target correlation time; targets with T_d of 1 and 5 sec were simulated.

All of these studies were conducted under nominally assumed conditions: as the parameters defining the real-world environment were changed, the filter was (artificially) provided knowledge of their values. Thus, there was no purposeful model mismatch between the filter and the actual tracking environment; such important robustness studies are described in Section IV,D. Also, the filter was implemented in open loop for this initial analysis: computed offsets were not fed to a pointing control system to be nulled out.

In order to optimize its performance, the filter must be tuned by adjusting the strengths both of the dynamic driving noises and the measurement-corruption noises. For the simulations conducted, the FLIR and background noises in Eqs. (68) and (69) were assumed independent, spatially and temporally uncorrelated, and Gaussian, so R in Eq. (71) was set equal to the sum of the variances for n_{jk} and b_{jk}. Adequate tuning results when the strength of the white noise terms and the correlation times for both the simulation and filter target dynamics models are set equal, and when the rms values for atmospheric jitter for both models (of different order) are equated. Figure 5 depicts the actual versus filter-computed error standard deviation committed in estimating atmospheric jitter in the horizontal direction for a typical case (S/N = 10; $\sigma_g = 3$; $\sigma_d = \sigma_a = 1$; $T_d = 1$). In this case and in all others, the adequacy of both the proposed filter tuning and the order reduction of the filter dynamics model is demonstrated by the good agreement between the two curves. When S/N is decreased to 1, the filter tends to underestimate its own errors (by about the same margin that it overestimates them in Fig. 5) using the tuning philosophy described, due to

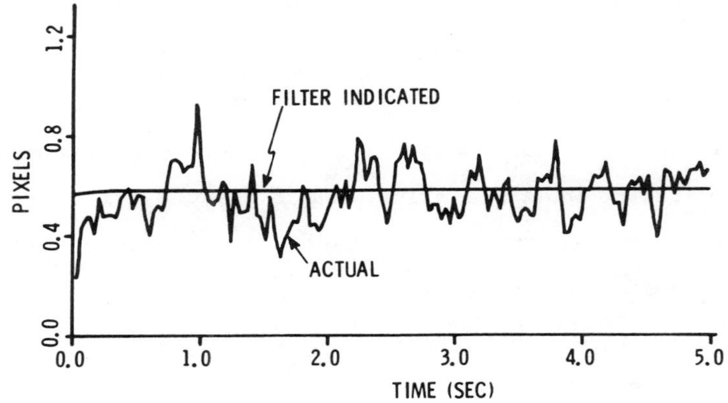

Fig. 5. $\hat{x}_a$ *Error standard deviation: actual versus filter-computed* ($S/N = 10$; $\sigma_g = 3$; $\sigma_d = \sigma_a = 1$; $T_d = 1$). *(From Ref. [58], by permission; ©1980 IEEE.)*

the mismatch between true and filter models becoming more apparent; this can readily be remedied by increasing the filter $\underline{Q}_d$ entries if desired. In fact, for a "conservative" or robust filter that is able to withstand modeling errors and yet can still provide good estimation performance (beyond the bare minimum of nondivergent characteristics [23]), one might want to tune the filter on purpose so that it overestimates its own errors somewhat. Had biased estimates been a problem for this application, it could have been combatted by tuning so as to match filter-computed error variances and actual mean square errors [21]; incorporating the "bias-correction term" from second-order filtering or implementing an entire second-order filter would be computationally prohibitive.

For the typical case and tuning philosophy depicted in Fig. 5, Fig. 6 portrays the sample mean error $\pm 1\sigma$ (standard deviation) committed by the filter in estimating the target true horizontal location. By comparison, Fig. 7 depicts the performance of the correlator algorithm under the same

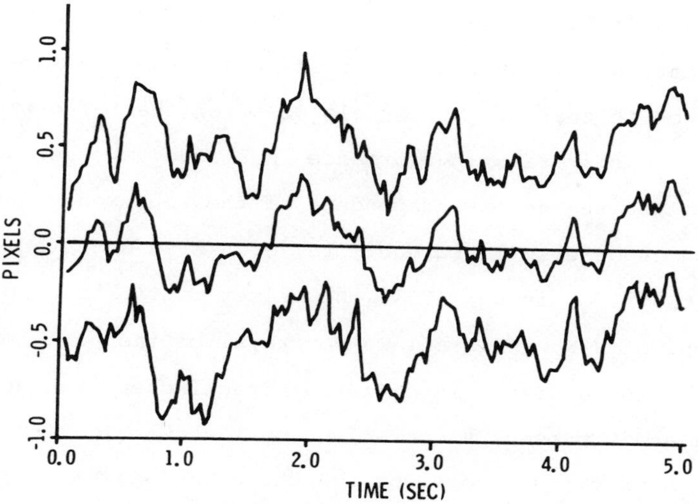

Fig. 6. $\hat{x}_d$ *Mean error* $\pm 1\sigma$ *(S/N = 10;* $\sigma_g = 3$*;* $\sigma_d = \sigma_a = 1$*;* $T_d = 1$*). (From Ref. [58], by permission; ©1980 IEEE.)*

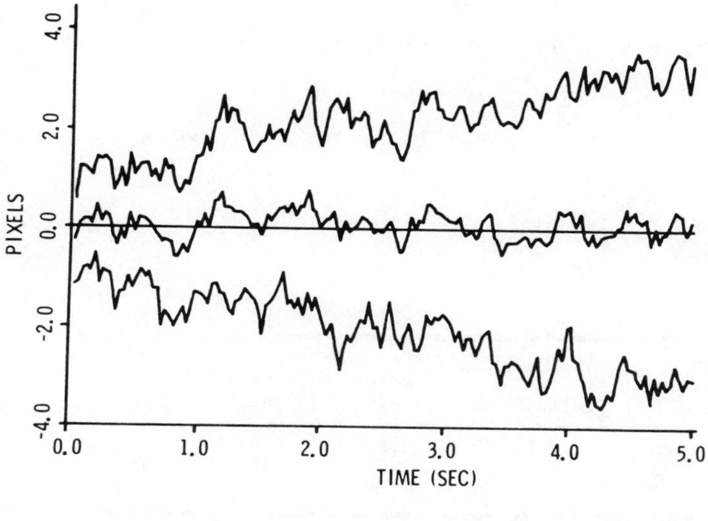

Fig. 7. Correlator target horizontal position mean error $\pm 1\sigma$ *(S/N = 10;* $\sigma_g = 3$*;* $\sigma_d = \sigma_a = 1$*;* $T_d = 1$*). (From Ref. [58], by permission; ©1980 IEEE.)*

conditions. In this case, both algorithms yield rather unbiased estimates, but the filter error standard deviation is only one-fourth that of the correlator after the 5-sec simulation (and the correlator performance is steadily worsening).

The filter tuning is independent of the Gaussian glint dispersion (spot size). Furthermore, if S/N is adjusted by changing only I_{max} in Eq. (75), the filter tuning is also independent of S/N. This allows portrayal of the performance of a singly tuned filter in different tracking environments. Tables IV and V present a comparison of the two algorithms in mean and 1σ tracking errors for the three S/N's examined, Table IV pertaining to the case of σ_g = 3 pixels and Table V to σ_g = 1 pixel. These are results at the end of the 5-sec simulations, and each represents an average of values generated from Monte Carlo simulations using the three different values of σ_d/σ_a. The extended Kalman filter performs well as S/N is lowered, with no noticeable change between the ratios 20 and 10, and exhibits only a slight degradation in performance at S/N = 1. It consistently outperforms the correlation tracker, especially at lower S/N's. In fact, the correlation algorithm

Table IV. Mean Error and 1σ Error Comparisons with σ_g = 3 pixel[a]

S/N	Correlation Tracker mean error (pixels)	Correlation Tracker 1σ error (pixels)	Extended Kalman Filter mean error (pixels)	Extended Kalman Filter 1σ error (pixels)
20	0.5	1.5	0.0	0.2
10	3.0	3.0	0.0	0.2
1	15.0	30.0	0.0	0.8

[a]*From [51], used with permission.*

Table V. Mean Error and 1σ Error Comparisons with σ_g *= 1 pixel*

S/N	Correlation Tracker mean error (pixels)	Correlation Tracker 1σ error (pixels)	Extended Kalman Filter mean error (pixels)	Extended Kalman Filter 1σ error (pixels)
20	7.0	8.0	0.0	0.2
10	8.0	10.0	0.0	0.2
1	15.0	30.0	0.0	0.8

[a] *From [51], used with permission.*

repeatedly exhibited a divergent characteristic in the more difficult tracking environments. As shown in Table V, decreasing the dispersion of the Gaussian intensity function seriously affected the correlator tracking, whereas the filter is essentially unaffected.

When the ratio of rms target motion to rms atmospheric jitter was decreased from 5 to 1, the mean filter error remained close to zero, but the 1σ value increased from 0.2 to 0.5 pixels (for the case of S/N = 20, $\sigma_g = 3$, $T_d = 1$). Decreasing it further to $\sigma_d/\sigma_a = 0.2$ resulted in a return to a level of about 0.2 pixels. This seems to imply that the filter is able to distinguish between true and apparent target motion more easily when there is a significant amplitude difference between the two effects. In all three corresponding cases, the correlation algorithm had a 1σ error of about 1 pixel, so that even in the worst case, the filter surpassed the tracking ability of the correlator by a wide margin.

Increasing the target correlation time from 1 to 5 sec had no discernible effect on the performance of either tracker. However, a large variation in T_d might well demonstrate that as the characteristics of the true target dynamics and atmospheric jitter become more distinctly different, the filter is better able to separate the effects and enhance tracking, whereas the correlator cannot perform this function.

D. *ROBUSTNESS OF FILTER*

The marked performance improvement over that attained by a correlation algorithm was achieved by a filter based on appropriate modeling assumptions, parameter values, and tuning. However, this raises the robustness issue of how much filter performance degrades when an accurate portrayal of the tracking problem differs from that assumed in the filter design. In this section, the sensitivity of the estimation performance to large variations in parameter values within assumed model forms is first depicted. Sensitivity to variations in the basic structure of the appropriate models is then presented. Finally, insights into required design modifications and on-line adaptation capability are summarized [60,61].

1. *Sensitivity to Model-Parameter Mismatches*

The extended Kalman filter was based upon the following nominal parameter values:

(1) maximum intensity level, I_{max} = 10 units (arbitrary scale);

(2) glint dispersion (spread), σ_g = 3 pixels;

(3) target dynamics rms value, $\sigma_d = \sigma_a$ (rms jitter) = 1 pixel;

(4) target dynamics correlation time, T_d = 1 sec; and

(5) S/N = 10 (i.e., rms background noise = 1 = $0.1I_{max}$).

When the actual environment was well modeled by these parameter values, the standard deviations of the errors in estimating target states x_d and y_d were each 0.56 pixel, and 0.55 pixel in estimating atmospheric jitter states x_a and y_a. Since all errors in these studies were essentially zero mean, these were also rms error values.

Table VI summarizes the effect of varying the true value of these parameters in the Monte Carlo simulation (20 runs per evaluation) without altering the values in the filter. The resulting actual error standard deviations (averaged over the 5-sec simulations) in estimating target position and atmospheric jitter are presented as each parameter is separately varied from the design conditions.

Table VI. Actual Estimation-Error Average Standard Deviations with Model-Parameter Mismatches [a]

True Parameter		Target σ (in pixels)	Jitter σ (in pixels)
I_{max} =	1	3.7	1.7
	10 [b]	.56	.55
	20	.70	1.5
σ_g =	.1	3.0	1.5
	3 [b]	.56	.55
	5	.65	.63
σ_d/σ_a =	.2	.38	.42
	1 [b]	.56	.55
	5	2.6	1.6
T_d =	.2	.66	.65
	1 [b]	.56	.55
	5	.43	.46
S/N =	1	3.8	8.0
	10 [b]	.56	.55
	20	.55	.57

[a] *From [51], used with permission.*

[b] *Design conditions, values assumed by filter.*

For the first two robustness studies, the real-world I_{max} and σ_g descriptors of the target intensity profile are allowed to vary. When I_{max} is 1, the real FLIR images are of a target much more highly masked by background noise than the filter assumes (S/N is actually 1 rather than 10), with resulting severe degradation. Such a low S/N in fact produces poor performance even without a parameter mismatch [58,59], so this result is expected. However, when I_{max} is increased to 20, the filter again has difficulty, apparently due to searching for the wrong shape of intensity profile due to mismodeled I_{max}. When the true target intensity is less spread out than the filter assumes (σ_g = 1 pixel), the real image can move substantially within the large envelope being sought by the filter, with significant deterioration in performance. On the other hand, when the real image is larger than assumed, estimation accuracy is acceptable: the intensity peak can be located rather precisely.

The filter assumed a rather benign target trajectory, as is appropriate for distant targets. In the next set of robustness studies, the rms values and correlation times of the first-order Gauss-Markov process were allowed to vary from design values. When σ_d/σ_a is set to 0.2, the real target-motion amplitudes are less than those assumed by the filter, and the estimation accuracy is acceptable (the filter over-estimates its own errors, and smaller errors could be achieved with correctly assumed σ_d). Unacceptably large errors are produced when the filter underestimates the dynamics amplitudes (σ_d/σ_a = 5). Correlation time variations by a factor of 5 have insignificant effect, yielding somewhat greater errors when the true target exhibits higher frequency motion than assumed, and smaller errors when the trajectories are more time correlated than anticipated.

Finally, mismatches in the background-noise model were investigated. As in the case of varying I_{max}, changing the rms value for background noise affects S/N, but the trends in performance differ for the two cases. Again, low S/N results in poor estimation (even without mismatches). When S/N is high and I_{max} is properly modeled, however, the assumed target-intensity shape is correct, whereas the corrupting noise is actually less than assumed and the filter tracks the target well.

2. *Sensitivity to Variations in Model Structure*

The filter under investigation was designed to track distant point targets with low angular rate and acceleration capabilities against a temporally and spatially uncorrelated background. Now we desire to establish the robustness of the filter to the structure of the assumed models, and we consider shorter range targets such that (1) the shape effects become significant, and (2) the target dynamics can become more violent, and we also consider scenarios in which background noise can be highly correlated, spatially and/or temporally. One does not necessarily expect accurate tracking by the filter under these very different conditions; rather, the goal is a prioritized list of the characteristics of the new scenario that cause the severest performance degradation.

In fact, rms errors double when true equal-intensity contours are ellipses with major axis dimension ten times that of the minor axis, instead of circular as assumed: such an intensity pattern would be representative of some air-to-air missile targets. Unmodeled or mismodeled target motion (especially involving persistent nonzero mean velocities and accelerations, or varying degrees of maneuvering in a single scenario) also have a very serious effect on tracking ability. Extensive performance analyses showed that loss of track occurs consistently whenever unmodeled motion allows the target to move out of the field of view in one or two sample periods, even with a closed-loop system assumed able to null out any estimated errors in a single sample period: the lack of a viable target velocity estimate is a critical shortcoming in this environment. Mismodeled background noise, misrepresented in spatial and temporal correlation as well as in rms value, does not have a significant effect at moderate expected values of S/N. For example, at the nominal S/N of 10, introducing exponential spatial correlation symmetrically in all directions with a correlation distance of 1.5 pixels increases the rms tracking error by 0.03 pixel, whereas introducing both this spatial correlation and a long temporal correlation (such that the correlation coefficient for a given pixel from one sample time to the next is 0.95) increases the rms error by only 0.1 pixel. When S/N is reduced to 1, such correlations cause consistent loss of track, but, as already seen, very low S/N degrades performance greatly, even in the absence of mismodeling in the filter.

3. *Insights from Robustness Analysis*

Thus, to generate a filter capable of tracking air-to-air missiles in background clutter, one must include the following aspects in the design:

(1) ability to estimate size, shape, and orientation of the target image;

(2) on-line estimation of target-intensity height I_{max}, since it is uncertain, varying, and important to filter residual generation and tracking performance;

(3) ability to predict future position by maintaining at least a velocity estimate in addition to a position estimate (acceleration estimates may well be required also);

(4) adaptation to maneuvers (detecting a maneuver not predicted by the filter, via residual monitoring, and responding appropriately as through gain changing).

Moreover, spatial and temporal correlation of background noise need not be modeled in the filter for expected S/N values. Sections VI.E and VI.F establish the design and capabilities of a filter with these features.

E. *ELLIPTICAL EQUAL-INTENSITY CONTOURS*

1. *Basic Model*

Analysis of real FLIR data indicated that air-to-air missile images could be well approximated by a bivariate Gaussian intensity pattern, but with elliptical, rather than circular, equal-intensity contours. The ratio of major and minor axis magnitudes [$(\sigma_{g1}/\sigma_{g2})$ as in Fig. 4] typically ranges from 1 to about 10, depending on the aspect angle of the missile. Moreover, the magnitude of σ_{g2} varies with the range from the target to the tracker.

For development of the filter [61,62], it was assumed that the semimajor axis of the ellipse could be aligned with the missile velocity vector (ignoring small angle of attack and sideslip angle). Since target velocity in the FLIR image plane is to be estimated, $\hat{v}_x$ and $\hat{v}_y$ are used to establish the angular orientation of the ellipse major axis. Letting Δx_1 and Δx_2 be measured from $[x_{peak}(t), y_{peak}(t)]$ along the principal axes, the target-intensity model [Eq. (64)] becomes

$$I_{target}(\Delta x_1, \Delta x_2, t) = I_{max} \exp\left\{-\frac{1}{2}\left[(\Delta x_1/\sigma_{g1})^2 + (\Delta x_2/\sigma_{g2})^2\right]\right\}, \tag{76}$$

where I_{max}, σ_{g1}, and σ_{g2} are treated as uncertain (slowly changing) parameters to be estimated simultaneously with the states. Various methods of estimating these uncertain parameters were considered [21,65-72], including treating them as additional states, multiple model Bayesian estimation for discretized parameters, full-scale and approximated maximum likelihood methods, and least-squares techniques.

2. *Estimation of* σ_{g1} *and* σ_{g2}

Very good performance and small computational burden were achieved by generating the estimates $\hat{\sigma}_{g1}(t_i)$ and $\hat{\sigma}_{g2}(t_i)$ that minimized the quadratic cost

$$C[\underline{Z}(t_i), \underline{a}] = \{\underline{z}(t_i) - \underline{h}[\hat{\underline{x}}(t_i^-), t_i; \underline{a}]\}^T \times\{\underline{z}(t_i) - \underline{h}[\hat{\underline{x}}(t_i^-), t_i; \underline{a}]\}, \tag{77}$$

as a function of $\underline{a}$, where $\underline{Z}(t_i)$ is the measurement history $\{\underline{z}(t_1), \ldots, \underline{z}(t_i)\}$, $\underline{a}$ is the vector of uncertain parameters to be estimated, and $\underline{h}$ is as defined in Eq. (69) but using

I_{target} as defined in Eq. (76). This can be viewed as a least-squares approximation to an estimate based on maximizing the likelihood function $\ln f[\underline{x}(t_i), \underline{z}(t_i) | \underline{Z}(t_{i-1}), \underline{a}]$ with respect to both $\underline{x}(t_i)$ and $\underline{a}$. Usually, one might seek a weighted sum of the quadratics of the most recent N residuals instead of a cost involving only the single current residual as in Eq. (77) for better performance, but the 64-dimensional measurement in this problem provides significant spatial averaging to supplant temporal averaging. In fact, use of Eq. (77) yields very acceptable results. A recursive gradient solution to minimizing Eq. (77) was implemented as

$$\hat{\underline{a}}(t_i) = \hat{\underline{a}}(t_{i-1}) + k(\partial C/\partial \underline{a})^T \Big|_{\hat{\underline{x}}(t_i^-), \hat{\underline{a}}(t_{i-1})}, \tag{78}$$

i.e., a single gradient step is taken each sample period, with k a scalar step-size control value (established empirically as 0.001) and with the partial derivative evaluated using the currently available state and parameter estimates $\hat{\underline{x}}[t_i^-; \hat{\underline{a}}(t_{i-1})]$ and $\hat{\underline{a}}(t_{i-1})$, respectively. Many terms required in the evaluation of this partial derivative are already available from the filter gain computations. Figure 8 is indicative of the performance of this simple algorithm; it displays the first half-second of a representative single sample time history of estimates of σ_{g1} and σ_{g2}, when true values were $\sigma_{g1} = 5$ pixels, $\sigma_{g2} = 1$ pixel, whereas the filter was initialized with $\hat{\sigma}_{g1} = \hat{\sigma}_{g2} = 3$ pixels. With these parameter values, the mean and standard deviation of errors in estimating σ_{g1} and σ_{g2} all assumed average values (time averaged over the 4.8 sec following the 0.2-sec transient period obvious in Fig. 8) of approximately 0.15 pixel. These results were obtained for

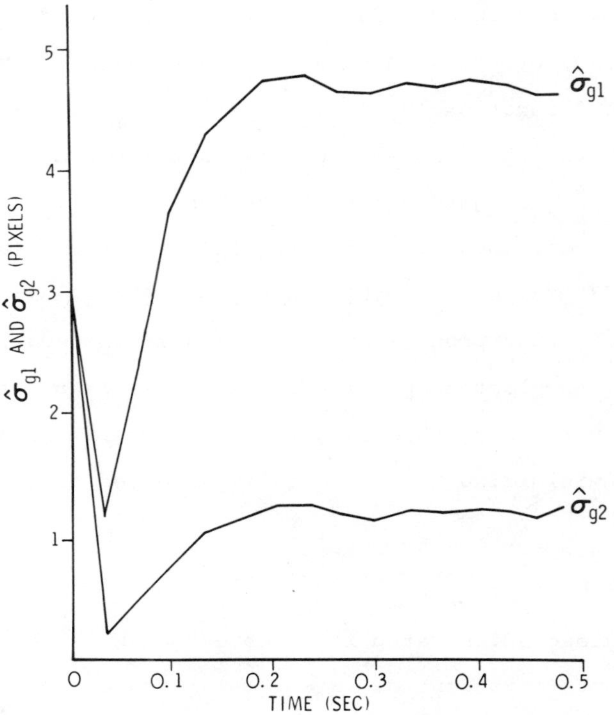

Fig. 8. Sample of estimates of σ_{g1} and σ_{g2}. (From Ref. [62], by permission; ©1981 IEEE.)

constant true σ_{g1} and σ_{g2}, for a trajectory at constant radius from the tracker; similarly good results were obtained when the aspect angle of the missile varied so that "true" σ_{g1} and σ_{g2} in fact varied.

3. Estimation of I_{max}

Although I_{max} could have been treated in a like manner, what was eventually implemented was a more direct use of measurement information that provided excellent performance with very small computational burden. Simply selecting the highest observed pixel intensity at time t_i as an estimate of I_{max} was explored, but it suffered due to both background-noise corruption effects and a bias even in the absence of noise. If there were no noise, the maximum pixel intensity is the average intensity over the pixel closest to the centroid of the Gaussian intensity profile, which is less than the value I_{max} at the centroid. This bias is a function of the centroid location, σ_{g1} and σ_{g2}, and can be substantial for small σ_{g1} and σ_{g2}. Assuming the centroid to be located at the center of the pixel, on the average, a bias function $b(\sigma_{g1}, \sigma_{g2})$ can be developed; for this feasibility study, a second-order polynomial fit approximation was used. Thus an estimate based on a single time sample of measurement data is

$$\hat{I}_1(t_i) = \max_k [z_k(t_i);\ 1 \le k \le 64] - b[\hat{\sigma}_{g1}(t_{i-1}), \hat{\sigma}_{g2}(t_{i-1})], \tag{79}$$

and this is time averaged with previous estimates to reduce the variance due to background noise:

$$\hat{I}(t_i) = c\hat{I}(t_{i-1}) + [1 - c]\hat{I}_1(t_i). \tag{80}$$

Performance capabilities were indicated by a set of simulations in which the missile was flown on an inertially straight trajectory such that at $t = 3$ sec; it was at a minimum range of 10 km from the tracker, with $v_x = 500$ m/sec and $v_y = 300$ m/sec as seen in the FLIR image plane (each pixel is a 20-μrad square). At that minimum distance, the "true" values were $\sigma_{g1} = 3$ pixels, $\sigma_{g2} = 1$ pixel, and for the whole simulation "true" $I_{max} = 25$. Selecting the highest pixel intensity yielded an I_{max} with mean of 24.47 and standard deviation of 1.12; the latter statistic is comparable to the rms background noise of $\sqrt{2}$. Just time averaging via Eq. (80) with $c = 0.8$

but with no bias correction yielded a mean and standard deviation of 24.53 and 0.33, respectively. Using bias correction only via Eq. (79) yielded 24.99 and 1.16, respectively, whereas using Eqs. (79) and (80) together resulted in a mean of 24.99 and a standard deviation of 0.30. These results were achieved with simultaneous estimation of σ_{g1} and σ_{g2}, with a precision comparable to that discussed earlier.

F. TARGET-MOTION COMPENSATION

1. Simple Six-State Filter

As indicated previously, at least the velocity of the target must be estimated in addition to its position in order to predict its position one sample period ahead for appropriate tracking-controller command generation. A velocity estimate was also required in the previous section to orient the elliptical intensity contours. The simplest possible dynamics model for FLIR plane motion that includes velocity states would be

$$\dot{\underline{x}}(t) = \underline{v}(t), \tag{81a}$$

$$\dot{\underline{v}}(t) = \underline{w}(t), \tag{81b}$$

with $\underline{w}$ white Gaussian noise with autocorrelation $E\{\underline{w}(t)\underline{w}^T(t + \tau)\} = \underline{Q}(t)\delta(\tau)$, and $\underline{Q}(t)$ chosen (adaptively) to provide an adequate representation of target maneuverability. Such a model only increases the filter state dimension from four to six, and the dynamics model remains linear. Though computationally simple, the filter based on such a model does not yield very good performance for this application [61,62]. For instance, Fig. 9 presents the mean error ±1 standard deviation in estimating the horizontal position for a 20-run

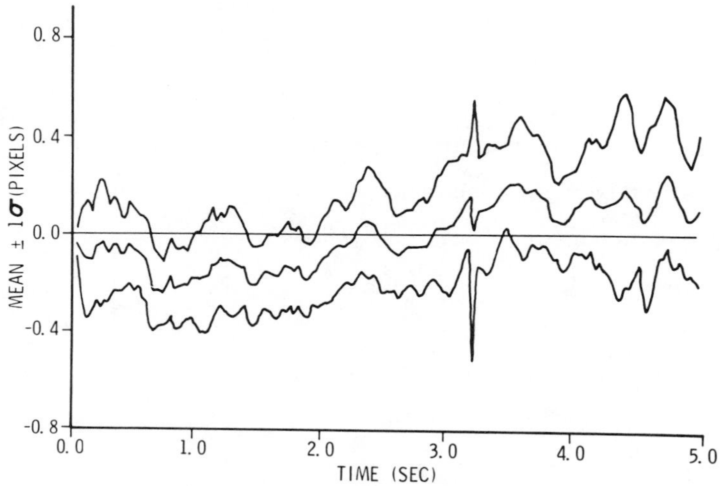

Fig. 9. Target horizontal position error mean ±1σ: six-state filter. (From Ref. [62], by permission; ©1981 IEEE.)

Monte Carlo simulation of the inertially straight trajectory described previously, with true $I_{max} = 25$, $\sigma_{g1} = 5$ pixels, $\sigma_{g2} = 1$ pixel, and background-noise rms value of 2. In fact, this plot corresponds to a case of estimating $\underline{Q}$ on-line after an acquisition phase, as discussed subsequently, but is representative of results in which $\underline{Q}$ is artificially tuned off-line at a constant value (after acquisition) for good performance on this type of trajectory. The projection of the inertially constant velocity into the FLIR image plane changes with time as the tracker rotates to maintain the target in the center of its field of view: an unmodeled noninertial acceleration is thus created, manifesting itself in the positive slope of the mean error depicted in Fig. 9. Moreover, velocity estimates diverge significantly over the last second, yielding eventual loss of track if the simulations were over longer periods. That the trend in Fig. 9 is due to noninertial acceleration was corroborated by tracking a missile at a constant range, yielding essentially zero-mean error and $\sigma \cong 0.2$ pixels for all time with no divergence. The tracker control signals which cause the noninertial acceleration could be made available for filter compensation and improved performance. However, less benign target trajectories further justified the need for a better dynamics model.

2. Preferable Eight-State Filter

As a result, an eight-state filter was generated [61,62] that estimated acceleration in the FLIR plane as well, as

$$\dot{\underline{x}}(t) = \underline{v}(t), \tag{82a}$$

$$\dot{\underline{v}}(t) = \underline{a}(t), \tag{82b}$$

$$\dot{\underline{a}}(t) = \underline{w}(t). \tag{82c}$$

Alternative models of acceleration, such as an exponentially time-correlated process model (which introduces an additional uncertain parameter, the correlation time) and a constant turn-rate model [73,74] of

$$\dot{\underline{a}}(t) = -\omega^2 \underline{v}(t) + \underline{w}(t), \tag{83a}$$

$$\omega = |\underline{v}(t) \times \underline{a}(t)| / |\underline{v}(t)|^2, \tag{83b}$$

(which yields nonlinear dynamics) were considered, but Eq. (82) was explored most fully because of its simplicity and performance potential. In a duplicate tracking environment as that used to generate Fig. 9, the eight-state filter produced a much improved tracking performance, as indicated in Fig. 10 (without being provided control signals for compensation).

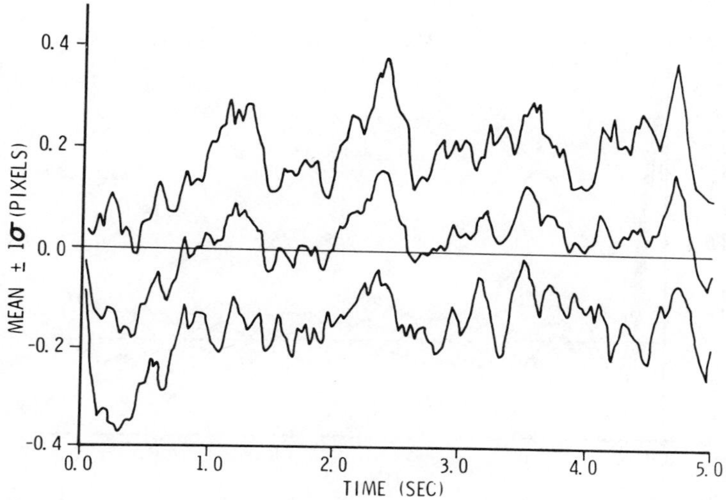

Fig. 10. Target horizontal position error mean ±1σ: eight-state filter. (From Ref. [62], by permission; ©1981 IEEE.)

3. Acquisition

The preceding results reflect a filter provided with perfect initial state knowledge, so recovery from realistic initial condition errors was investigated. To provide acquisition capability, the filter initial covariance $\underline{P}_0$ was assumed diagonal with large entries corresponding to target states: 25 pixel^2, 2000 pixels^2/sec^2, and 100 pixels^2/sec^4, respectively. Further, the $\underline{Q}$ values were maintained at a high value (600 pixels^2/sec^5) for 0.5 sec after initialization. With 8-m/sec true initial velocity error in each direction, performance was as depicted in Fig. 11: acquisition is accomplished in about half a second, followed by tracking capability as portrayed previously.

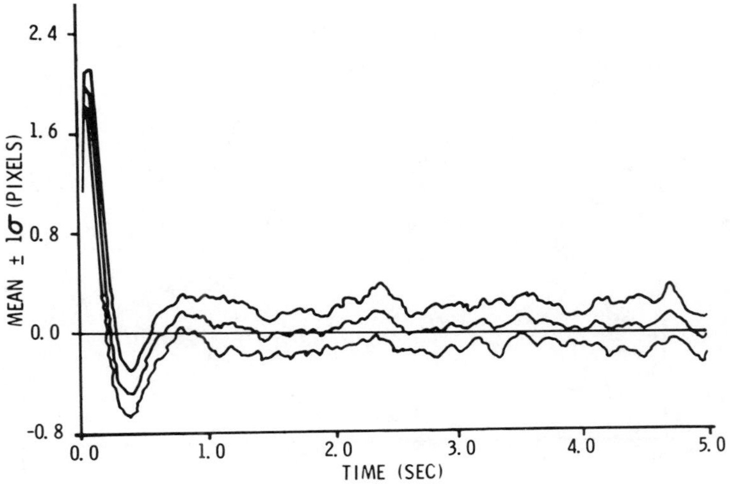

Fig. 11. Target horizontal position error mean ±1σ: eight-state filter; recovery from initialization errors. (From Ref. [62], by permission; ©1981 IEEE.)

4. Adaptive Tuning

Adaptive estimation of the dynamics noise covariance matrix was investigated to allow self-tuning to an uncertain and dynamically changing environment. The ability to adjust the filter bandwidth on-line was considered necessary because an air-to-air missile can exhibit a wide range of dynamic characteristics. Various methods of covariance estimation were considered, including maximum likelihood, multiple model Bayesian adaptation, and correlation and covariance matching techniques [21,65-72,75-77]. Due to performance and computational considerations, the approximation to maximum likelihood estimation first described in [75] was employed: if the filter covariance propagation and update equations are as given in Eqs. (13), (16) and (70), then an estimate of $\underline{Q}_d(t_i)$ is provided by

$$\underline{Q}_d(t_i) = N^{-1} \sum_{j=i-N+1}^{i} \left[\underline{\delta x}(t_j)\, \underline{\delta x}^T(t_j) + \underline{P}(t_j^+) - \underline{\Phi}P(t_{j-1}^+)\underline{\Phi}^T\right], \tag{84}$$

where

$$\underline{\delta x}(t_j) \equiv \hat{\underline{x}}(t_j^+) - \hat{\underline{x}}(t_j^-). \tag{85}$$

Equation (84) can also be derived heuristically by noting that

$$E\left\{\underline{\delta x}(t_j)\, \underline{\delta x}^T(t_j)\right\} = \underline{K}(t_j)\underline{H}(t_j)\underline{P}(t_j^-), \tag{86}$$

and by substituting Eqs. (13), (70), and (86) into Eq. (16), and approximating the ensemble average in Eq. (86) by a temporal average over the most recent N sample periods. To reduce storage requirements, a fading-memory approximation to the finite-memory result (84) was implemented as

$$\hat{\underline{Q}}_d(t_i) = k\hat{\underline{Q}}_d(t_{i-1}) + [1 - k]\hat{\underline{Q}}_{d1}(t_i) \tag{87}$$

where $\hat{\underline{Q}}_{d1}(t_i)$ is a single term from the summation in Eq. (84). The parameter k was empirically set to 0.8 as a tradeoff: $k \in (0.8, 1.0)$ provides smoother estimates, whereas $k \in (0, 0.8)$ provides more rapid response to true changes in dynamics. On the inertially straight trajectory and similar benign trajectories, the filter with adaptive $\underline{Q}_d$ estimation performed approximately the same as a filter with artificial off-line tuning to a given trajectory.

However, this adaptation was insufficient for abrupt significant maneuvers. In one set of simulations, the missile initiated a 20-g pullup at t = 4 sec of the previously defined trajectory. With a field of view of 160 × 160 μrad, such an acceleration can move the image from 3 to 4 pixels laterally in two sample periods. Moreover, virtually all of the position information for the lateral direction (i.e., region of high-intensity profile gradients) is within 1 or 2 times σ_{g2} (equal to 1 pixel here). The $\hat{\underline{Q}}_d$, appropriately low for the benign portion of the trajectory, did not respond fast enough to preclude loss of track. Although the filter residuals were of large magnitude when the maneuver was conducted, the gains were too low to weight them enough; by the time the gains grew, there was little overlap of the actual and predicted intensity profiles, so the residuals were of questionable usefulness.

5. *Significant Maneuver Indication and Appropriate Filter Response*

To maintain track required several matrix coefficients (filter gain and/or covariance matrix $\underline{P}$, as well as $\underline{Q}_d$) and some state estimates to change significantly in a single period: for instance, true elevation-acceleration changes from 0 to 2400 pixels/sec^2 when the lateral maneuver begins. One possible variable for reliable and rapid indication and quantification of a maneuver is the scalar

$$\underline{\delta x}(t_i)^T \, \underline{\delta x}(t_i) = \mathrm{tr}\left[\underline{\delta x}(t_i) \, \underline{\delta x}^T(t_i)\right], \tag{88}$$

where

$$\underline{\delta x}(t_i) = \underline{P}(t_i^+)\underline{H}^T(t_i)\underline{R}^{-1}(t_i)\{\underline{z}(t_i) - \underline{h}[\hat{\underline{x}}(t_i^-), t_i]\}, \tag{89}$$

and the filter gain shown in Eq. (89) is used because of dimensionality considerations, as discussed in Section VI,B. Since inappropriately small $\underline{P}(t_i^+)$ values are part of the maneuver compensation problem, and since $\underline{R}(t_i)$ is assumed diagonal, alternative indicators are the magnitude or separate components of the available vector

$$\underline{\delta y}(t_i) = \underline{H}^T(t_i)\{\underline{z}(t_i) - \underline{h}[\hat{\underline{x}}(t_i^-), t_i]\}, \tag{90}$$

where $\underline{\delta x}(t_i) = \underline{P}(t_i^+)\,\underline{\delta y}(t_i)/R(t_i)$. At the sample instant after initiation of the 20-g maneuver, at t = 4.03 sec, both Eq. (88) and the elevation-position component of Eq. (90) increased by an order of magnitude, then returned to their normal magnitudes on the following sample instant, t = 4.07 sec (because the true and projected images had already diverged far enough laterally, about 5 pixels, to generate essentially no overlap and thus very small residuals). Therefore, a maneuver was detected by one of these indicators surpassing a magnitude threshold, with the components of $\underline{\delta y}(t_i)$ providing direction information about the unmodeled maneuver as well.

Upon maneuver detection the appropriate response is (1) to increase the filter gain directly rather than to allow slow increase via $\underline{Q}_d$ estimation, (2) to incorporate updated state estimates for reprocessing state estimate time propagation over the previous sample period and for future propagation, and (3) to expand the field of view (e.g., treat averaged intensities of 2 × 2 arrays of pixels, instead of individual pixels, as filter measurements). Increased gain was introduced by reverting to an acquisition cycle of very high reinitialized $\underline{P}$ and high $\underline{Q}_d$ for 0.5 sec thereafter. To reprocess the state propagation, a curve-fit function was established for unmodeled position displacements as a function of σ_{g1}, σ_{g2}, and the first two components of $\underline{\delta y}(t_i)$; these displacements were assumed to be the results of an unmodeled acceleration acting over the previous sample period. If a maneuver is detected at time t_i, the acceleration-state estimates of $\hat{\underline{x}}(t_{i-1}^{+})$ are modified by these calculated increments and $\hat{\underline{x}}(t_i^{-})$ recomputed. Incorporating these changes postponed divergence for about 15 sample periods. A further ad hoc adaptation used the six target state components of $\left[\hat{\underline{x}}(t_i^{+}) - \hat{\underline{x}}(t_i^{-})\right]$ throughout the acquisition period as an indicator of unmodeled target dynamics, which was then added during the next sample period to the standard propagation equations. This allowed nondivergent results for the entire simulation period. Expansion of the field of view was not evaluated, but it is a useful means of maintaining track at the expense of some resolution.

Although these modifications allowed track to be maintained, the required artificial introduction of nonzero acceleration estimates points out an important shortcoming of zero-mean acceleration models as in Eq. (82) or exponentially time-correlated process descriptions. The constant turn-rate model [Eq. (83)] has been shown to be more representative of many airborne targets at close range [73,74], so current efforts are considering its incorporation into the filter structure.

G. CONCLUSIONS FROM FILTER DESIGN AND PERFORMANCE ANALYSIS

A simple four-state extended Kalman filter has been developed to track a distant point-source target with benign dynamics, using outputs from an FLIR sensor as measurements. As shown in part by Figs. 6 and 7, it consistently outperforms the currently used correlation tracker, with the most substantial improvement being gained in scenarios with low S/N and/or small target spot size relative to detector (pixel) size. The filter exploits knowledge unused by the correlation tracker (size, shape, and motion characteristics of the target, atmospheric jitter spectral description, and background and sensor noise characteristics) to yield the enhanced performance. However, robustness studies have revealed a serious degradation in tracking performance when the filter-assumed model does not represent the actual tracking environment well, indicating appropriate design modifications for generating a filter capable of tracking less benign targets in a realistic and more uncertain environment.

Figures 10 and 11 are indicative of the performance capabilities of the resulting eight-state adaptive tracker for realistic but not overly harsh trajectories of a missile viewed at short range. Good tracking performance is achieved on the basis of estimating target velocity and acceleration as well as position, assuming elliptical intensity profile contours having the major axis aligned with the estimated velocity vector and adaptively estimating I_{max}, σ_{g1}, σ_{g2}, and $\underline{Q}_d$. To address more dynamic environments, detection and appropriate response to maneuver initiation were investigated with some success, but rather tenuous ad hoc modifications were required due to assumed zero-mean acceleration models. Current research is concentrated on better target-acceleration models and on different filter forms to exploit these models, such as the multiple model adaptive filtering algorithm that probabilistically weights the outputs of a bank of filters, each based on one of the alternative models. Work is also being accomplished on a generalization in which target-intensity patterns are uncertain or irregular enough to discount a bivariate Gaussian model and instead preprocess the measurements to provide the entire $\underline{h}$ function adaptively to the filter, such as through spatial modal decomposition [78].

VII. CONCLUSION

Attaining an adequate model upon which to base a Kalman filter or nonlinear estimator is an essential aspect of designing an operational on-line filter algorithm. Numerous methods have been presented for generating models and filters of substantially different levels of complexity, state dimension, and performance potential. Another integral part of a systematic design approach is the realistic evaluation of the performance of any proposed filter in estimating quantities of interest when subjected to the real-world environment. Such performance analysis capability has also been described, and once again the adequacy of modeling efforts, here in the form of producing a "truth model" that accurately depicts the real world regardless of its required complexity, is shown to be an issue of primary importance. The design process itself is composed of iteratively proposing alternative filter designs, tuning each for best performance admitted by its structure, evaluating error budgets and sensitivities to parameter variations (incorporating adaptive estimation of particular parameters if the uncertainty in the knowledge of their values could yield unacceptable performance degradation), and trading-off performance capabilities and computer loading to yield the final algorithm for implementation.

REFERENCES

1. P. S. MAYBECK, "Stochastic Models, Estimation and Control," Vol. 1, Academic Press, New York, 1979.

2. G. HIRZINGER and G. KREISSELMEIER, "On Optimal Approximation of High-Order Linear Systems by Low-Order Models," *Int. J. Control 22*, No. 23, 399-408 (1975).

3. V. LARSON and P. W. LIKINS, "Optimal Estimation and Control of Elastic Spacecraft," *in* "Control and Dynamic Systems," Vol. 13 (C. T. Leondes, ed.), Academic Press, New York, 1977.

4. P. W. LIKINS, Y. OHKAMI, and C. WONG, "Appendage Modal Coordinate Truncation in Hybrid Coordinate Dynamic Analysis," *J. Spacecraft 13*, No. 10, 611-617 (1976).

5. G. T. SCHMIDT, "Linear and Nonlinear Filtering Techniques," *in* "Control and Dynamic Systems," Vol. 12 (C. T. Leondes, ed.), Academic Press, New York, 1976.

6. G. T. SCHMIDT, (ed.), *Practical Aspects of Kalman Filtering Implementation, AGARD-LS-82*, NATO Advisory Group for Aerospace Research and Development, London, May 1976.

7. K. W. SIMON and A. R. STUBBERUD, "Reduced Order Kalman Filter," *Int. J. Control 10*, 501-509 (1969).

8. R. E. SKELTON, P. C. HUGHES, and H. HABLANI, "Order Reduction for Models of Space Structures Using Modal Cost Analysis," *AIAA J. Guid. Control 5*, 351-357 (1982).

9. R. E. SKELTON and P. W. LIKINS, "Techniques of Modeling and Model Error Compensation in Linear Regulator Problems," *in* "Advances in Control and Dynamic Systems," Vol. 14 (C. T. Leondes, ed.), Academic Press, New York, 1978.

10. E. C. Y. TSE, J. V. MEDANIC, and W. R. PERKINS, "Generalized Hessenberg Transformations for Reduced Order Modeling of Large Scale Systems," *Int. J. Control 27*, No. 4, 493-512 (1978).

11. V. C. KLEMA and A. J. LAUB, "The Singular Value Decomposition: Its Computation and Some Applications," *IEEE Trans. Autom. Control AC-25*, No. 2, 164-176 (1980).

12. B. C. MOORE, "Principal Component Analysis in Linear Systems: Controllability, Observability, and Model Reduction," *IEEE Trans. Autom. Control AC-26*, No. 1, 17-32 (1981).

13. N. R. SANDELL, JR., P. VARAIYA, M. ATHANS, and M. G. SAFONOV, "Survey of Decentralized Control Methods for Large Scale Systems," *IEEE Trans. Autom. Control AC-23*, No. 2, 108-128 (1978).

14. M. J. BALAS, "Observer Stabilization of Singularly Perturbed Systems," *AIAA J. Guid. Control 1*, No. 1, 93-95 (1978).

15. A. J. CALISE, "A New Boundary Layer Matching Procedure for Singly Perturbed Systems," *IEEE Trans. Autom. Control AC-23*, No. 3, 434-438 (1978).

16. A. H. HADDAD and P. V. KOKOTOVIC, "Stochastic Control of Linear Singularly Perturbed Systems," *IEEE Trans. Autom. Control AC-22*, No. 5, 815-821 (1976).

17. P. V. KOKOTOVIC, R. E. O'MALLEY, JR., and P. SANNUTI, "Singular Perturbations and Order Reduction in Control Theory--An Overview," *Automatica 12*, 123-132 (1976).

18. H. E. RAUCH, "Order Reduction in Estimation with Singular Perturbation," Fourth Symposium on Nonlinear Estimation and its Applications, San Diego, September, 1973.

19. D. TENEKETZIS and N. R. SANDELL, JR., "Linear Regulator Design for Stochastic Systems by a Multiple Time Scales Method," *IEEE Trans. Autom. Control AC-22*, No. 4, 615-621 (1977).

20. A. H. JAZWINSKI, "Stochastic Processes and Filtering Theory," Academic Press, New York, 1970.

21. P. S. MAYBECK, "Stochastic Models, Estimation and Control," Vols. 2 and 3, Academic Press, New York, 1982.

22. T. P. McGARTY, "Stochastic Systems and State Estimation," Wiley, New York, 1974.

23. M. G. SAFONOV and M. ATHANS, "Robustness and Computational Aspects of Nonlinear Stochastic Estimators and Regulators," *IEEE Trans. Autom. Control AC-23*, No. 4, 717-725 (1978).

24. M. ATHANS, R. P. WISHNER, and A. BERTOLINI, "Suboptimal State Estimators for Continuous-Time Nonlinear Systems from Discrete Noisy Measurements," *IEEE Trans. Autom. Control AC-13*, No. 5, 504-518 (1968).

25. A. GELB, (ed.), "Applied Optimal Estimation," MIT Press, Cambridge, Massachusetts, 1974.

26. J. A. D'APPOLITO, "The Evaluation of Kalman Filter Designs for Multisensor Integrated Navigation Systems," Tech. Rept. AFAL-TR-70-271, The Analytic Sciences Corp., Reading, Massachusetts, January, 1971.

27. E. L. HAMILTON, G. CHITWOOD, and R. M. REEVES, "An Efficient Covariance Analysis Computer Program Implementation," *Proc. IEEE Nat. Aerosp. Electron. Conf.*, Dayton, Ohio, 340-345 (1976).

28. S. H. MUSICK, "SOFE — A Computer Program for Kalman Filter Design," *Proc. IEEE Nat. Aerosp. Electron. Conf.*, Dayton, Ohio, 742-749 (1981); also "SOFE: A Generalized Digital Simulation for Optimal Filter Evaluation, User's Manual," Tech. Rept. AFWAL-TR-80-1108, Air Force Wright Aeronautical Labs., Wright-Patterson AFB, Ohio, October 1980.

29. K. R. BRITTING, "Inertial Navigation System Analysis," Wiley, New York, 1971.

30. W. G. HELLER, "Models for Aided Inertial Navigation System Sensor Errors," Tech. Rept. TR-312-3, The Analytic Sciences Corp., Reading, Massachusetts, February, 1975.

31. C. T. LEONDES, (ed.), *Theory and Applications of Kalman Filtering, AGARDograph* No. 139, NATO Advisory Group for Aerospace Research and Development, London, February, 1970.

32. J. C. PINSON, "Inertial Guidance for Cruise Vehicles," *in* "Guidance and Control of Aerospace Vehicles" (C. T. Leondes, ed.), McGraw-Hill, New York, 1963.

33. W. S. WIDNALL and P. A. GRUNDY, "Inertial Navigation System Error Models, " Tech. Rept. TR-03-73, Intermetrics, Inc., Cambridge, Massachusetts, May 1973.

34. B. FRIEDLAND, "On the Effect of Incorrect Gain in the Kalman Filter," *IEEE Trans. Autom. Control AC-12*, No. 5, 610 (1967).

35. R. E. GRIFFIN and A. P. SAGE, "Sensitivity Analysis of Discrete Filtering and Smoothing Algorithms," *AIAA J. 7*, No. 10, 1890-1897 (1969).

36. H. KWAKERNAAK, "Sensitivity Analysis of Discrete Kalman Filters," *Int. J. Control 12*, 657-669 (1970).

37. R. A. NASH and F. B. TUTEUR, "The Effect of Uncertainties in the Noise Covariance Matrices on the Maximum Likelihood Estimate of a Vector," *IEEE Trans. Autom. Control AC-13*, No. 1, 86-88 (1968).

38. R. J. FITZGERALD, "Divergence of the Kalman Filter," *IEEE Trans. Autom. Control AC-16*, No. 6, 736-747 (1971).

39. C. F. PRICE, "An Analysis of the Divergence Problem in the Kalman Filter," *IEEE Trans. Autom. Control AC-13*, No. 6, 699-702 (1968).

40. F. H. SCHLEE, C. J. STANDISH, and N. F. TODA, "Divergence in the Kalman Filter," *AIAA J. 5*, No. 6, 1114-1120 (1967).

41. J. A. D'APPOLITO and C. E. HUTCHINSON, "Low Sensitivity Filters for State Estimation in the Presence of Large Parameter Uncertainties," *IEEE Trans. Autom. Control AC-14*, No. 3, 310-312 (1969).

42. J. C. DOYLE and G. STEIN, "Robustness with Observers," *IEEE Trans. Autom. Control AC-24*, No. 4, 607-611 (1979).

43. C. E. HUTCHINSON, J. A. D'APPOLITO, and K. J. ROY, "Applications of Minimum Variance Reduced-State Estimators," *IEEE Trans. Aerosp. Electron. Syst. AES-11*, No. 5, 785-794 (1975).

44. J. VAGNERS, "Design of Numerically Stable Flight Filters from Minimum Variance Reduced Order Estimators," *Proc. of IEEE Nat. Aerosp. Electron. Conf.*, Dayton, Ohio, 577-581, May 1979.

45. R. R. CLARK, "Performance Sensitivity Analysis of a Kalman Filter Using Adjoint Functions," Tech. Rept. NAFI TR-1767, Naval Avionics Facility, Indianapolis, Indiana, February 1972.

46. G. J. BIERMAN, "Factorization Methods for Discrete Sequential Estimation," Academic Press, New York, 1977.

47. N. A. CARLSON, "Fast Triangular Formulation of the Square Root Filter," *AIAA J. 11*, No. 9, 1259-1265 (1973).

48. P. G. KAMINSKI, A. E. BRYSON, JR., and S. F. SCHMIDT, "Discrete Square Root Filtering: A Survey of Current Techniques, *IEEE Trans. Autom. Control AC-16*, No. 6, 727-735 (1971).

49. A. FOOTE, C. VELLENGA, J. PRICE, and W. BUCHHOLZ, "Applications of Covariance Analysis Simulation to Avionics Flight Testing," *Proc. IEEE Nat. Aerosp. Electron. Conf.*, Dayton, Ohio, 750-756, May 1981.

50. "Position Update Filter Function," Radiometric Area Correlation Guidance Captive Flight Test R&D Status Rept. LMSC-D434550, Lockheed Missiles and Space Co., Inc., Sunnyvale, California, November 1975.

51. P. S. MAYBECK, "Performance Analysis of a Particularly Simple Kalman Filter," *AIAA J. Guid. Control 1*, 391-396 (1978).

52. R. MORRISON, H. GARRET, and B. WALLS, "A Strapdown Laser Gyro Navigator," *Proc. IEEE Nat. Aerosp. and Electron. Conf.*, Dayton, Ohio, May 1974.

53. D. J. PASIK, M. I. GNESES, and G. R. TAYLOR, "A Ring Laser Gyro Strapdown Inertial Navigation System: Performance Analysis and Test Results," AIAA Paper, 75-1075, Boston, Massachusetts, August 1975.

54. C. L. RICHARDS, "Correlation Tracking Algorithm," SAMRT-76-0076 Eng. Data Release, Aeronutronic Ford Corp., Newport Beach, California, July 1976.

55. C. L. RICHARDS, "Results of HAWK Image Tracking Experiment," SAMRT-76-0087 Eng. Data Release, Aeronutronic Ford Corp., Newport Beach, California, August 1976.

56. C. L. RICHARDS, "Correlation Tracking Software," SAMRT-76-0088 Eng. Data Release, Aeronutronic Ford Corp., Newport Beach, California, August 1976.

57. C. L. RICHARDS, "Precision Line and Point Reticle Location," SAMRT-77-0006 Tech. Data Release, Ford Aerospace and Commun. Corp., Newport Beach, California, March 1977.

58. P. S. MAYBECK and D. E. MERCIER, "A Target Tracker Using Spatially Distributed Infrared Measurements," *IEEE Trans. Autom. Control AC-25*, No. 2, 222-225 (1980).

59. D. E. MERCIER, "An Extended Kalman Filter for Use in a Shared Aperture Medium Range Tracker," M.S. Thesis, Air Force Institute of Technology, Wright-Patterson AFB, Ohio, December 1978.

60. P. S. MAYBECK, D. A. HARNLY, and R. L. JENSEN, "Robustness of a New Infrared Target Tracker," *Proc. IEEE Nat. Aerosp. Electron. Conf.*, Dayton, Ohio, 639-644, May 1980.

61. R. L. JENSEN and D. A. HARNLY, "An Adaptive Distributed-Measurement Extended Kalman Filter for a Short Range Tracker," M.S. Thesis, Air Force Institute of Technology, Wright-Patterson AFB, Ohio, December 1979.

62. P. S. MAYBECK, R. L. JENSEN, and D. A. HARNLY, "An Adaptive Extended Kalman Filter for Target Image Tracking," *IEEE Trans. Aerosp. Electron. Syst. AES-17*, No. 2, 173-180 (1981).

63. C. B. HOGGE and R. R. BUTTS, "Frequency Spectra for the Geometric Representation of Wavefront Distortions Due to Atmospheric Turbulence," *IEEE Trans. Antenna and Propagat. AP-24*, 144-154 (1976).

64. "Advanced Adaptive Optics Control Techniques," Tech. Rept. TR-996-1, The Analytic Sciences Corp., Reading, Massachusetts, January 1978.

65. K. J. ÅSTRÖM and P. EYKHOFF, "System Identification--A Survey," *Automatica 7*, 123-162 (1971).

66. M. ATHANS and C. B. CHANG, "Adaptive Estimation and Parameter Identification Using Multiple Model Estimation Algorithm," Tech. Note 1976-28, ESD-TR-76-184, Lincoln Lab., Lexington, Massachusetts, June 1976.

67. R. ISERMAN, U. BAUR, W. BAMBERGER, P. KNEPPO, and H. SIEBERT, "Comparison of Six On-Line Identification and Parameter Estimation Methods," *Automatica 10*, 81-103 (1974).

68. T. KAILATH, (ed.), (special issue on "System Identification and Time-Series Analysis"), *IEEE Trans. Autom. Control AC-19*, No. 6 (1974).

69. P. S. MAYBECK, "Combined Estimation of States and Parameters for On-Line Applications," Ph.D. Dissertation, Massachusetts Institute of Technology, Tech. Rept. T-557, Cambridge, Massachusetts, February 1972.

70. P. S. MAYBECK, "Parameter Uncertainties and Adaptive Estimation," unpublished, Air Force Institute of Technology, Wright-Patterson AFB, Ohio, 1978.

71. G. N. SARIDIS, "Comparison of Six On-Line Identification Algorithms," *Automatica 10*, 69-79, 1974.

72. K. I. YARED, "On Maximum Likelihood Identification of Linear State Space Models," Ph.D. Dissertation, LIDS-TH-920, Massachusetts Institute of Technology, Cambridge, Massachusetts, July 1979.

73. "Firefly III IFFC Fire Control System," Tech. Rept. 19008 ACS 12004, General Electric Co., Aircraft Equipment Div., Binghamton, New York, December 1979 (revised, January 1981).

74. W. H. WORSLEY, "Comparison of Three Extended Kalman Filters for Air-to-Air Tracking," M.S. Thesis, Air Force Institute of Technology, Wright-Patterson AFB, Ohio, December 1980.

75. P. D. ABRAMSON, JR., "Simultaneous Estimation of the State and Noise Statistics in Linear Dynamic Systems," Ph.D Dissertation, Massachusetts Institute of Technology, Rept. TE-25, Cambridge, Massachusetts, May 1968.

76. P. R. BELANGER, "Estimation of Noise Covariance Matrices for a Linear Time-Varying Stochastic Process," *Automatica 10*, 267-275, 1974.

77. R. K. MEHRA, "Approaches to Adaptive Filtering," *IEEE Trans. Autom. Control AC-17*, 693-698, October 1972.

78. P. S. MAYBECK and S. K. ROGERS, "Adaptive Tracking of Dynamic Multiple Hot-Spot Target IR Images," *Proc. of IEEE Conf. on Decision and Control*, Orlando, Florida, 1145-1151, December 1982.

Application of Model Switching and Adaptive Kalman Filtering for Aided Strapdown Navigation Systems

W. LECHNER

DFVLR Institut für Flugführung
Federal Republic of Germany

I. INTRODUCTION

Inertial navigation systems are often used in civil and military aviation and are needed in all cases where autonomous navigation is essential (space flight, missiles, navigation on land and at sea). However, accuracy levels of inertial systems are frequently insufficient, and for this reason additional external measurements are used, such as those provided by radar equipment, TACAN facilities, and microwave landing systems (MLS). Combinating data from the inertial navigation system (INS) with radio signals is often carried out by using the methods of Kalman filtering. Here it is important that the dynamic error behavior of the INS be carefully modeled,

ISBN 0-12-012720-2

i.e., described mathematically. The conformity of the error model with the real-error behavior of the INS is of major importance for the accuracy level of an aided INS. In the development of suitable error models it is necessary to find a compromise between, on the one hand, a mathematically simple description of the error behavior that satisfies real-time computation requirements and as far as possible creates no numerical problems and, on the other hand, an accurate description of the real-error behavior including all the important error sources.

In the case of a strapdown mechanization of an INS [1], it is rather difficult to find such a compromise, since the errors of the gyros and accelerometers, and therefore the system errors as well, depend to a very large extent on the dynamic environment of a strapdown navigation system (SDS). An error model that conforms to the real SDS error behavior for all possible cases of a dynamic environment (extreme maneuver, terrain-following flight path, linear and angular vibrations, etc.) will thus generally lead to an unacceptably sophisticated error model with regard to the real-time computations or numerical problems involved.

In the following contribution we attempt to solve the problem by using the technique of model switching between predefined low-order sensor-error models and by application of the methods of adaptive Kalman filtering. Several examples are presented and the corresponding results discussed.

II. THE TECHNIQUE OF MODEL SWITCHING FOR STRAPDOWN NAVIGATION SYSTEMS

The general state-space notation of a linear error model [2] is given by

$$\dot{\underline{x}} = \underline{\underline{A}}\underline{x} + \underline{w}, \tag{1}$$

where $\underline{x}$ is a state vector, $\underline{\underline{A}}$ a transition matrix or linear error model, and $\underline{w}$ a random-noise vector. The elements of the state vector $\underline{x}$ can often be subdivided into two parts:

$$\underline{x}^T = \left(\underline{x}^T_{system}, \underline{x}^T_{sensor}\right), \tag{2}$$

where $\underline{x}_{system}$ is the time-dependent part of the state vector superimposed by random noise, and $\underline{x}_{sensor}$ is the sensor-error coefficients modeled as constants.

We use the following abbreviations: $\underline{\omega}$ is the angular rate, $\underline{a}$ the acceleration signal, the subscript b is the body-fixed coordinate frame, and δ the symbol for error expressions.

As far as strapdown error models are concerned, the state vector $\underline{x}$ contains the following error sources:

$\epsilon_N, \epsilon_E, \epsilon_D$	Angular misalignment of the north, east, and down navigational axes
$\delta v_N, \delta v_E, \delta v_D$	Velocity errors with respect to the navigational axes
$\delta\phi, \delta\lambda, \delta h$	Position errors in terms of geographical latitude and longitude, and height
$\epsilon^{gy}_x, \epsilon^{gy}_y, \epsilon^{gy}_z$	Angular misalignment of the gyros with respect to the body-fixed axes
D^0_x, D^0_y, D^0_z	Fixed gyro drifts
D^g_x, D^g_y, D^g_z	Mass unbalance drifts of the gyros
$D^{gg}_x, D^{gg}_y, D^{gg}_z$	Anisoelasticity drifts of the gyros

D_x^{ω}, D_y^{ω}, D_z^{ω}	Fixed scale-factor errors of the gyros
$D_x^{\omega\omega}$, $D_y^{\omega\omega}$, $D_z^{\omega\omega}$	Quadratic nonlinearity scale-factor errors of the gyros
$D_x^{\lvert\omega\rvert}$, $D_y^{\lvert\omega\rvert}$, $D_z^{\lvert\omega\rvert}$	Asymmetric scale-factor errors of the gyros
$D^{\Delta\omega}$	Angular acceleration drifts of the gyros
$D^{2\omega}$	Anisoinertia drifts of the gyros
ϵ_x^{ac}, ϵ_y^{ac}, ϵ_z^{ac}	Angular misalignment of the accelerometers with respect to the body-fixed axes
B_x^0, B_y^0, B_z^0	Accelerometer bias
B_x^g, B_y^g, B_z^g	Fixed scale-factor errors
$B_x^{\lvert g\rvert}$, $B_y^{\lvert g\rvert}$, $B_z^{\lvert g\rvert}$	Asymmetric scale-factor errors
B_x^{gg}, B_y^{gg}, B_z^{gg}	Quadratic nonlinearity scale-factor errors
B_x^{3g}, B_y^{3g}, B_z^{3g}	Cubic nonlinearity scale-factor errors of the accelerometers
B^{2g}	Cross-coupling coefficient of the accelerometers
δhbar	Bias of a barometric altimeter necessary for the computation of the height and vertical velocity

If all the error sources are taken into account, the state vector contains a total of 9 system errors and 43 sensor errors. Therefore the rank of the transition matrix is 52. The system errors are time-dependent (Schuler loop), but the sensor errors are by definition constants.

According to the dynamic environment of a SDS, it is possible not only for a few isolated sensor errors but also for a large number of different sensor errors to have a non-negligible effect at system-error level. The order of magnitude of the contribution of each sensor-error coefficient to the system-error budget can be calculated by use of the sensor-error models.

The gyro error model is given by Eq. (3)

$$\delta\underline{\omega}_b = \underline{\underline{S}}^{gy}\underline{x}^{gy} = \left[\underline{\underline{S}}_1^{gy}, \ldots, \underline{\underline{S}}_7^{gy}, \underline{S}_8^{gy}, \underline{S}_9^{gy}\right]\begin{bmatrix} \underline{x}_1^{gy} \\ \vdots \\ \underline{x}_7^{gy} \\ x_8^{gy} \\ x_9^{gy} \end{bmatrix}, \tag{3}$$

$$\underline{\underline{S}}_1^{gy}\underline{x}_1^{gy} = \begin{bmatrix} 0 & -\omega_z & \omega_y \\ \omega_z & 0 & -\omega_x \\ -\omega_y & \omega_x & 0 \end{bmatrix}\begin{bmatrix} \varepsilon_x^{gy} \\ \varepsilon_y^{gy} \\ \varepsilon_z^{gy} \end{bmatrix}, \quad \underline{\underline{S}}_2^{gy}\underline{x}_2^{gy} = \begin{bmatrix} 1 & 0 & 0 \\ 0 & 1 & 0 \\ 0 & 0 & 1 \end{bmatrix}\begin{bmatrix} D_x^0 \\ D_y^0 \\ D_z^0 \end{bmatrix},$$

$$\underline{\underline{S}}_3^{gy}\underline{x}_3^{gy} = \begin{bmatrix} a_x & 0 & 0 \\ 0 & a_y & 0 \\ 0 & 0 & a_z \end{bmatrix}\begin{bmatrix} D_x^g \\ D_y^g \\ D_z^g \end{bmatrix},$$

$$\underline{\underline{S}}_4^{gy}\underline{x}_4^{gy} = \begin{bmatrix} a_x a_z & 0 & 0 \\ 0 & a_y a_z & 0 \\ 0 & 0 & a_z a_x \end{bmatrix}\begin{bmatrix} D_x^{gg} \\ D_y^{gg} \\ D_z^{gg} \end{bmatrix},$$

$$\underline{\underline{S}}_5^{gy}\underline{x}_5^{gy} = \begin{bmatrix} \omega_x & 0 & 0 \\ 0 & \omega_y & 0 \\ 0 & 0 & \omega_z \end{bmatrix}\begin{bmatrix} D_x^\omega \\ D_y^\omega \\ D_z^\omega \end{bmatrix},$$

$$\underline{\underline{S}}_6^{gy}\underline{x}_6^{gy} = \begin{bmatrix} \omega_x^2 & 0 & 0 \\ 0 & \omega_y^2 & 0 \\ 0 & 0 & \omega_z^2 \end{bmatrix} \begin{bmatrix} D_x^{\omega\omega} \\ D_y^{\omega\omega} \\ D_z^{\omega\omega} \end{bmatrix},$$

$$\underline{\underline{S}}_7^{gy}\underline{x}_7^{gy} = \begin{bmatrix} |\omega_x| & 0 & 0 \\ 0 & |\omega_y| & 0 \\ 0 & 0 & |\omega_z| \end{bmatrix} \begin{bmatrix} D_x^{|\omega|} \\ D_y^{|\omega|} \\ D_z^{|\omega|} \end{bmatrix},$$

$$\underline{S}_8^{gy}x_8^{gy} = \begin{bmatrix} -\omega_y \\ \omega_x \\ \omega_y \end{bmatrix} [D^{\Delta\omega}], \quad \underline{S}_9^{gy}x_9^{gy} = \begin{bmatrix} \omega_x\omega_z \\ \omega_y\omega_z \\ \omega_z\omega_x \end{bmatrix} [D^{2\omega}].$$

The error model for the accelerometers can be described by Eq. (4):

$$\delta\underline{a}_b = \underline{S}^{ac}\underline{x}^{ac} = \left[\underline{\underline{S}}_1^{ac}, \ldots, \underline{\underline{S}}_6^{ac}, \underline{S}_7^{ac}\right] \begin{bmatrix} \underline{x}_1^{ac} \\ \vdots \\ \underline{x}_6^{ac} \\ x_7^{ac} \end{bmatrix} \tag{4}$$

$$\underline{\underline{S}}_1^{ac}\underline{x}_1^{ac} = \begin{bmatrix} 0 & -a_z & a_y \\ a_z & 0 & -a_x \\ -a_y & a_x & 0 \end{bmatrix} \begin{bmatrix} \epsilon_x^{ac} \\ \epsilon_y^{ac} \\ \epsilon_z^{ac} \end{bmatrix}, \quad \underline{\underline{S}}_2^{ac}\underline{x}_2^{ac} = \begin{bmatrix} 1 & 0 & 0 \\ 0 & 1 & 0 \\ 0 & 0 & 1 \end{bmatrix} \begin{bmatrix} B_x^0 \\ B_y^0 \\ B_z^0 \end{bmatrix},$$

$$\underline{\underline{S}}_3^{ac}\underline{x}_3^{ac} = \begin{bmatrix} a_x & 0 & 0 \\ 0 & a_y & 0 \\ 0 & 0 & a_z \end{bmatrix} \begin{bmatrix} B_x^g \\ B_y^g \\ B_z^g \end{bmatrix}, \quad \underline{\underline{S}}_4^{ac}\underline{x}_4^{ac} = \begin{bmatrix} |a_x| & 0 & 0 \\ 0 & |a_y| & 0 \\ 0 & 0 & |a_z| \end{bmatrix} \begin{bmatrix} B_x^{|g|} \\ B_y^{|g|} \\ B_z^{|g|} \end{bmatrix},$$

$$\underline{\underline{S}}_5^{ac}\,\underline{x}_5^{ac} = \begin{bmatrix} a_x^2 & 0 & 0 \\ 0 & a_y^2 & 0 \\ 0 & 0 & a_z^2 \end{bmatrix}\begin{bmatrix} B_x^{gg} \\ B_y^{gg} \\ B_z^{gg} \end{bmatrix}, \quad \underline{\underline{S}}_6^{ac}\,\underline{x}_6^{ac} = \begin{bmatrix} a_x^3 & 0 & 0 \\ 0 & a_y^3 & 0 \\ 0 & 0 & a_z^3 \end{bmatrix}\begin{bmatrix} B_x^{3g} \\ B_y^{3g} \\ B_z^{3g} \end{bmatrix},$$

$$\underline{S}_7^{ac} x_7^{ac} = \begin{bmatrix} a_x a_z \\ a_y a_x \\ a_z a_x \end{bmatrix} [B^{2g}].$$

The predominant error sources can be roughly estimated by,

$$\delta\omega_{max} = \max\left[|s_{ij}^{gy} x_j^{gy}|\right] = |s_{\nu\eta}^{gy} x_\eta^{gy}|; \quad i = 1, 2, 3, \quad j = 1, \ldots, 23, \tag{5}$$

$$\delta a_{max} = \max\left[|s_{ij}^{ac} x_j^{ac}|\right] = |s_{\alpha\beta}^{ac} x_\beta^{ac}|; \quad i = 1, 2, 3, \quad j = 1, \ldots, 19. \tag{6}$$

If many i, j terms exist for which the conditions (7) and (8) are fulfilled,

$$|s_{ij}^{gy} x_j^{gy}| << \delta\omega_{max}; \quad i \neq \nu, \quad j \neq \eta, \tag{7}$$

$$|s_{ij}^{ac} x_j^{ac}| << \delta a_{max}; \quad i \neq \alpha, \quad j \neq \beta, \tag{8}$$

then low-order sensor-error models describe the real world with sufficient accuracy. If ν, η, α, and β change during a flight, then different low-order sensor-error models can be used to apply successfully the technique of model switching.

In order to discuss in visual terms the technique of model switching, the existence of only two different low-order sensor-error models I and II has been assumed:

$$\underline{\underline{A}}_{I/II} = \begin{bmatrix} \underline{\underline{A}}_{i,j} & \underline{\underline{A}}_{i,I/II} \\ 0 & 0 \end{bmatrix}; \quad i, j = 1, 2, \ldots, 9, \tag{9}$$

$$\underline{x}^T = \left(x_1^T, \ldots, x_9^T, x_{I/II}^T\right). \tag{10}$$

If the technique of model switching is used within a Kalman filtering algorithm, the covariance matrix $\underline{\underline{P}}$

$$\underline{\underline{P}} = E[(\hat{\underline{x}} - \underline{x})(\hat{\underline{x}} - \underline{x})^T], \tag{11}$$

where $\underline{x}$ is the true state vector and $\hat{\underline{x}}$ the estimated state vector, can be written in four parts:

$$\underline{\underline{P}}_{I/II} = \begin{bmatrix} \underline{\underline{P}}_{i,j} & \underline{\underline{P}}^a_{I/II} \\ \left(\underline{\underline{P}}^a_{I/II}\right)^T & \underline{\underline{P}}^b_{I/II} \end{bmatrix}; \quad i, j = 1, 2, \ldots, 9. \tag{12}$$

Figure 1 shows the principle of the technique of model switching. The transition matrices $\underline{\underline{A}}_{I/II}$, the covariance matrices $\underline{\underline{P}}_{I/II}$, and the state vectors $\underline{x}_{I/II}$ are stored in the buffer of the computer. The procedure may start with a rms value of $|\underline{\omega}_b| < 1° \sec^{-1}$ and therefore all terms having the subscript I are active. At this moment $\underline{x}_I$, and $\underline{\underline{P}}_I$ allow for the fixed gyro drifts, for example, because no maneuver is performed. However, 3 min later, the angular rate $|\underline{\omega}_b|$ reaches the rms value of $2° \sec^{-1}$, i.e., a maneuver is performed and the criterion for switching has been fullfilled. The state vector $\underline{x}_I$, the transition matrix $\underline{\underline{A}}_I$, and the covariance matrix $\underline{\underline{P}}_I$ are at this moment stored in the computer buffer, and the vector $\underline{x}_{II}$ and the matrices $\underline{\underline{A}}_{II}$ and $\underline{\underline{P}}_{II}$ are retrieved from the buffer. Now, $\underline{x}_{II}$, $\underline{\underline{A}}_{II}$, and $\underline{\underline{P}}_{II}$ might contain, for example, in addition to the system errors, three fixed scale-factor errors of the gyros. The system errors $\underline{x}_{system}$, of course, are only shifted in the case of model switching. After a further 3 min, the rms value of the angular rate $|\underline{\omega}_b|$ again decreases to zero, and the storage procedure

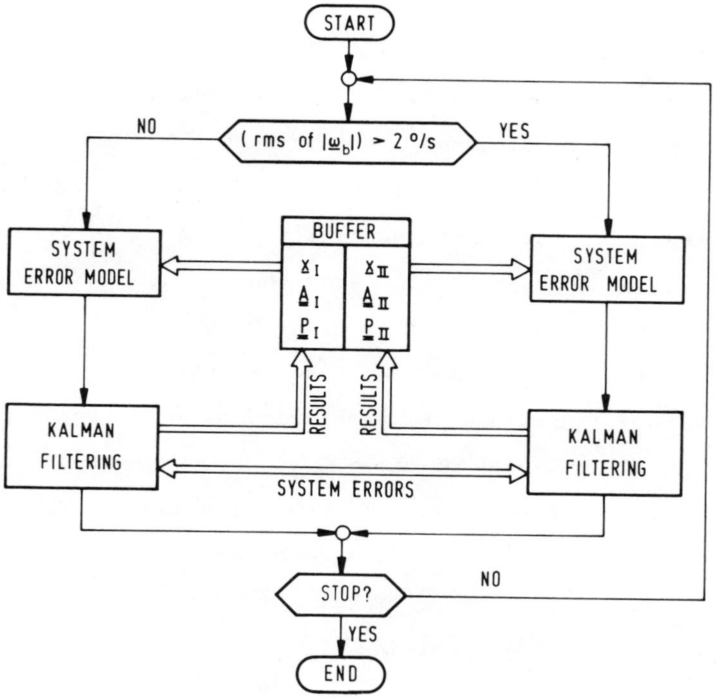

Fig. 1. Principle of model switching.

is then repeated in reverse; i.e., $\underline{x}_{II}$, $\underline{\underline{A}}_{II}$, and $\underline{\underline{P}}_{II}$ are stored in a buffer and $\underline{x}_I$, $\underline{\underline{A}}_I$, and $\underline{\underline{P}}_I$ are used again as initial conditions.

The purpose of the technique of model switching is constantly to take into account in a low-order error model those error sources that predominate in the error budget. Moreover, since the Kalman filtering algorithms use the results of the last estimates as initial conditions when certain sensor-error coefficients are used again, it is sufficient to have relatively short, though frequently recurring, periods in order to improve the covariance matrix $\underline{\underline{P}}$.

Example 1.

To demonstrate the technique of model switching, SDS data were calculated by simulation [3]. Figure 2 shows the selected lateral path of a simulated straight flight of ≈100 min duration, containing four full turns and take-off and landing procedures. The corresponding altitude profile is given in Fig. 3. This flight path simulates the structure of a civil airliner flying from point A to point B as directly as possible. The ground speed was ≈300 kt, the turns were performed within 3 min, and the accelerations were less than ±0.3 g. The simulation of the SDS is based on the usual values for the error coefficients of mechanical sensors. The magnitudes are listed in Table I. The sensor errors cause misalignments or velcoty errors at the system-error level corresponding to the integrals

$$\underline{\epsilon}_n = \int_0^t \underline{\underline{C}}_{nb}(t)\,\delta\underline{\omega}_b(t)\,dt, \tag{13}$$

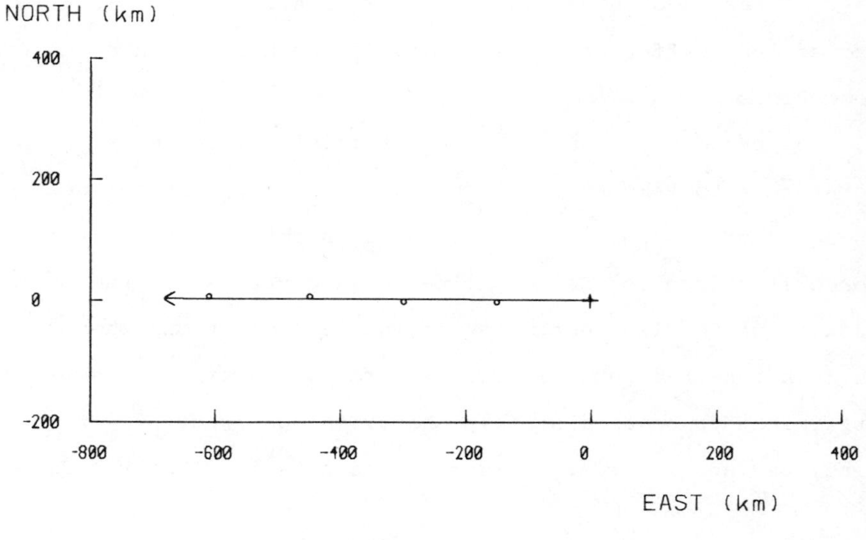

Fig. 2. Simulated lateral path (Example 1).

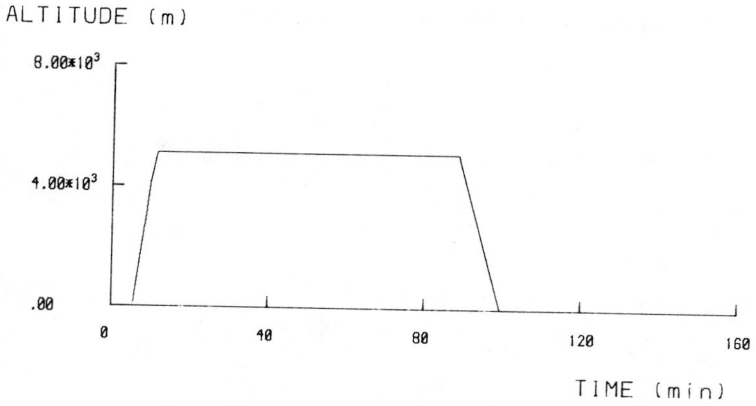

Fig. 3. Simulated altitude profile (Example 1).

$$\delta \underline{v}_n = \int_0^t \underline{\underline{C}}_{nb}(t)\, \delta \underline{a}_b(t)\, dt, \tag{14}$$

where $\underline{\underline{C}}_{nb}$ is the transformation matrix from the body-fixed to the navigational coordinate frame.

Table I. Sensor-Error Coefficients

gyro error coefficients			accelerometer error coeffficients		
type	magnitude	dependent on	type	magnitude	dependent on
ε^{gy}	6 arcs	ω	ε^{ac}	6 arcs	a
D^{o}	0.01°/h	-	B^{o}	1.E-4 g	-
D^{g}	0.02°/h/g	a	B^{g}	1.E-5	a
D^{gg}	0.03°/h/g²	a^2	$B^{\|g\|}$	1.E-5	a
D^{ω}	3.E-5	ω	B^{gg}	1.E-5/g	a^2
$D^{\omega\omega}$	3.E-5	ω^2	B^{3g}	1.E-6/g²	a^3
$D^{\|\omega\|}$	3.E-6	ω	B^{2g}	1.E-5/g	a^2
$D^{\Delta\omega}$	4.E-4 s	ω			
$D^{2\omega}$	4.E-4 s	ω^2			

The calculation of error budgets by means of Eqs. (3), (4), (13), (14) leads to the main error sources: fixed gyro drifts D_x^0, D_y^0, D_z^0; axes misalignments ϵ_x^{gy}, ϵ_y^{gy}; fixed scale-factor error D_z^ω of the z gyro; and the biases B_x^0, B_y^0, B_z^0 of the accelerometers. Therefore the following sensor-error models were compared:

$$\underline{\underline{S}}_1^{gy} = \begin{bmatrix} 1 & 0 & 0 \\ 0 & 1 & 0 \\ 0 & 0 & 1 \end{bmatrix}; \quad \underline{\underline{S}}_1^{ac} = \underline{\underline{0}}; \qquad \underline{x}_{10,11,12}^T = \left(D_x^0,\ D_y^0,\ D_z^0\right),$$

$$\underline{\underline{S}}_2^{gy} = \underline{\underline{0}}; \qquad \underline{\underline{S}}_2^{ac} = \begin{bmatrix} 1 & 0 & 0 \\ 0 & 1 & 0 \\ 0 & 0 & 1 \end{bmatrix}; \quad \underline{x}_{10,11,12}^T = \left(B_x^0,\ B_y^0,\ B_z^0\right),$$

$$\underline{\underline{S}}_3^{gy} = \begin{bmatrix} 0 & -\omega_z & 0 \\ \omega_z & 0 & 0 \\ -\omega_y & \omega_x & \omega_z \end{bmatrix}; \quad \underline{\underline{S}}_3^{ac} = \underline{\underline{0}}; \qquad \underline{x}_{10,11,12}^T = \left(\epsilon_x^{gy},\ \epsilon_y^{gy},\ D_z^\omega\right),$$

where $\underline{\underline{S}}_4^{gy}$ is the model switching between the models $\underline{\underline{S}}_1$ and $\underline{\underline{S}}_3$, and $\underline{\underline{S}}_5^{gy}$ the reference sensor-error model, including all 43 sensor errors.

Figure 4 contains the time histories of the angular misalignment ϵ_D for the five different sensor-error models mentioned above. It can be seen how the overall system error is produced by the individual sensor-error coefficients: the linear increase of ϵ_D is caused by the fixed gyro drift (model $\underline{\underline{S}}_1$) and the system error contributions of the fixed scale-factor error and the axes misalignment (model $\underline{\underline{S}}_3$) correspond clearly to the maneuvers simulated. During the turns the fixed scale-factor error leads to a system misalignment that

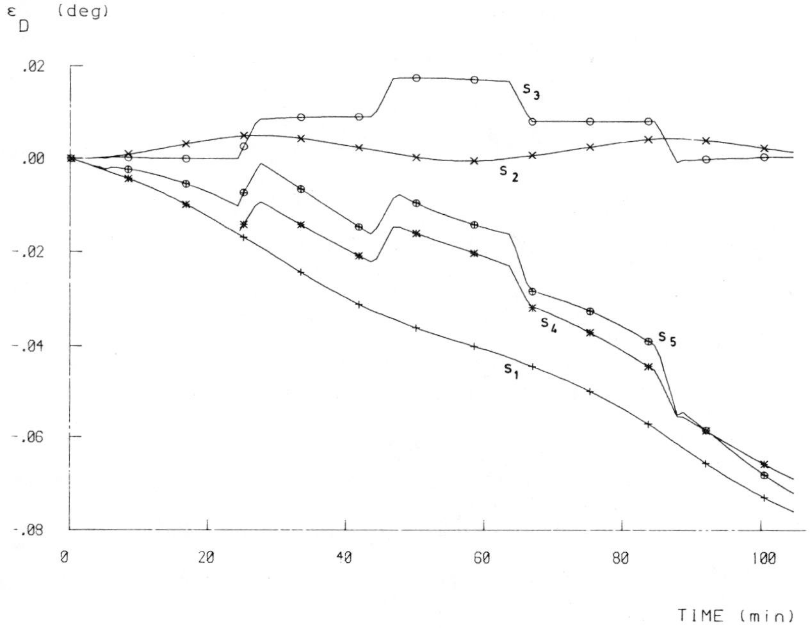

Fig. 4. System misalignment ϵ_D with respect to sensor-error models S_1 to S_5 (Example 1).

could be calculated as follows:

$$\epsilon_D = D_z^{\omega}\omega_z \,\Delta T = 3 \times 10^{-5} \times (360°/3\ \text{min}) \times 3\ \text{min} \approx 0.01°. \tag{15}$$

This value can be read off directly from the height of the steps in the time histories of the system misalignment caused by model $\underline{\underline{S}}_3$. During the straight lines of the flight-path model, $\underline{\underline{S}}_3$ does not produce any additional error contributions. Because the contributions of the accelerometer bias (model $\underline{\underline{S}}_2$) are rather small, model $\underline{\underline{S}}_4$, which is able to switch between model $\underline{\underline{S}}_1$ and $\underline{\underline{S}}_3$, fits the reference-error behavior of model $\underline{\underline{S}}_5$ best. The rank of $\underline{\underline{S}}_4$ is only 3.

Example 2

For the second example of model switching a flight path was constructed by simulation that included many extreme maneuvers. The lateral flight path is given in Fig. 5. It is the result of a sophisticated simulation [4] and was selected to represent a flight path of a remotely piloted vehicle (RPV). The altitude profile shown in Fig. 6 contains a simulated "terrain-following" section. The flight path is based on the following parameters:

(1) catapult takeoff with a flight-path angle of 20° and acceleration to a speed of 275 m/sec;

(2) total flying distance, ≈280 km; flying time, ≈40 min;

(3) altitude profile during the mission: high-low-low-high, with a total of two low-level stages (schematized terrain-following) having a total length of ≈31 km;

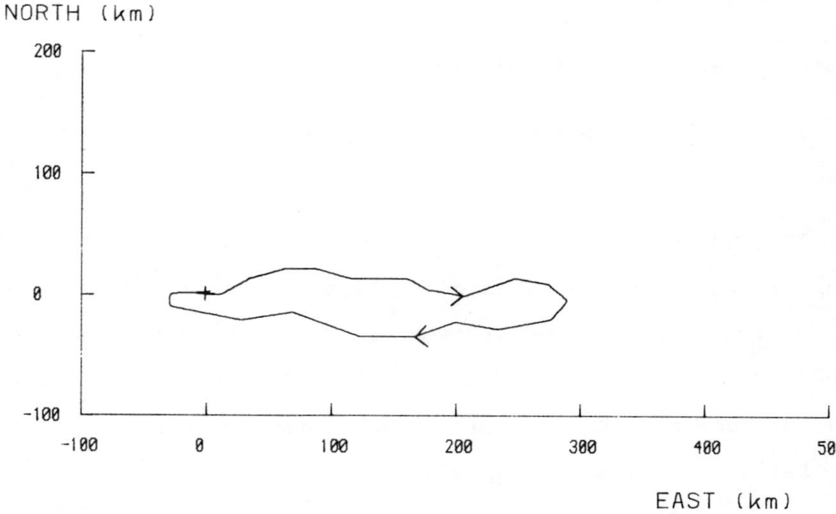

Fig. 5. Simulated lateral path (Example 2).

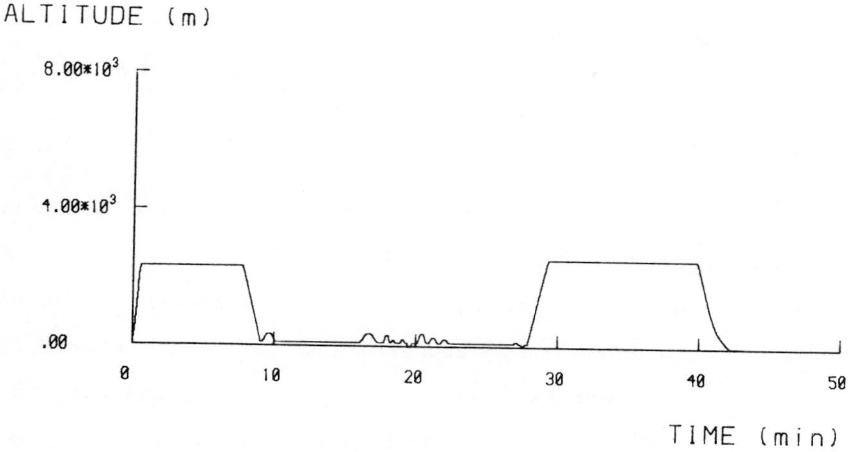

Fig. 6. Simulated altitude profile (Example 2).

(4) vertical maneuvers of up to ≈2 g;

(5) horizontal turns of up to ≈3 g.

These extreme maneuvers produce bank rates of up to ±50°/sec, and accelerations of up to 5 g.

The calculation of error budgets produces the following sensor-error models:

$$\underline{\underline{S}}_6^{ac} = \underline{\underline{S}}_7^{ac} = \underline{\underline{S}}_8^{ac} = \underline{\underline{S}}_9^{ac} = \underline{\underline{0}},$$

$$\underline{\underline{S}}_6^{gy} = \begin{bmatrix} 1 & 0 & 0 \\ 0 & 1 & 0 \\ 0 & 0 & 1 \end{bmatrix}; \qquad \underline{x}_{10,11,12}^T = \left(D_x^0,\ D_y^0,\ D_z^0\right),$$

$$\underline{\underline{S}}_7^{gy} = \begin{bmatrix} \omega_x & 0 \\ 0 & \omega_z \end{bmatrix}; \qquad \underline{x}_{10,11}^T = \left(D_x^\omega,\ D_z^\omega\right),$$

$$\underline{\underline{S}}_8^{gy} = \begin{bmatrix} -\omega_x \\ \omega_y \\ \omega_x \end{bmatrix}; \qquad \underline{x}_{10}^T = D^{\Delta\omega},$$

$\underline{\underline{S}}_9^{gy}$ is the model switching between

$$\underline{\underline{S}}_6^{gy} \quad \text{and} \quad \begin{bmatrix} \omega_x & \omega_z & -\omega_x \\ 0 & 0 & \omega_y \\ 0 & 0 & \omega_x \end{bmatrix}; \qquad \underline{x}_{10,11,12}^T = \left(D_x^0, D_y^0, D_z^0\right) \text{ or } \left(D_x^\omega, D_z^\omega, D^{\Delta\omega}\right),$$

and $\underline{\underline{S}}_{10}^{gy}$ is the reference sensor-error model that includes all 43 sensor errors.

The effect of error contributions with different signs at system level is especially noticeable in the time histories of the east-position errors shown in Fig. 7. While the contribution of the anisoertia term (model $\underline{\underline{S}}_8$) increases up to approximately -4 km, the fixed scale factor errors (model $\underline{\underline{S}}_7$) produce a position error of up to ≈1 km. The effect of the fixed gyro drift is negligible in the simulated RPV flight path (model $\underline{\underline{S}}_6$). Sensor-error model $\underline{\underline{S}}_9$, which is switched between the error models defined above, describes with sufficient accuracy the

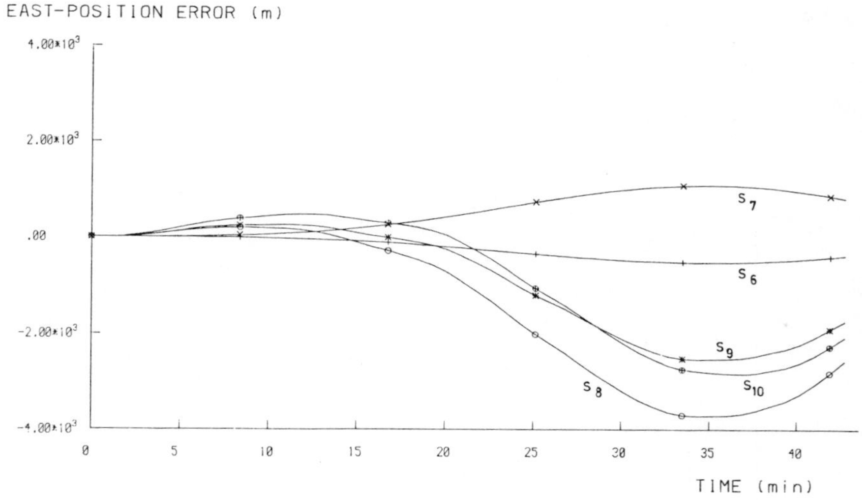

Fig. 7. Position error with respect to sensor-error models S_6 to S_{10} (Example 2).

position errors caused by all the different sensor errors. The rank of the sensor-error model $\underline{\underline{S}}_9$ is only 3.

Example 3

For Example 3 a flight path flown by an F104 combat aircraft was used [5]. A SDS made by the Teledyne company was part of the instrumentation system. The maneuvers were performed at a speed of ≈700 kt. The lateral flight path is shown in Fig. 8. The altitude profile given in Fig. 9 contains climb and descent phases, with vertical speeds up to ≈100 kt. These maneuvers produce bank rates of up to 80° sec^{-1} and cross accelerations of up to 4 g. Noise terms whose standard deviations can be estimated at ≈7° sec^{-1} or 0.1 g are superimposed on the sensor signals.

The following sensor-error models determined by Eqs. (3), (4), (13), and (14) are now compared:

$$\underline{\underline{S}}^{ac}_{11,12,13,14} = 0,$$

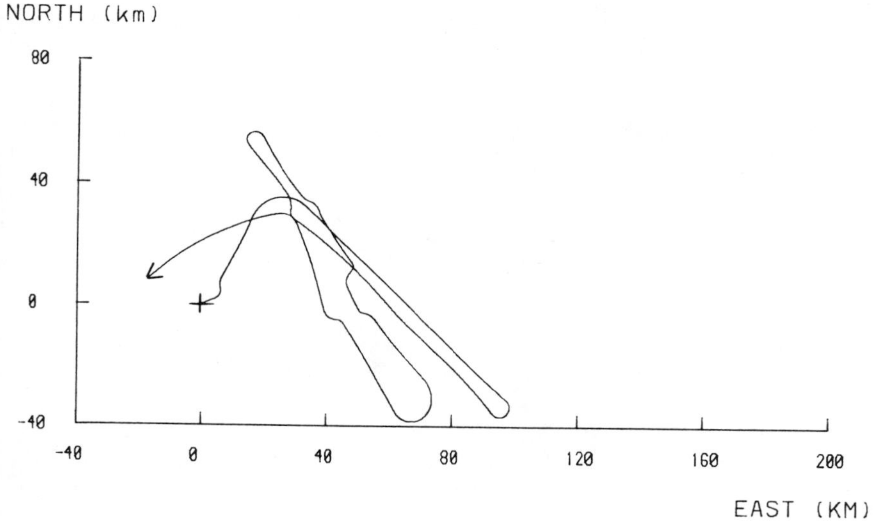

Fig. 8. Lateral path flown by an F104 (Example 3).

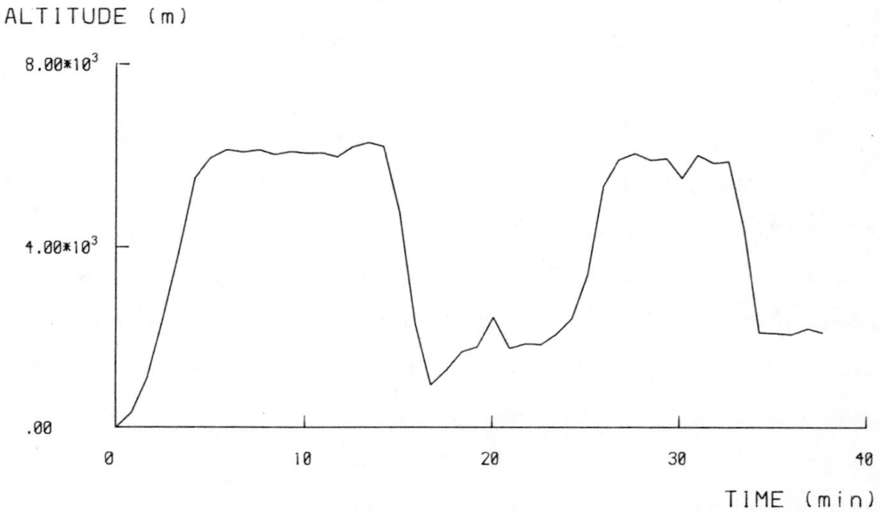

Fig. 9. Altitude profile performed by an F104 (Example 3).

$$\underline{\underline{S}}_{11}^{gy} = \begin{bmatrix} 1 & 0 & 0 \\ 0 & 1 & 0 \\ 0 & 0 & 1 \end{bmatrix}; \qquad \underline{x}_{10,11,12}^{T} = \left(D_x^0,\ D_y^0,\ D_z^0\right),$$

$$\underline{\underline{S}}_{12}^{gy} = \begin{bmatrix} \omega_x & |\omega_x| \\ 0 & 0 \end{bmatrix}; \qquad \underline{x}_{10,11}^{T} = \left(D_x^{\omega},\ D_x^{|\omega|}\right),$$

$$\underline{\underline{S}}_{13}^{gy} = \begin{bmatrix} -\omega_x \\ \omega_y \\ \omega_x \end{bmatrix}; \qquad \underline{x}_{10}^{T} = D^{\Delta\omega},$$

$\underline{\underline{S}}_{14}^{gy}$ is the model switching between

$$\underline{\underline{S}}_{11}^{gy} \text{ and } \begin{bmatrix} \omega_x & |\omega_x| & -\omega_x \\ 0 & 0 & \omega_y \\ 0 & 0 & \omega_x \end{bmatrix}; \qquad \underline{x}_{10,11,12}^{T} = \left(D_x^0,\ D_y^0,\ D_z^0\right) \text{ or } \left(D_x^{\omega},\ D_x^{|\omega|},\ D^{\Delta\omega}\right),$$

$\underline{\underline{S}}_{15}^{gy}$ is the reference sensor-error model that includes all 43 sensor errors.

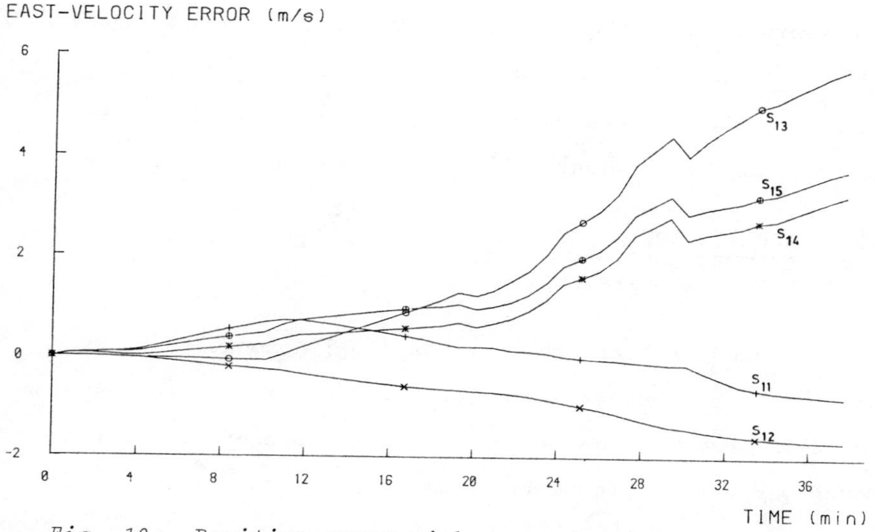

Fig. 10. Position error with respect to sensor-error models S_{11} to S_{15} (Example 3).

Figure 10 shows the time histories of the north velocity errors. The error model $\underline{\underline{S}}_{13}$ provides a velocity error that is too large compared to the reference values (model $\underline{\underline{S}}_{15}$). The fixed gyro drift (model $\underline{\underline{S}}_{11}$) and the scale-factor errors (model $\underline{\underline{S}}_{12}$) produce velocity errors with negative signs. The time history of the error behavior caused by the switchable sensor-error model $\underline{\underline{S}}_{14}$ is nearest to the reference. At the end of this real flight of ≈40 min, the error budget given in Table II is obtained.

The effect whereby some sensor errors are canceled out depends on the sign of the sensor-error coefficients and the type of maneuvers flown. If the aircraft executes contrary

Table II. North-Velocity Errors for Models S_{11} to S_{15} (Example 3).

sensor error model	S_{11}	S_{12}	S_{13}	S_{14}	S_{15}
north velocity error (m/s)	-0.7	-1.7	5.8	3.3	3.8

maneuvers such as the following bank-angle commands 0°/30°/0°/-30°/0°, then some errors will always cancel each other out to some extent. In this case a position error can be partly reduced during a flight by selecting appropriate maneuvers.

III. APPLICATION OF ADAPTIVE KALMAN FILTERING FOR AIDED STRAPDOWN NAVIGATION SYSTEMS

In Kalman filter applications [6,7] nonmodeled or even unknown error sources are often interpreted as random system noise in terms of the elements of the system-noise matrix $\underline{\underline{Q}}$. Roughly speaking, the covariance propagation

$$\underline{\underline{P}}(k+1) = \underline{\underline{\phi}}(k)\underline{\underline{P}}(k)\underline{\underline{\phi}}^T(k) + \underline{\underline{Q}}(k), \tag{16}$$

where $\underline{\underline{\phi}}$ is the time-discrete transition matrix or error model, supplies overoptimistic values in the case of nonmodeled error sources. This effect can be compensated for by a corresponding increase in the elements of the system-noise matrix $\underline{\underline{Q}}$. However, this technique leads to problems if essential error contributions dependent on the sign of the sensor signals are interpreted as unbiased random signals. For example, in the case of a fixed scale-factor error of the gyro this means that if the aircraft performs first a left-hand turn and then a right-hand turn, the system misalignments caused by these sensor-error coefficients cancel each other out to some extent. The interpretation of these sensor-error coefficients as system noise would make the covariance matrix worse, regardless of the particular direction of the turns. Therefore this technique leads to overpessimistic covariance matrices in the case of contrary maneuvers.

Another disadvantage of this technique is the need to determine a system-noise matrix $\underline{\underline{Q}}$ that corresponds to the nonmodeled or even unknown error sources. If the time-discrete transition matrix $\underline{\underline{\phi}}$ is approximated by means of the identity matrix $\underline{\underline{I}}$ for a sufficiently short sampling period T_a, then the following applies for the angular misalignments $\underline{\epsilon}_n$ and the velocity errors $\delta\underline{v}_n$:

$$\underline{\epsilon}_n(k+1) = \underline{\epsilon}_n(k) + T_a\underline{\underline{C}}_{nb}(k)\,\delta\underline{\omega}_b(k), \tag{17}$$

$$\delta\underline{v}_n(k+1) = \delta\underline{v}_n(k) + T_a\underline{\underline{C}}_{nb}(k)\,\delta\underline{a}_b(k), \tag{18}$$

or in statistical terms,

$$\underline{\sigma}^2_\epsilon(k+1) = \underline{\sigma}^2_\epsilon(k) + T^2_a\underline{\underline{C}}_{nb}E\left[\delta\underline{\omega}_b(k)\,\delta\underline{\omega}^T_b(k)\right]\underline{\underline{C}}^T_{nb}, \tag{19}$$

$$\underline{\sigma}^2_v(k+1) = \underline{\sigma}^2_v(k) + T^2_a\underline{\underline{C}}_{nb}E\left[\delta\underline{a}_b(k)\,\delta\underline{a}^T_b(k)\right]\underline{\underline{C}}^T_{nb}. \tag{20}$$

The calculation of the expectation values leads to problems because the sensor signals consist generally of a low-frequency part that describes the flight path and superimposed high-frequency vibrations [8]. The sensor signals represent a nonstationary time series, and the calculation of the expectation values consequently poses considerable problems. One can try to give rough estimates for the system-noise matrix $\underline{\underline{Q}}$, but if the values are too large, the level of system accuracy decreases, and if the values are too small, the problem of Kalman-filter divergence can arise. The cause of this divergence lies in an overoptimistic covariance matrix $\underline{\underline{P}}$, which reduces the elements of the gain matrix $\underline{\underline{K}}$ and thus, roughly speaking, ignores the measurements being received. In the case of SDS, the calculation of constant system-noise matrices $\underline{\underline{Q}}$ must allow for the worst dynamic environment of the SDS. For example, a large number of sensor-error coefficients effective only during a short maneuver are able to initiate the divergence of the Kalman filter.

It is easier to solve the problem of nonmodeled or even unknown error sources by using the methods of adaptive Kalman filtering. The matrix $\underline{\underline{Q}}$ then becomes time variant and depends in the case of a SDS on the actual maneuvers flown by the aircraft. The calculation of the elements of the system-noise matrix $\underline{\underline{Q}}$ takes into account the statistics of the filter residuals. The basic relationship between the measurements $\underline{z}$, the covariance matrix $\underline{\underline{R}}$ that describes the statistics of the errors of, for example, a radar unit, the measurement matrix $\underline{\underline{H}}$, and the unknown noise matrix $\underline{\underline{Q}}$ can be formulated as follows:

$$E[(\underline{z} - \underline{\underline{H}}\underline{x}')(\underline{z} - \underline{\underline{H}}\underline{x}')^T](k) = \underline{\underline{R}}(k) + \underline{\underline{H}}[\underline{\underline{P}}'(k) + \underline{\underline{Q}}(k)]\underline{\underline{H}}^T. \tag{21}$$

The estimates $\underline{x}$ and the covariance matrix $\underline{\underline{P}}$ correspond to the predicted expressions $\underline{x}'$, $\underline{\underline{P}}'$ via Eqs. (24) and (25).

$$\underline{x}'(k) = \underline{\underline{\phi}}(k)\underline{x}(k - 1), \tag{22}$$

$$\underline{\underline{P}}'(k) = \underline{\underline{\phi}}(k)\underline{\underline{P}}(k)\underline{\underline{\phi}}^T(k) + \underline{\underline{Q}}(k). \tag{23}$$

In visual terms Eq. (21) means that the difference between measured and predicted state variables are described statistically by the corresponding covariance matrices $\underline{\underline{P}}$, $\underline{\underline{R}}$, and $\underline{\underline{Q}}$. The result is a variable system-noise matrix $\underline{\underline{Q}}$ or a corresponding effect on the gain matrix $\underline{\underline{K}}$ of the Kalman filter.

From the large number of possible adaptive Kalman filtering algorithms [9], the one based on the work of Jazwinski [10] was selected because it requires a particularly small number of calculations and is thus especailly suitable for real-time applications. In this algorithm the expectation values of the filter residuals are calculated on the basis of n measurements backward in time history. If these expectation values do not correspond to the sum of the covariance matrices $\underline{\underline{P}}$ and $\underline{\underline{R}}$, this can be compensated for via the noise matrix $\underline{\underline{Q}}$. According to [11,12], for a matrix $\underline{\underline{B}}$,

$$\underline{\underline{B}} = E[(\underline{z} - \underline{\underline{H}}\underline{x}')(\underline{z} - \underline{\underline{H}}\underline{x}')^T] - \underline{\underline{R}} - \underline{\underline{H}}\underline{\underline{P}}'\underline{\underline{H}}^T, \qquad (24)$$

the following criterian apply: If

$$B_{i,i} > 0, \quad \text{then } Q_{i,i} = B_{i,i}; \quad i = 1, 2, \ldots, m, \qquad (25)$$

where m is the rank of the measurement vector $\underline{z}$. If

$$B_{i,i} \leq 0, \quad \text{then } Q_{i,i} = 0. \qquad (26)$$

By use of this relatively simple algorithm, the system-noise matrix $\underline{\underline{Q}}$ continuously adapts itself to the predicted statistics of the Kalman filter. However, the elements of the matrix $\underline{\underline{Q}}$ can only be calculated at the level of the measurements. An extension of the adaptive Kalman filtering algorithm in order to calculate all the elements of the noise matrix $\underline{\underline{Q}}$ increases the computational borders drastically [13,14].

IV. SOFTWARE DESIGN FOR ERROR-MODEL TESTING

A software package was developed in order to test the technique of model switching and the application of the methods of adaptive Kalman filtering for aided SDS. Figure 11 shows the main parts of this software:

(1) the simulation of an unaided SDS, including the calculation of the reference flight path;

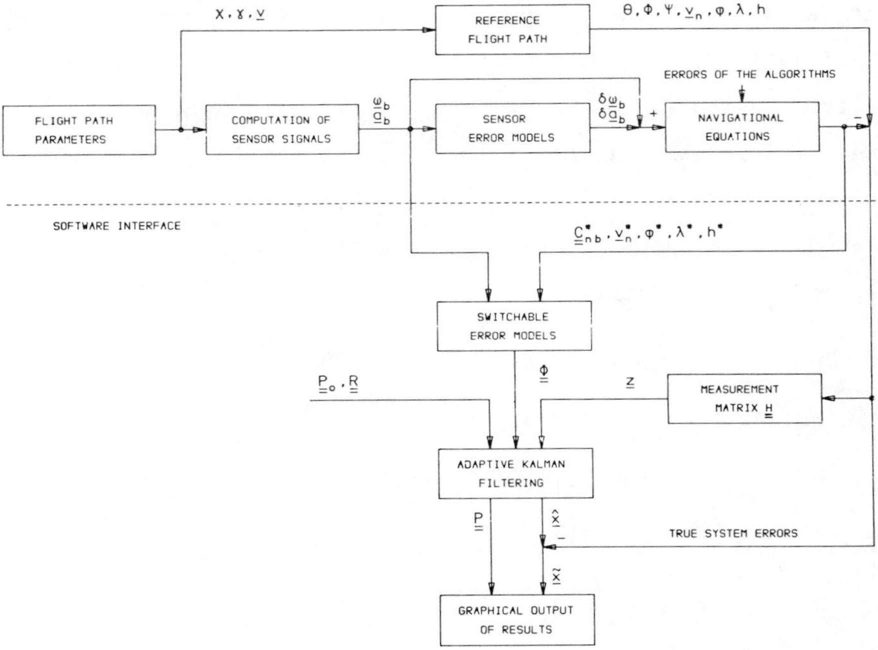

Fig. 11. Construction of the software for error-model testing ($x^* = x + \delta x$).

(2) the design of switchable sensor-error models;

(3) the adaptive Kalman filtering algorithms; and

(4) the comparison of assumed sensor-error coefficients or of system errors determined from the simulation, with errors estimated by the adaptive Kalman filter.

The simulation of the SDS shown in the upper part of Fig. 11 begins with the selection of tracks, flight-path angles, and velocities. Based on this input the sensor signals are calculated for the gyros and the accelerometers in terms of angular or velocity increments and are then fed into the sensor-error model. The corresponding errors of position, velocity, attitude, and heading angles are then obtained by comparing the results of the subsequent navigation calculation with the data of the reference flight path. All these values are stored on a magnetic disk for further use.

The adaptive Kalman filtering algorithms that now follow use the data from the simulated SDS and are based on the switchable sensor-error models developed by the calculation of error budgets. The state vector consists of three position errors, three velocity errors, and three angular errors, as well as a certain number of predefined sensor-error coefficients for model switching. The measurements required for the adaptive Kalman filtering algorithms can be obtained from the position signals of the simulated reference flight path, which is known exactly. In this case the reference flight path is considered to be the external position measurements carried out by a tracking-radar system, for example. Together with the initial covariance matrix $\underline{\underline{P}}_0$ and the covariance matrix $\underline{\underline{R}}$ assumed for the errors of the simulated measurements, the adaptive Kalman filters have all the necessary input data at their disposal. The results of the filtering are the estimation vector $\underline{x}$ and the covariance matrices $\underline{\underline{P}}$ and $\underline{\underline{Q}}$.

Now the comparison can be made between the results of the adaptive Kalman filtering and the sensor and system errors known by the simulation calculations and the corresponding assumptions for the magnitudes of the sensor-error coefficients. The differences determined in this way correspond to the so-called "true estimation errors" and, according to the theory of Kalman filtering, must satisfy the following relation:

$$\underline{\underline{P}}_{\text{Kalman}} = E\Big[(\hat{\underline{x}}_{\text{Kalman}} - \underline{x}_{\text{simulation}}) \times (\hat{\underline{x}}_{\text{Kalman}} - \underline{x}_{\text{simulation}})^T\Big], \tag{27}$$

where $\underline{\underline{P}}_{Kalman}$ is the covariance matrix corresponding to the self-diagnosis of the adaptive Kalman filter; $\hat{\underline{x}}_{Kalman}$ is the estimated state vector based on switchable low-order sensor error models; and $\underline{x}_{simulation}$ is the state vector known by simulation and the assumptions for the sensor-error coefficients.

Roughly speaking, Eq. (27) means that the estimation errors must lie within the 1σ limits defined by the trace of the covariance matrix $\underline{\underline{P}}$ calculated by the adaptive Kalman filtering algorithms. The aim when testing low-order sensor-error models is to use as few state variables as possible while still satisfying Eq. (27) and in doing so obtain acceptable values for the 1σ limits.

Example 4

Figure 12 shows the results for the component of the north-position error and is based on the simulated flight path of a civil airliner described in Example 1. The estimation error

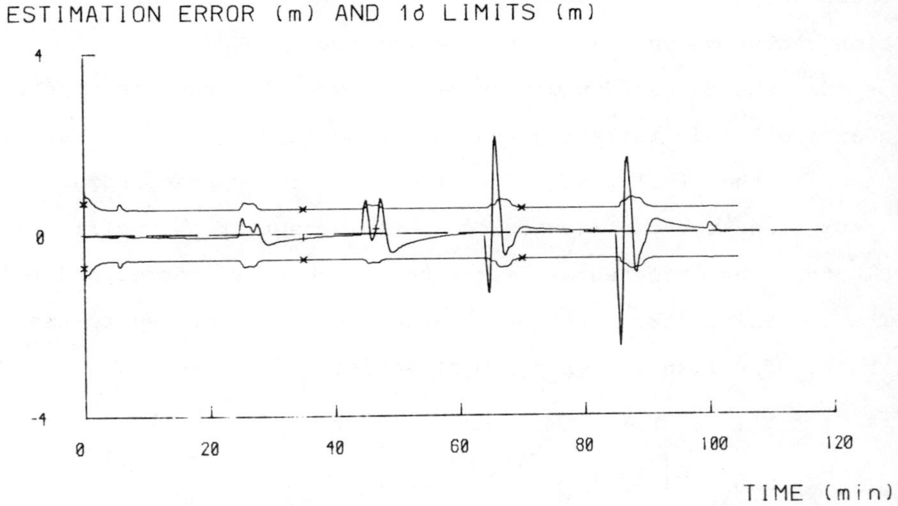

Fig. 12. North-position error with respect to sensor-error model S_4 (Example 4).

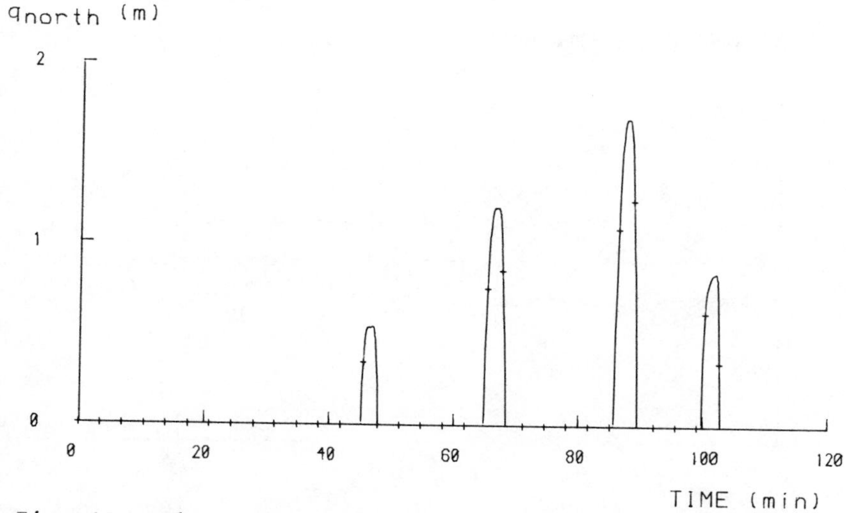

Fig. 13. Element q_{north} of the noise matrix $\underline{Q}$ (Example 4).

caused by sensor-error model $\underline{\underline{S}}_4$ is plotted together with the corresponding 1σ limits. The peaks noticeable in the time history of the estimation error correspond to the maneuvers that have been included in the simulated flight path. For the duration of these maneuvers there are nonmodeled sensor errors effective at system level. Therefore the statistics of the filter residuals and the predicted statistics of the adaptive Kalman filter no longer agree. The corresponding element q_{north} which compensates for this effect is shown in Fig. 13.

Example 5

For this example, the simulted RPV flight path described in Example 2 was used. The north position error based on sensor-error model $\underline{\underline{S}}_9$ was plotted. Figure 14 shows the time histories of the estimation error and the corresponding 1σ limits. The 1σ limits are the results of the self-diagnosis of the adaptive Kalman-filtering algorithms. Figure 15 presents the corresponding element q_{north}. Only during the

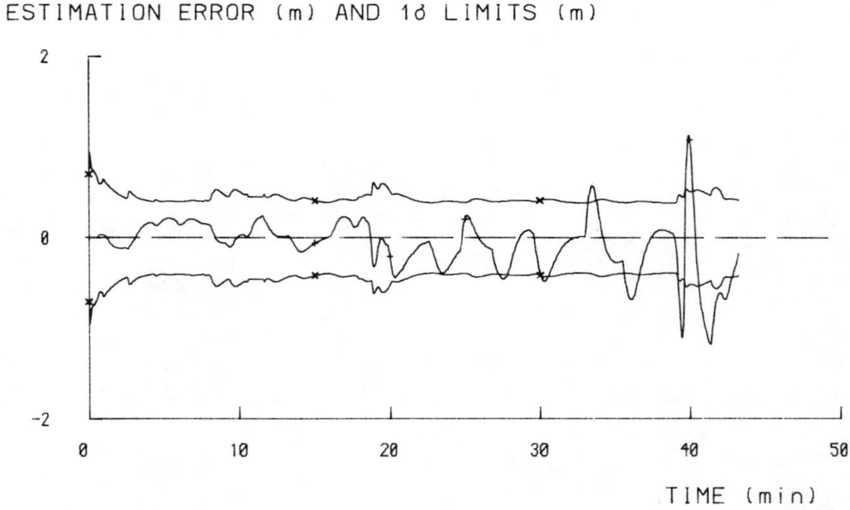

Fig. 14. North position error with respect to sensor-error model S_q (Example 5).

last 10 min are elements $q_{north} \neq 0$ necessary in order to adapt the predicted statistics to the statistics of the filter residuals. The complex error behavior caused by the large number of extreme maneuvers of this simulated RPV flight path

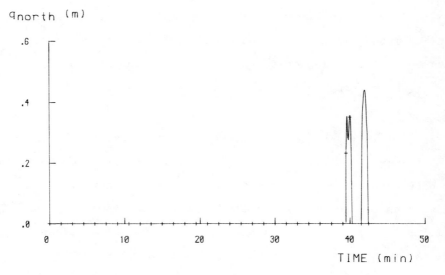

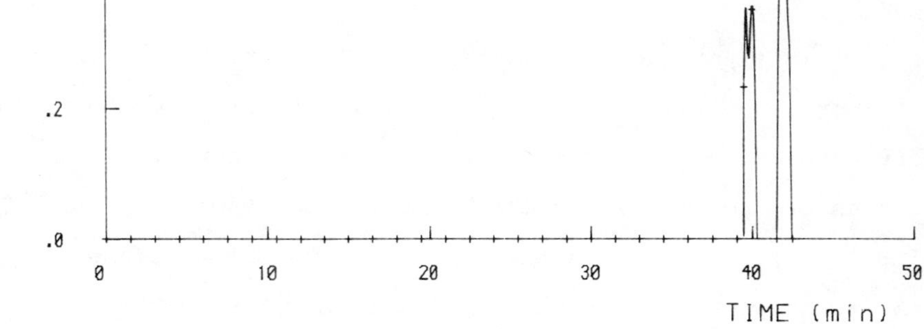

Fig. 15. Element q_{north} of the noise matrix $\underline{Q}$ (Example 5).

can be acceptably described by the technique of model switching and the method of adaptive Kalman filtering. The results are based on nine system errors and three switchable sensor errors, i.e., the rank of the state vector is only 12.

V. SUMMARY

The basic problem in the design of error models for aided SDS is the need to provide, in a low-order error model, a sufficiently realistic mathematical description of a large number of sensor-error coefficients which, depending on the maneuvers flown, can be effective at system-error level. If the flight path can be divided into sections with different structures where only a few sensor errors are effective at system-error level, it is possible to give a sufficiently good description of the real system-error behavior by switching between predefined low-order sensor-error models. In the case of sensor errors that cannot be modeled although they are effective at system-error level, the system-noise matrix $\underline{\underline{Q}}$ was correspondingly varied by application of the method of adaptive Kalman filtering. Several examples illustrated the advantages of the technique of model switching and the method of adaptive Kalman filtering algorithms for the improvement of accuracy of aided strapdown navigation systems.

REFERENCES

1. K. BRITTING, "Inertial Naviagation System Analysis," Wiley, New York, 1971.
2. A. GELB, "Applied Optimal Estimation," MIT Press, Cambridge, Massachusetts, 1974.
3. V. WETZIG, "Simulationen zum Fehlerverhalten eines Strapdown-Navigations-systems auf einer RPV-Flugbahn ohne überlagerte Vibrationen," DFVLR, Braunschweig, 1977.

4. Vereinigte Flugtechnische Werke VFW, "Grundform für das RPV-Missions-Profil," VFW, Bremen, 1976.

5. W. J. KUBBAT, "Application of Strapdown Inertial Navigation to High Performance Fighter Aircraft," *AGARD Lecture Series No. 95*, 1978.

6. B. STIELER, W. LECHNER, "Calibration of an INS Based on Flight Data," *AGARD Conf. Proc. No. 220*, 1976.

7. B. STIELER, and H. WINTER, "Advanced Instrumentation and Data Evaluation Techniques for Flight Tests," XI ICAS Congress, Lisboa, 1978.

8. N. LOHL, "Vermessung und Modellierung der Flugzeugbewegungen sowie deren Auswirkung auf die Navigationsgenauigkeit eines Strapdown-Systems," Dissertation, Technical University, Braunschweig, 1982.

9. R. K. MEHRA, "Approaches to Adaptive Filtering," *IEEE Trans. Autom. Control AC-17*, October 1972.

10. A. H. JAZWINSKI, "Stochastic Processes and Filtering Theory," Academic Press, New York, 1970.

11. A. H. JAZWINSKI, "Adaptive Filtering," *Automatica 5*, 1969.

12. C. B. CHANG, R. H. WHITING, and M. ATHANS, "On the State and Parameter Estimation for Maneuvering Reentry Vehicles, *IEEE Trans. Autom. Control AC-22*, February 1977.

13. T. LEE, "A Direct Approach to Identify the Noise Covariances of Kalman Filtering," *IEEE Trans. Autom. Control AC-25*, August 1980.

14. S. GODBOLE, "Kalman Filtering with No a priori Information About Noise," *IEEE Trans. Autom. Control AC-17*, October 1972.

Use of Filtering and Smoothing Algorithms in the Analysis of Missile-System Test Data

EDWARD M. DUIVEN
CHARLES L. MEDLER
JOSEPH F. KASPER, JR.
The Analytic Sciences Corporation
Reading, Massachusetts

THE PURPOSE

The increasing complexity of modern weapon systems demands a corresponding increase in the sophistication of the approaches used to test these systems. This article discusses advanced techniques for the processing of missile-system test data. In Section II, data from multiple references are used

ISBN 0-12-012720-2

in a postflight analyzer that is based in large part on a smoothing algorithm. The objectives of the processing are to obtain the best estimate of overall system accuracy and to recover the maximum information about individual guidance-system error contributors. In Section III, a procedure for validating the models used in filtering and smoothing algorithms is presented. The procedure checks model validity using data from multiple-system tests. It employs well-known statistical hypothesis-testing methods in an innovative manner.

I. INTRODUCTION

Modern weapon systems -- particularly ballistic missiles -- have grown in complexity by a significant amount over the past 20 to 30 years. Designers and developers now concern themselves with the total system aspect of missile development. Obtaining a broad system-level understanding of the missile and its environment has become vital.

Increasingly, system-level understanding is supported by modern analytic methods including applications of filtering and smoothing theory. Advances in the theory have taken place in concert with weapon-system development. Two interrelated elements of the modern analytic approach are system modeling and system testing. Models, which are mathematical representations of the physical characteristics of a system, have a number of uses in the system-development process.

Models for the errors associated with various system components and subsystems are formulated and then combined to create an overall weapon-system error model. Such a model can be used to generate performance projections (e.g., weapon-system accuracy) even before the weapon system has been built and deployed. Parameters of the model can also be varied about the nominal values to illustrate where the overall system is most sensitive to variations in subsystem performance. In this way, critical elements in the system design can be identified and given extra attention in the development effort.

Prior to testing, the weapon-system error model can be exercised to determine how well a proposed test procedure supports understanding of weapon-system behavior. Knowing the ability of a given test to isolate key system performance characteristics is a valuable aid in test-program management. Once testing has been performed, data are available to support validation of the various models. Quite often, conditions existing in the test environment must necessarily be different than those which would exist in the operational environment. Models provide the mathematical bridge which enables accurate extrapolation from performance under test conditions to performance under operational conditions.

Finally, models for system behavior are the vehicle which supports development of next-generation, advanced systems. By efficiently characterizing system behavior, models serve as the building blocks for future system-design activities. In many ways, they represent the "legacy" of a system-development program.

The keys to overall weapon-system modeling are proper formulation of component and subsystem models, sufficient testing to obtain data which are representative of all system characteristics, and a reliable model validation procedure to ensure that the mathematical representation corresponds faithfully to the actual system. Sections II and III both address the application of model-based modern analytic methods to ballistic missile development.

Section II is concerned with the Minuteman III flight-test program. In particular, Section II discusses the use of external reference information to enable determination of specific error characteristics which make up the model for the missile guidance system. It is shown that the ability to identify elements of the model is strongly influenced by the nature of the available reference systems and the chosen test plan. An algorithm based on a generalized likelihood ratio (GLR) test is seen to be effective in isolating certain non-linear error phenomena, provided that adequate reference data are available.

Section III is concerned with validation of the models for multiple phases in the operation of a ballistic missile system. A procedure based on statistical hypothesis-testing methods is presented. The procedure can be used to determine whether a proposed test program is capable of isolating bias-error phenomena. Alternatively, when data from multiple tests have been collected, the procedure provides a statistical assessment of the presence of bias-error phenomena in the system being tested.

II. BALLISTIC MISSILE GUIDANCE-SYSTEM EVALUATION USING MULTIPLE REFERENCES

A. *INTRODUCTION*

Historically, ballistic missile-system performance evaluation has been accomplished by postflight processing of guidance-system telemetry and radar measurements. This was adequate when the goal of system testing was weapon-system accuracy estimation. However, as guidance systems became more accurate, the goal of system testing shifted to the characterization of guidance-system errors in the "operational" environment, and it became necessary to upgrade range instrumentation quality.

As a consequence, instrumentation and postflight data-processor development activities aimed at upgrading guidance-system test methodologies were instituted [1-3]. Section II focuses on the test programs initiated by the U.S. Air Force (USAF) in 1970 that culminated in the launch of the last Minuteman III Production Verification Missile (PVM) in March, 1980. Over the 10 years, a series of programs directed at improved guidance-system characterization and advances in the quality and availability of external reference systems were initiated.

Section II.B is an overview of the USAF test programs. In *Sections II.C and II.D*, a discussion of the methodology and performance-evaluation studies undertaken to "optimize" the recovery of guidance-system error characteristics is presented. *Section II.E* discusses a data processor -- the postflight analyzer (PFA) -- developed to evaluate data from a series of test programs. The processing of the flight-test data, and the associated results, are described in Section II.F. Finally, Section II.G is a summary and suggests enhancements that may be desirable for future ballistic missile testing.

B. BACKGROUND

In 1971, with the Minuteman III test program approximately two-thirds complete, a significant decision was made by the USAF; it resulted in the termination of system testing at the Eastern Test Range (ETR) for cost reduction. Prior to this, approximately one-half of the test missiles had been launched at the ETR. Subsequently, flight tests were conducted only at the Western Test Range (WTR). The high-accuracy tracking capability and the good geometry characteristics available at the ETR were sacrificed.

The guidance-analysis community began to recognize the limitations of the test methodology in operation. The level of accuracy desired from the test program could not be achieved with the external reference systems available at the WTR. Also, the quantization levels associated with guidance telemetry data were not consistent with the levels required for guidance-system error characterization. The USAF began to look at alternative reference systems that could overcome test limitations.

At approximately the same time, the Charles Stark Draper Laboratory (CSDL) was actively developing a floated inertial reference platform, known as AIRS, the advanced inertial reference sphere [4]. The instruments developed for AIRS were designed to provide system quality an order of magnitude better than the primary Minuteman III guidance system (the NS-20).

The AIRS development schedule and the need for an improved reference system were nearly coincident. As a result, the USAF instituted the missile-performance measurement system (MPMS) program. An AIRS platform was incorporated in a separate wafer[1] along with its associated electronics, power supplies, telemetry unit, cooling system, etc. The primary guidance-system computer was modified to allow for the time-tagging of guidance-system outputs (integrated specific force). Time-tagging was a means of eliminating the impact of large quantization levels on the recovery of guidance-system errors; it reduced quantization-induced errors by approximately an order of magnitude.

Although originally planned as a multimissile test program, only one MPMS missile was flown. The test was conducted on Special Test Missile No. 11 (STM-11) on 15 July 1976. AIRS functioned well and much was learned about the performance of the AIRS hardware as well as NS-20 instrument-error characteristics. However, cost considerations dictated that that program be limited. MPMS led to the FLY-2 Program in which the AIRS platform was replaced by a second NS-20.

In principal, the FLY-2 concept would appear less than optimal. In most test programs it is desirable that the measuring device be an order of magnitude more accurate than the system being tested. However, by taking advantage of the NS-20 instrument orientations (Figs. 1 and 2) and the fact that the platforms can be aligned in azimuth to any desired orientation, within gimbal constraints (Fig. 3), the reliance on "identical" systems can be minimized. Thus, for FLY-2, it became a question of how to orient the platforms to achieve "optimal" recovery of a set of "primary error sources." Optimization-study results are discussed in Sections II.C and II.D.

[1]*Minuteman III is capable of carrying one or more insertable missile-body sections (wafers) between the fourth-stage motor and the payload section.*

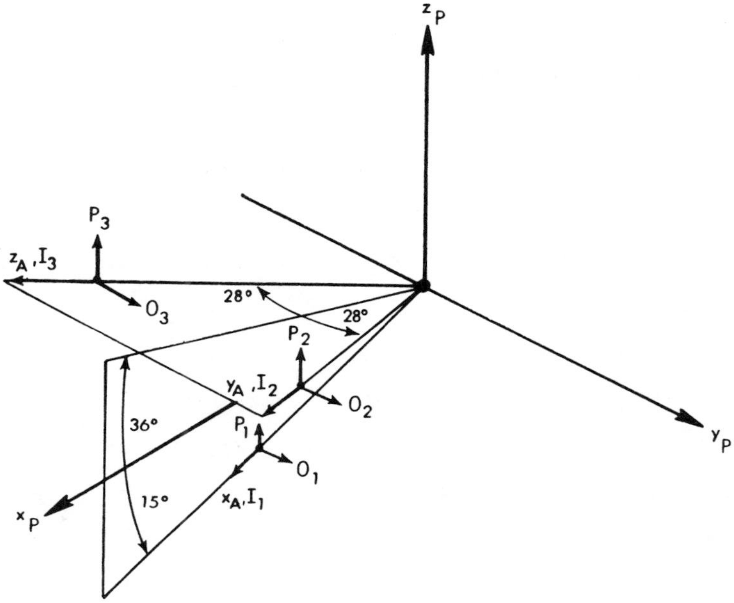

Fig. 1. Accelerometer-input axes: x_A, y_A, z_A. *Platform axes:* x_P, y_P, z_P.

A series of three FLY-2 missiles were flown between November 1976 and June 1977. Data from the three flights provided significant insight into a number of error contributors not previously included as part of the system-error model. However, FLY-2 was limited in its performance-assessment capabilities due to the lack of an independent reference with an accuracy superior to the WTR radars.

This shortcoming was resolved with the introduction of a GPS[2] receiver within the FLY-2 wafer. The original intent of GPS Receiver Test Program (GPS/RTP or FLY-2/GPS) was to demonstrate that the receiver could provide an accurate

[2]*Global Positioning System, a satellite-navigation system being developed by a triservice Joint Program Office [5].*

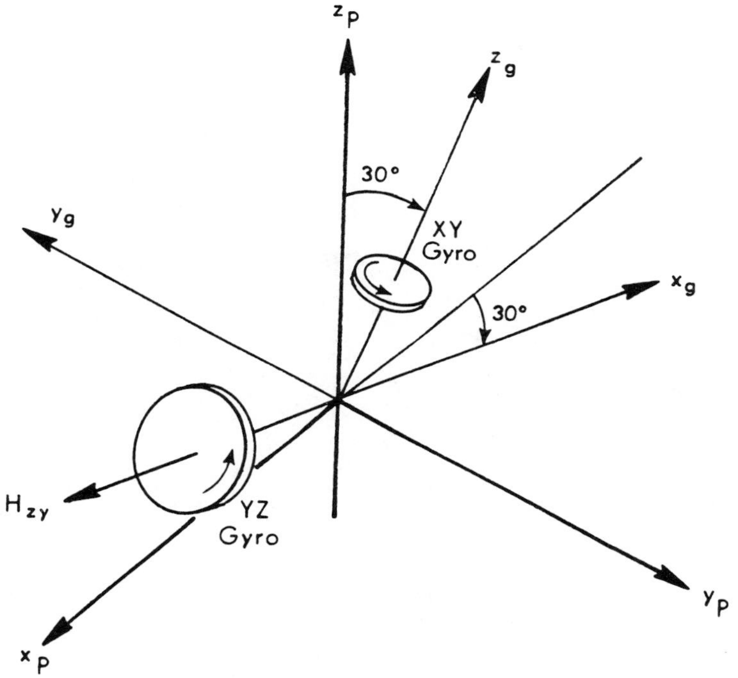

Fig. 2. Gyro-input axes: x_g, y_g, z_g. *Platform axes:* x_p, y_p, z_p.

postboost update in the ballistic missile environment. Since it was projected that the receiver would maintain lock[3] on the signals transmitted by the satellites, it was determined that the range and range-rate measurements should be used for postmission evaluation.

Two test flights were performed as part of the Minuteman III test program. Test missiles PVM-18 and PVM-19 were launched on 31 January 1980 and 27 March 1980. The presence of an accurate external reference, in addition to the FLY-2

[3] *Except during the staging events when high-acceleration rates are present due to motor shutdown and startup.*

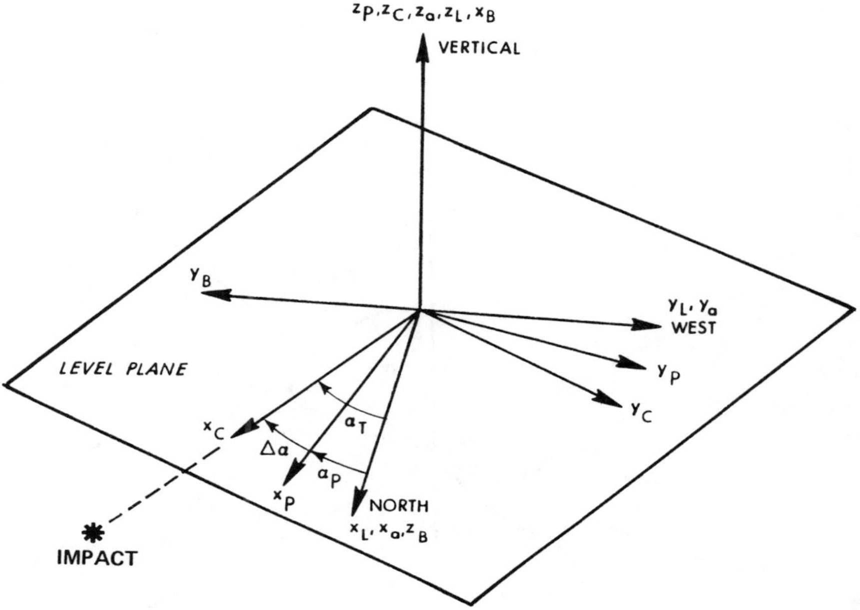

Fig. 3. Inertial measurement-unit frames. Launch-site frames: $x_L(x_L, y_L, z_L)$. Computer frame: $x_C(x_C, y_C, z_C)$. Platform frame: $x_P(x_P, y_P, z_P)$. Gyro-compass frame: $x_a(x_a, y_a, z_a)$. Missile-body frame: $x_B(x_B, y_B, z_B)$.

configuration, provided the best data collected during the Minuteman III test program. In summary, the USAF had pursued a course that led to ever-increasing test capability without having to make major changes to an overall test philosophy.

C. EVALUATION METHODOLOGY

The methodology used to "optimize" FLY-2 (and subsequently FLY-2/GPS) performance is very strongly tied to the objectives set forth for the test programs. Thus, it is important that these objectives be presented and the test program goals be put into perspective. The goals of FLY-2 were the following:

(1) to validate the effect on system accuracy of preflight software (Ground Program) modifications introduced as a consequence of the Guidance Improvement Program[4];

(2) to increase the understanding of a number of *"priority" error sources* included in the guidance-system error model;

(3) to detect and identify *"unmodeled" error sources;*

(4) to identify *source of anomalous performance* using the unique data characteristics available from the FLY-2 instrumentation system.

The same goals were established for FLY-2/GPS with the additional goal of demonstrating GPS receiver performance in the "operational" environment.

The priority error sources are (1) initial azimuth misalignment, (2) accelerometer cross-axis compliance, (3) gyro g^2 and g^4 coefficients, and (4) platform compliance. The error mechanisms for these quantities are included in the Minuteman III guidance-error model. However, the coefficients typically could not be separated during static testing[5]; sled testing does not provide the appropriate dynamics for coefficient observability. Thus, these quantities may be "observed" only during powered flight. The goal of FLY-2 and FLY-2/GPS was to provide data to assist in characterizing these priority error sources.

[4] *One in a series of accuracy upgrades made to the Minuteman III guidance system between 1970 and 1976.*

[5] *Static testing implies all testing in a 1-g field, including tumble and vibration testing.*

The unmodeled errors of interest can actually be called mismodeled errors. There had been speculation that certain of the "bias"-error coefficients have time-varying characteristics, specifically shifts and/or ramps. This type of error, if present in the guidance system, could have a significant impact on weapon system accuracy. In addition to the bias shift/ramp type of error, additional unmodeled errors include gyro g^2- and g^4-sensitive error coefficients. These "unmodeled" errors could be addressed using FLY-2 and/or FLY-2/GPS data -- once suitable models had been developed for them.

Finally, sources of anomalous performance are those error characteristics that were not anticipated but had been discovered as a result of data analysis. A variety of these surfaced during the test programs. However, no evaluation studies had been undertaken, ahead of time, to assess the ability to detect and isolate sources of anomalous performance.

Based on the objectives discussed above, there are two criteria by which the test program may be assessed (optimized): (1) recovery of the priority error sources in a postmission data-evaluation environment, and (2) detection and identification of unmodeled (or improperly modeled) error characteristics.

The USAF test-program objectives called for postmission processing of test data to extract information about the priority error sources and the "unmodeled" errors. It was determined that the processor would be based on a Kalman filter [6,7]. The filter estimates the priority error sources and the "unmodeled" errors incorporated in the filter, to some level of confidence. To address the question of the presence of instrument-error coefficient shifts and/or ramps, a new methodology was developed. The technique referred to as the generalized likelihood ratio (GLR) test is a direct extension of the Kalman filter. The GLR test uses filter residuals to determine whether there are any unmodeled errors (bias shifts and/or ramps) that would cause the residuals to be other than a zero-mean white-noise sequence.

Figure 4 depicts the flow of data through the postflight evaluation software. The filter processes the radar, dual NS-20 guidance telemetry, and, if available, GPS measurements to estimate the errors in the filter model. The filter minimizes, in a mean-squared error sense, the error between the actual measurements and those predicted by the model. The NS-20 error model assumes that the principal instrument errors are biases over the period of powered flight. It is well known [6] that the sequence of measurement residuals will be a zero-mean white-noise sequence if the filter models are correct.

However, if certain of the error coefficients display sudden shifts or ramping characteristics, the model is not correct, and the measurement residuals will not be white and of zero mean. The GLR algorithm tests the mean and whiteness of the filter residuals [8]. The test is a two-step process. The first step determines whether a shift in one (or more) of the coefficients has taken place. This is referred to as the *detection* process. Detection is performed by forming a weighted sum of the last M measurement residuals[6] and using this quantity as a test statistic in a binary hypothesis test. If the test statistic l is greater than a specified threshold ϵ, a shift is detected; if it is smaller than ϵ, no shift is assumed to be present.

[6] *The quantity M is referred to as the GLR detection-window length.*

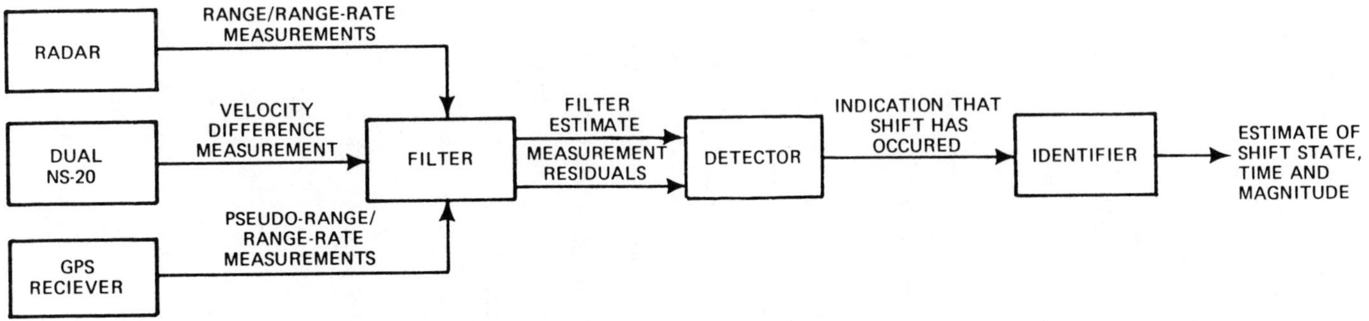

Fig. 4. Postflight evaluation software-data flow.

The second step is *identification*. The GLR formulation results in an algorithm that generates an estimate of the state that shifted, the time of the shift, and the shift magnitude. Under the assumption of no a priori knowledge about the jump characteristic, the GLR estimate is "optimal." The capability to estimate the jump characteristics makes GLR more attractive than other residual-based detection processes [9].

The critical parameters of the GLR test design are the probability of false alarm (P_F) and the probability of detection (P_D). The probability of false alarm is defined as the probability that a shift will be detected when no shift occurs. It is shown in [8] that the higher the value of ϵ selected, the lower the probability of false alarm; however, that is not the only tradeoff.

The probability of detection, defined as the probability that a jump (if present) will be detected, is a function of the shift-detection threshold ϵ and the window length M, as

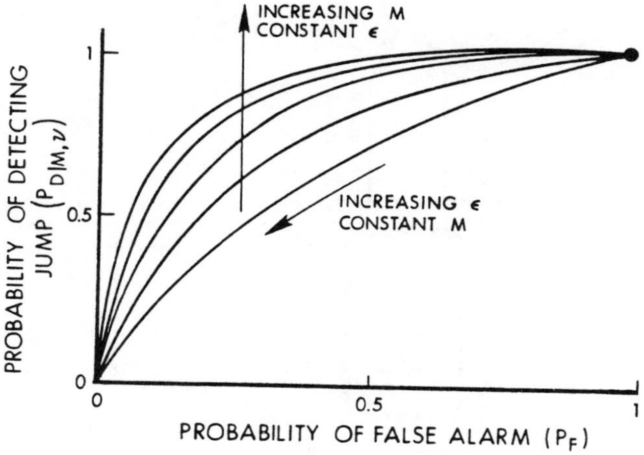

Fig. 5. General relationship between P_D and P_F as a function of M and ϵ.

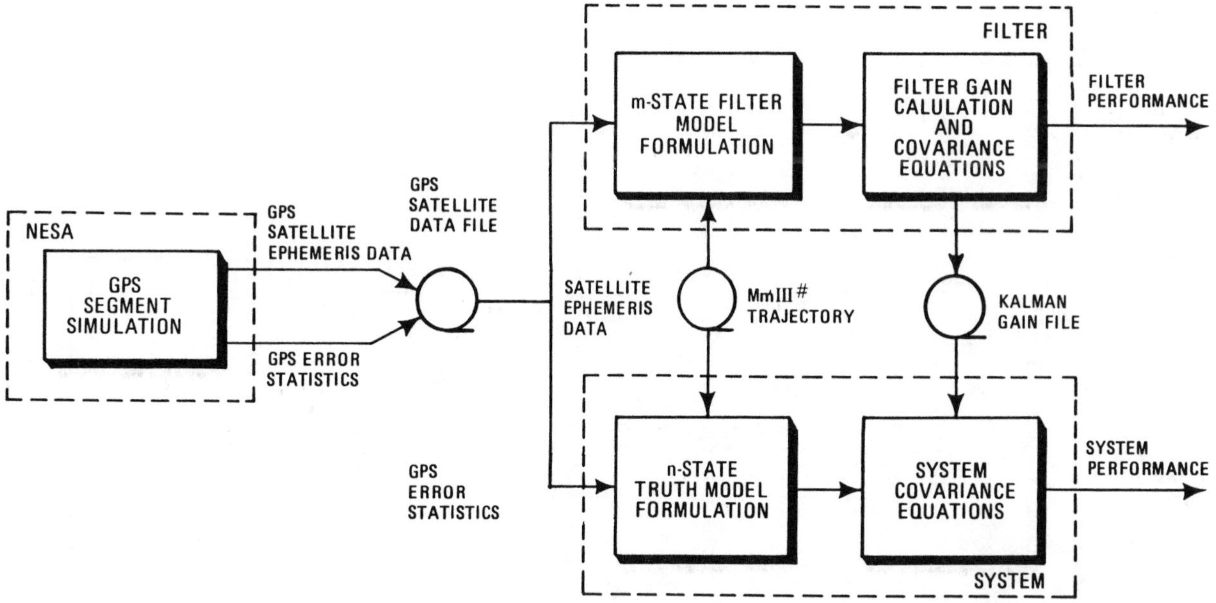

Fig. 6. GPS/User satellite performance projection methodology.

well as the magnitude of the jump itself, v [8]. As seen in Fig. 5, the longer the detection window, the higher the probability of detection for a given P_F. However, the length of the window is limited by the missile flight time, computational capabilities of the hardware used for postflight processing, and the fact that multiple jumps may occur during the flight.

The methodology used for evaluation of the FLY-2 and FLY-2/GPS flight-test programs is depicted in Fig. 6. The same error covariance analysis procedures were used for both the FLY-2 and FLY-2/GPS studies. Only the FLY-2/GPS simulation is discussed here.

There are three steps involved in the generation of projected FLY-2/GPS performance estimates. The first step is simulation of the GPS segment. It is necessary for two reasons:

(1) to develop a time history of GPS satellite orbital positions and velocities so that proper accounting is made for GPS/missile geometry;

(2) to generate the GPS satellite position, velocity, and clock calibration error covariances.

In Fig. 6, the FILTER module represents the second step, recursive solution of the filter error covariance propagation and update equations. These equations are solved once for a specific GPS satellite-measurement schedule. The outputs of the FILTER module are time histories of filter-indicated performance and the Kalman gain matrices.

The third step in the evaluation process, the SYSTEM module in Fig. 6, involves recursive solution of the linear *system* error covariance equations. These equations are solved repeatedly to produce an error budget, using the same Kalman-gain file each time. When all error contributiors have been evaluated, the overall measurement system performance projection can be calculated from the detailed error-source-by-error-source breakdown. This analysis produces the following benefits:

(1) *determination of key error contributors*, indicating where to focus attention for subsequent performance improvements;

(2) *identification of insignificant error contributors*, indicating where a less costly (i.e., poorer quality) subsystem might be substituted with minimal performance degradation.

The methodology presented in this section was used for "optimization" of FLY-2/GPS performance. A more detailed discussion of the error covariance methodology can be found elsewhere [5,10].

The FLY-2/GPS error covariance simulations determine the Kalman filter estimation error covariance matrix based on a sequence of measurements. There are three sets of measurements associated with the GPS/RTP. The first set is the difference between the two inertial measuring-unit (IMU) velocity measurements; the second set of measurements are those associated with the range radars; and the third set results from processing of the GPS measurements.

Table I. IMU Error Summary

ERROR OR ERROR SOURCE NAME	NUMBER OF STATES FULL MODEL	TRUTH MODEL	FILTER MODEL
PRIMARY			
Position Errors	3	3	3
Velocity Errors	3	3	3
Alignment Errors	3	3	3
Initial Alignment Errors	3	3	3
PRIMARY - MEW			
Differential Position Errors	3	3	3
Differential Velocity Errors	3	3	3
Differential Alignment Errors	3	3	3
Differential Initial Alignment Errors	3	3	3
PRIMARY IMU INSTRUMENT ERRORS SOURCES			
Accelerometers			
Uncorrelated Bias	3	3	3
Scale Factor	3	-	-
Input g^2 Nonlinearity	3	-	-
Input g^3 Nonlinearity	3	-	-
Input Axis Misalignments	6	-	-
Cross-Axis Nonlinearity	3	-	-
Q-Matrix Calibration Errors	9	9	9
Platform Compliance Errors	27	-	-
Gyros			
Bias	3	3	3
Mass Unbalance	4	2	2
Anisoelasticity	6	3	3
Gyro g^4 Coefficients	8	3	3
Temperature Dependent Drift	3	-	-
MEW IMU INSTRUMENT ERROR SOURCES			
Accelerometers			
Uncorrelated Bias	3	3	3
Scale Factor	3	-	-
Input g^2 Nonlinearity	3	-	-
Input g^3 Nonlinearity	3	-	-
Input Axis Misalignments	6	-	-
Cross-Axis Nonlinearity	3	-	-
Q-Matrix Calibration Errors	9	9	9
Platform Compliance Errors	27	-	-
Gyros			
Bias	3	3	3
Mass Unbalance	4	2	2
Anisoelasticity	6	3	3
Gyro g^4 Coefficients	8	3	3
Temperature Dependent Drift	3	-	-
TOTAL NUMBER OF STATES	186	70	70

The error sources for FLY-2/GPS are those associated with the two IMUs, the radar, and the GPS satellites. Table I lists the errors modeled for each of the IMUs and selected for use in the filter model and truth (i.e., system) model formulations.

Table II. Radar Error-Model Summary

ERROR SOURCE NAME	NUMBER OF STATES		
	FULL MODEL	TRUTH MODEL	FILTER MODEL
RANGE MEASUREMENTS			
Bias Error	1	1	1
Scale Factor Error	1	1	1
Random Error	1	1	1
Measurement Noise	1	1	1
Survey Errors	0	0	0
RANGE-RATE MEASUREMENTS			
Bias Error	1	1	1
Scale Factor	1	1	1
Random Error	1	1	1
Measurement Noise	1	1	1
Survey Errors	0	0	0

Table II lists the error sources associated with the WTR measurements. Error sources associated with the GPS satellite, propagation delays, and the missile receiver are given in Table III. The uncertainties in satellite position, velocity, etc., are provided by a program that simulates the GPS satellite ground-tracking process and determines the estimation

Table III. GPS Error-Model Summary

ERROR SOURCE NAME	NUMBER OF STATES		
	FULL MODEL	TRUTH MODEL	FILTER MODEL
SATELLITE ERRORS			
Position	3	3	0
Velocity	3	3	0
Solar Radiation Force	1	1	0
Gravitation Constant	1	1	0
Satellite Clock	3	3	0
PROPAGATION ERRORS	2	0	0
RECEIVER ERRORS			
Missile Clock	5	3	3
Carrier and Code Loop	2	0	0

error covariance for the GPS satellites. The propagation errors and carrier and code-loop errors listed in Table III are modeled as white-measurement-noise sequences in the simulation and are not estimated.

D. PERFORMANCE PROJECTIONS

FLY-1 (or single IMU versus radar) performance was evaluated using several trajectories that emulated nominal missions flown from Vandenberg Air Force Base (VAFB) to the Kwajalein Atoll. FLY-1 performance was developed as a baseline against which FLY-2 and FLY-2/GPS performance may be compared. The nominal ground track and specific force profiles for these trajectories are shown in Figs. 7 and 8, respectively. For these analyses, the azimuth offset angle $\Delta\alpha$ (Fig. 3) is assumed to be zero. Range measurements from the South Vandenberg Air Force Base, Point Mugu, and Pillar Point radars

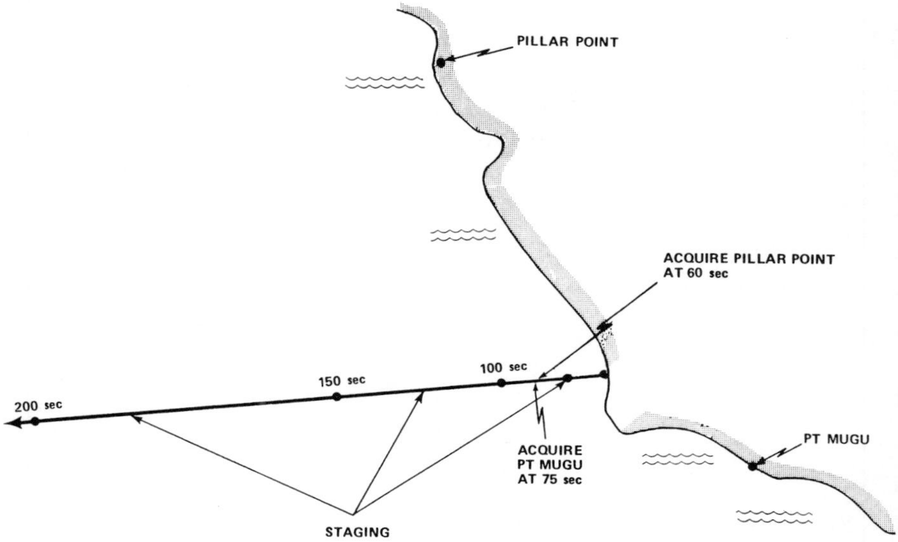

Fig. 7. Typical Minuteman III test trajectory.

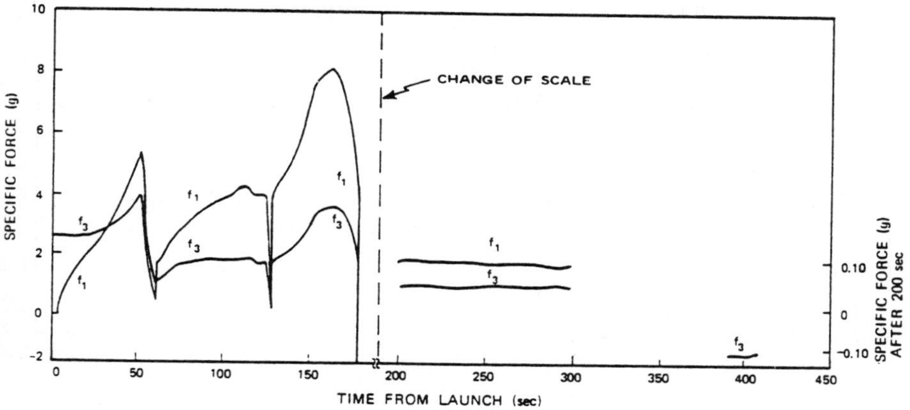

Fig. 8. Typical specific force time history: f_1 = down range component; f_3 = up component.

were assumed available every 1/2 sec beginning 15, 40, and 50 sec into the mission, respectively.

FLY-1 results are presented in terms of normalized (unitless) quantities called recovery ratios. Two types of recovery ratios are of interest: (1) *guidance error recovery ratio* and (2) *error coefficient* recovery ratio. The former is defined as

$$R_G = \frac{\text{rms error in estimate of guidance quantity}}{\text{rms guidance error in absence of tracking}}. \tag{1}$$

These are obtained for the following:

(1) downrange, cross-track, vertical position, and velocity errors at reentry vehicle deployment;

(2) downrange and cross-track miss distances;

(3) CEP [11]; and

(4) initial azimuth misalignment.

Recovery ratios for these quantities are always less than or equal to 1.00; the smaller the value, the better the recovery of the error of interest.

Table IV. FLY-1 Guidance-Error Recovery Ratios at Boost Burnout

REENTRY ANGLE	DOWN-RANGE POSITION ERROR	CROSS-TRACK POSITION ERROR	DOWN-RANGE VELOCITY ERROR	CROSS-TRACK VELOCITY ERROR	PREDICTED CROSS-TRACK MISS	PREDICTED CEP
Low	0.98	0.56	0.99	0.63	0.63	0.82
Medium	0.99	0.53	0.99	0.56	0.56	0.76
High	0.99	0.55	0.99	0.62	0.63	0.79

The error coefficient recovery ratio (R_C) is the ratio of the final rms uncertainty in the estimate of the error coefficient σ_F to the initial rms or a priori uncertainty σ_0. That is,

$$R_C = \sigma_F/\sigma_0. \tag{2}$$

Downrange and cross-track guidance-error recovery ratios for FLY-1 are given in Table IV. Vertical position and velocity ratios (not shown) are essentially identical to the downrange numbers. The processing of combined radar and NS-20 data yields cross-track error reductions of 40 to 50%. Cross-track miss distance recovery is essentially equal to cross-track velocity error recovery because cross-track velocity error at boost-burnout is the major source of cross-track miss. Unfortunately, processing of the combined radar and single NS-20 data *does not* produce any significant improvement in downrange (or vertical) guidance-error estimation as a consequence of radar accuracy and geometry relative to the missile trajectory. The Vandenberg and Point Mugu stations essentially provide only downrange information. However, the NS-20 IMU is more accurate in the determination of downrange position than the WTR radars. Thus, the NS-20

Table V. Best FLY-1 Priority Error-Source Coefficient Recovery Ratios

ACCELEROMETER COEFFICIENTS			GYRO COEFFICIENTS				INITIAL AZIMUTH ERROR
1ST ORDER NONLINEARITY (δF_{i1})	CROSS-TRACK g^2 (Bc2)	PLATFORM COMPLIANCE	BIAS	g-DRIFT	g^2-DRIFT	g^4-DRIFT	
0.99	0.99	0.99	0.99	0.99	0.96	0.98	0.80

"calibrates the downrange radars." Pillar Point provides good cross-track information and is the source of recovery for these errors. The reduction in error of the predicted impact point (i.e., CEP recovery) results solely from the reduction in cross-track miss prediction error.

Priority error source recovery ratios for FLY-1 are summarized in Table V, which lists the smallest recovery ratio attained for a given coefficient over all simulated flights. Since the radar data basically yields only cross-track information, a 20% reduction in initial azimuth error is attained. However, processing of FLY-1 data produces no significant recovery of any of the remaining priority error sources.

The guidance error and error coefficient recovery ratios are excellent measures of flight-test performance; however, considered individually they are too numerous to use in a meaningful optimization criterion. Furthermore, there is no single flight-test configuration which simultaneously minimizes all recovery ratios of interest. Instead, two simple measures of performance, one for guidance-error recovery and a second for error coefficient recovery were developed.

Table VI. Best FLY-2 Priority Error-Source Coefficient Recovery Ratios

ACCELEROMETER COEFFICIENTS			GYRO COEFFICIENTS						
1ST ORDER NONLINEARITY (δF_{il})	CROSS-TRACK g^2 (Bc2)	PLATFORM COMPLIANCE	BIAS	g DRIFT		g^2 DRIFT		g^4 DRIFT	
				δC	δD	δB	δE	P	J
0.93	0.96	0.93	0.99	0.76	0.81	0.48	0.18	0.07	0.22

In the course of the optimization studies, approximately 150 FLY-2 flights were simulated. Table VI lists, for each priority error source, the best (i.e., smallest) coefficient recovery ratio attained over all flights. It must be emphasized that no one flight simulation yielded all these results.

If a particular error source coefficient strongly influenced the error behavior of an IMU, simply *averaging* the outputs of two systems (under the assumption that the error sources in both systems are equal in rms value and uncorrelated) would reduce the effect of that error source on system error by a factor of $1/\sqrt{2}$ or 0.71. It could be argued that coefficient recovery ratios greater than 0.71 are not significant. Table VII shows that FLY-2 produces no significant recovery of accelerometer or platform compliance coefficients. The same is true for gyro bias and g-dependent drift rates. In fact, of all the priority error source coefficients only gyro g^2- and g^4-dependent drift rates are recovered at a significant level. For these coefficients it is convenient to define a composite coefficient recovery ratio:

$$R_{COMP} = \frac{1}{4}[\min R_{\delta E} + \min R_{\delta B} + \min R_J + \min R_P], \tag{3}$$

Table VII. Effect of Azimuth-Offset Variations on Error Recovery -- FLY-2/GPS

DIFFERENTIAL AZIMUTH OFFSET $\lvert\Delta\alpha_1-\Delta\alpha_2\rvert$ (deg)	INDIVIDUAL AZIMUTH OFFSETS (deg)		COMPOSITE COEFFICIENT RECOVERY	GUIDANCE CEP RECOVERY
	$\Delta\alpha_1$	$\Delta\alpha_2$		
30	0	30	0.29	0.62
	-15	15	0.47	0.65
45	0	45	0.32	0.63
	-15	30	0.44	0.72
	-22.5	22.5	0.49	0.76

where min R is the smallest recovery ratio attained for a given coefficient in a given run; δE, δB signify gyro g^2-dependent drift coefficients; J, P signify gyro g^4-dependent drift coefficients; and R_{COMP} and R_G are used as measures of FLY-2 performance for optimization purposes.

A major concern was selection of primary and secondary NS-20 IMU azimuth offsets and trajectory reentry angle to optimize (i.e., minimize) the guidance error CEP and composite coefficient recovery ratios. Three-axis velocity difference data and radar-tracking data were processed every 4.5 sec throughout the boost phase using a Kalman filter algorithm to estimate guidance errors, instrument and platform error coefficients, and initial alignment errors.

With regard to azimuth offset angle ($\Delta\alpha$) optimization, one might assume that simultaneous offset of both IMUs is desirable. However, for the optimization criteria selected, this is not the case. To illustrate, the results of two test cases from the series of medium-reentry-angle studies are summarized in Table VII. The flights had a fixed azimuthal *difference* of either 30° or 45° between the two systems, but the orientation of the primary guidance system (System 1) varied about the $\Delta\alpha = 0°$ orientation. The composite coefficient recovery ratio and the CEP recovery ratio for these flights are also presented.

For a fixed azimuthal difference, superior recovery always occurs when one system is launched with zero offset. This was observed to be the case at all reentry angles. In this orientation the gyro and accelerometer errors contribute the least to guidance errors. When both IMUs are offset so that their individual contributions to guidance errors are comparable, the optimal postflight data processor cannot distinguish between the two systems. Thus, recovery ratios are poor. Conversely, when one system is placed on-axis, its contribution to guidance errors is greatly reduced, and the errors of the off-axis system become more observable. The on-axis IMU becomes the reference through which errors in the off-axis system are recovered.

Azimuth-angle offset optimization studies were performed, with one platform always at zero offset, for low, medium, and high reentry angles with results shown in Figs. 9-11. All three sets of results are quite similar and demonstrate that initial azimuth error recovery shows little variation with

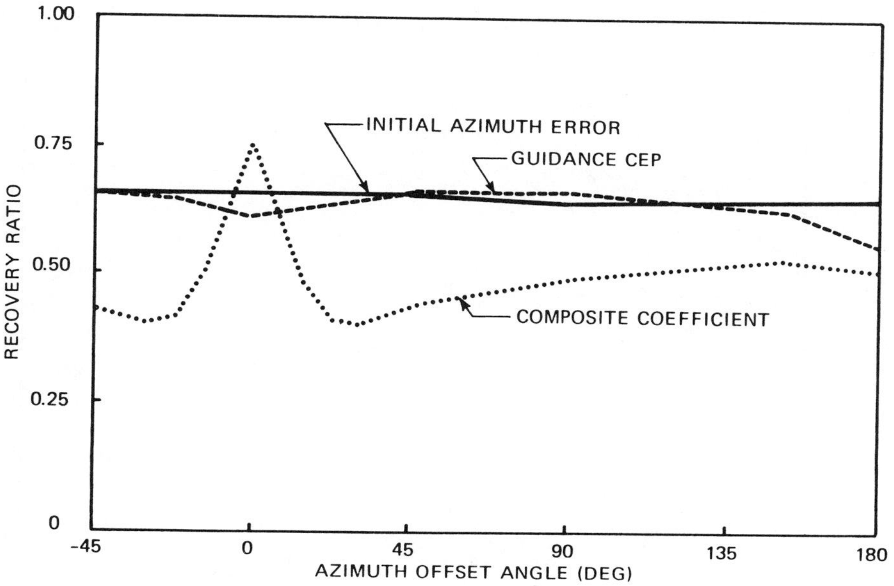

Fig. 9. Recovery ratio as a function of secondary IMU azimuth offset angles (low reentry angle).

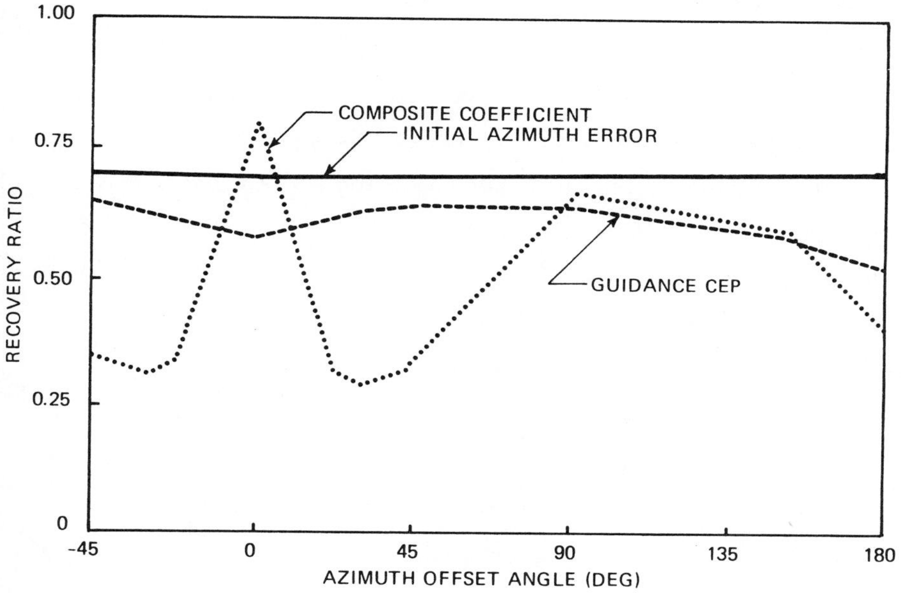

Fig. 10. Recovery ratio as a function of secondary IMU azimuth offset angle (medium reentry angle).

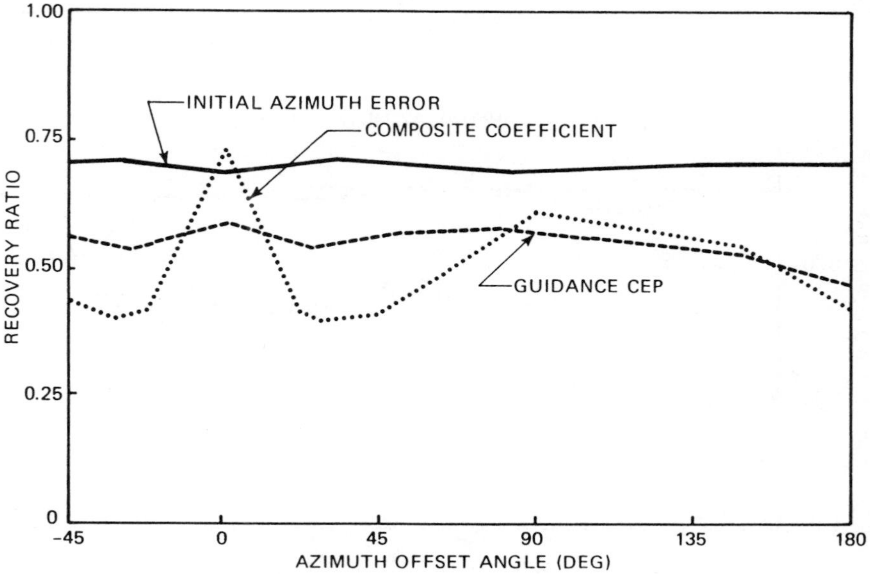

Fig. 11. Recovery ratio as a function of secondary IMU azimuth offset angle (high reentry angle).

offset angle. This is because much of the initial azimuth-error recovery comes from radar-tracking data and not IMU velocity difference data.

The guidance CEP recovery ratio shows some variation with azimuth offset angle, but the variation is not pronounced. Guidance CEP recovery is minimum when $\Delta\alpha = 180°$, i.e., when the level-platform axes for the two systems are antiparallel. However, actual implementation of this configuration is not possible due to guidance-system gimbal constraints.

Referring again to Figs. 9 to 11, the composite coefficient recovery ratio shows the greatest variation with azimuth offset angle of any of the recovery ratios considered. Furthermore, for all reentry angles considered, this ratio reaches a minimum with a 30° offset of the secondary IMU. This minimum is fairly broad, however, providing low composite coefficient ratios in the range of 22.5° to 45°. Also, the composite coefficient recovery ratio plot is symmetric at about $\Delta\alpha = 0°$ so that both positive and negative offsets are useful.

As a consequence of these optimization studies, the following conclusions were drawn:

(1) The primary guidance system should be aligned to the target azimuth ($\Delta\alpha = 0°$).

(2) The secondary guidance platform should be offset 22.5° to 45° from the primary guidance system

(3) The reentry angles for FLY-2 should be in the middle of the capability range of the system.

The first two recommendations were followed on all three FLY-2 flights. However, a range of reentry angles was selected so that specific error-coefficient recovery could be emphasized rather than minimization of the composite performance index.

Having addressed the "optimization" issues associated with FLY-2, it is possible to assess GLR test performance. The GLR test was specifically designed to detect and identify shifts and/or ramps in certain guidance-system instrument-error coefficients. Attention is directed here to the detection and identification of shifts in the accelerometer bias and/or gyro bias-drift coefficients. The results are based on the same model used in the optimization studies. In addition, two forms of the GLR test mechanization are considered: fixed lag and fixed interval.[7]

[7] *The terms fixed interval and fixed lag were selected because of the close association of the formulations to the fixed-interval and fixed-lag smoothers [6].*

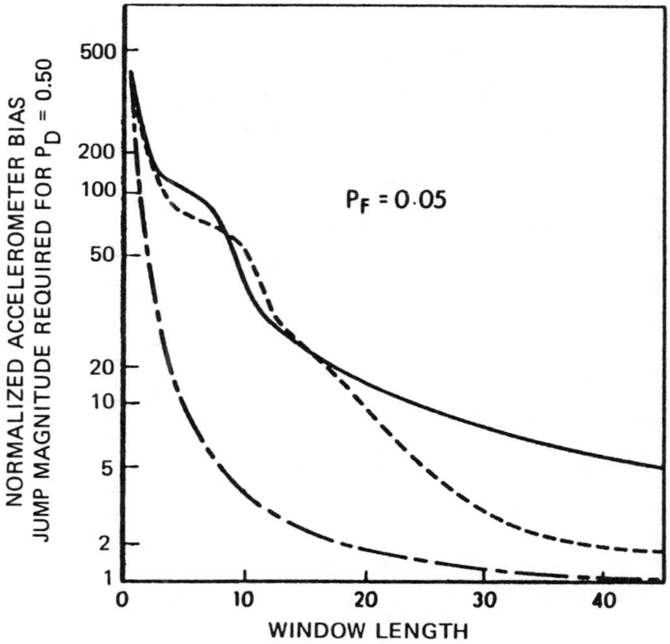

Fig. 12. Accelerometer bias jump detection versus window length, using fixed-lag GLR. Solid line, jump time = 0 sec; short dashes, jump time = 100 sec; long-short dashes, jump time = 200 sec.

Fixed-lag GLR is based on a data window M of fixed length. The relationship between window length and detectable jump magnitude is shown in Figs. 12 and 13. For shifts in both accelerometer bias and gyro-bias drift, there is an asymptotic relationship between detectable jump magnitude and window length. The minimum acceptable window length is approximately 20 (100 sec for the 5-sec sampling interval). However, maximum detectability for all possible jump times would require window lengths on the order of 45 (225 sec). Figure 12 indicates that accelerometer shifts on the order of 10σ (σ is the initial rms uncertainty) are detectable, with a false-alarm probability

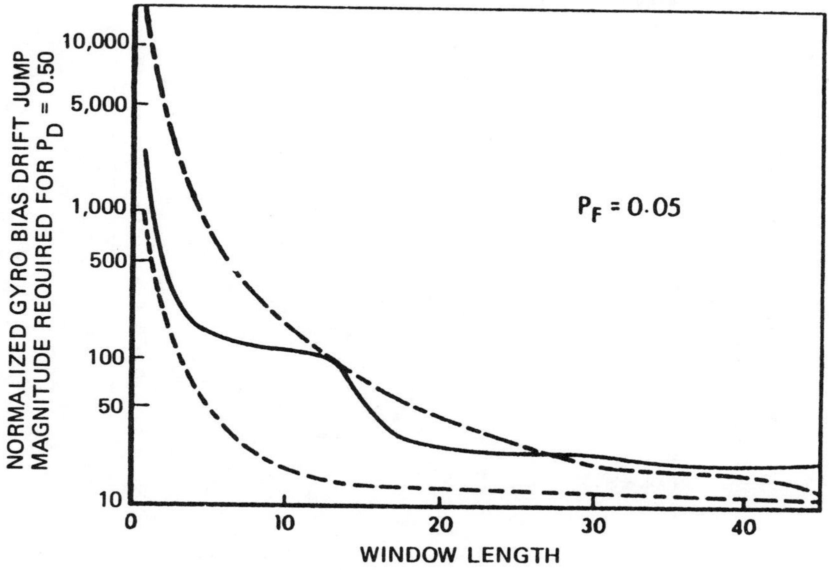

Fig. 13. Gyro-bias-drift jump detection versus window length, using fixed-lag GLR. Solid line, jump time = 0 sec; short dashes, jump time = 100 sec; long-short dashes, jump time = 200 sec.

P_F of 0.05 and a detection probability P_D of 0.50. For gyro bias drift, shifts on the order of 50σ are detectable if they occur prior to third-stage-thrust termination.

The regions of superior shift detectability are shown in Figs. 14 and 15.[8] Accelerometer bias shifts are most detectable if they occur after burnout. The poor performance prior to burnout is caused by the large specific force components exciting the higher-order accelerometer and gyro-error terms. Thus, bias shifts must be large relative to the specific force effects on the g-dependent errors if they are to be observable.

[8] *Fixed-lag and fixed-interval results are shown in Figs. 14 and 15 for comparison; only the latter are discussed.*

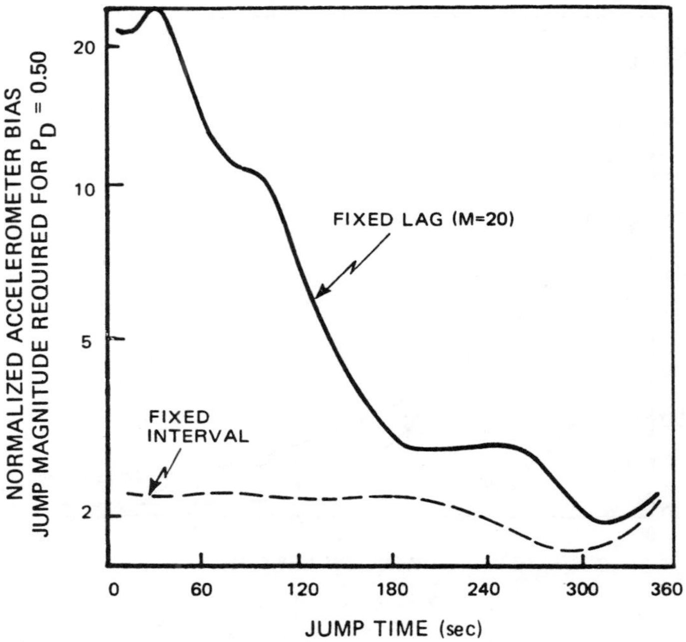

Fig. 14. Accelerometer bias jump detection versus jump time; $P_F = 0.05$.

After thrust termination, the detection of smaller shifts is possible (for the same P_D) because of the lower specific force component magnitudes.

It is well known [11-14] that gyro-bias-drift errors enter guidance-velocity error through the term $\underline{\psi} \times \underline{f}$, where $\underline{\psi}$ is the platform-misalignment vector resulting from gyro-drift errors, and $\underline{f}$ is the specific force vector. It follows that gyro-bias-drift coefficient shift detection should be the best during the period of powered flight when $\underline{f}$ is maximum. The data plotted in Fig. 15 substantiates this premise.

Fixed-interval GLR uses a variable-length window which runs from the candidate jump time to the end of the data interval. Figures 12 and 13 show the effect of the increased

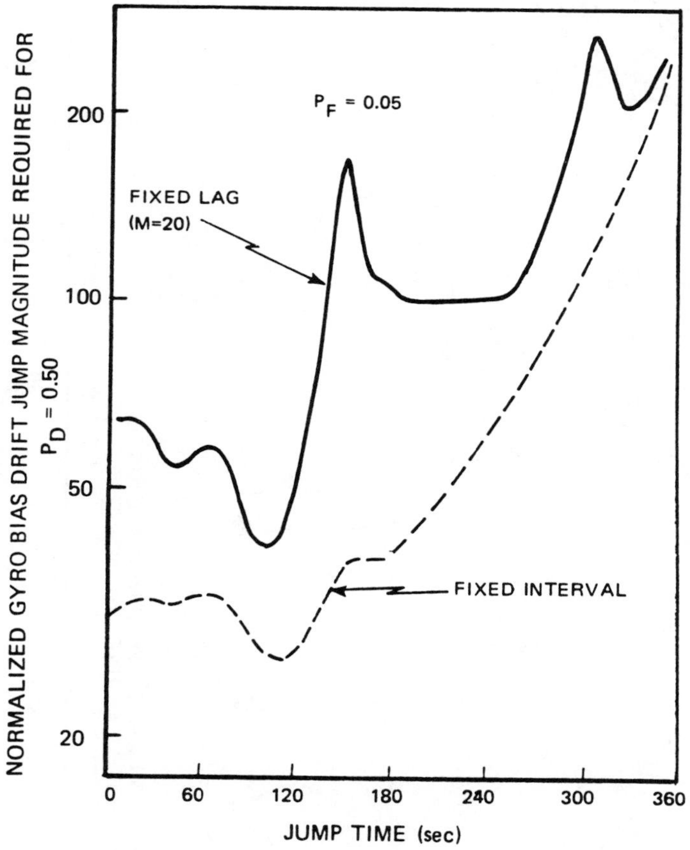

Fig. 15. Gyro-bias-drift jump detection versus jump time; $P_F = 0.05$.

window length on jump detection. The projected detection performance of fixed-interval GLR is presented in Figs. 14 and 15 for comparison with the fixed-lag algorithm. These figures show the jump magnitude required to produce a detection probability of 0.50 when the threshold is set for a false-alarm rate of 0.05. Naturally, the larger windows result in improved performance for all cases; however, the improvement is most dramatic for accelerometer jumps prior to burnout (200 sec).

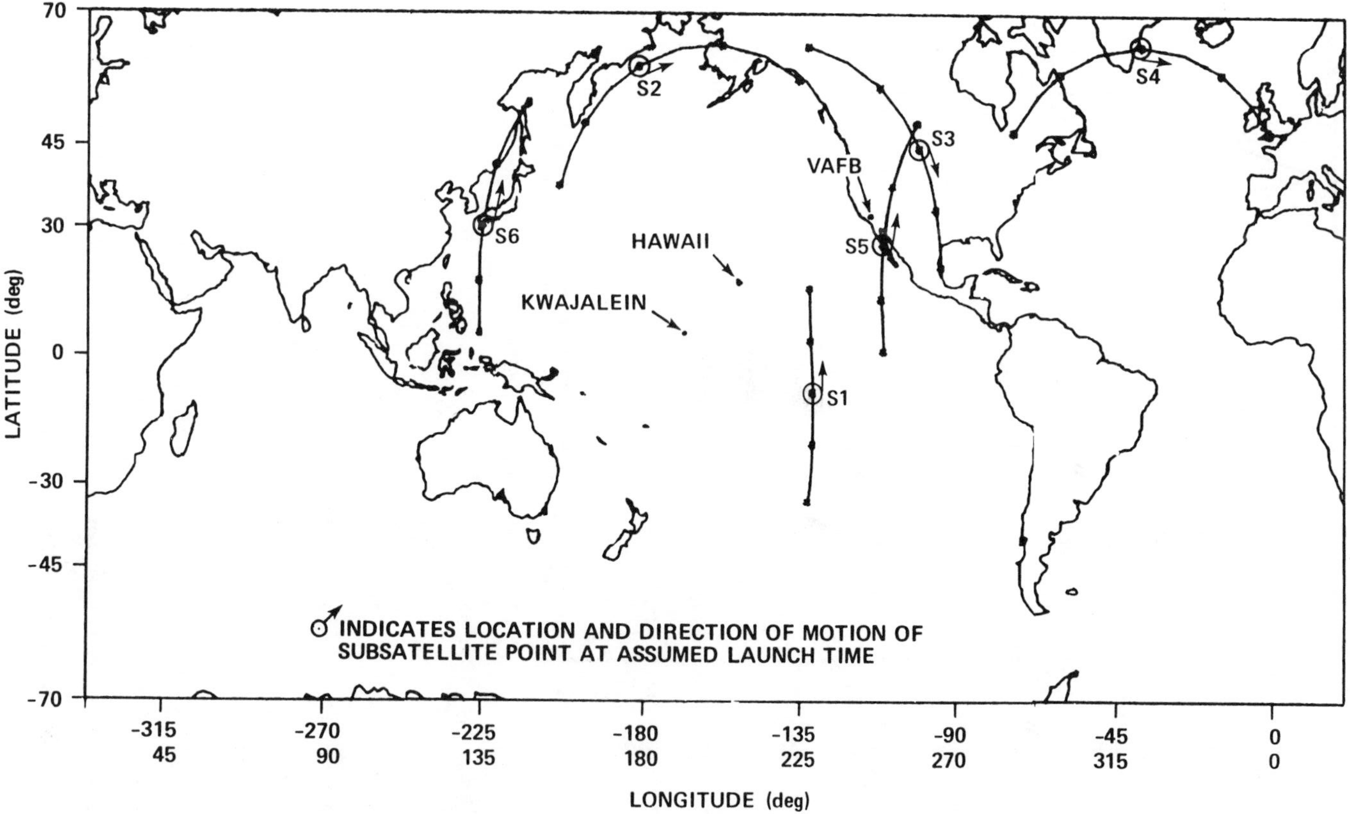

Fig. 16. Phase 1 GPS satellite configuration.

Accelerometer bias jumps of about 2σ are uniformly detectable throughout the flight. The significant difference between the two GLR mechanizations in detecting jumps before burnout is explained as follows. The fixed-interval algorithm always has available the filter residuals after burnout where the effect of an earlier accelerometer shift is highly observable. The fixed-lag version lacks this information and is unable to identify a small shift in the presence of large g-sensitive error coefficients.

Significant information concerning a variety of the priority errors may be obtained using FLY-2 flight-test data. However, a number of shortcomings were identified based on insights gained during the performance evaluation and optimization studies. These shortcomings were borne out during subsequent data-processing activities.

Principal among the shortcomings is the inability to distinguish between certain error sources whose signatures, in measurement space, are nearly identical. It is impossible, for example, to separate initial primary and secondary IMU azimuth misalignments; consequently, the need for an accurate, independent position/velocity reference is apparent. The advent of the GPS-Receiver Test Program (GPS/RTP) was most timely since it provided the potential for uniquely accurate reference-system measurements. Figure 16 shows the GPS satellite geometry anticipated for the missile-test dates.

The incorporation of the GPS measurements significantly improves the capability to estimate guidance-system-induced deployment errors as well as initial azimuth misalignment. Table VIII summarizes the results of the FLY-2/GPS performance-evaluation study. These results represent those associated

Table VIII. Summary of Guidance-Error Recovery Ratios at Boost Burnout

INSTRUMENTATION CONFIGURATION	GUIDANCE RECOVERY RATIOS				
	DOWN-RANGE POSITION ERROR	CROSS-TRACK POSITION ERROR	DOWN-RANGE VELOCITY ERROR	CROSS-TRACK VELOCITY ERROR	INITIAL AZIMUTH ERROR
FLY-1/Radar	0.98	0.56	0.99	0.63	0.80
FLY-2/Radar	0.71	0.50	0.71	0.60	0.60
FLY-2/GPS	0.01	0.02	0.02	0.03	0.36

with a medium reentry-angle trajectory. The secondary system was offset 45° from the primary. Table VIII also contains the projected performance for FLY-1/Radar and FLY-2/Radar. It is apparent that overall weapon-system test-program performance could be greatly enhanced via the use of GPS data.

Recovery of the priority error sources is also improved. Table IX presents the secondary system guidance error coefficient recovery capability for a particular FLY-2/GPS mission. These are the error sources that demonstrate the significant recovery capability. FLY-1/Radar and FLY-2 performance projections are also included.

Certain of the recovery ratios tend to remain large (poor recovery), regardless of the measurement type or quality. This is a consequence of the processor's inability to separate the various error sources. Consequently, for evaluation of future systems, a new methodology to define filter models, filter dimensions, etc., that recognizes the limitation of "optimal" data processors should be developed. In addition, prelaunch and flight-test data must be processed in a complementary manner to provide maximum system understanding relative to each type of data.

Table IX. Secondary Guidance-System Priority Gyro Error Source Coefficient Recovery Ratios

INSTRUMENTATION CONFIGURATION	RECOVERY RATIOS			
	δB	δE	P	J
FLY-1/Radar	0.98	0.96	0.98	0.99
FLY-2/Radar	0.54	0.33	0.22	0.56
FLY-2/GPS	0.51	0.25	0.15	0.37

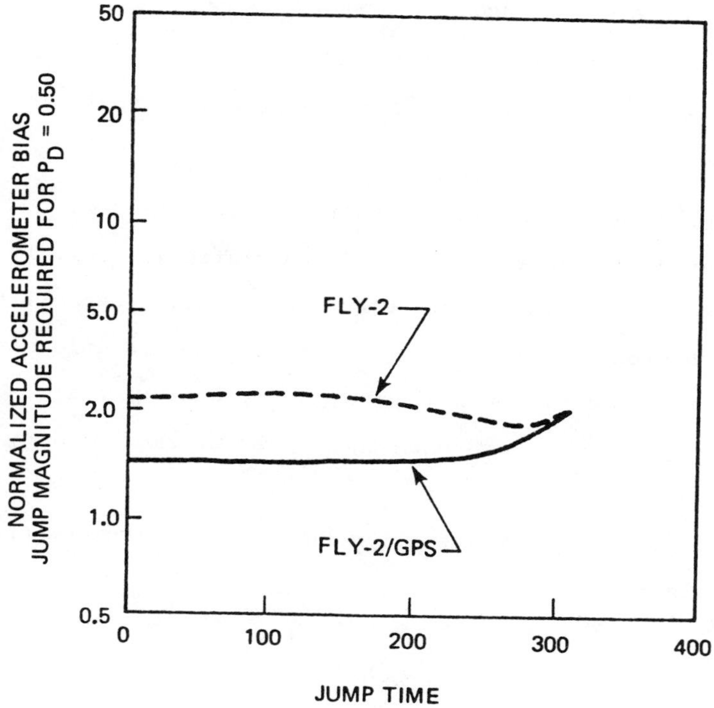

Fig. 17. Normalized accelerometer bias jump detection versus jump time; $P_F = 0.05$.

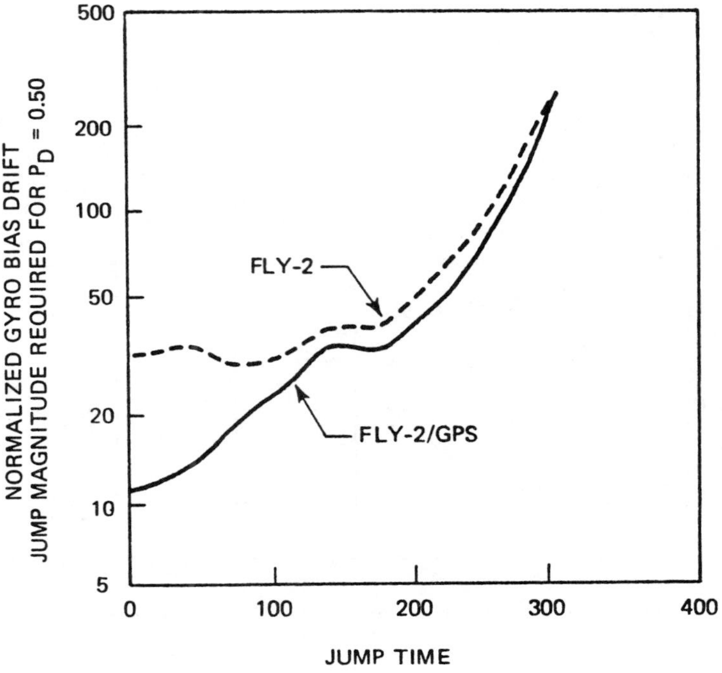

Fig. 18. Normalized gyro bias-drift jump detection versus jump time; $P_F = 0.05$.

The value of GPS measurements in the detection of instrument coefficient shifts is demonstrated in Figs. 17 and 18. A factor of 2 to 3 improvement in detection capability can be achieved with the incorporation of the GPS information. Other than this improvement, however, the characteristics of the detection process are unchanged. The GLR methodology must be modified to account for the inability of the GLR test to identify, with high confidence, a number of instrument-error characteristics.

E. DATA-PROCESSOR STRUCTURE

The top-level structure of the postflight analyzer (PFA) is depicted in Fig. 19. The PFA is structured such that guidance-system initial condition errors and instrument-error coefficient shifts are determined using a five-step process:

(1) data preprocessing;

(2) filter analysis;

(3) model analysis;

(4) jump detection and identification;

(5) decision making.

In *data preprocessing*, telemetry data from two NS-20s, the GPS measurements, and data from several radars are sorted, time synchronized, compensated for deterministic errors, rotated to appropriate coordinate frames for comparison, and combined such that all relevant high-rate data is reduced to a rate suitable for the advanced-analysis tools. Since this step involves substantial computation, the PFA allows parallel processing of each data type, thereby decreasing the preprocessor timeline substantially.

The *filter analysis* programs take the sequence of range and range-rate-difference measurements (GPS and/or radar) and velocity difference measurements (between the two NS-20s) provided by the preprocessor and calculate estimates of NS-20 error coefficients (primary and secondary systems), GPS errors, and radar errors. The estimation process is carried out with a suboptimal Kalman filter augmented with smoothing capabilities for key epoch times of the missile flight (e.g.,

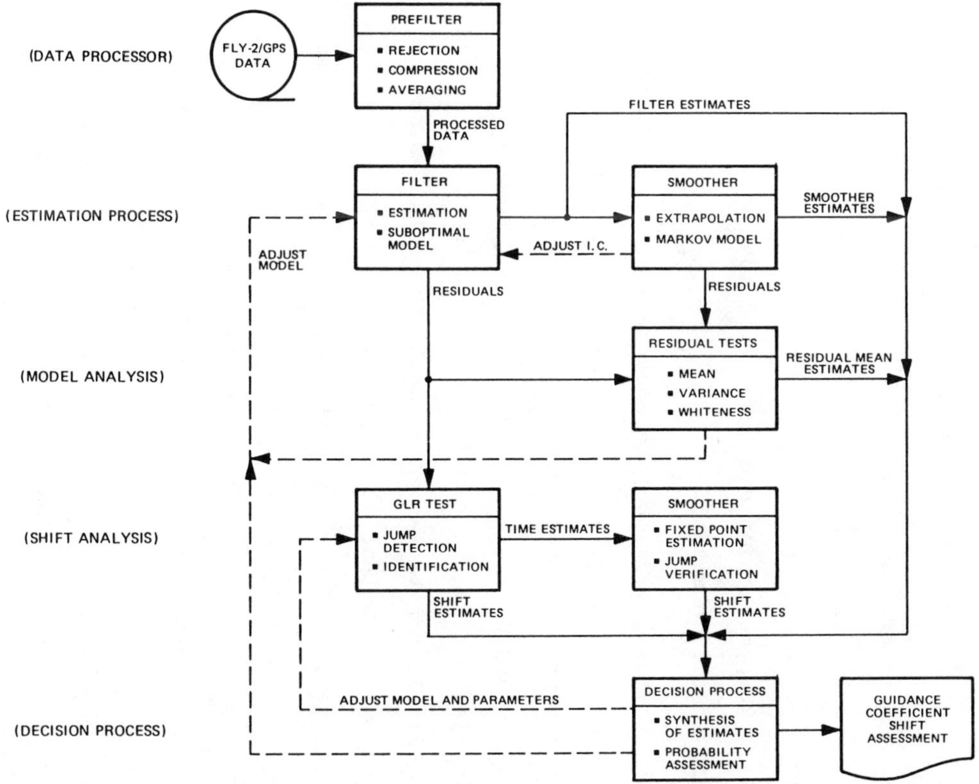

Fig. 19. Postflight analyzer data flow.

deployment). The residual differences between the measurements and the estimates form the basis for the model- and shift-analysis tests which follow.

The *model-analysis* programs characterize the residual differences provided by the filter. In particular, tests are performed to determine if the residuals are a zero-mean white-noise process with a variance predicted by the filter model. If these tests are passed, the mathematical model imbedded in the filter is consistent with the true system dynamics. If the "whiteness" tests are failed, further analyses into the nature of the failure are initiated.

Jump detection and identification analysis is used to seek one or more instrument-parameter shifts consistent with the filter residual characteristics. The GLR test provides the primary means of instrument-coefficient jump detection and identification.

1. *Data Preprocessing*

A number of important steps must be taken to prepare raw recorded data so that it may be efficiently and accurately analyzed. The software that performs these steps is depicted in Fig. 20.

The *PIGA*[9] *prefilter* calculates the specific velocity sensed by the primary NS-20 and the indicated velocity difference between NS-20s. Seven categories of deterministic errors are compensated:

(1) The six PIGA pulse sums are adjusted (using the telemetered time of last pulse) to reduce the effects of

[9] *The accelerometers used on Minuteman III are PIGAs or pendulous integrating gyroscopic accelerometers [11].*

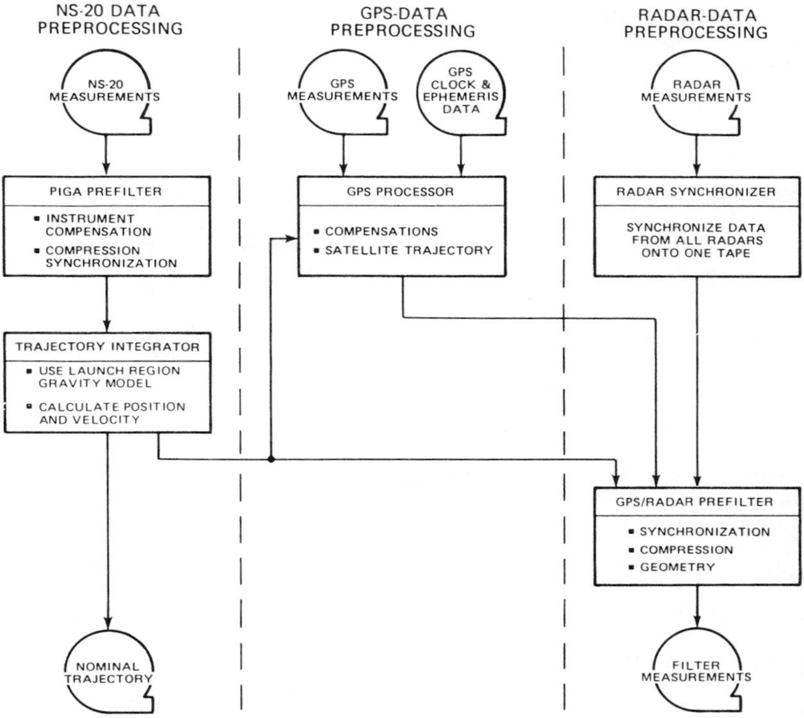

Fig. 20. Data flow for preprocessing steps.

quantization and sample time differences. Compensations are also made to account for timing differences due to the asynchronous sampling of the PIGAs and due to guidance-computer clock drift rate.

(2) The six PIGA pulses are compensated for errors due to "coning," the result of a misalignment between the PIG float and PIAG input axes. The misalignment angle and phase are calibrated using prelaunch telemetry data.

(3) The PIGA pulses are subsequently passed through a digital low-pass filter to reduce the residual random errors resulting from quantization and timing uncertainties. The result is the "best estimate" of all six PIGA pulse sums.

(4) The PIGA pulses are compensated with preflight estimates of bias and nonlinearity errors and then transformed into a velocity vector in NS-20 computational coordinates.

(5) The velocity vector is then corrected for platform-to-computer misalignments. The misalignments are based on the prelaunch values of gyro g^2 and g^4 error coefficients. Initial misalignment, due to gyro torquer limit cycling, is also taken into account.

(6) Platform compliance errors are compensated next using a 27-term platform-bending model.

(7) Finally, the velocity of the secondary NS-20 relative to the primary NS-20 (lever-arm effect) is subtracted from the sensed velocity of the secondary system. This compensation is based upon the telemetered NS-20 gimbal angles which have been interpreted, smoothed, and differentiated.

The results at this point in the NS-20 processing are two measurements of the integrated specific force[10] (specific velocity), as sensed by the two sets of instruments, compensated for all known deterministic errors. The specific velocity vectors are provided to the trajectory integrator.

The *trajectory integrator* calculates the position and velocity of the missile, based on the best available gravity model and the sensed specific velocity. To allow for refinements in the trajectory (as bad data is removed and errors are estimated) without repeating the long integration process required by this program, the total gravity gradient matrix is also calculated.

[10] *Specific force is the sum of all forces acting on the vehicle except for gravity [11].*

Radar data is preprocessed using two programs. The *radar synchronizer* performs the function of merging data: range-measurement data from up to 10 tracking radars are extracted from the raw-data tapes, put in common engineering units, and time synchronized. The result is a single sequential file containing all available radar data.

The *radar prefilter* determines the difference between measured radar range and range-rate and computed range and range-rate based on the NS-20-indicated position and velocity time history generated by the trajectory integrator. High-frequency measurement noise is reduced by averaging all range differences over a 4.5-sec time interval. The geometry of each measurement is also determined in order to properly weight the one-dimensional range and range-rate-difference measurements in the estimation of three-dimensional position and velocity vectors.

Two types of GPS measurement data are available: preflight data and inflight data. The primary purpose of the preflight processing is to calibrate GPS-related errors, most notably receiver-clock errors. These estimates are then applied to the inflight data.

The data-tape records contain a mixture of parameter values from receiver-generated "high-rate" and "low-rate" data tables; two separate programs extract the required components from each table. The first reads selected values from the low-rate table and prepares the data for input to the calculation of pseudorange.[11] These data items, such as master time delays or user and satellite epoch count differences, are either

[11] *Pseudorange measurements contain "true" slant range plus the receiver clock-phase offset.*

constant or slowly time-varying quantities. The required high-rate data-table items are accessed by a second program. The items include the replica code-counter states, vernier range corrections, range rates, and status and identification tags for each channel. The program uses this data, along with that supplied from the low-rate table, to form the receiver-to-satellite pseudorange measurement and also scales the range rates and corrects for the range-rate computational delay prior to outputting time-tagged, satellite-indexed, corrected pseudorange and range-rate measurements.

The GPS measurements are compensated for the following calibratable errors:

(1) satellite-clock errors;

(2) receiver-clock gravity-sensitive trending;

(3) tropospheric propagation delays;

(4) relative position and velocity offset between GPS antenna-phase center and the primary IMU; and

(5) relativistic effects, both special and general, between GPS receiver and ground-based user.

A final preprocessing program determines the differences between the measured and computed range and range rate using the receiver- and satellite-indicated position and velocity. The satellite state vector is computed at each time-of-signal transmission using the best estimate of the "Block II" ephemeris data provided by the GPS Joint Project Office [15]. The receiver position and velocity are determined from the best estimate trajectory interpolated to the time-of-signal reception. The resulting difference measurements are then

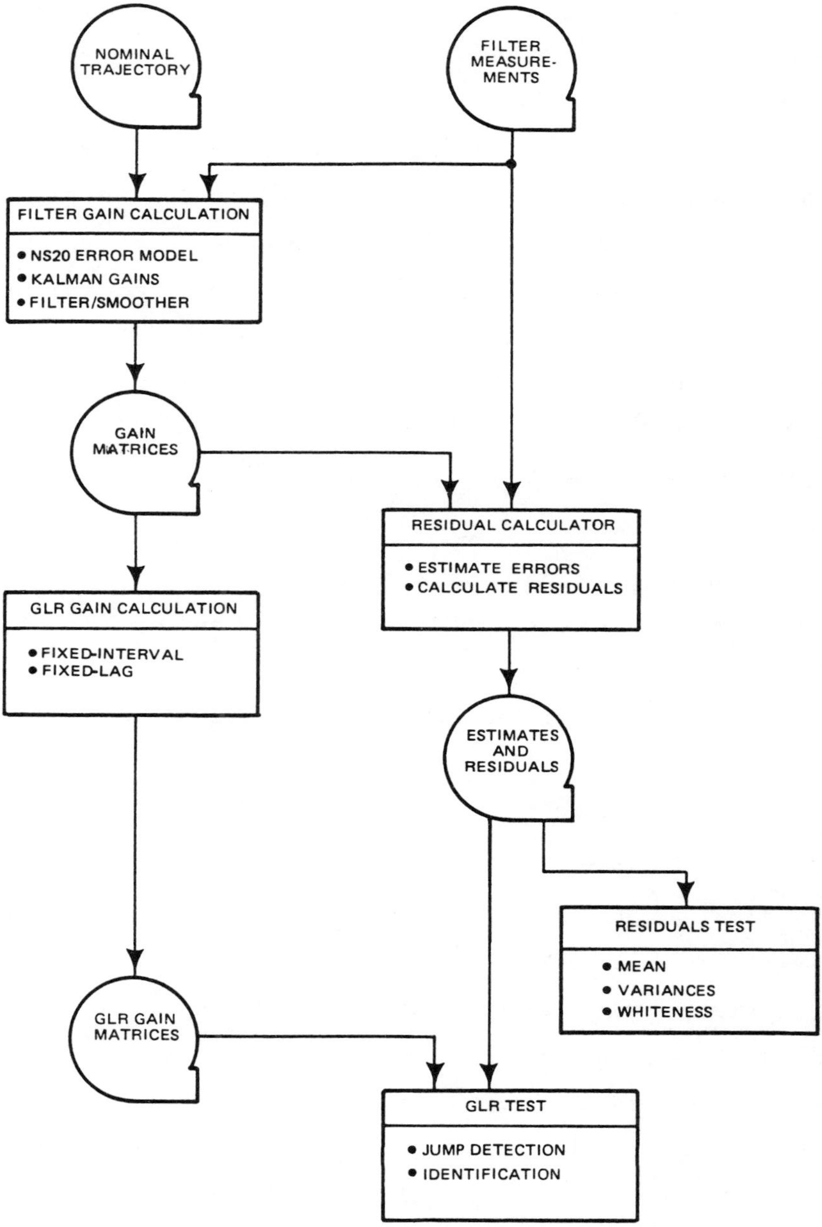

Fig. 21. Data flow for residual calculation and evaluation.

compressed to suppress measurement-noise effects. These range and range-rate differences, along with the computed measurement geometry, are the final preprocessor outputs.

2. *Filter Analysis*

The filter calculations use the sequence of range and range-rate differences (GPS and/or radar) and velocity differences (between NS-20s) to calculate the best estimate of NS-20 guidance coefficients, GPS errors, and radar errors based on a priori error statistics. The residual differences between the measurements and estimates are the basic inputs to the GLR tests. Data flow is shown in Fig. 21. The residual calculations are divided into two separate sets of programs for computational efficiency. The first, *gain calculation*, requires the straightforward, although lengthy, computation of Kalman gains based on the nominal trajectory, the system-error model and the measurement sequence.

Two forms of *smoother* may be used. The fixed-point smoother [16] allows the computationally efficient estimation of a limited number of smoothed states at selected times. This is particularly attractive if only certain candidate states are suspected to be time varying. The fixed-interval smoother [6] allows the smoothed estimation of all parameters but requires more computations. Both have a place in the search for unmodeled-parameter changes.

The second program set, *residual calculator*, uses the gains to interpret the measurements from the data preprocessor. During preliminary data editing, the relatively simple residual calculations can be performed many times, using the same set of gains, without significant loss of accuracy. The more lengthy gain calculations need be repeated only after "bad" data has been removed or whenever the filter model is changed.

3. *Model Analysis and Jump Detection/Identification*

The primary jump detection is performed using the GLR test. The Kalman-filter residuals are used in the GLR test. The GLR test computations are divided into two routines: the first calculates the GLR gain matrices; the second performs the GLR test on the data. (The GLR gain matrices need to be recomputed only when the filter gain matrices are recomputed.) The GLR test routines use the gain matrices to determine whether the filter residuals are consistent with the model. In the event of a jump detection, the time and identity of the parameter(s) that changed (jumped) are estimated. These jump estimates may then be used to change the model, and the residual calculations may be repeated.

Residual tests are performed on the filter and smoother outputs. If the models are correct, the residuals will be zero-mean uncorrelated random sequences with variance as predicted by the model. Thus, the sample mean and variance calculations provide some clues as to the nature of the modeling errors. The residual tests provide a "quick-look" capability for identifying missions with possible parameter jumps.

F. *DATA-PROCESSING EVALUATION RESULTS*

Data processing included evaluation of data from the three FLY-2 flights and the first FLY-2/GPS mission. Here, the processing results from one FLY-2 flight (STM-13W) and the

Table X. Flight-Test Parameters

PARAMETER	STM-13W	PVM-18
Launch Date	31 January 1977	31 January 1980
Launch Time	05:05:00 PST	05:40:00 PST
Reentry Angle	Low	Medium
Primary Azimuth Offset	0 deg	0 deg
Secondary Azimuth Offset	45 deg	0 deg

FLY-2/GPS flight (PVM-18) are highlighted. Table X summarizes the principal characteristics of each flight.

The STM-13W data analysis focused on jump detection and identification. A quick-look technique for determining the possibility of PIGA and/or gyro-error coefficient shifts was developed based on the velocity-difference data generated by the dual IMUs. Figure 22 is a plot of sensed velocity differences over the first 1500 sec of powered flight. Three distinct phases are evident. During the first, or powered-flight phase (0 to 180 sec), uncompensated acceleration-dependent errors cause parabolic error growth. Over the second phase (180 to 500 sec), no error growth is evident since the vehicle is experiencing a nearly zero specific force. The third phase (after 500 sec) provides a clear indication of a PIGA bias shift.

The PIGA bias shift is easily detected by the GLR algorithm. However, in order to identify a gyro-error (e.g., bias drift) coefficient shift during the powered-flight phase, a closer look at the data over the first interval is required. Rather than velocity differences, it is more enlightening to examine

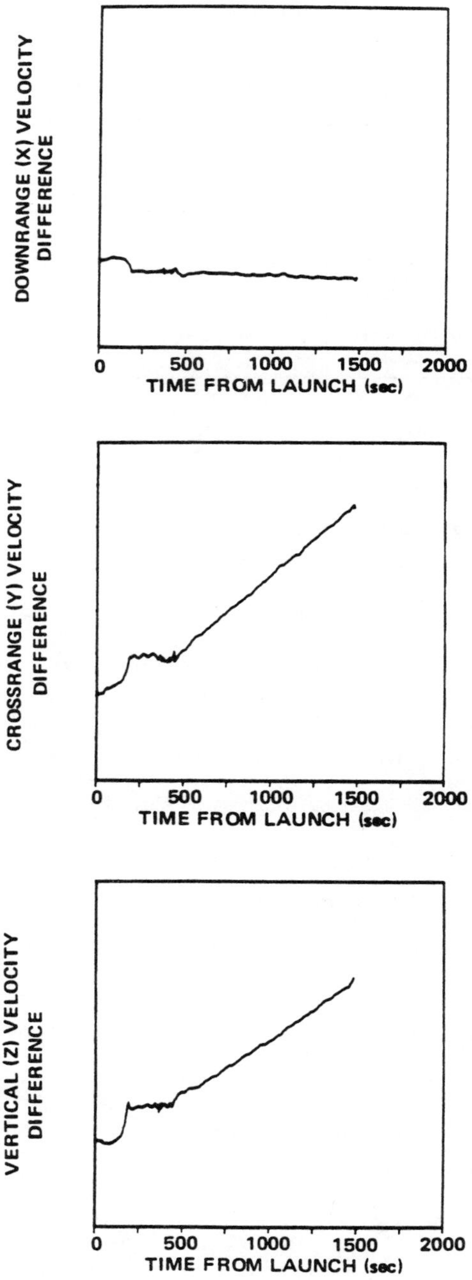

Fig. 22. Sensed-velocity comparison (primary minus secondary in computer coordinates).

platform-to-computer misalignment angles $\underline{\psi}$. These angles can be obtained by recalling that, over a very short time interval Δt,

$$\int_{t_0}^{t_0+\Delta t} (\underline{\psi} \times \underline{f})\, dt = \underline{\Delta v}, \tag{4}$$

where $\underline{\Delta v}$ is the difference in measured velocity. If $\underline{\psi}$ is assumed constant over the interval Δt,

$$\underline{\psi} \times \int_{t_0}^{t_0+\Delta t} (\underline{f})\, dt = \underline{\Delta v} = -[A]\underline{\psi}, \tag{5}$$

where [A] is the skew-symmetric matrix of integrated specific force components. Consequently,

$$\underline{\psi} = -[A^{-1}]\, \underline{\Delta v}. \tag{6}$$

Figure 23 presents the estimates of the three components of $\underline{\psi}$ in computer axes (downrange, cross track, and up). Straight-line approximations to the curves correspond to the assumption that the gyro drift is caused by a bias only (possibly with a jump change in magnitude). The curves in Fig. 23 indicate the possibility of gyro-bias-error breaks occurring at approximately 60 and 135 sec. However, the shifts are not large and may be accounted for by the NS-20 error model.

It was anticipated that a PIGA bias shift would be evident in the GLR output, and perhaps one or more gyro bias shifts would be detected. It should be recalled that the GLR test answers the question: What is the relative likelihood that a given guidance coefficient experienced a shift at a given time, compared to the null hypothesis (no shift)? The likelihood

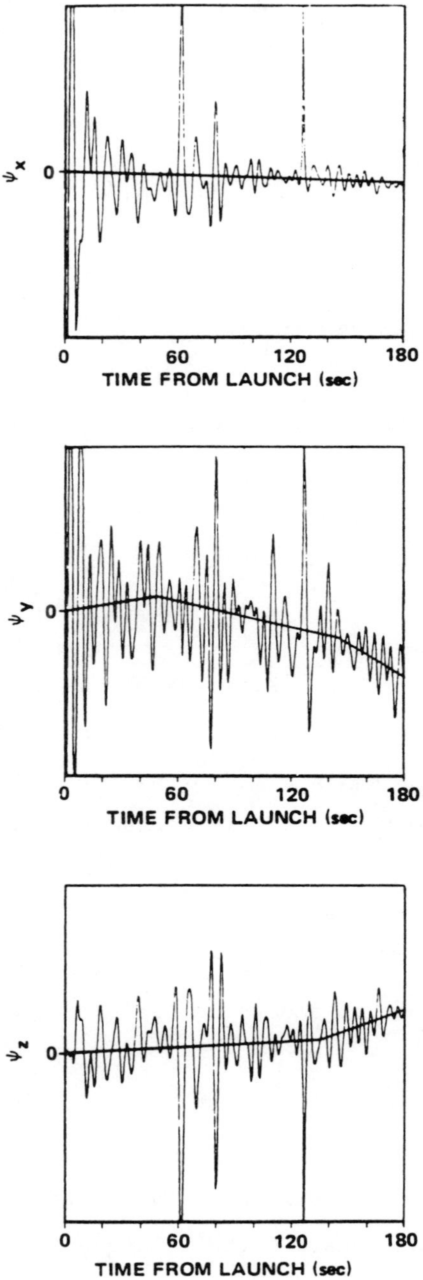

Fig. 23. ψ-Angle estimates.

ratio l is the quantity used to quantify the alternative hypotheses. Large l implies a significant jump in the parameter of interest. Values of $l < 10$ are not significant as indicators of a jump at the $P_F = 0.05$ level. Results were obtained using both the fixed-lag GLR algorithm, with a 100-sec data window, and the fixed-interval GLR algorithm, incorporating data up to 600 sec into the flight. For brevity, only fixed-lag results are presented here.

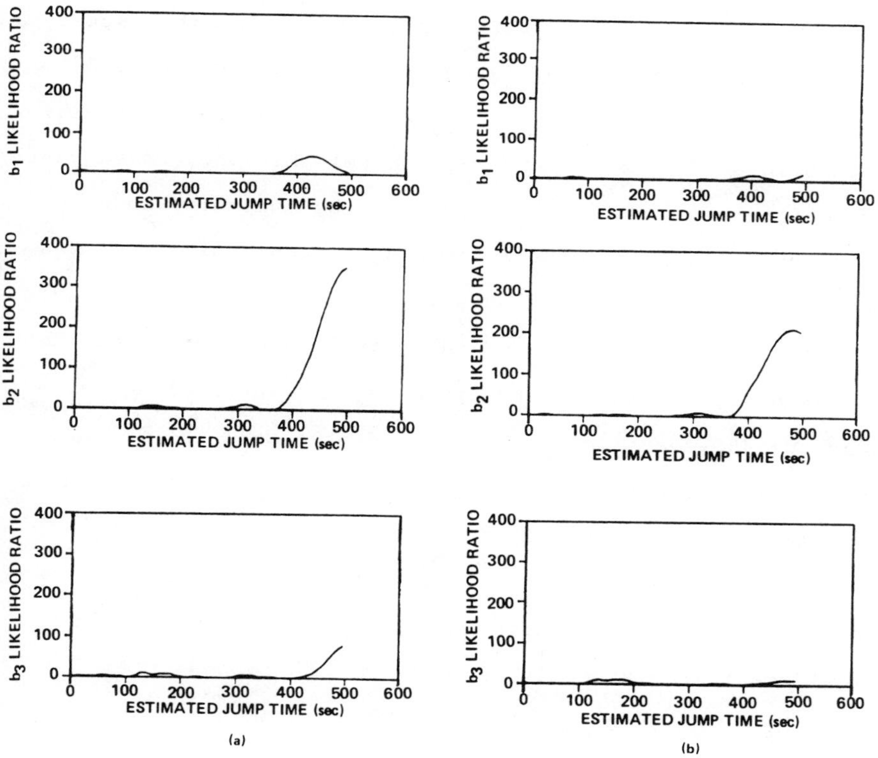

Fig. 24. Fixed-lag likelihood ratios for primary system PIGA bias shifts: (a) primary NS-20; (b) MEW NS-20.

The fixed-lag GLR results (Fig. 24) display a weak PIGA bias anomaly at 140 sec which falls well below the $l = 10$ threshold. Consequently, this weak anomaly was not deemed to be significant. A strong anomaly is evident in the postboost phase. Although this anomaly has minimal impact on system accuracy (because of its time of occurrence), it was evaluated in detail. The conclusion of the analysis is that all three PIGAs in the primary system experience shifts in their bias level near 450 sec.

Fixed-lag gyro bias-drift likelihood ratios demonstrate a false response due to the large PIGA bias shifts (Fig. 25). Only two of the three gyro bias-drift states are presented; the third drift state is nearly unobservable and, consequently, of no interest. Indepth analysis of the telemetry and radar data indicates that no detectable gyro bias-drift anomalies occurred during the boost phase.

Results of the STM-13W-data analysis are typical of those for each FLY-2 flight. The presence of a large PIGA bias shift near the 450-sec time point was evident on all the flights. In addition, there was no indication of a detectable PIGA or gyro anomaly during boost.

It was concluded that anomalous guidance-system performance, in the form of shifts in instrument parameters, is not significant statistically or in terms of weapon-system accuracy. Thus, for the FLY-2/GPS data-processing activity, the focus shifted to guidance-coefficient estimation and GPS receiver-performance assessment.

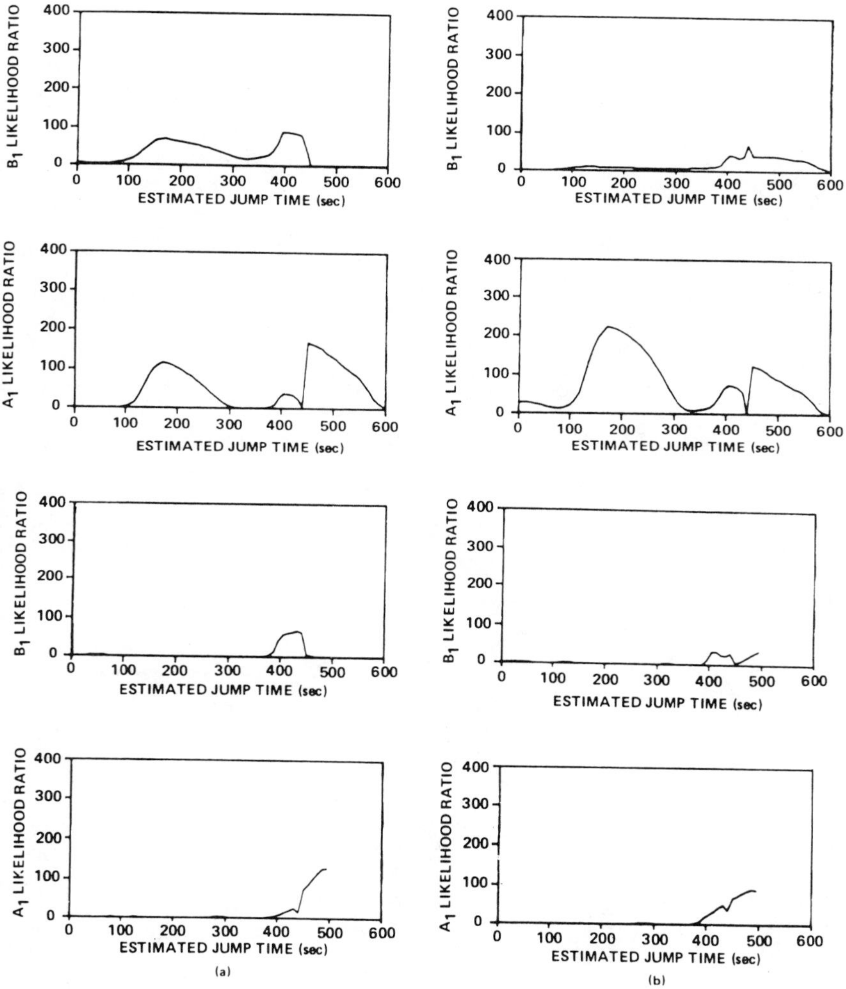

Fig. 25. Fixed-lag likelihood ratios for primary gyro bias drift (false indication resulting from large PIGA bias shift at 450 sec): (a) primary NS-20; (b) MEW NS-20.

For the PVM-18 mission, four GPS satellites provided range and range-rate measurements. The subsatellite points for each satellite are indicated in Fig. 26. The signals from the satellites were acquired approximately 5 sec after launch and, except during staging events, provided accurate information to approximately 1000 sec. Satellites No. 1 and No. 2 yielded

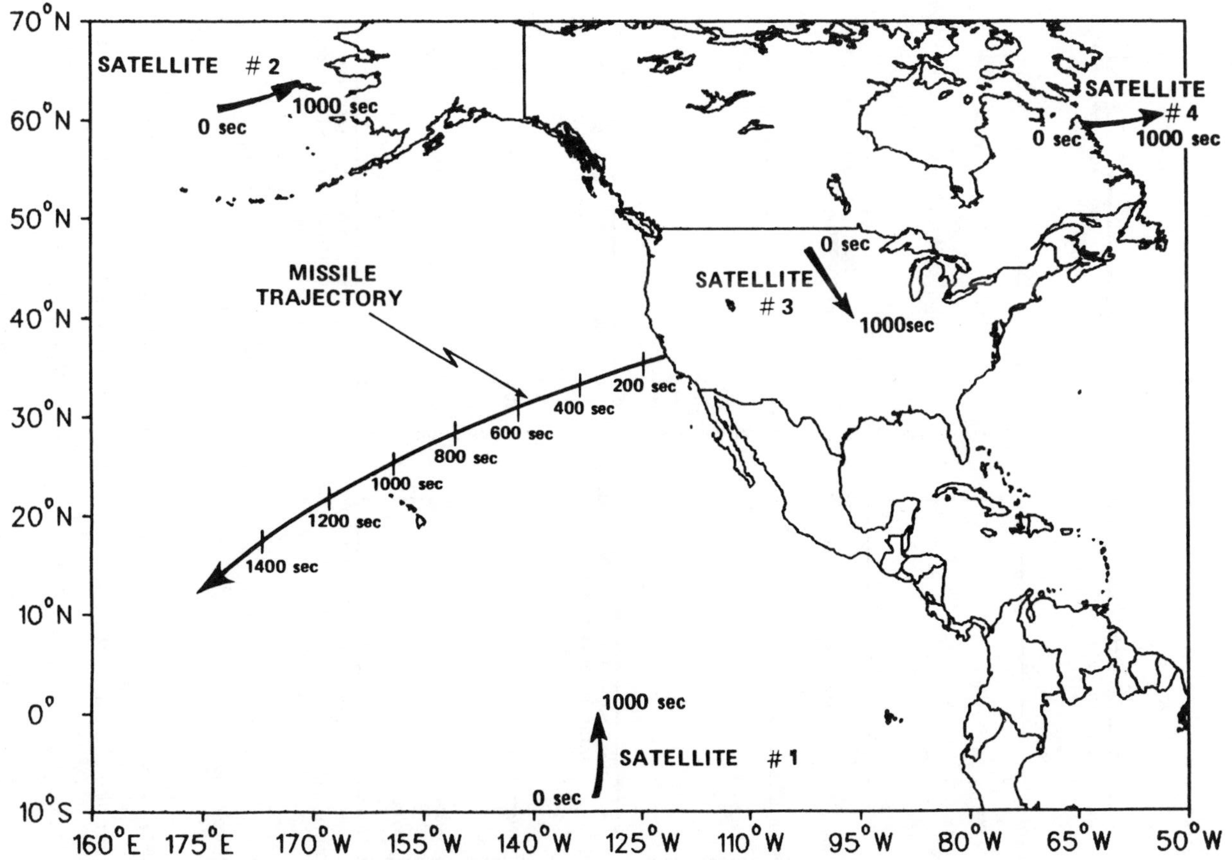

Fig. 26. GPS satellite orbits during PVM-18 flight test.

very good cross-range information, while Satellites No. 3 and No. 4 contributed primarily to downrange information. Overall, geometric dilution of precision (GDOP) [5] was approximately 4 to 5 over the flight, with the vertical channel having the poorest GDOP. The cross-track axis had a single-channel GDOP less than 1.0. Values of azimuth, as measured from north, and elevation above the local-horizontal plane of the satellite relative to the receiver are summarized in Table XI.

The primary-minus-secondary IMU velocity differences for PVM-18 are presented in Fig. 27. The three phases of error growth (i.e., powered flight, free flight, and post-PIGA bias shift) are evident.

Table XI. GPS Satellite/Receiver Geometry

SATELLITE NUMBER	GEOMETRY[a]	
	AZIMUTH (deg)	ELEVATION (deg)
1	198.0	34.8
2	324.0	32.0
3	42.8	66.0
4	36.3	36.5

[a] *At time of launch.*

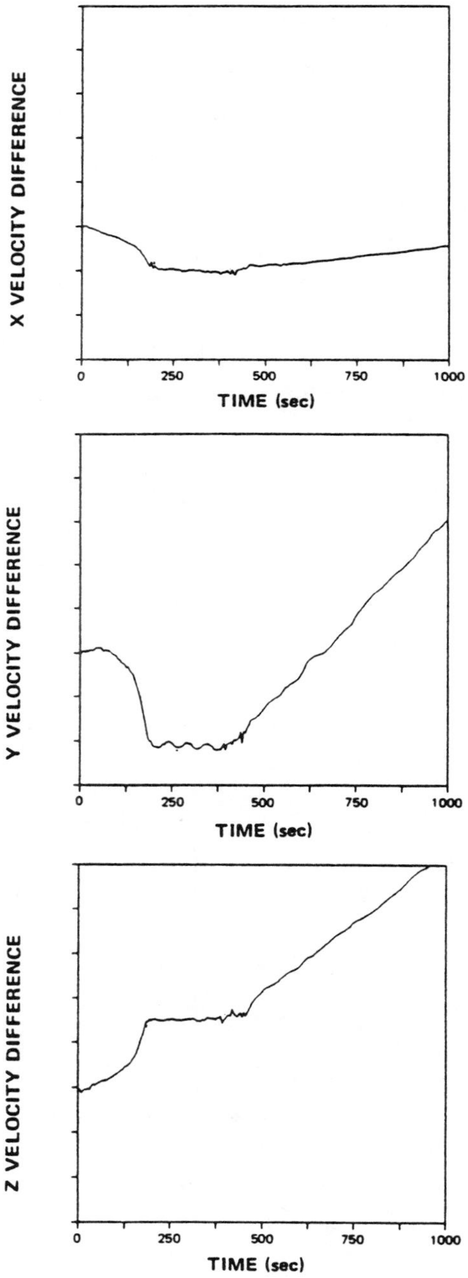

Fig. 27. Primary-minus-secondary IMU velocity difference (computer coordinates).

The velocity differences are quite small through the first 125 sec of flight (the first and second stages of missile thrusting). A rapid divergence occurs during third-stage thrusting, leveling off in all three axes at thrust termination. The nature of the third-stage divergence, occurring most noticeably in the cross-track direction and with an obvious thrust dependence, is indicative of large residual gyro errors (or possibly PIGA misalignments) in one or both systems. Cross-track sensitivity to gyro errors is extremely high in Minuteman III due to the exclusively in-plane (x-z plane) thrusting pattern utilized. The sensitivity to errors about azimuth is further accentuated by the particular trajectory flown.

Range- and range-rate-difference measurements along the Satellite No. 1 line of sight are presented in Figs. 28 and 29, respectively. The dotted line represents the high-frequency measurement data and the solid line represents the "smooth" difference measurements used in the subsequent data analysis. These are typical of the range and range-rate measurements provided by all four satellites. (The large spikes in the range-rate measurements occur during periods when the tracking algorithm is in frequency track only.)

The continuous GPS measurement availability and excellent measurement quality made it possible to improve the postmission analysis results. The S_{A1} and F_{S1} gyro errors were identified as the primary sources of the observed impact error for PVM-18. This conclusion is based on the fact that the postflight analysis is in excellent agreement with preflight predictions of the miss-distance contributions of the S_{A1} and F_{S1} error sources. However, even with the excellent GPS measurement

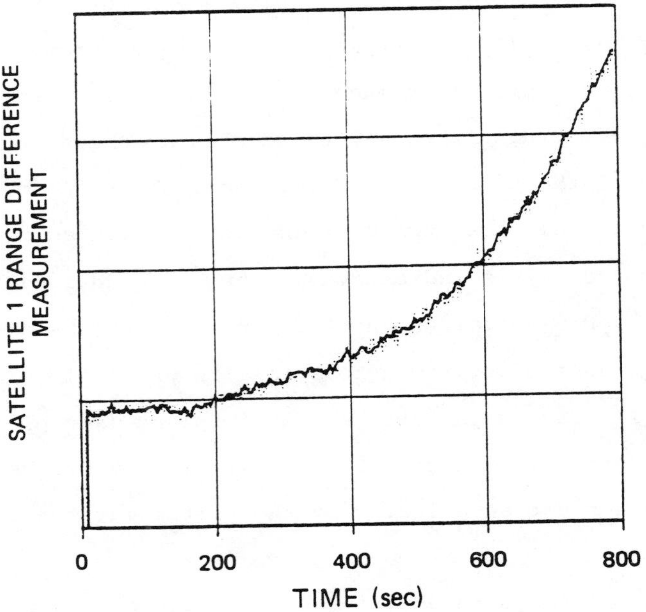

Fig. 28. GPS-primary satellite 1 range-difference measurements.

quality, the inherent capability for accurately separating the individual error contributions of the S_{A1} and F_{S1} instrument errors is still in question. This separability problem was demonstrated based on results of a sensitivity study performed as part of the PVM-18 analysis. This study examined the sensitivity of the estimated impact-error contribution of critical gyro-error sources to their initial rms uncertainties. Results of this study show significant variations in the estimated miss distance resulting from the individual gyro-error sources, whereas total impact error displays minimal net variation. This behavior is indicative of a basic inability to isolate individual gyro-error source contributors.

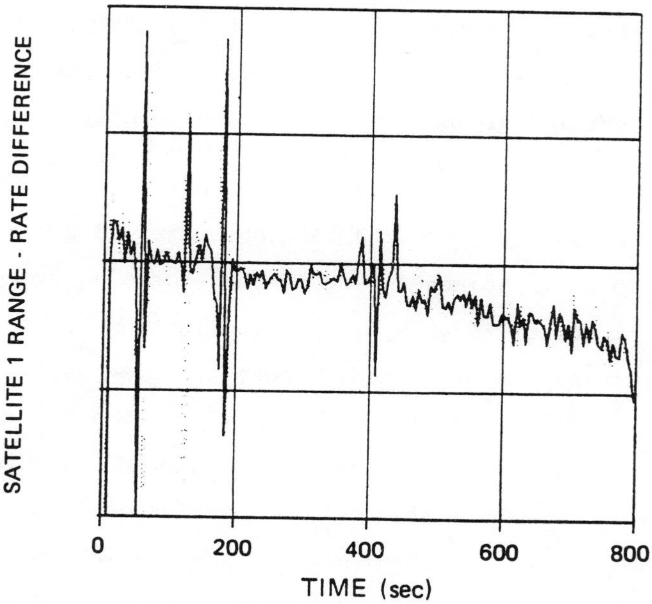

Fig. 29. GPS-primary satellite 1 range-rate-difference measurements.

Postflight evaluation of Minuteman performance based on GPS test measurements indicates that GPS is an excellent absolute reference for both position and velocity. Estimation of initial platform misalignment is also improved. In addition, qualitative insight into PIGA performance can also be obtained through examination of IMU/GPS velocity differences. A performance issue that impacts future utilization of GPS must still be addressed, however. This issue is the proper use and interpretation of data that is extremely accurate at the position and velocity levels but, due to the complexity of the underlying guidance error model, does not provide unique insight into the magnitudes of specific instrument-related error mechanisms. In other words, the model observability problem must be addressed as it becomes necessary to work to finer levels of detail in generating system understanding. The capabilities of filtering and smoothing analysis offer a great deal to the evaluation of complex weapon systems, but only to a certain threshold which must be identified.

G. SUMMARY

Over the past 10 years the USAF has upgraded the accuracy of Minuteman III. To assess and further these accuracy upgrades, a number of flight-test program instrumentation enhancements were incorporated. These include postflight processing of multiple-IMU test data (the MPMS and FLY-2 programs) and the use of GPS data (the FLY-2/GPS program). This series of flight-test programs was planned and executed in a logical manner to minimize cost/schedule impacts.

The Minuteman III flight-test program enhancements have been successful. A number of significant error mechanisms were identified and isolated using data obtained during the MPMS, FLY-2, and FLY-2/GPS programs. With the improved accuracy objectives associated with the next-generation ICBM system, problems of flight-test optimization and postmission processing will continue to provide challenging opportunities over the years ahead. There will almost assuredly be further advances in filtering and smoothing theory to support the needed growth in system understanding.

III. VALIDATION OF FILTER/SMOOTHER MODELS

A. *INTRODUCTION*

1. *Motivation for Model Validation*

The importance of the model used in the design of a Kalman filter/smoother is well recognized. In practical applications, tradeoffs inevitably exist between complex models, which represent the real world with great fidelity, and simplified approximate models, which lead to less costly implementations. To the system analyst, the question of model validity is of great importance for two reasons. First, if Kalman-filtering results are to be interpreted with confidence, it is essential that the model be a valid representation of the physical system. Second, and perhaps even more important, the model often represents a baseline design of the system with associated baseline-system performance characteristics. If that model is not a valid representation of the actual system being tested, there is an implication that the system does not match its baseline design and therefore may not meet its baseline performance characteristics.

In Section III, a procedure for model validation is described. The procedure is based on statistical hypothesis tests focused on the question: Are the estimates generated by a Kalman smoother from system test data consistent with the system model? The procedure is a multiple-test approach; filter/smoother estimates from several system tests are combined in a common data base on which the statistical hypothesis tests are performed.

The model-validation procedure discussed is based on well-known statistical hypothesis testing methods [17,18]. The contributions presented are, first, a problem formulation and second, analysis and data-reduction procedures which lead to efficient application of the statistical hypothesis tests. Another approach to the model-validation problem which is potentially applicable to the same class of systems is based on maximum-likelihood parameter identification procedures [19,20]. In each of those methods, expectation-maximization (E-M) algorithms [21] are used to obtain maximum-likelihood estimates of statistical parameters. Those estimates are then available for use in the calculation of test statistics for hypothesis testing similar to that discussed here.

Another approach to model validation is based on direct examination of residual sequences resulting from an ensemble of test results [22-24]. Procedures based on this approach are designed only to detect the presence of data/model inconsistency; unlike the procedures described in Section III, they do not attempt to *isolate* the source of the inconsistency to specific system parameters. Kashyap and Rao [22] discuss the model-validation problem from this viewpoint with an emphasis on much smaller systems than those considered here and under the restrictive assumption that all tests are based on identical scenarios. Goodrich and Cains [23] consider the statistical parameter identification problem based on likelihood functions formed directly from the innovations (i.e., filter residuals) of each test. Baram [24] approaches the model-validation problem by generating test statistics from normalized residual sequences from each test. Although these latter approaches have considerable potential because of their generality, they are computationally very costly and do not lead to the development of an expanding data base available for use by the test designer/analyst.

2. *The Model-Validation Problem For Linear Discrete-Time Systems*

The models used in the design of posttest data processors are typically developed via a two-step procedure. First, models using algebraic and differential (or difference) equations are developed for each component and error source of the complete system based on physical understanding. Second, specific numerical values for the various parameters of these models are determined through laboratory tests, analysis of previous field tests, and engineering judgment. This procedure leads to a formulation of the model-validation problem based on the model structure and parameters shown in Fig. 30.

In this discrete-time formulation, the structure of the model, including the order of the difference equations describing the dynamic model, is assumed to be correct. The various model parameters shown in Fig. 30 are less certain and are to be validated. The vector $\underline{\epsilon}$ is referred to as the initialization vector for the model. Use of a separate symbol for $\underline{\epsilon}$ (which is exactly $\underline{x}_0$ in Fig. 30) is motivated by the multiple-phase models discussed in Section II.B.4. Note that a separate block has been shown representing the measurement system because the measurement-system model is an essential part of the overall model-validation question. If dynamic states are used in the measurement-system model, they must be included in the $\underline{x}_l$ vector representing system dynamics in Fig. 30.

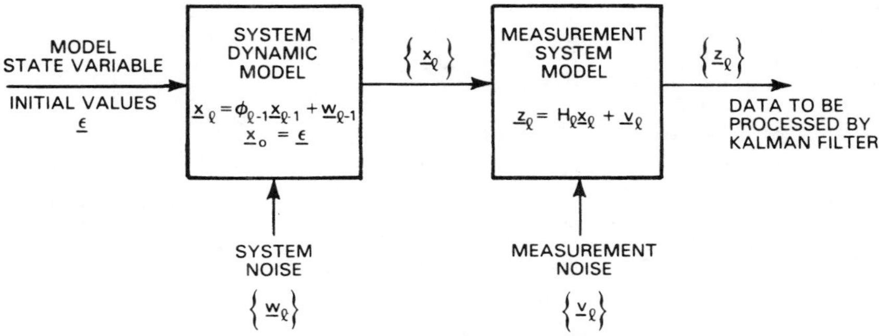

SYMBOL	DEFINITION	FILTER BASELINE MODEL
$\underline{b}, \Sigma$	MEAN-VALUE AND COVARIANCE OF $\underline{\epsilon}$	$\underline{b} = 0, \Sigma = \Sigma_o$
ϕ_ℓ	SYSTEM STATE-TRANSITION MATRICES	$\phi_\ell = \phi_\ell^o$
$\underline{m}_w, Q_\ell$	MEAN-VALUE AND COVARIANCE OF $\underline{w}_\ell$	$\underline{m}_w = 0, Q_\ell = Q_\ell^o$
$\underline{m}_v, R_{v\ell}$	MEAN-VALUE AND COVARIANCE OF $\underline{v}_\ell$	$\underline{m}_v = 0, R_{v\ell} = R_{v\ell}^o$

Fig. 30. Model structure and parameters.

The model parameters fall into two categories: *structural parameters*, which define the elements of matrices ϕ_l and H_l, and *statistical parameters*, which define the normal density functions which model $\underline{\epsilon}$, $\underline{w}_l$, and $\underline{v}_l$. The approach described here is directed only at $\underline{b}$ and $\underline{\Sigma}$, the statistical parameters associated with $\underline{\epsilon}$. For typical systems, these parameters are among the most crucial in determining overall performance. In a ballistic missile system, for example, nonzero values of $\underline{b}$ lead directly to a bias in the impact distribution; similarly, off-nominal values of $\Sigma(\neq\Sigma_0)$ lead directly to an off-nominal circular error probable (CEP) for the system. The other statistical parameters and the structural parameters in Fig. 30 should not be dismissed as unimportant, but they are generally somewhat better known than $\underline{b}$ and Σ. Exceptions to this, and an area of current research, are the parameters associated with Markov-error models often used to represent various system-error sources. Approaches to validating these parameters have been presented in the literature [23,24], but algorithms which are practical for use in large-system test-data analysis have not yet been developed.

The model-validation problem addressed in this section is as follows:

(1) given models as defined by the matrices Σ_0, ϕ_l^k, H_l^k, Q_l^k, and R_{vl}^k, where $k = 1, \ldots, N$ is the number of tests, $l = 1, \ldots, l_f(k)$ is the number of Kalman updates for test k, and given optimal smoothed estimates $\hat{\underline{x}}_0^{sk}$ of the initial state vector of each test $\underline{x}_0^k$,

(2) evaluate the consistency of the model assumptions $\underline{b} = 0$, $\Sigma = \Sigma_0$ with the estimates $\hat{\underline{x}}_0^{sk}$, assuming that the remainder of the model is correct.

Only the initial-mean model-validation procedures are described in this section. Validation of the model initial covariance matrix is based on the same input data and involves similar but not identical algorithms. A summary of covariance-matrix validation procedures is given in Section III.D.

B. VALIDATION OF THE MODEL INITIAL MEAN

In this section, details of the model-mean validation procedures are presented. This section provides a description of a "data equation" representation of smoothed estimates from a Kalman filter/smoother. Sections III.B.2 and III.B.3 describe algorithms for data processing and capability analysis that are based on the data equation.

1. The Data Equation

Efficient computation of all test statistics and probabilities described in this section is based on a single equation, called the *data equation*, for each test result. The data equation defines the explicit relationship between smoothed estimates calculated by a Kalman filter/smoother algorithm and $\underline{\epsilon}$, the initialization vector of the dynamic model state. Figure 31 illustrates the relationship between the data equation and the model structure of Fig. 30. The smoothed estimate of $\underline{x}_0$ which appears on the left-hand side of the data equation can be interpreted as a noisy measurement of $\underline{\epsilon}$. The response matrix D describes the cross-coupling which exists between initialization errors and estimates, and the noise term $\underline{e}'$ represents the accumulated effect of the assumed zero-mean dynamic-system and measurement-system noise processes $\{\underline{w}_l\}$ and $\{\underline{v}_l\}$.

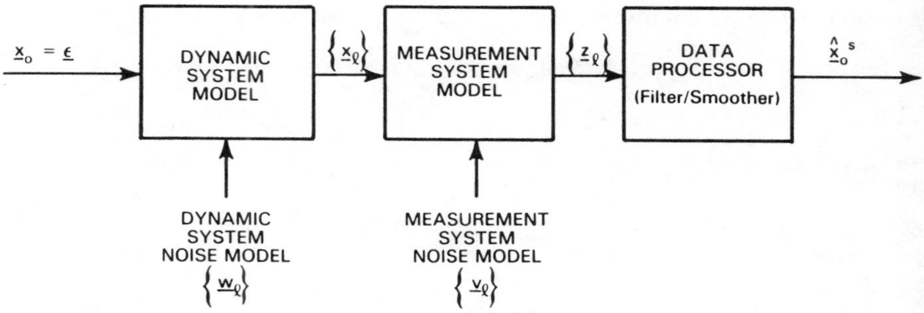

Fig. 31. Data-equation description of complete system structure: $\hat{x}_0^s = D\underline{\epsilon} + \underline{e}'$.

All of the data-processing procedures which are used for validating statistical parameters (Σ_0 and $\underline{b}$) of $\underline{\epsilon}$ are based on using only $\hat{\underline{x}}_0^s$, D, and R as input data. It can be shown that, in fact, $\hat{\underline{x}}_0^s$ is a *sufficient statistic* for Σ_0 and $\underline{b}$. That is, one could not infer any more about the probability density function of $\underline{\epsilon}$ by any type of processing on the original data sequence $\{\underline{z}_l\}$ than by correctly processing $\hat{\underline{x}}_0^s$ alone. This compression of the thousands of individual measurements contained in typical data sequences into a single vector estimate makes the validation procedures described in this section attractive.

In the following discussion, the data equation for each test k (k = 1, ..., N) is described. The superscript k is suppressed to avoid unnecessary notational complexity, but it should be remembered that, in general, different data-equation matrices (D^k, R^k) result for each test.

a. Data equation for initial mean validation

Let the initialization vector in Fig. 31 be rewritten as

$$\underline{\epsilon} = \underline{b} + \underline{\epsilon}^r, \tag{7}$$

where $\underline{b} = E[\underline{\epsilon}]$, the actual initial mean $n \times 1$, and $\underline{\epsilon}^r \sim N(0, \Sigma_0)$, where Σ_0 is assumed known. The data equation in Fig. 31 can be rewritten as

$$\hat{\underline{x}}_0^s = D\underline{b} + \underline{e}, \tag{8}$$

where

$$\text{cov}(\underline{e}) = D\Sigma_0 D^T + \text{cov}(\underline{e}'), \tag{9}$$

and we define $R = \text{cov}(\underline{e}) = \text{cov}\left(\hat{\underline{x}}_0^s\right)$. For an optimal filter/smoother

$$\mathrm{cov}(\underline{x}_0) = \mathrm{cov}\left(\hat{\underline{x}}_0^s + \tilde{\underline{x}}_0^s\right) \quad \text{or} \quad \Sigma_0 = R + P^s, \tag{10}$$

where P^s is the error covariance of the fixed-point smoothed estimate of $\underline{x}_0$. Furthermore, for an optimal filter/smoother, and for $\underline{\epsilon} = \underline{x}_0$,

$$E\left[\hat{\underline{x}}_0^s \underline{\epsilon}^T\right] = E[(D\underline{\epsilon} + \underline{e}')\underline{\epsilon}^T] = D\Sigma_0$$

$$= E\left[\hat{\underline{x}}_0^s\left(\hat{\underline{x}}_0^s + \tilde{\underline{x}}_0^s\right)^T\right] = R.$$

Therefore, provided the inverse exists,

$$D = R\Sigma_0^{-1}. \tag{11}$$

So, given the a priori covariance Σ_0 and the Kalman-smoother error covariance P^s, one can ideally use Eqs. (10) and (11) to find matrices R and D, necessary to define Eq. (8).

Unfortunately, for many system models of interest, observability of the various components of $\underline{x}_0$ varies widely. The effect is that R is a very poorly conditioned matrix, and computation of R via

$$R = \Sigma_0 - P^s \tag{12}$$

is very inaccurate. The inaccuracy is due both to the finite word-length effect on the subtraction and to round-off error during computation of P^s in typical filter/smoother algorithms. This drawback, combined with the requirement for inverting Σ_0 in Eq. (11), has motivated the use of recursive equations for the direct computation of the D and R matrices. These equations are presented in the Appendix, along with an outline of their derivation.

b. The normalized data equation

Although data-processing procedures based on statistical hypothesis tests could be developed directly from Eq. (8), there are two practical reasons for not doing this. First, test statistics based on $\hat{\underline{x}}_0^s$ in Eq. (8) would not be distributed according to standard probability distributions for which efficient computational procedures already exist. Second, as mentioned earlier, limited model observability results in a poorly conditioned R matrix, i.e., a high degree of linear dependency among the components of $\hat{\underline{x}}_0^s$. Both of these difficulties can be overcome by a normalization procedure which will result in a reduced number of normalized estimates z_i, which will be pairwise uncorrelated. Test statistics based on these normalized estimates will be central or noncentral χ^2 random variables under the hypotheses considered in Section III.B.2.

To obtain the normalized data equation, Eq. (8) is premultiplied by a matrix M chosen so that the resulting noise term $M\underline{e}$ will have identity covariance. If we let

$$R = R^{1/2}(R^{1/2})^T, \tag{13}$$

where $R^{1/2}$ is any positive semidefinite square root of R, then M can be computed from

$$MR^{1/2} = I. \tag{14}$$

Because of the ill-conditioned nature of typical R matrices, M will usually be a pseudoinverse of $R^{1/2}$. One procedure which has proved satisfactory for computing M is based on the use of a singular value decomposition algorithm to obtain matrices U and S such that

$$R = USU^T, \tag{15}$$

where

$$S = \mathrm{diag}\{s_1, s_2, \ldots, s_n\}, \tag{16}$$

and U is an $n \times n$ matrix of eigenvectors of R^TR. The transformation M can therefore be computed using the formula

$$M = (S^{1/2})^- U^T, \tag{17}$$

where $(\ )^-$ denotes a pseudoinverse matrix, and

$$(S^{1/2})^- = \left[\begin{array}{cccc|c} s_1^{-1/2} & & & 0 & \\ & s_2^{-1/2} & & & \\ & & \ddots & & 0_{m\times(n-m)} \\ 0 & & & s_m^{-1/2} & \end{array}\right] \tag{18}$$

is a rank m pseudoinverse of $S^{1/2}$. Multiplying Eq. (8) on the left by M yields the following normalized data equation for the bias problem:

$$\underline{z} = H\underline{b} + \underline{v}, \tag{19}$$

where

$$\underline{z} = M\underline{\hat{x}}_0^s \tag{20}$$

is an $m \times 1$ vector of normalized estimates and

$$H = MD \tag{21}$$

is an $m \times n$ normalized-response matrix. The covariance of the noise term in Eq. (19) is $\mathrm{cov}(\underline{v}) = \mathrm{cov}(M\underline{e}) = MRM^T = I_{m\times m}$ as desired.

2. Data Processing Procedures

Data processing for model-mean validation consists of a four-step procedure designed to evaluate consistency. The four steps are (1) model acceptance, (2) error detection, (3) error isolation, (4) and parameter estimation. Each of the steps is based on quantities derived from the cumulative, normalized data equation

$$\underline{z} = H\underline{b} + \underline{v}, \tag{22}$$

where $\underline{z}$, H, and $\underline{v}$ now represent collections of elements from single-test-data equations,

$$\underline{z} = \begin{bmatrix} \underline{z}^1 \\ \vdots \\ \underline{z}^N \end{bmatrix}, \quad H = \begin{bmatrix} H^1 \\ \vdots \\ H^N \end{bmatrix}, \quad \underline{v} = \begin{bmatrix} \underline{v}^1 \\ \vdots \\ \underline{v}^N \end{bmatrix}. \tag{23}$$

a. Hypothesis-testing procedures

Model acceptance is designed to test the validity of the normalization process. If some of the model matrices (ϕ_l, H_l, Q_l, R_{vl}) do not accurately model the system which generated the data processed by the Kalman filter, then each $\underline{v}^k$ in Eq. (23) may not have identity covariance. This would cause subsequent statistical hypothesis tests to be unreliable because of deviations from the assumed χ^2 (central or non-central) distributions.

The hypothesis to be tested is

$$H_A: \quad \underline{v} \sim N(0, I). \tag{24}$$

The test statistic to be used is

$$\Lambda_A = \|\underline{z} - H\hat{\underline{b}}\|^2, \tag{25}$$

where $\underline{\hat{b}}$ is the least squares (also maximum likelihood under H_A) estimate of $\underline{b}$ based on Eq. (22). The hypothesis test is

$$\Lambda_A \underset{\text{Accept}}{\overset{\text{Reject}}{\gtrless}} \lambda_A, \tag{26}$$

where the threshold λ_A is determined from a specified level of significance α such that

$$\Pr\{\Lambda_A > \lambda_A | H_A \text{ is true}\} = \alpha. \tag{27}$$

The threshold λ_A is determined from Eq. (27) using the fact that if H_A is true, then

$$\Lambda_A \sim \chi_p^2, \tag{28}$$

where degrees of freedom p = (m - rank H) and m is the dimension of $\underline{z}$. Rejection of H_A means that, with high confidence, there exists a modeling error *other than* $\underline{b} \neq 0$, and the succeeding analysis procedures may yield misleading results. Nonrejection of H_A, of course, does not preclude the possibility of other modeling errors. It does imply that if such errors exist, they have not caused $\underline{z}$ to deviate significantly from its baseline statistical distribution.

Error detection is designed to detect the presence of an error of the type considered, a nonzero mean in this case. The hypothesis to be tested is simply

$$H_D: \ \underline{b} = 0, \tag{29}$$

and the test statistic used is derived from the same least squares solution used in the model-acceptance test,

$$\Lambda_D = ||H\underline{\hat{b}}||^2. \tag{30}$$

The bias-detection hypothesis test becomes

$$\Lambda_D \underset{\text{Accept}}{\overset{\text{Reject}}{\gtrless}} \lambda_D, \tag{31}$$

where the threshold λ_D is again based on a specified level of significance α,

$$\Pr\{\Lambda_D > \lambda_D | H_D \text{ is true}\} = \alpha. \tag{32}$$

Under hypothesis H_D,

$$\Lambda_D \sim \chi_p^2, \quad p = \text{rank } H, \tag{33}$$

enabling calculation of the threshold λ_D from the central χ^2 distribution. This test, like the model-acceptance test, is a significance test; rejection of H_D means that, with high confidence, a nonzero bias exists in the system.

Figure 32 is helpful in interpreting detection and isolation test results. The triangle shows the relationship between the data $\underline{z}$; its projection on the linear space spanned by possible bias vectors, which has length $\Lambda_D^{1/2}$ (called "explained sum of squares" or ESS); and the residual vector, which has length $\Lambda_A^{1/2}$ (called "residual sum of squares" or RSS). For the isolation tests discussed later, the projection of $\underline{z}$ on a *subspace* of that spanned by all possible biases is considered.

Another interpretation of Λ_D is as a generalized likelihood ratio (GLR) which could be used as a GLR test statistic to select one of the two alternative hypotheses: H_D: $\underline{b} = 0$ or H_D^C: $\underline{b} \neq 0$.

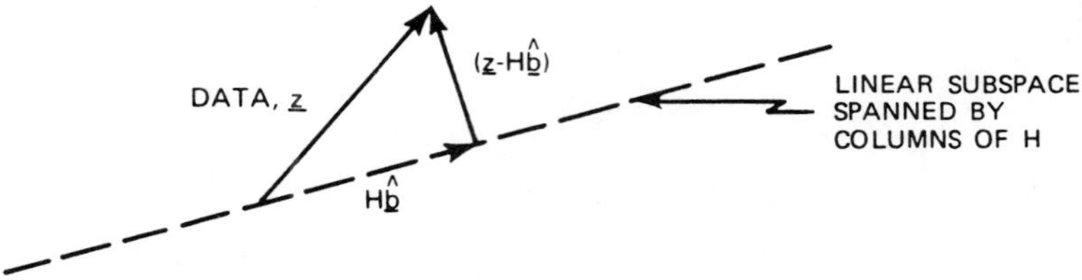

Fig. 32. Decomposition of data into explained and residual portions.

The third and fourth steps of the consistency evaluation are done simultaneously following detection of a modeling error. In the *error-isolation* step, the analyst attempts to isolate the error to a subset of the components of $\underline{b}$. The following notation is used to describe the isolation procedure:

$$B(J) = \{\underline{b}: n \times 1 \text{ vector}, b_j \text{ is arbitrary if } j \in J, \quad b_j = 0 \text{ if } j \notin J\}, \tag{34}$$

where $J = \{1 \leq j_1 < j_2 \cdots < j_q \leq n\}$ is an index set with $q \leq n$ elements. Selection of the index sets J could be based on engineering judgment or on automatic set-selection procedures.

The hypothesis to be tested for each J can be written as

$$H_J: \underline{b} \in B(J), \tag{35}$$

and an appropriate test statistic is

$$\Lambda_J = \Lambda_D - \|H\hat{\underline{b}}_J\|^2, \tag{36}$$

where $\hat{\underline{b}}_J$ is the least squares (and maximum likelihood) solution of the overdetermined set of equations

$$H_J\underline{b}_J \cong \underline{z}. \tag{37}$$

In H_J, columns of H whose indices are not in J are replaced by zeros.

The form of the isolation test is

$$\Lambda_J \underset{\text{Accept}}{\overset{\text{Reject}}{\gtrless}} \lambda_J, \tag{38}$$

where the threshold λ_J is determined from

$$\Pr\{\Lambda_J > \lambda_J | H_J \text{ is true}\} = \alpha. \tag{39}$$

Under hypothesis H_J, it can be shown that

$$\Lambda_J \sim \chi^2_p, \quad p = \text{rank } H - \text{rank } H_J, \tag{40}$$

so that the threshold computation is again based on a central χ^2 distribution.

Each isolation-test statistic Λ_J can be interpreted as a GLR. The two alternative hypotheses for each J are H_U: $\underline{b}$ unconstrained and H_J: $\underline{b} \in B(J)$.

The fourth component of the evaluation is the *estimate* $\hat{\underline{b}}_J$ generated for each of the sets tested. Engineering judgment is of utmost importance in the interpretation of the $(\Lambda_J, \hat{\underline{b}}_J)$ pairs; Λ_J is a measure of how much of the ESS Λ_D is explained by biases in B(J). A perfect score, $\Lambda_J = 0$, would indicate "certain" isolation of the bias. In actual data processing, random effects are aliased by various bias sources; different bias sources may have similar signatures in the data space. As a result, the analyst may "accept" (i.e., fail to reject) two or more sets B(J) as explaining the data. Selection of the most likely bias candidates from among those accepted is based on statistical scoring techniques and, most important, good engineering judgment.

b. Output information from hypothesis tests

Output information from a computer program which implements the hypothesis tests must include test statistics and thresholds for each of the tests, along with the least squares estimates for each alternative index set J. A sophisticated isolation algorithm should also include a ranking system for determining which of the alternatives are the best candidates for explaining the data. A discussion of criteria for ranking the alternatives is beyond the scope of this article.

3. Capability Analysis

Procedures for calculating probabilities associated with the detection and isolation tests just described are now presented. These probabilities are of great importance to the system analyst. First, during the planning stage of system tests and test instrumentation, it is important to learn as much as possible about the observability of various system errors, if they in fact exist, under the proposed test program. Second, capability analysis based on these probabilities provides a guide for planning and interpreting the data-processing procedures and results.

a. Scaling the bias errors

Capability-analysis results are based on the probability density functions of the test statistics. These densities are completely determined by the original model and specification of model errors which are assumed to exist. The procedure to be used to specify error sources considered in capability analysis is to select errors which are "significant" according to a well-defined system-performance criterion. This is called scaling the error sources.

For model-mean validation, system errors are nonzero components in the initialization error-bias vector $\underline{b}$. The scaling criterion has the form

$$||\underline{b}||_E^2 = \underline{b}^T E \underline{b}, \tag{41}$$

where

$$E = N^{-1} \sum_{k=1}^{N} J_k^T J_k, \tag{42}$$

N is the number of tests from which data are to be processed, and $J_k = [\partial \underline{r}_k / \partial \underline{\epsilon}]s \times n$ is a gradient matrix defining the sensitivity of an $s \times 1$ output vector $\underline{r}$ to the initialization-error vector $\underline{\epsilon}$.

b. Evaluating detection and isolation probabilities

Probabilities associated with the detection and isolation tests are calculated from the known probability density functions for test statistics Λ_D and Λ_J. Let $\underline{b}_T$ represent a hypothesized true bias in the a priori distribution of $\underline{\epsilon}$. Then the cumulative data vector $\underline{z}$ in Eq. (22) would be

$$\underline{z} = H\underline{b}_T + \underline{v}. \tag{43}$$

Therefore $\underline{z}$ would be distributed normally with mean $H\underline{b}_T$ and covariance I, denoted $\underline{z} \sim N(H\underline{b}_T, I)$. Let the least squares (and maximum likelihood) estimate of $\underline{b}_T$ be written

$$\hat{\underline{b}} = H^- \underline{z}, \tag{44}$$

where H^- represents a pseudoinverse of H. Therefore the detection-test statistic defined in Eq. (30) can be written

$$\Lambda_D = \underline{z}^T[H^{-T}(H^TH)H^-]\underline{z}. \tag{45}$$

Since the bracketed matrix is idempotent and $\underline{z}$ is normal with identity covariance, Λ_D is a noncentral χ^2 random variable denoted by $\Lambda_D \sim \chi^2(p, \delta^2)$, where p is the degree of freedom, equal to rank H, and δ^2 is a noncentrality parameter equal to $\|H\underline{b}_T\|^2$. The probability of detecting the hypothesized bias $\underline{b}_T$ is given by

$$P_D(\underline{b}_T) = \Pr\{\chi^2(p, \delta^2) > \lambda_D\}, \tag{46}$$

where the threshold λ_D satisfies Eq. (32). This probability can be evaluated using well-known procedures for noncentral χ^2 densities.

For the error probabilities associated with isolation tests, the situation is slightly more complex, but again results in evaluating probabilities from a noncentral χ^2 density function. The constrained estimate $\hat{\underline{b}}_J$ can be denoted

$$\hat{\underline{b}}_J = H_J^-\underline{z}. \tag{47}$$

Combining Eq. (36) with Eqs. (45) and (47), we have

$$\Lambda_J = \underline{z}^T[H^{-T}(H^TH)H^- - H_J^{-T}(H^TH)H_J^-]\underline{z}. \tag{48}$$

The bracketed matrix is again idempotent so that

$$\Lambda_J \sim \chi^2\left(p', \delta_J^2\right), \tag{49}$$

where

$$p' = \text{rank } H - \text{rank } H_J, \tag{50}$$

$$\delta_J^2 = \left\|\left(I - H_J H_J^-\right) H\underline{b}_T\right\|^2.$$

For a specified index set and hypothesized true bias $\underline{b}_T$, the probability of not rejecting (i.e., accepting) set J as possibly containing the bias is

$$P_J(\underline{b}_T) = \Pr\left\{\chi^2\left(p', \delta_J^2\right) < \lambda_J\right\}, \tag{51}$$

where the threshold λ_J satisfies Eq. (39). If $\underline{b}_T$ is, in fact, contained in set B(J), then $\delta_J^2 = 0$ and

$$P_J(\underline{b}_T) = 1 - \alpha, \tag{52}$$

where α is the level of significance used to select λ_J.

Although Λ_D and Λ_J can be interpreted as GLRs, they were developed from a geometrical viewpoint.[12] Λ_J can be interpreted as the square of the distance from the point $(H\underline{b}_T + \underline{v})$ in $\underline{z}$ space to the set HB(J) defined by

$$HB(J) = \{\zeta\colon \zeta = H\underline{b}_J,\ \underline{b}_J \in B(J)\}. \tag{53}$$

Then, $P_J(\underline{b}_T)$ can be interpreted as the probability that this distance is less than a threshold distance λ_J, which defines an "acceptance region" around HB(J).

c. Output information from capability analysis

For capability analysis, biases $\underline{b}_T$ which satisfy

$$\|\underline{b}_T\|_E = d \tag{54}$$

[12] *Developed by J. E. Sacks.*

for a specified error magnitude d are considered. There are many ways in which probabilities associated with specified alternative sets B(J) can be calculated and presented. One which has been successfully implemented is to consider true biases $\underline{b}_T$, which are in the set

$$B(I,\ d) = \{\underline{b}_T\colon\ \underline{b}_T \in B(I) \quad \text{and} \quad \|\underline{b}_T\|_E = d\}, \tag{55}$$

where I is a specifed index set. Then, maximum and minimum probabilities

$$P_{max,min}(J,\ I) = \max,\ \min\{P_J(\underline{b}_T)\} \text{ over } \underline{b}_T \in B(I,\ d) \tag{56}$$

can be computed; they define the range of probabilities of accepting set B(J) as explaining a bias caused by $\underline{b}_T \in B(I, d)$. Examples of results of this type are presented in Section III.C.

4. *Software-System Implementation*

This section describes an efficient software system implementing the procedures presented here. Extension of the procedures to multiple-phase models is discussed first since this extension has a significant impact on the software design. The remaining sections summarize major design considerations and organization of the complete software system.

a. *Multiple-phase models*

The system model considered in Section III.B is specified by the system- and measurement-model equations in Fig. 30. For some systems, however, a complete model of a complex system can be most efficiently represented by two or more sets of system and model equations, each set representing one "phase" of system operation. The relationships between variables describing system operation during two adjacent phases is defined at a specific value of the independent variable, called the interface time, by Eq. (57):

$$\underline{x}_{j0} = \Lambda_{j,j-1}\underline{x}_{j-1}(T_{j-1}) + \Lambda_{j0}\underline{\epsilon}_j, \tag{57}$$

where $\underline{x}_{j0}$ is the initial condition of phase j; $\underline{x}_{j-1}(T_{j-1})$ is the state of phase j - 1 at interface time T_{j-1}; $\Lambda_{j,j-1}$, Λ_{j0} are known transformation matrices; and $\underline{\epsilon}_j \sim N\left(0, \Sigma_0^j\right)$ is the initialization error for phase j. Equation (57) provides the motivation for distinguishing between $\underline{\epsilon}$ and $\underline{x}_0$ in Section III.B; the statistical parameters of $\underline{x}_{j0}$ vary from one test to another because of variations in $\Lambda_{j,j-1}$ and/or the distribution of $\underline{x}_{j-1}(T_{j-1})$, but $\underline{\epsilon}_j$ is modeled by a probability distribution which can reasonably be assumed to be the same for all tests.

Distinct measurement systems will generally be used during distinct phases and the resulting measurements processed in distinct filter/smoother runs, resulting in a collection of smoothed estimates $\hat{\underline{x}}_0^{sj}$, j = 1, ..., N_p, where N_p is the number of phases for which estimates are available. Therefore, N_p data equations must be combined to form a single, normalized data equation for the entire test. Another important difference in the multiple-phase case is that in order to account correctly for correlations which must exist between estimates of initial conditions in different phases, smoothed estimates (along with corresponding D and R matrix elements) of a subset of the state vector of the earlier phase at interface time must be included in the data equation.

For a two-phase model, the composite data equation (before normalization) is

$$\begin{bmatrix} \hat{\underline{x}}^{s1} \\ --- \\ \hat{\underline{x}}_0^{s2} \end{bmatrix} = \left[\begin{array}{c|c} D_1 & 0 \\ \hline D_2\Lambda_{2,1}\phi_1^* & D_2\Lambda_{20} \end{array}\right] \begin{bmatrix} \underline{b}_1 \\ --- \\ \underline{b}_2 \end{bmatrix} + \begin{bmatrix} \underline{e}_1 \\ --- \\ \underline{e}_2 \end{bmatrix}, \tag{58}$$

where

$$\hat{\underline{x}}^{s1} = \begin{bmatrix} \hat{\underline{x}}_0^{s1} \\ --- \\ \hat{\underline{x}}_i^{s1} \end{bmatrix}, \qquad \phi_1^* = \phi(T_1, t_0), \tag{59}$$

and $\underline{x}_i^1$ is the subset of the phase-one state vector at the interface time corresponding to nonzero columns of $\Lambda_{2,1}$. The composite covariance matrix is

$$R^c = \mathrm{cov}\begin{bmatrix} \hat{\underline{x}}^{s1} \\ \\ \hat{\underline{x}}_0^{s2} \end{bmatrix} = \left[\begin{array}{c|c} R_1 & (\text{symmetric}) \\ \hline D_2\Lambda_{2,1}R_1' & R_2 \end{array}\right], \tag{60}$$

where

$$R_1' = \mathrm{cov}\left(\hat{\underline{x}}_i^{s1}, \hat{\underline{x}}^{s1}\right). \tag{61}$$

Since

$$R_1 = \mathrm{cov}\begin{bmatrix} \hat{\underline{x}}_0^{s1} \\ \\ \hat{\underline{x}}_i^{s1} \end{bmatrix} = \left[\begin{array}{c|c} R_{10} & R_{10i} \\ \hline \multicolumn{2}{c}{R_1'} \end{array}\right], \tag{62}$$

R_1' is a submatrix of the R_1 matrix for phase one based on the augmented estimate defined in Eq. (59).

The fact that the smoothed estimate of $\underline{x}_{1i}$ provides critical information is not surprising. In fact, it can be shown [25] that in order to obtain sufficient statistics for estimating statistical parameters in a two-phase system, a third estimate (in addition to $\hat{\underline{x}}_0^{sj}$, j = 1, 2) is necessary. In [25], it is shown that $\left(\hat{\underline{x}}_0^{s1}, \hat{\underline{x}}_i^{s1}, \hat{\underline{x}}_0^{s2}\right)$ are sufficient statistics for the parameter estimation and validation problem of interest in this article.

b. Important design considerations

The procedures described in Section III.B are based on the normalized data-equation elements ($\underline{z}_k$, H_k) for each test result. The extent to which calculations of ($\underline{z}_k$, H_k) should be formalized depends on several factors. Some of the most important are (1) size (i.e., number of states) and observability of the models; (2) number of phases in the model; and (3) number of tests available for analysis. For highly observable (i.e., well-conditioned R) single-phase models and a small number of tests (say up to 10), little formal data organization is necessary. Data-equation matrices (D, R) could be computed from closed-form formulas [Eqs. (11) and (12)] or from recursive formulas (given in the Appendix) implemented concurrently with the filter/smoother equations. One additional program would be required to compute and store normalized data-equation elements ($\underline{z}_k$, H_k). Subsequent analysis (data processing or capability analysis) could then be performed by specially developed programs, possibly using subroutines from standard regression-analysis packages. For more complex cases, however, especially when multiple-phase models are involved, a more formal approach is essential to obtain the maximum benefit from the analysis techniques.

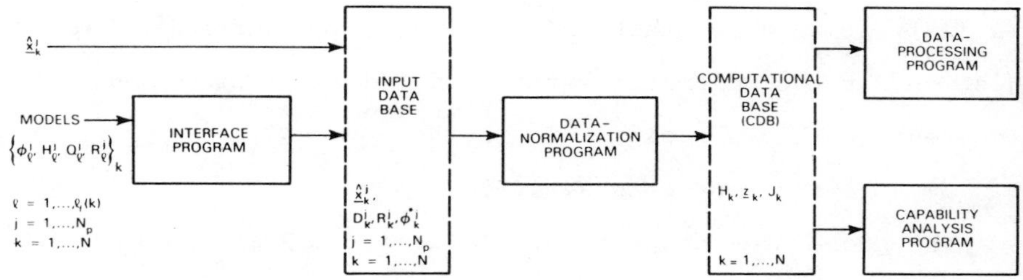

Fig. 33. Software-system organization.

The organization of the software system presented in Fig. 33 includes four distinct program segments and two data-base segments. The first of the program segments, the interface program, is optional depending on the choice of method for computing D and R matrices. If closed-form formulas are used, or if the recursive equations are integrated with the filter/smoother, then resulting (D, R) matrices can be written directly to the input data base. Alternatively, the interface program, which implements the recursive equations for D and R, can read a file stored by the filter/smoother which completely describes the model used in the data processing. The minimum set of matrices which must be stored in that file is shown in Fig. 33. The interface program must also compute and store the cumulative state transition matrix for phase j of test k.

The second program segment, data normalization, performs two functions. First, for multiple-phase models, it assembles the composite data-equation matrices and the error-response matrix J_k for each test $k = 1, \ldots, N$. Second, for all models, it normalizes the composite data-equation elements and stores the resulting ($\underline{z}_k$, H_k) along with J_k on the computational data base (CDB). All subsequent analyses deal *only* with data on the CDB. Calculations performed by the interface and phase combination programs are relatively expensive, but are performed only once for each phase of each test. Therefore, repeated calculations using the last two program segments can be performed at relatively low cost. The CDB contains sufficient statistics for model validation.

The data processing and capability analysis programs contain implementations of the statistical hypothesis tests and probability computations discussed in Section III.B. These two segments share many subroutines and are complementary in that one, capability analysis, assesses the capability of the other, data processing, to solve the problem. User inputs and possible outputs for the two segments are summarized in Table XII. Required inputs for the capability analysis program do

Table XII. Comparison of Analysis Programs

	DATA PROCESSING PROGRAM	CAPABILITY ANALYSIS PROGRAM
USER INPUTS	• (H_k, $\underline{z}_k$) FOR TESTS TO BE ANALYZED • LEVEL-OF-SIGNIFICANCE, α • ALTERNATIVE INDEX SETS $\{J_i,\ i = 1, 2, \ldots\}$	• H_k FOR TESTS TO BE ANALYZED • LEVEL-OF-SIGNIFICANCE, α • ALTERNATIVE INDEX SETS $\{J_i,\ i = 1, 2, \ldots\}$ • HYPOTHESIZED TRUE BIASES, $\{\underline{b}_{Tj},\ j = 1, 2, \ldots\}$
TYPICAL OUTPUT DATA	• HYPOTHESIS TEST RESULTS (acceptance, detection, isolation) • RANKED LIST OF ALTERNATIVE SETS, $\{J_i,\ i = 1, 2, \ldots\}$	• DETECTION PROBABILITIES $P_D(\underline{b}_T)$ • ISOLATION PROBABILITIES $P_J(\underline{b}_T)$

not include normalized data $\underline{z}_k$; that is, all of the computations necessary to perform capability analysis can be done before data are actually collected. This program can therefore be used as a powerful observability analysis tool in the evaluation of proposed test programs. In the capability analysis program, details of how the hypothesized true biases $\underline{b}_T$ are to be selected are not indicated. One method was discussed in Section III.B.2; example results are included in III.C.

C. *EXAMPLE: INITIAL MEAN VALIDATION IN A TWO-PHASE SYSTEM*

This example is based on a simple two-phase model of a ballistic missile system. The dynamic equations represent error models of inertial navigation systems (INSs), which might be used in a mobile missile launcher (prelaunch) and onboard a missile (postlaunch). Numerical values used are for illustration only and are not based on a specific weapon system. The parameters to be validated are the components of the assumed zero mean of the state initialization vector for each phase

$$\underline{b}_j = E[\underline{\epsilon}_j] = \underline{0}_j, \quad j = 1, 2. \tag{63}$$

1. *Baseline Models*

a. *Prelaunch (Phase 1) model*

The 14 states in this model are summarized in Table XIII, along with the 1σ uncertainty of the initialization vector and time constants associated with the Markov error models. This model represents errors in a local-level velocity-damped (damping constant, 1.0) INS moving in a path tangential to the earth's surface at velocities small relative to earth rotation

Table XIII. Phase 1 Model-State Vector and Initialization Error Model

STATE NUMBER	VARIABLE NAME			σ_{io}=INITIAL UNCERTAINTY	MARKOV TIME CONSTANT
1	δL	Position Error	INS Errors	0.5 nmi[a]	
2	$\delta\lambda$	Position Error	INS Errors	0.5 nmi	
3	δV_N	Velocity Error	INS Errors	0.2 kt[b]	
4	δV_E	Velocity Error	INS Errors	0.2 kt	
5	θ_N	Misalignment	INS Errors	0.3 $\widehat{\text{min}}$	
6	θ_E	Misalignment	INS Errors	0.3 $\widehat{\text{min}}$	
7	δH	Misalignment	INS Errors	2.0 $\widehat{\text{min}}$	
8	ε_N	Gyro Drift Rate	Error Source Models	0.1 $\widehat{\text{min}}$/hr	18 hr
9	ε_E	Gyro Drift Rate	Error Source Models	0.1 $\widehat{\text{min}}$/hr	18 hr
10	ε_Z	Gyro Drift Rate	Error Source Models	0.1 $\widehat{\text{min}}$/hr	18 hr
11	$\delta A_{VD(N)}$	Vertical Deflection	Error Source Models	0.25 $\widehat{\text{min}}$	50 hr
12	$\delta A_{VD(E)}$	Vertical Deflection	Error Source Models	0.25 $\widehat{\text{min}}$	50 hr
13	$\delta V_{REF(N)}$	Velocity Reference	Error Source Models	0.5 kt	(Bias Error)
14	$\delta V_{REF(E)}$	Velocity Reference	Error Source Models	0.5 kt	(Bias Error)

[a] *nmi = nautical miles.*
[b] *Kt = nautical miles per hour.*

[13]. Three representative error sources are modeled: gyro drift rates, accelerometer sensing errors due to deflection of the local vertical, and velocity reference errors.

Measurements processed by a Kalman filter/smoother for state estimation in Phase 1 are to be generated by subtracting INS-indicated position from an externally derived position measurement. Measurement noise is assumed to be 100 ft (1σ) in each horizontal direction (north, east).

b. Postlaunch (Phase 2) model

Table XIV describes the 17 states used to represent a space-stable INS with orthogonal axes parallel to an earth-centered coordinate system. Table XIV also includes 1σ

Table XIV.   Phase 2 Model-State Vector and Initialization Error Model

STATE NUMBER	VARIABLE NAME			σ_{oi} =INITIAL UNCERTAINTY
1	r_x ⎫			50 ft
2	r_y ⎬ Position Error			100 ft
3	r_z ⎭			100 ft
4	v_x ⎫		INS	0.5 ft/sec
5	v_y ⎬ Velocity Error		Errors	0.5 ft/sec
6	v_z ⎭			0.5 ft/sec
7	ψ_x ⎫			0.5 $\widehat{\min}$
8	ψ_y ⎬ Misalignment			0.2 $\widehat{\min}$
9	ψ_z ⎭			0.2 $\widehat{\min}$
10	a_x ⎫			0.02 ft/sec^2
11	a_y ⎬ Accelerometer Errors			0.02 ft/sec^2
12	a_z ⎭			0.02 ft/sec^2
			Error Source Models	
13	ε_x ⎫			8 $\widehat{\min}$/hr
14	ε_y ⎬ Gyro Drift Rate			8 $\widehat{\min}$/hr
15	ε_z ⎭			8 $\widehat{\min}$/hr
16	ε_{fx} g-Sensitive			10 $\widehat{\min}$/hr/g
17	ε_{fz} Gyro Drift Rate			10 $\widehat{\min}$/hr/g

uncertainties of the components of $\underline{\epsilon}_2$. Two representative error sources are modeled: accelerometer bias errors due to miscalibration and uncompensated gyro drift-rate errors. The latter include biases in each coordinate axis (three gyros assumed) and two terms representing thrust-dependent bias errors in the x and z directions.

Position measurements for phase 2 are assumed to be similar to those in Phase 1 so that $\underline{z}$ consists of measurements of INS position error along each coordinate axis with additive noise, which has a 1σ value of 30 ft.

c. Phase interface model

The following transformation matrices define a simple model of the process by which the phase 2 INS is initialized by the phase 1 INS at interface time just prior to launch. The complete initial state vector for phase 2 can be written

$$\underline{x}_{20} = \Lambda_2 \Lambda_1 \underline{x}_1(t_i) + \underline{\epsilon}_2, \tag{64}$$

where Λ_1 defines a 7×1 output vector from phase 1,

$$\underline{y}_{1i} = \Lambda_1 \underline{x}_1(t_i), \tag{65}$$

where

$$\Lambda_1 = (\Lambda_{11} \mid 0_{7\times 7}), \tag{66}$$

$\Lambda_{11} = \text{diag}(1, \cos L, 1, 1, 1, 1, -1)$, and L is the latitude at launch. Next, Λ_2 contains the necessary scale factors and coordinate trnsformations to map $\underline{y}_{1i}$ into the phase 2 INS errors:

$$\underset{17\times 7}{\Lambda_2} = \left[\begin{array}{c|c|c} \Lambda_{21} & & \\ \hline & \Lambda_{22} & \\ \hline & & \Lambda_{23} \\ \hline \multicolumn{3}{c}{0_{8\times 7}} \end{array}\right], \tag{67}$$

where

$$\Lambda_{21} = C_1 \begin{bmatrix} 0 & 0 \\ -\sin\beta & \cos\beta \\ \cos\beta & \sin\beta \end{bmatrix}, \quad \Lambda_{22} = C_2 \begin{bmatrix} 0 & 0 \\ -\sin\beta & \cos\beta \\ \cos\beta & \sin\beta \end{bmatrix},$$

$$\Lambda_{23} = \begin{bmatrix} 0 & 0 & -1 \\ -\sin\beta & \cos\beta & 0 \\ \cos\beta & \sin\beta & 0 \end{bmatrix}.$$

In these matrices, β represents the launch direction (azimuth) and C_1, C_2 are position and velocity unit-conversion factors. The 17×1 vector $\underline{\epsilon}_2$ in Eq. (64) represents initialization errors in the phase 2 INS introduced during the transfer alignment process and phase 2 INS instrument errors (biases). These errors are assumed to be uncorrelated with $\underline{x}_1(t_i)$. The mean value of $\underline{\epsilon}_2$ is to be validated.

2. *Description of the Tests*

For this example, 10 test scenarios were simulated using standard covariance-analysis procedures. Parameters which summarize the test scenarios are tabulated in Table XV. The 10 tests describe a mix found in a typical test program, some yielding much better observability of system-error sources than others. No one mission would provide a clear test of the correctness of the zero-mean assumption for the initialization vectors of the model. Only by processing data from an ensemble of missions can a determination be made with a high degree of confidence.

Table XV. Parameters of the Test Scenarios

TEST NUMBERS	MODEL PARAMETERS				BASELINE MODEL PREDICTED PERFORMANCE CEP (feet)
	Phase 1	Phase 2			
	LATITUDE L	LAUNCH AZIMUTH β	LAUNCH ELEVATION θ	RANGE R(nmi)[a]	
1,4	30°	135°	45°	850	8400
2	30°	135°	30°	2400	15000
3	30°	135°	65°	1500	14200
5,8	0°	135°	45°	850	8800
6	0°	135°	30°	2400	15200
7	0°	135°	65°	1500	14200
9,10	30°	180°	45°	1900	8900

[a]*nmi = nautical miles.*

3. *Capability Analysis Results for the Example System*

a. *Bias-detection capability*

Table XVI contains bias-detection capability results for several cases. Five different hypothesized "true" bias sources are considered. Each bias is identified by the state variables in the left-hand column which indicate that the corresponding element of $\underline{\epsilon}_1$ or $\underline{\epsilon}_2$ is biased by the indicated magnitude. The a priori sigmas are from Tables XII and XIII. For the two cases which contain more than one biased component, two probabilities are printed corresponding to the worst ($P_{D(min)}$) and best ($P_{D(max)}$) cases among all those biases satisfying the error constraint $||\underline{b}_T||_E = d$. This error is the rms miss distance across the ensemble of ten tests which would be caused by each hypothesized bias. The two values of d, for

Table XVI. Bias-Detection Capability Results

TRUTH SET CONTAINING BIAS AND A PRIORI SIGMA	ERROR MAGNITUDE d (ft)	$P_{D(MIN)}$[a] NUMBER OF TESTS			BIAS AT $P_{D(MIN)}$	$P_{D(MAX)}$[a] NUMBER OF TESTS			BIAS AT $P_{D(MAX)}$
		5	10	20		5	10	20	
$\{\delta V_N\}$,0.2 kt	1000	1.0	1.0	1.0	3.29[b]	(ONLY ONE VALUE OF SINGLE-COMPONENT BIAS YIELDS REQUIRED d)			
	2000	1.0	1.0	1.0	6.58[b]				
$\{\delta H\}$,2.0 $\widehat{\text{min}}$	1000	α	α	0.11	0.209[c]				
	2000	0.11	0.11	0.12	0.419[c]				
$\{\varepsilon_N\}$,0.1 $\frac{\widehat{\text{min}}}{\text{hr}}$	1000	0.18	0.29	0.53	0.086				
	2000	0.52	0.86[d]	1.0	0.172				
$\{\delta A_{VD(N,E)}\}$ 0.25 $\widehat{\text{min}}$	1000	0.14	0.19	0.29	-0.124 0.124	0.26	0.44	0.77	0.235 0.259
	2000	0.29	0.52	0.86	-0.245 0.250	0.78	0.99	1.0	0.471 0.517
$\{a_x, a_y, a_z\}$ 0.02 ft/sec^2	1000	α	α	0.11	-0.0020[c] 0 -0.0019	0.14	0.18	0.27	-0.0072 0 0.0075
	2000	0.11	0.12	0.14	-0.0040[c] 0 -0.0038	0.27	0.48	0.82	-0.014 0 0.015

[a] *Based on thresholds for level of significance* $\alpha = 0.10$. *In table entries,* α *indicates no detectability of the hypothesized bias.*

[b] $b_i >> \sigma_i$ *Implies low system sensitivity to* ϵ_i.

[c] $b_i < \sigma_i$ *Implies high system sensitivity to* ϵ_i.

[d] *Simulated data-processing results for this case are discussed in the text.*

which results are given in the tables (1000 and 2000 ft), are relatively small for the example system, which has an average CEP across the 10 tests of 11,000 ft (see Table XV). Thus, the probabilities presented correspond to a system bias which would be difficult to detect in the impact domain defined by downrange and cross-range error based on the 10-test ensemble.

For each case (i.e., each bias source and each d value), three probabilities are given corresponding to the number of test results assumed to be available for processing. The five-test case assumes that only tests 1 to 4 and 9 are available, and the 20-test case assumes that each of the 10 tests described in Table XIV is conducted twice.

The various cases in Table XVI can be grouped into three broad categories. For some cases, indicated by footnote *b* in Table XVI, the bias magnitude required to produce a significant d is far greater than the modeled prior uncertainty. Such a bias, if it existed in the system, would represent a severe system anomaly and would be easily detected by the data-processing algorithm if the associated state variable is observable in the classical control/estimation theory sense. For the north-velocity-bias case shown, the smoothed estimates of the system initial velocity for the 10-test ensemble would clearly indicate the presence of the bias; the model-validation data-processing software would not be necessary.

A second category is typified by the cases indicated by footnote *c* in Table XVI. Here, the system-performance measure is extremely sensitive to the hypothesized bias so that, for the $\{\delta H\}$ case, for example, a bias of only one-tenth of the a priori uncertainty would cause a 1000-ft rms error. For these cases, even after perfect measurement of the states of interest, one would have great difficulty in distinguishing between the unbiased a priori model and the actual, slightly biased density function.

The third category includes the rest of the cases in Table XVI and the majority of cases in practical applications. For these cases, system sensitivity is moderate, relative to the d of interest, and the unique capability of the data-processing algorithm based on data from multiple tests is of maximum advantage. The steadily increasing probabilities as the numbers of tests increases is clearly evident.

b. Bias isolation capability

Table XVII contains bias isolation capability results. Here are used three of the hypothesized bias sets for which detection capability results were presented previously in Table XVI. The probability of accepting each of six alternative sets is computed for each case. As with the detection capability results, for multiple-component hypothesized biases, worst-case ($P_{J(MAX)}$) and best-case ($P_{J(MIN)}$) probabilities are computed for each case. The effect of increasing d (from 2000 to 4000 ft) or the number of tests (from 10 to 20) is shown for each truth/alternative pair.

Table XVII. Bias Isolation Capability Results

TRUTH SET CONTAINING BIAS	ALTERNATIVE SETS[a]							
	d	N	$\{\varepsilon_N, \varepsilon_E, \varepsilon_Z\}$	$\{\underline{\delta A}_{VD}\}$	$\{\underline{\delta V}_{REF}\}$	$\{\underline{\psi}\}$	$\{\underline{a}\}$	$\{\underline{\varepsilon}, \underline{\varepsilon}_f\}$
$\{\varepsilon_N\}$	2000	10	1-α[b]	0.13	0.13	0.13	0.12	0.11
	2000	20	1-α	0	0	0	0	0
	4000	10	1-α	0	0	0	0	0
$\{\delta A_{VD(N,E)}\}$	2000	10	0.48/0.03	1-α	0.90/0.89[c]	0.57/0.02	0.46/0.01	0.48/0.01
	2000	20	0.14/0.01	1-α	0.90/0.88	0.25/0	0.13/0	0.15/0
	4000	10	0.03/0	1-α	0.89/0.86	0.02/0	0./0	0./0
$\{\underline{a}\}$	2000	10	0.88/0.50	0.88/0.50	0.88/0.51	0.88/0.50	1-α	0.88/0.49
	2000	20	0.86/0.17	0.86/0.17	0.86/0.17	0.86/0.17	1-α	0.85/0.16
	4000	10	0.84/0.01	0.81/0.01	0.81/0.01	0.81/0.01	1-α	0.80/0.01

[a] *Pr {Accept the alternative set} (see footnote b) (for multiple-component true biases, $P_{J(MAX)}/P_{J(MIN)}$ are shown.*

[b] *Based on thresholds for level of significance α = 0.10; in table entries, 1 - α is the designed probability that an alternative set containing the truth be accepted for these cases.*

[c] *Probability 0.90 = 1 - α indicates extreme difficulty of distinguishing between this truth/alternative pair.*

A general feature of the results is that for alternative sets which do not contain the hypothesized bias, the probabilities of acceptance (i.e., the probabilities of misisolation) do not vary much from one alternative set to another. This result is typical of misisolation probabilities which have been computed for many weapon-system models. Exceptions to this general feature do occur, however; one such case is indicated by footnote *b* in the table. That result (misisolation probability = $1 - \alpha$) means that for this example, biases in the vertical deflection errors and the velocity reference errors have almost identical signatures in the data space. It can be shown that by using engineering judgment in interpreting isolation test results, incorrect acceptance of $\underline{\delta V}_{REF}$ as a bias source can almost certainly be avoided.

4. Data-Processing Results

In order to illustrate applications of data-processing algorithms to the example two-phase system, a sequence of simulated, normalized, biased data $\{\underline{z}^k\}$ was generated. The bias simulated corresponds to a case considered in the previous bias capability analysis results and would cause d = 2000 ft of rms error:

$$\underline{b}_T\colon \{b_8 = E[\epsilon_N(0)] = 0.172\ \widehat{\text{min}}/\text{hr}\}.$$

The sequence $\{\underline{z}^k\}$ was made up of 12 sets of 10 $\{\underline{z}^k\}$ (representing results of each of the 10 test scenarios).

This single-component bias is highly detectable ($P_D = 0.86$) and easily isolated ($P_J \approx 0.13$ for J, not including ϵ_N). In 10 of the 12 trials, the hypothesis $\underline{b} = 0$ was rejected at the $\alpha = 0.1$ level, an experimental detection rate of 0.83.

Table XVIII. Bias Isolation Results

ALTERNATIVE SET (J)	NUMBER OF TRIALS FOR WHICH SET J WAS ACCEPTED (N_J)	ACCEPTANCE RATE ($N_J/12$)	PREDICTED PROBABILITY (P_J)
$\{\varepsilon_N, \varepsilon_E, \varepsilon_Z\}$	12	1.0	$(1-\alpha)$
$\{\delta A_{VD(N,E)}\}$	3	0.24	0.13
$\{\delta V_{REF(N,E)}\}$	3	0.25	0.13
$\{\underline{\psi}\}$	4	0.33	0.13
$\{\underline{a}\}$	3	0.25	0.12
$\{\underline{\varepsilon}, \underline{\varepsilon}_f\}$	3	0.25	0.11

Isolation results for the six alternative sets considered earlier (Table XVII) are summarized in Table XVIII. Acceptance rates of incorrect alternative sets for this small number of trials are higher than predicted, but for each set, two of the false acceptances occurred in the trials in which the detection test failed to reject the $\underline{b} = 0$ hypothesis. Thus, use of engineering judgment in these cases would help to avoid an incorrect conclusion: after failure of a detection test, the analyst should not conclude that a bias exists in any of the (falsely) isolated sets without careful examination of the bias estimates $\hat{\underline{b}}_J$ produced for each set.

D. SUMMARY AND EXTENSIONS

A formal, organized approach to validation of the statistical parameters of initialization errors in linear dynamic system models used by Kalman filter/smoothers has been presented. The approach for the mean-value (bias) parameters has been discussed in detail; a similar approach which has been developed for initial covariance-matrix validation is discussed briefly in the following paragraph. The bias-validation procedures include statistical hypothesis tests for detecting and isolating bias errors based on data-processing results and capability-analysis formulas for calculating probabilities of detecting and isolating (or misisolating) hypothesized model bias errors. All of the analysis procedures are based on a data-equation representation of the overall system which transforms an initialization vector $\underline{\epsilon}$ into a smoothed estimate vector $\hat{\underline{x}}_0^s$ (Fig. 31).

Analysis procedures for the covariance problem are also based on the data equation of Fig. 31, but normalization for this problem is done with respect to the covariance of $\underline{e}'$ (process and measurement-noise effects) rather than with respect to the covariance of $\hat{\underline{x}}_0^s$. Hypothesis tests for covariance-matrix validation are based on quadratic forms in normal random variables. Another difference in the covariance problem is the way in which errors are scaled during capability analysis. Since a model error for this problem is of the form $\Delta\Sigma_0$, the effect of this error on the system output vector is a change $\Delta\Sigma_f$ in the covariance matrix of the system output. A variety of scalar measures might be used as norms on $\Delta\Sigma_f$; one which would be appropriate for weapon systems such as the example in Section III.C is the change in CEP due to $\Delta\Sigma_0$.

The procedures have potential application beyond the basic model-validation problem. For example, if the model is viewed as describing an ideal system design, the procedures can be used as system-parameter-estimation tools. Since parameter estimates are generated from sufficient statistics for *all* the data, the algorithms provide an efficient method for compressing and storing the data generated by an ensemble of tests. For situations in which both bias and covariance errors exist in the system model, the algorithm can be used recursively to successively adjust estimates in the data equations as improved estimates of model parameters are generated.

APPENDIX. RECURSIVE CALCULATION OF DATA-EQUATION MATRICES

In this Appendix, recursive equations are presented which can be used to compute matrices (D, R) associated with the smoothed estimate data equation for a single-phase model as discussed in Section III.B. An outline of the derivation is also presented.

D, R FOR A SINGLE-PHASE MODEL

Let the linear discrete-time system model be represented for each $l = 0, 1, \ldots, l_f$ by

$$\underline{x}_{l+1} = \phi_l \underline{x}_l + \underline{w}_l, \quad \text{cov}(\underline{w}_l) = Q_l, \quad \underline{x}_0 = \underline{\epsilon} \sim N(0, \Sigma_0), \tag{A1}$$

$$\underline{z}_{l+1} = H_{l+1}\underline{x}_{l+1} + \underline{v}_{l+1}, \quad \text{cov}(\underline{v}_{l+1}) = R_{vl+1}. \tag{A2}$$

Then, matrices D_l, R_l such that

$$\hat{\underline{x}}_l = D_l \underline{x}_0 + \underline{e}_l, \quad l = 0, 1, \ldots, l_f \tag{A3}$$

$$R_l = \text{cov}(\hat{\underline{x}}_l) = D_l \Sigma_0 D_l^T + \text{cov}(\underline{e}_l), \tag{A4}$$

(where $\hat{\underline{x}}_l$ is the optimal filtered estimate at time l) can be computed from the formulas

$$D_{l+1} = (I - K_{l+1}H_{l+1})\phi_l D_l + K_{l+1}H_{l+1}\phi^*_{l+1}, \quad D_0 = 0, \tag{A5}$$

$$R_{l+1} = \phi_l R_l \phi_l^T + K_{l+1}\psi_{l+1}K_{l+1}^T, \quad R_0 = 0, \tag{A6}$$

where

$$\phi_{l+1}^{*} = \phi(l+1,\ 0) = \phi_l \phi_{l-1} \cdots \phi_0, \tag{A7}$$

$$\psi_{l+1} = H_{l+1}P_{l+1/l}H_{l+1}^T + R_{vl+1}, \tag{A8}$$

and K_{l+1} is the Kalman gain and $P_{l+1/l}$ the one-step prediction-error covariance.

Equations (A5) and (A6) can be derived by an induction procedure. The zero initial conditions are a result of the filter initialization

$$\hat{\underline{x}}_0 = E[\underline{x}_0] = 0. \tag{A9}$$

The induction procedure is based on the Kalman filter update formulas and uses the orthogonality property of an optimal filter

$$\text{cov}(\hat{\underline{x}}_{l+1},\ \underline{\nu}_{l+1}) = 0, \tag{A10}$$

where

$$\underline{\nu}_{l+1} = \underline{z}_{l+1} - H_{l+1}\phi_l \hat{\underline{x}}_l \tag{A11}$$

is the innovation at time $l + 1$. The ϕ_{l+1}^{*} factor in Eq. (A5) results from the following representation of the state at $l + 1$:

$$\underline{x}_{l+1} = \phi_{l+1}^{*}\underline{x}_0 + \underline{w}_{l+1}^{*}, \tag{A12}$$

where $\underline{w}_{l+1}^{*}$ is the cumulative effect of all process noise.

Now, let Eqs. (A1) and (A2) be replaced by an augmented-state model:

$$\underline{x}^a_{l+1} = \phi^a_l \underline{x}^a_l + \underline{w}^a_l, \tag{A13}$$

$$\underline{x}^a_0 = \begin{bmatrix} \underline{x}_0 \\ \underline{x}_0 \end{bmatrix},$$

$$\underline{z}^a_{l+1} = H^a_{l+1} \underline{x}^a_{l+1} + \underline{v}_{l+1}, \tag{A14}$$

where

$$\underline{x}^a_l = \begin{bmatrix} \underline{x}_l \\ \underline{x}_0 \end{bmatrix}, \quad \phi^a_l = \begin{bmatrix} \phi_l & 0 \\ 0 & I \end{bmatrix}, \quad \underline{w}^a_l = \begin{bmatrix} \underline{w}_l \\ 0 \end{bmatrix},$$

$$H^a_{l+1} = (H_{l+1} \quad 0). \tag{A15}$$

A filtered estimate of this augmented-state system is therefore

$$\hat{\underline{x}}^a_l = \begin{bmatrix} \hat{\underline{x}}_l \\ \hat{\underline{x}}_{0/l} \end{bmatrix} \tag{A16}$$

where $\hat{\underline{x}}_{0/l}$ is the optimal smoothed estimate of $\underline{x}_0$.

The data equation for the smoothed estimate $\hat{\underline{x}}_{0/l}$ is

$$\hat{\underline{x}}_{0/l} = D^s_l \underline{x}_0 + \underline{e}_l, \quad l = 0, 1, \ldots, \tag{A17}$$

where

$$D^s_{l+1} = D^s_l - K^s_{l+1} H_{l+1} \left(\phi_l D_l - \phi^*_{l+1} \right), \quad D^s_0 = 0. \tag{A18}$$

Corresponding covariance matrices are

$$R^s_l = \mathrm{cov}(\hat{\underline{x}}_{0/l}), \quad R^c_l = \mathrm{cov}(\hat{\underline{x}}_l, \hat{\underline{x}}_{0/l}), \tag{A19}$$

which satisfy recursions

$$R^c_{l+1} = \phi_l R^c_l + K_{l+1}\psi_{l+1}\left(K^s_{l+1}\right)^T, \quad R^c_0 = 0, \tag{A20}$$

$$R^s_{l+1} = R^s_l + K^s_{l+1}\psi_{l+1}\left(K^s_{l+1}\right)^T, \quad R^s_0 = 0. \tag{A21}$$

Equations (A18) to (A21) are derived directly from Eqs. (A5) and (A6) by replacing each matrix by an augmented form, including

$$R^a = \begin{bmatrix} R & R^c \\ R^{cT} & R^s \end{bmatrix}, \quad D^a = \begin{bmatrix} D \\ D^s \end{bmatrix}, \tag{A22}$$

and then equating corresponding partitions of the two equations.

To summarize for a single-phase system in which the smoothed data-equation matrices (D^s, R^s) are required, the necessary recursive equations are Eqs. (A5), (A18), and (A21). Matrices R and R^c are not required for this case. The matrices denoted (D, R) in Section III.B are the *smoothed* data-equation matrices $\left(D^s_l, R^s_l\right)$ in this Appendix, evaluated after the last update at time l_f.

ACKNOWLEDGMENTS

The data-processing methodology described in the first part of this article, as well as the performance evaluation and data-analysis software, is the result of a dedicated effort by a number of staff members of The Analytic Sciences Corporation. The original GLR test methodology was formulated by H. L. Jones and refined by K. S. Tait. The performance-evaluation software was developed by J. A. D'Appolito, C. M. Ermer, L. M. Hawthorne, and D. J. Meyer. C. J. Vahlberg and D. J. Meyer developed the data-processing software.

Design and development of the procedures described in the second part of this article and of a software system which implements them has been the work of several individuals at The Analytic Sciences Corporation. The original concept was developed by J. L. Center and P. J. Olinski. Design of the bias capability procedures was primarily by J. E. Sacks and covariance matrix validation procedures were developed by F. K. Sun. The software system, including the data-base design, was developed by S. L. Rubin.

REFERENCES

1. E. M. DUIVEN *et al.*, "Detection of Anomalous Guidance System Performance Using FLY-2 and GPS Measurements," *Proc. 8th Biennial Guidance Test Symp.*, Holloman Air Force Base, October 1979.

2. R. FUSSELL *et al.*, "A Method for Determining the Performance of a Precision Inertial Guidance System," *Proc. 1979 AIAA Guidance and Control Conf.*, Boulder, Colorado, August 1979.

3. T. THOMPSON, "Performance of the SATRACK/GPS Trident I Missile Tracking System," *Proc. 1980 Position Location and Navig. Symp.*, Atlantic City, New Jersey, December 1980.

4. "AIRS Description Document," Honeywell, Inc., Rept. No. 0972-11167-A, February 1973.

5. "Global Positioning System," *J. Navig. 25*, No. 2 (1978).

6. A. GELB, ed., "Applied Optimal Estimation," MIT Press, Cambridge, Massachusetts, 1974.

7. C. T. LEONDES, ed., "Theory and Application of Kalman Filtering," *NATO-AGARDograph* No. 139, Bradford House, London, England, 1970.

8. A. S. WILLSKY and H. L. JONES, "A Generalized Likelihood Ratio Approach to the Detection and Estimation of Jumps in Linear Systems," *IEEE Trans. Autom. Control AC-21*, No. 2, 108-112 (1976).

9. A. S. WILLSKY, J. J. DEYST, and B. S. CRAWFORD, "Adaptive Filtering and Self-Test Methods for Failure Detection and Compensation," *Joint Autom. Control Conf.*, Austin, Texas, June 1970.

10. E. M. DUIVEN, "Suboptimal Linear Filtering," *AIAA Journal 2*, No. 3, 196-198 (1974).

11. G. R. PITMAN, ed., "Inertial Guidance," Wiley, New York, 1962.

12. C. E. HUTCHINSON and R. A. NASH, "Comparison of Error Propagation in Local Level and Space Stable Systems," *IEEE Trans. Aerosp. Electron. Syst. AES-7*, No. 6, 1138-1142 (1971).

13. C. T. LEONDES, ed., "Guidance and Control of Aerospace Vehicles," McGraw-Hill, New York, 1963.

14. K. R. BRITTING, "Inertial Navigation Systems Analysis," Wiley, New York, 1971.

15. "Space Vehicle Navigation Subsystem and NTS PRN Navigation Assembly/User System Segment and Monitor Station," GPS Joint Project Office, Rept. No. MH08-00002-400 (revised), October 1979.

16. K. K. BISWAS and A. K. MAHALANABIS, "An Approach to Fixed-Point Smoothing Problems," *IEEE Trans. Aerosp. Electron. Syst. AES-8*, No. 5, 676-682 (1972).

17. T. W. ANDERSON, "An Introduction to Multivariate Statistical Analysis," Wiley, New York, 1958.

18. C. R. RAO, "Linear Statistical Inference and Its Application," Wiley, New York, 1973.

19. L. J. LEVY, R. H. SHUMWAY, D. E. OLSEN, and F. C. DEAL, JR., "Model Validation from an Ensemble of Kalman Filter Tests," *Proc. of the 21st Midwest Symp. on Circuits and Systems*, August 1978.

20. F. K. SUN, "An Alternative Approach for Maximum Likelihood Identification," *Proc. of the 18th Conf. on Decision and Control*, Ft. Lauderdale, Florida, 1979.

21. A. P. DEMPSTER, N. M. LAIRD, and D. B. RUBIN, "Maximum Likelihood from Incomplete Data via the EM Algorithm," *J. Statist. Soc. 39*, November 1977.

22. R. L. KASHYAP and A. R. RAO, "Dynamic Stochastic Models from Empirical Data," Academic Press, New York, 1976.

23. R. L. GOODRICH and P. E. CAINS, "Linear System Identification from Nonstationary Cross-Sectional Data," *IEEE Trans. Autom. Control AC-24*, No. 3 (1979).

24. Y. BARAM, "Nonstationary Model Validation from Finite Data Records," *IEEE Trans. Autom. Control AC-25*, No. 1 (1980).

25. F. K. SUN, "Statistical Inference Regarding Unknown Random Changes in Linear Dynamic Systems Using Cross-Sectional Data," to appear in *IEEE Trans. Autom. Control*.

Inertial Navigation System Error-Model Considerations in Kalman Filtering Applications

JAMES R. HUDDLE

Litton Guidance and Control Systems Division Woodland Hills, California

ISBN 0-12-012720-2

I. INTRODUCTION

The application of modern linear estimation techniques requires an "adequate" model of the system whose states are to be estimated. The adequacy of a particular model of a physical system is usually determined by digital computer simulation. In these simulations as accurate a model as is obtainable is employed to represent the physical system, and the subset of its states which are of interest in the application are estimated using a Kalman filter based on a "design model" [1] of this system. The adequacy of the design model is ascertained by observing how well the state estimates track the actual states of the simulated physical system using the root mean square (rms) difference between them as a criterion. Some designers also compare the standard deviations from the estimator covariance matrix to these rms values as an indicator of design adequacy. A more absolute judgement of estimator performance is obtainable by comparing the rms estimate errors with the standard deviations from the covariance matrix for the estimator based on the exact model of the simulated system: the so-called real-world model covariance analysis approach. To economize on mechanization requirements it is usually desirable to simplify the latter complete estimator design model, motivating the examination of various simplified candidate design models.

Regardless of the estimator design criterion employed, the work of estimator design involves a "tuning" process in which states are added or deleted, dynamic intercouplings are changed, and white-noise components are altered. The subject of this article deals with an aspect of this latter process for the case of inertial navigation systems. Herein it is shown that the analytical model for propagation of error in the navigation variables of position, velocity, and attitude have alternative forms with various degrees of approximation. The model differences are important in that they imply different real-time digital computer mechanization requirements in terms of memory and duty cycle. These models have been employed in oeprational systems and have been proved effective for differing application requirements.

II. LOCAL-LEVEL COORDINATE-SYSTEM NAVIGATION EQUATIONS

The process of terrestrial navigation using inertial equipment involves the measurement of force by a usually orthogonal triad of accelerometers whose orientation relative to the earth is established and maintained by three usually orthogonal gyroscopic axes. Since the orientation of the accelerometers relative to the earth is known, the force due to gravity can be removed from these measurements by using an analytical model to obtain the acceleration of the inertial system center of mass relative to inertial space. Correction of these measurements obtained or expressed in some reference navigation-coordinate frame for Coriolis accelerations due to the effects of earth and reference-frame rotation rate relative to inertial space, yields the rate of change of system velocity relative to the earth with respect to the reference navigation-coordinate frame. Integration of these variables with proper initialization then yields the velocity of the inertial system relative to the earth. Transformation of the velocity components to an earth fixed frame and subsequent integration yield system position change relative to the earth thus accomplishing the navigation objective. To make these statements more specific, the navigation equations that are mechanized for most aircraft inertial navigation systems assume as the navigation reference-coordinate frame [x, y, z] a local-level system with "wander azimuth angle" α, as illustrated in Fig. 1. This coordinate frame resides at the center of mass

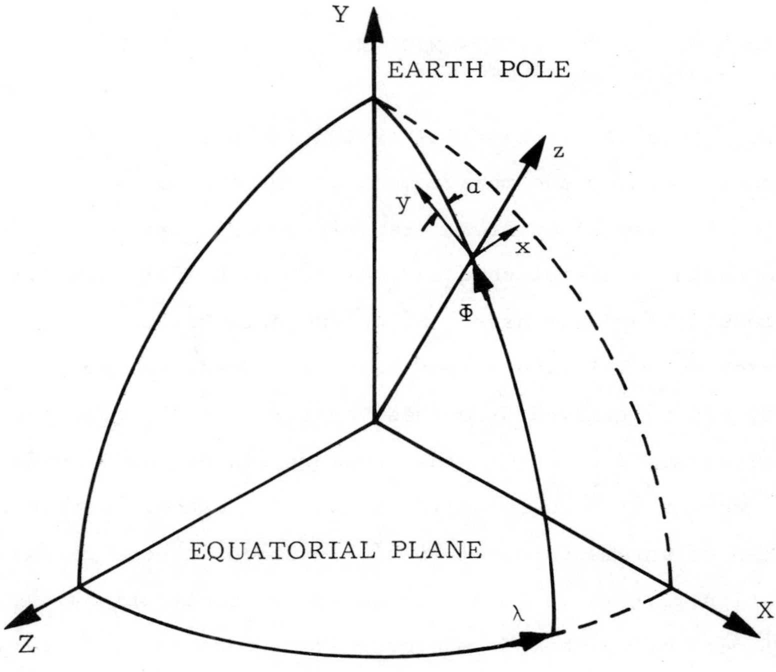

Fig. 1. Illustration of the local-level navigation reference-coordinate frame [x, y, z] and an earth-fixed [X, Y, Z] reference-coordinate frame.

of the inertial system and is maintained in the local-level orientation as the system is moved relative to the earth. Alternative mechanizations for the behavior of the wander angle are possible. For example, if $\alpha(t) \equiv 0$ for all t, then the navigation equations correspond to the north-slaved mechanization since the y axis is always directed northward. In this case the x and y axes are coincident with the local east and north axes, whereas the z axis still remains coincident with the local vertical.

III. COORDINATE FRAMES FOR ERROR-MODEL DEVELOPMENT

The local-level navigation coordinate equations that are implemented in the real-time digital computer have been derived in detail elsewhere [2] and are summarized in extended form in the appendix to be readily employed later. The development of the describing error equations presented here is more conceptual than mathematically rigorous so as to simplify presentation of the material. The development is facilitated by the introduction of two additional orthogonal coordinate systems to that depicted in Fig. 1. The frame shown there is hereafter referred to as the reference frame and is local level at the true position of the inertial system with the azimuth angle α.

A. PLATFORM FRAME

The first additional frame is called the platform frame and is slightly misaligned from the reference frame via small attitude-error angles as defined by the skew-symmetric transformation

$$\begin{bmatrix} x \\ y \\ z \end{bmatrix}_p = [I + \phi]\begin{bmatrix} x \\ y \\ z \end{bmatrix}, \tag{1}$$

where[1]:

$$\phi = \begin{bmatrix} 0 & \phi_z & -\phi_y \\ -\phi_z & 0 & \phi_x \\ \phi_y & -\phi_x & 0 \end{bmatrix},$$

where the angles are positive counterclockwise about their respective axes, the variables $\phi_{x,y}$ representing the tilt of the platform coordinates and the azimuth variable ϕ_z representing the difference

$$\phi_z \triangleq \alpha_p - \alpha. \tag{2}$$

B. SYSTEM-COMPUTED LOCAL GEODETIC FRAME

The second orthogonal coordinate frame used in the error description is called the system-computed local geodetic frame and differs in angular orientation from the reference-coordinate frame by three small, independent nonorthogonal rotations due to errors in system-computed geodetic position and the wander angle:

(1) $\delta\Phi \triangleq \Phi_c - \Phi = -\delta\theta_E$ is the error in system-computed geodetic latitude positive clockwise about the local east axis.

[1]*The notation convention in this article normally identifies scalar quantities with subscripts except where the text defines vector quantities. Square brackets are employed to identify matrices which are all defined explicitly in the text. Variables with no subscripts are normally vectors which are defined explicitly in the text and where relevant the text indicates the coordinate system in which the vector is assumed to be expressed.*

Note that $\delta\theta_E$ is positive counterclockwise about the east axis.

(2) $\delta\lambda \triangleq \lambda_c - \lambda$ is the error in system-computed longitude positive counterclockwise about the earth's polar axis. Note that this error can be projected onto the local north and vertical axes knowing the system latitude as

$$\delta\theta_N \triangleq \delta\lambda \cos \Phi, \qquad \delta\theta_V \triangleq \delta\lambda \sin \Phi.$$

(3) $\delta\alpha \triangleq \alpha_c - \alpha$ is the difference between the system-computed wander angle and that of the reference-coordinate system.

The three sources of angular rotation can be expressed about the reference-coordinate axes, knowing the wander angle as

$$\delta\theta_x \triangleq \delta\theta_E \cos \alpha + \delta\theta_N \sin \alpha, \qquad \delta\theta_y \triangleq \delta\theta_N \cos \alpha - \delta\theta_E \sin \alpha,$$
$$\delta\theta_z \triangleq \delta\lambda \sin \Phi + \delta\alpha. \tag{4}$$

These three rotations describe completely the difference in orientation of a coordinate system described by the direction cosine matrix $[D]_c$ defined in the Appendix, based on the computed latitude, longitude, and wander angle $[\Phi, \lambda, \alpha]_c$ of a local-level coordinate frame relative to the reference local-level coordinate frame:

$$\begin{bmatrix} x \\ y \\ z \end{bmatrix}_c = [I + \delta\theta] \begin{bmatrix} x \\ y \\ z \end{bmatrix}, \tag{5}$$

where

$$[\delta\theta] \triangleq \begin{bmatrix} 0 & \delta\theta_z & -\delta\theta_y \\ -\delta\theta_z & 0 & \delta\theta_x \\ \delta\theta_y & -\delta\theta_x & 0 \end{bmatrix}. \tag{6}$$

C. *ALTERNATIVE INSTRUMENT MECHANIZATIONS OF INERTIAL SYSTEMS*

Several mechanizations can be employed for obtaining the inertial instrument measurements. Regardless of the instrumentation approach employed, the local-level coordinate-system formulation of the navigation-mechanization equations can be employed to accomplish the navigation function so long as the accelerometer measurements can be expressed along the local-level coordinate axes. In all mechanizations the attitude error ϕ between the platform frame and the local-level frame is minimized prior to use of the inertial system for navigation by a process called alignment.

1. *Schuler-Tuned Platform Mechanization*

The Schuler-tuned platform mechanization of the inertial instrumentation has been employed for several decades. The attempt in this approach is to maintain the accelerometer-sensing axes coincident with the local-level frame by appropriate precessing of the system gyros. The commonly mounted gyros and accelerometers comprise what is called the stable element, which is isolated from the angular motion of the carrying vehicle by a gimbal set. Once initial alignment of the accelerometer-sensing axes with the local-level frame coordinates has been achieved, this orientation is maintained by precessing the gyros, relative to inertial space, by the system-computed spatial rate ω_c of the local-level frame. This term is the sum of the system-computed angular rate of the local-level frame relative to the earth ρ_c and the system-computed rotation rate of the earth relative to inertial space Ω_c:

$$\omega_c = \rho_c + \Omega_c. \tag{7}$$

The platform frame in this mechanization is the orientation defined by the accelerometer-sensing axes, which are ideally maintained coincident with the local-level reference frame. Consequently, the angular rate of the platform-coordinate frame relative to the instrument-sensing axes expressed in the local-level frame ν_c is mechanized as zero.

2. *Strapdown and Space-Stable Inertial Instrument Mechanizations*

More generally, as in the case of an alternative gimbaled inertial system or a strapdown inertial system mechanization, the platform-coordinate frame is a computed orientation relative to that where the accelerometer axes actually exist that is determined using the inertial instrument measurements. In the errorless case the platform frame is, of course, again coincident with the local-level reference frame. In a strapdown system where there is no gimbal set and where the inertial instruments are "strapped" to the carrying-vehicle frame, the transformation matrix between the platform frame and the instrument frame is computed using the system computed spatial rate of the local-level frame ω_c, minus the gyro measurements of angular rate of the vehicle frame relative to inertial space ω_g, both expressed in the local-level frame

$$\nu_c = \omega_c - [P]_c\omega_g. \tag{8}$$

For an alternative gimbaled inertial system such as space-stable system where the instruments remain fixed relative to inertial space, the platform-to-instrument frame-transformation matrix is obtained as the system-computed spatial angular rate, expressed in the local-level frame ω_c:

$$\nu_c = \omega_c, \tag{9}$$

since the accelerometer axes are presumed fixed relative to inertial space.

In all of the mechanizations discussed thus far, the linear transformation or direction-cosine matrix from the accelerometer coordinate frame $[x, y, z]_a$ to the platform frame can be computed once initialization by alignment has been achieved, by integration of the matrix differential equation

$$[\dot{P}]_c = [\nu]_c [P]_c, \tag{10}$$

where the antisymmetric matrix of relative angular rates of the platform frame relative to the instrument frame in platform axes is defined as

$$[\nu]_c \triangleq \begin{bmatrix} 0 & \nu_z & -\nu_y \\ -\nu_z & 0 & \nu_x \\ \nu_y & -\nu_x & 0 \end{bmatrix}_c = \begin{cases} 0, & \text{Schuler-tuned platform,} \\ [\omega_c - [P]_c \omega_g], & \text{strapdown system} \\ [\omega_c], & \text{space-stable platform,} \end{cases}$$

$$\begin{bmatrix} x \\ y \\ z \end{bmatrix}_p = [P]_c \begin{bmatrix} x \\ y \\ z \end{bmatrix}_a, \tag{11}$$

$$[P]_c \triangleq \begin{bmatrix} \langle x_p, x_a \rangle & \langle x_p, y_a \rangle & \langle x_p, z_a \rangle \\ \langle y_p, x_a \rangle & \langle y_p, y_a \rangle & \langle y_p, z_a \rangle \\ \langle z_p, x_a \rangle & \langle z_p, y_a \rangle & \langle z_p, z_a \rangle \end{bmatrix}_c .$$

IV. ERROR-MODEL DEVELOPMENT

Using the three coordinate systems just defined, we may now develop a set of ten linear differential equations describing the propagation of error for the local-level coordinate-system navigation equations and the three different inertial instrument implementations just discussed. These ten equations describe the time rate of change of velocity difference δV, attitude error ϕ, position error $\delta\theta$, and elevation error δh.

A. *ERROR IN THE SYSTEM-COMPUTED VELOCITY*

The rate of change of velocity difference is obtained by first differencing the representation of the mechanized version of this equation employing actual values in the system computer [Eq. (A11) of the Appendix], with the representation of the acceleration equation for the local-level reference navigation frame [Eq. (A1) of the Appendix]. Since the accelerometer measurements are expressed in the platform-coordinate frame, their difference from the accelerometer measurements expressed in the reference frame due to the effects of attitude error is

$$\delta a \triangleq A_p - A = [\phi]A. \quad (12)$$

The system-computed Coriolis acceleration components are all determined from variables which reside in registers in the system computer. These system-computed values differ from the values of the same variables that correspond to the reference navigation-coordinate frame as defined here:

$$\delta V \triangleq V_c - V = \begin{bmatrix} \delta V_x \\ \delta V_y \\ \delta V_z \end{bmatrix}, \tag{13}$$

$$\delta \rho \triangleq \rho_c - \rho = \begin{bmatrix} \delta \rho_x \\ \delta \rho_y \\ \delta \rho_z \end{bmatrix}, \tag{14}$$

$$\delta \Omega \triangleq \Omega_c - \Omega = \begin{bmatrix} \delta \Omega_x \\ \delta \Omega_y \\ \delta \Omega_z \end{bmatrix}, \tag{15}$$

which upon examination of Eqs. (A2) and (A12) and ignoring the small effects of error in the computed radii of curvature, yields

$$\delta \rho_x = -\delta V_y R^{-1}, \quad \delta \rho_y = \delta V_x R^{-1}, \quad \delta \rho_z = \delta \dot{\alpha} + \delta \rho_V, \tag{16}$$

$$\delta \rho_V \triangleq \rho_{N_c} \tan \Phi_c - \rho_N \tan \Phi = \delta \rho_N \tan \Phi + \rho_N \, \delta \Phi \sec^2 \Phi,$$

$$\delta \rho_N = \delta \rho_x \sin \alpha + \delta \rho_y \cos \alpha + \rho_E \, \delta \alpha,$$

where to first order, R can be assumed to be a nominal radius for the earth. Further, to first-order,

$$\begin{aligned} \delta \Omega_x &= -\Omega \sin \Phi \sin \alpha \, \delta \Phi + \Omega \cos \Phi \cos \alpha \, \delta \alpha, \\ \delta \Omega_y &= -\Omega \sin \Phi \cos \alpha \, \delta \Phi - \Omega \cos \Phi \sin \alpha \, \delta \alpha, \\ \delta \Omega_z &= \Omega \cos \Phi \, \delta \Phi, \end{aligned} \tag{17}$$

which with Eq. (4) can be written as

$$\begin{aligned} &\delta \Omega_x = \Omega_y \, \delta \theta_z - \Omega_z \, \delta \theta_y, \quad \delta \Omega_y = \Omega_z \, \delta \theta_x - \Omega_x \, \delta \theta_z, \\ &\delta \Omega_z = \Omega_x \, \delta \theta_y - \Omega_y \, \delta \theta_x, \end{aligned} \tag{18}$$

or

$$\delta\Omega = [\delta\theta]\Omega = \Omega \times \delta\theta. \tag{19}$$

Combining Eqs. (12) thru (18), we may write an equation for the difference between (A11) and (A1) to first order as

$$\delta\dot{V} \triangleq \dot{V}_c - \dot{V} = \begin{bmatrix} \delta\dot{V}_x \\ \delta\dot{V}_y \\ \delta\dot{V}_z \end{bmatrix}$$

$$\approx [\phi]A + [\delta\rho + 2\,\delta\Omega]V - [\delta V](\rho + 2\Omega) + \delta\gamma + \nabla, \tag{20}$$

where the following skew-symmetric matrix definitions have been employed:

$$[\delta\rho + 2\,\delta\Omega] \triangleq \begin{bmatrix} 0 & [\delta\rho + 2\,\delta\Omega]_z & -[\delta\rho + 2\,\delta\Omega]_y \\ -[\delta\rho + 2\,\delta\Omega]_z & 0 & [\delta\rho + 2\,\delta\Omega]_x \\ [\delta\rho + 2\,\delta\Omega]_y & -[\delta\rho + 2\,\delta\Omega]_x & 0 \end{bmatrix},$$

$$[\delta V] \triangleq \begin{bmatrix} 0 & \delta V_z & -\delta V_y \\ -\delta V_z & 0 & \delta V_x \\ \delta V_y & -\delta V_x & 0 \end{bmatrix}, \tag{21}$$

and

$$\delta\gamma = \begin{bmatrix} \delta\gamma_x \\ \delta\gamma_y \\ \delta\gamma_z \end{bmatrix} = \gamma - \gamma_c \tag{22}$$

represents the error in the computation of the gravity vector from the analytical model due solely to error in the system-computed geodetic position and elevation. If an ellipsoidal equipotential surface is assumed for the gravity model, $\delta\gamma_x = \delta\gamma_y = 0$, and $\delta\gamma_z$ is in error due only to error in system-computed latitude and elevation.

$$\nabla = \begin{bmatrix} \nabla_x \\ \nabla_y \\ \nabla_z \end{bmatrix}$$

represents the generalized accelerometer measurement error due to all instrument-related error sources transformed onto the reference local-level coordinate frame plus the difference between actual gravity and that represented by the gravity model. Note that if an ellipsoidal equipotential surface is assumed for the gravity model, error exists along the level axes due to the deflection of the vertical to the geoid relative to that of the ellipsoid [3]. The error exists along the vertical due to model error for the intensity of the gravity.

At this point, some remarks should be made about the meaning of the various quantities previously defined. Generally, the definition of "error" that has been selected stands for the simple difference between the value of the variable as it physically exists in the system computer and the value of the variable as interpreted in the reference local-level navigation coordinate system when determined without error. For the case of the earth rate, the error [Eq. (18)] corresponds to the difference between the earth rate determined in the computer coordinates and that for the reference coordinates. For velocity error [Eqs. and (13) and (20)], this is not the case, for by construction, the velocity error which arises from the integration of Eq. (20) results from the transformation error ϕ between the platform and reference-coordinate systems, the errors in the computed Coriolis acceleration, and the gravity vector components and, of course, any measurement errors associated with the accelerometers.

If, as occurs in some applications, one desires to express the acceleration measurement in an earth-fixed coordinate frame prior to integration, as [X, Y, Z] shown in Fig. 1, then the total transformation error must include the effects of the position error $\delta\theta$ of Eq. (4), because the measurements A_p must be transformed through the system-computed direction-cosine matrix $[D]_c$ of the Appendix to the earth-fixed frame. In this case, however, the mechanization equations which are integrated to compute the system velocity are different from Eq. (A1) because the earth-fixed frame in which the integration is performed is obviously not rotating with respect to the earth as is the local-level navigation frame. The correct mechanization equation for the rate of change of inertial system velocity relative to the earth with respect to earth-fixed coordinates is, in error-free vector form,

$$\dot{V}_e = A_e - 2\Omega_e \times V_e - \gamma_e, \tag{23}$$

where

$$\dot{V}_e \triangleq \begin{bmatrix} \dot{V}_X \\ \dot{V}_Y \\ \dot{V}_Z \end{bmatrix}$$

denotes the rate of change of velocity relative to the earth with respect to the earth-fixed frame which when integrated in the earth-fixed frame yields system velocity with respect to the earth in the earth-fixed frame;

$$A_e \triangleq \begin{bmatrix} A_X \\ A_Y \\ A_Z \end{bmatrix}$$

is the specific force measured by the accelerometers due to the true system acceleration and the modeled gravity at the true system position, expressed in the earth-fixed frame;

$$\Omega_e \triangleq \begin{bmatrix} 0 \\ \Omega \\ 0 \end{bmatrix}$$

is the earth rotation rate expressed in the earth-fixed frame of Fig. 1; and

$$\gamma_e \triangleq \begin{bmatrix} \gamma_X \\ \gamma_Y \\ \gamma_Z \end{bmatrix}$$

is the projection of the modeled gravity vector at the true system position onto the earth-fixed frame. One mechanized version of Eq. (23) that would be integrated in the system computer is

$$\dot{V}_{e_c} = [D]_c^T A_p - 2\Omega_e \times V_{e_c} - \gamma_{e_c},$$

where all components are expressed in the earth-fixed coordinate system prior to integration. Note that the earth-rate components are known exactly in the earth-fixed frame, but that the direction and magnitude of the gravity-vector components relative to these coordinates are a function of the system-computed latitude, longitude, and elevation and hence are subject to the errors in these variables. The equation for the difference between Eqs. (23) and (24) is then to first order

$$\delta V_e \triangleq V_{e_c} - V_e \approx [D]^T[\psi]A - 2[\delta V_e]\Omega_e$$
$$+ [D]^T\{[\delta\theta]\gamma + \delta\gamma\} + \nabla_e, \qquad (25)$$

where relative to the local-level reference frame,

$$[\psi] \triangleq \begin{bmatrix} 0 & (\phi - \delta\theta)_z & -(\phi - \delta\theta)_y \\ -(\phi - \delta\theta)_z & 0 & (\phi - \delta\theta)_x \\ (\phi - \delta\theta)_y & -(\phi - \delta\theta)_x & 0 \end{bmatrix} \tag{26}$$

represents angular error incurred in the transformation of the accelerometer measurements from the platform frame to an earth-fixed frame. Because $\delta\theta$ is small, we have here

$$\begin{bmatrix} x \\ y \\ z \end{bmatrix} = [I - \delta\theta] \begin{bmatrix} x \\ y \\ z \end{bmatrix}_c . \tag{27}$$

Note that the computer frame is not an earth-fixed frame but is related to an earth-fixed frame through the computed position and wander angle $[\Phi, \lambda, \alpha]_c$. Further,

$$\begin{bmatrix} x \\ y \\ z \end{bmatrix}_p = [I + \phi][I - \delta\theta] \begin{bmatrix} x \\ y \\ z \end{bmatrix}_c \approx [I + \psi] \begin{bmatrix} x \\ y \\ z \end{bmatrix}_c . \tag{28}$$

B. ERROR IN THE SYSTEM-COMPUTED POSITION AND ELEVATION

Because the direction cosine matrix $[D]_c$ defines the system-computed latitude, longitude, and wander angle, the perturbation of this matrix due to error in these three independent variables is of interest. From definition (A5), the following perturbations relative to $[\delta\lambda, \delta\Phi, \delta\alpha]$ can be obtained directly, and upon employing the definition, (A5,4) yields, not surprisingly, the second equivalence:

$$
\begin{aligned}
\delta\langle X, x\rangle &= -\delta\lambda(\cos\alpha\sin\lambda + \sin\alpha\sin\Phi\cos\lambda)\\
&\quad - \delta\alpha(\sin\alpha\cos\lambda + \cos\alpha\sin\Phi\sin\lambda)\\
&\quad - \delta\phi(\sin\alpha\cos\Phi\sin\lambda),\\
&= \delta\theta_z\langle X, y\rangle - \delta\theta_y\langle X, z\rangle,\\
\delta\langle X, y\rangle &= \delta\lambda(\sin\alpha\sin\lambda - \cos\alpha\sin\Phi\cos\lambda)\\
&\quad + \delta\alpha(\sin\alpha\sin\Phi\sin\lambda - \cos\alpha\cos\lambda)\\
&\quad - \delta\Phi(\cos\alpha\cos\Phi\sin\lambda),\\
&= \delta\theta_x\langle X, z\rangle - \delta\theta_z\langle X, x\rangle,\\
\delta\langle X, z\rangle &= \delta\Phi(\cos\Phi\sin\lambda) + \delta\lambda(\cos\Phi\cos\lambda),\\
&= \delta\theta_y\langle X, x\rangle - \delta\theta_x\langle X, y\rangle,\\
\delta\langle Y, x\rangle &= -\delta\alpha(\cos\alpha\cos\Phi) - \delta\Phi(\sin\alpha\sin\Phi),\\
&= \delta\theta_z\langle Y, y\rangle - \delta\theta_y\langle Y, z\rangle,\\
\delta\langle Y, y\rangle &= -\delta\alpha(\sin\alpha\cos\Phi) - \delta\Phi(\cos\alpha\sin\Phi),\\
&= \delta\theta_x\langle Y, z\rangle - \delta\theta_z\langle Y, x\rangle,\\
\delta\langle Y, z\rangle &= \delta\Phi\cos\Phi = \delta\theta_y\langle Y, x\rangle - \delta\theta_x\langle Y, y\rangle,\\
\delta\langle Z, x\rangle &= \delta\lambda(\sin\alpha\sin\Phi\sin\lambda - \cos\alpha\sin\lambda)\\
&\quad + \delta\alpha(\sin\alpha\sin\lambda - \cos\alpha\sin\Phi\cos\lambda)\\
&\quad - \delta\Phi(\sin\alpha\cos\Phi\cos\lambda),\\
&= \delta\theta_z\langle Z, y\rangle - \delta\theta_y\langle Z, z\rangle,\\
\delta\langle Z, y\rangle &= \delta\lambda(\sin\alpha\cos\lambda + \cos\alpha\sin\Phi\sin\lambda)\\
&\quad + \delta\alpha(\cos\alpha\sin\lambda + \sin\alpha\sin\Phi\cos\lambda)\\
&\quad - \delta\lambda(\cos\alpha\cos\Phi\cos\lambda),\\
&= \delta\theta_x\langle Z, z\rangle - \delta\theta_z\langle Z, x\rangle,\\
\delta\langle Z, z\rangle &= -\delta\lambda(\cos\Phi\sin\lambda) - \delta\Phi(\sin\Phi\cos\lambda),\\
&= \delta\theta_y\langle Z, x\rangle - \delta\theta_x\langle Z, y\rangle.
\end{aligned}
\tag{29}
$$

Clearly,

$$[\delta D] \triangleq [D]_c - [D] \approx [\delta\theta][D], \tag{30}$$

$$\begin{bmatrix} x \\ y \\ z \end{bmatrix} = [D_c - \delta D] \begin{bmatrix} X \\ Y \\ Z \end{bmatrix}.$$

Thus, as stated previously, we have confirmed that the perturbation vector angle $\delta\theta$ represents a rotation from the local-level reference frame to the computed geodetic frame. Proceeding formally, we may differentiate the first-order approximation in Eq. (30) to obtain

$$[\dot{\delta D}] = [\delta\dot{\theta}][D] + [\delta\theta][\dot{D}] \tag{31}$$

which from Eq. (A4),

$$[\dot{D}] = [\rho][D], \tag{32}$$

yields for Eq. (31),

$$[\dot{\delta D}] = \{[\delta\dot{\theta}] + [\delta\theta][\rho]\}[D], \tag{33}$$

and, further, differentiating Eq. (30) and using definitions, we obtain to first order,

$$[\dot{\delta D}] \approx [\delta\rho][D] + [\rho][\delta D] \triangleq [\dot{D}]_c - [\dot{D}], \tag{34}$$

where

$$[\delta\rho] \triangleq [\rho]_c - [\rho], \tag{35}$$

using Eq. (30) yields:

$$[\dot{\delta D}] \approx \{[\delta\rho] + [\rho][\delta\theta]\}[D]. \tag{36}$$

Note that $\delta\rho$ denotes the difference in the angular rate of the system-computed geodetic frame and the local-level frame, both taken with respect to the earth frame, whereas $\delta\dot{\theta}$ denotes the angular rate of change of the system-computed geodetic frame taken with respect to the local-level geodetic frame. Because [D] is invertible, we obtain from Eqs. (31) and (36)

$$[\delta\dot{\theta}] = [\delta\rho] + [\rho][\delta\theta] - [\delta\theta][\rho], \tag{37}$$

or in scalar form on expansion,

$$\begin{aligned} \delta\dot{\theta}_x &= \delta\rho_x + \rho_z\,\delta\theta_y - \rho_y\,\delta\theta_z, \\ \delta\dot{\theta}_y &= \delta\rho_y + \rho_x\,\delta\theta_z - \rho_z\,\delta\theta_x, \\ \delta\dot{\theta}_z &= \delta\rho_z + \rho_y\,\delta\theta_x - \rho_x\,\delta\theta_y, \end{aligned} \tag{38}$$

or in vector form,

$$\delta\dot{\theta} = \delta\rho - \rho \times \delta\theta. \tag{39}$$

Equation (39) merely indicates that the rate of change of angular error of the system-computed geodetic frame relative to the local-level reference frame $\delta\dot{\theta}$ is simply the sum of the rate of change of this angular error relative to the earth, $\delta\rho$ or $\delta\dot{\theta}_e$, and the Coriolis effect due to the rotation rate between the computed geodetic frame and the earth. The second term in Eq. (39) can also be viewed as the error in resolving the correct relative angular rate vector ρ from the earth-fixed frame to the local-level reference frame due to the error $\delta\theta$ given knowledge of its orientation when the system-computed latitude, longitude, and wander angle are employed.

The final position-error equation is that for the elevation of the system relative to the earth. Elevation error is obtained by integrating the difference between the system-computed and actual system velocity relative to the earth as projected onto the local vertical axis:

$$\delta\dot{h}_c = V_{z_c} - V_z \triangleq \delta V_z. \tag{40}$$

C. ERROR IN THE PLATFORM-FRAME ORIENTATION

To derive the dynamics of the attitude error ϕ of the platform frame relative to the local-level reference frame, we can proceed in a manner analogous to that given earlier for the angular position error. First, the difference between the system-computed platform- to instrument-frame transformation $[P]_c$ and the local-level- to instrument-frame transformation $[P]$ is derived:

$$[\delta P] \triangleq [P]_c - [P] = [\phi][P], \tag{41}$$

where

$$\begin{bmatrix} x \\ y \\ z \end{bmatrix} = [P]\begin{bmatrix} x \\ y \\ z \end{bmatrix}_a, \quad \begin{bmatrix} x \\ y \\ z \end{bmatrix}_p = [I + \phi]\begin{bmatrix} x \\ y \\ z \end{bmatrix}, \quad \begin{bmatrix} x \\ y \\ z \end{bmatrix}_p \triangleq [P]_c\begin{bmatrix} x \\ y \\ z \end{bmatrix}_a, \tag{42}$$

have been used. Differentiation of Eq. (41) yields

$$[\delta\dot{P}] = \{[\dot{\phi}] + [\phi][\nu]\}[P], \tag{43}$$

where $[\dot{\phi}]$ is expressed and differentiated with respect to the local-level frame. Further,

$$\begin{aligned} [\delta\dot{P}] &= [\dot{P}]_c - [\dot{P}] \\ &= [\nu]_c[P]_c - [\nu][P] \approx \{[\delta\nu] + [\nu][\phi]\}[P], \end{aligned} \tag{44}$$

where

$$[\delta\nu] \triangleq [\nu]_c - [\nu] \tag{45}$$

is the difference between the angular rate of the system-computed platform frame with respect to the instrument frame expressed in the platform frame $[\nu]_c$ and the angular rate of the local-level frame with respect to the instrument frame $[\nu]$

expressed in the local-level frame. Equating Eqs. (43) and (44) using the invertibility of [P] yields

$$[\dot{\phi}] = [\delta\nu] + [\nu][\phi] - [\phi][\nu], \tag{46}$$

which yields the vector form

$$\dot{\phi} = \delta\nu + \phi \times \nu. \tag{47}$$

It is of interest to specify Eq. (47) for the three instrumentation mechanizations discussed earlier: Schuler tuned, space stable, and strapdown. In the case of a Schuler-tuned mechanization, the platform frame is the instrument frame, hence ν_c is zero. However, the instrument frame rotates relative to the local-level frame as the gyros are precessed at the computed spatial rate ω_c applied about the platform-frame coordinates as opposed to the local-level frame coordinates. The instrument frame also rotates relative to the local-level frame due to the generalized drift rate of the gyros ϵ, hence,

$$\delta\nu = \delta\omega + \phi \times \omega + \epsilon = \dot{\phi}, \tag{48}$$

where $\delta\omega$ denotes the scalar difference of the components of the vectors ω_c and ω:

$$\delta\omega \triangleq \begin{bmatrix} \omega_{x_c} - \omega_x \\ \omega_{y_c} - \omega_y \\ \omega_{z_c} - \omega_z \end{bmatrix} = \delta\rho + \delta\Omega, \tag{49}$$

and $\phi \times \omega$ expresses the rotation rate of the platform frame relative to the local-level frame when the local-level spatial angular rate components are applied in the misaligned platform frame even if they are well known.

For the space-stable mechanization,

$$\nu_c \triangleq \omega_c, \tag{50}$$

whereas the angular rate of the local-level frame relative to the instrument frame is

$$\nu = \omega - \epsilon, \tag{51}$$

where the components of ν are about the local-level-frame coordinates. Hence for the space-stable mechanization using Eqs. (47), (50), and (51), we have

$$\dot{\phi} = \delta\omega + \phi \times \omega + \epsilon. \tag{52}$$

For the strapdown mechanization,

$$\nu_c \triangleq \omega_c - [P]_c \dot{\theta}_g, \tag{53}$$

whereas the angular rate of the local-level frame relative to the instrument frame is

$$\nu = \omega - [P]\dot{\theta}, \tag{54}$$

where we define the generalized gyro drift rate about the instrument axes ϵ_g as the difference between the actual instrument-frame-rotation rate relative to inertial space $\dot{\theta}$ and the gyro output measurements $\dot{\theta}_g$:

$$\epsilon_g \triangleq \dot{\theta} - \dot{\theta}_g, \tag{55}$$

which yields the generalized drift rate about the local-level coordinates as

$$\epsilon = [P]\epsilon_g. \tag{56}$$

Hence, using Eqs. (41), (55), and (56) and differencing Eqs. (53) and (54), we have to first-order

$$\delta\nu = \delta\omega - [\phi][P]\dot{\theta} + \epsilon. \tag{57}$$

Consequently, using Eqs. (47), (51), and (57) we have
$\dot{\phi} = \delta\omega - [\phi][P]\dot{\theta} + \epsilon + \phi \times \{\omega - [P]\dot{\theta}\}$, which as

$$[\phi][P]\dot{\theta} = -\phi \times [P]\dot{\theta}, \tag{58}$$

yields

$$\dot{\phi} = \delta\omega + \phi \times \omega + \epsilon \tag{59}$$

to describe the dynamics of the attitude error for the strap-down-instrument mechanization. We note in summary that regardless of the three mechanizations employed, the dynamics of the attitude-error propagation [Eqs. (48), (52), and (59)] are identical in form. Note, however, that the generalized drift-rate vector ϵ employed in these equations is obtained by transforming the drift rate about the instrument axes to the local-level frame coordinate axes.

D. *ANGULAR ROTATION BETWEEN THE PLATFORM AND SYSTEM-COMPUTED GEODETIC FRAMES*

The dynamics of the angular rotation from the system-computed geodetic frame to the platform frame

$$\psi \triangleq \phi - \delta\theta \tag{60}$$

relative to the local-level frame can be obtained by differencing the corresponding individual rates as derived earlier [Eqs. (39) and (59):

$$\dot{\psi} \triangleq \dot{\phi} - \delta\dot{\theta} = \delta\rho - \delta\theta \times \Omega + \phi \times \omega + \epsilon - \delta\rho - \delta\theta \times \rho, \tag{61}$$

or

$$\dot{\psi} = \psi \times \omega + \epsilon. \tag{62}$$

The advantage of Eq. (62) is that it is simpler to propagate than the attitude-error expression [Eq. (59)]. Knowledge of ψ and $\delta\theta$ allows determination of ϕ at any instant of time by

Eq. (60). Noting that in Eq. (62) the time rate of change of ψ is relative to the local-level frame that rotates with angular rate ω with respect to inertial space, we can conclude that

$$\dot{\psi}_I \triangleq \dot{\psi} + \omega \times \psi = \epsilon, \tag{63}$$

where $\dot{\psi}_I$ denotes the time rate of change of ψ relative to inertial space. In other words, the rate of change of ψ viewed from inertial space is simply the generalized drift rate of the system gyros projected onto the inertial frame coordinate axes [4].

V. RELATIONSHIP BETWEEN COORDINATE FRAMES

The correspondence between the coordinate frames discussed previously can be summarized conveniently in Fig. 2. Here, the arrows indicate which direction the transformation denoted is used in obtaining the ensuing coordinate frame. Because

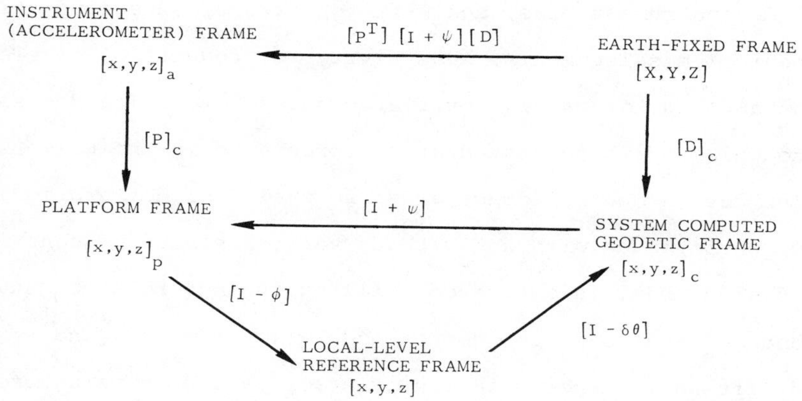

Fig. 2. Relationship between coordinate frames.

all transformations are orthogonal, however, the inverse transformation is realized by the transpose.

VI. KALMAN FILTER MODELING CONSIDERATIONS

Having developed the fundamental linear differential equations that describe the error propagation for inertial navigation systems, we are now in a position to discuss various simplifications that have been made to implement operational Kalman filter designs. The objective of such simplifications in a specific application is to reduce the computer memory and duty-cycle requirements without incurring unacceptable degradation in the performance of the operational filter.

Simplifications that are investigated by Kalman-filter design engineers generally fall into two categories. The first of these categories deals with the question of how many of the modelable instrument-error states present in the error-projection vectors for accelerometer measurement error ∇ and generalized gyro drift rate ϵ need to be included as states in the Kalman filter. The elemental states to be considered include instrument bias, scale-factor errors, sensitive axis mechanical misalignments, sensitivity to products of acceleration and angular rates, correlated noise, etc. The decision as to which of these states are incorporated in the Kalman filter design model is made after several design iterations in which performance with and without various states present in the design model is evaluated, "filter tuning" to accommodate absence of states in the design model is performed, and tradeoffs in the specification of error-parameter values for the actual system have been investigated. Such a design process is usually lengthy and requires the use of highly sophisticated simulation software. These issues do not concern us further here.

The second category of simplifications addresses the error dynamics of the navigation-system errors [Eqs. (20), (39), and (59)] and is what interests us here. Two types of simplification are of interest: (1) reduction of the modeled error states as previously mentioned, and (2) reduction of the dynamic coupling between the error states that are retained. Simplifications that have proved especially useful in operational filter design are the following:

(1) vertical axis model elimination;

(2) level-axes Coriolis acceleration elimination;

(3) use of the "ψ equation" [Eq. (62)]; and

(4) alternative definitions of azimuth error;

and these are discussed in detail in the following sections.

A. *VERTICAL AXIS MODEL ELIMINATION*

The subset of the error-model equations given previously that describes the propagation of error for the vertical axis of the local-level coordinate-frame navigation equations is

$$\delta\dot{h} = \delta V_z, \qquad \delta\dot{V}_z = \phi_y A_x - \phi_x A_y + \delta C_z + \delta\gamma_z + \nabla_z, \tag{64}$$

where the error in the system-computed Coriolis acceleration component along the vertical axis is

$$\begin{aligned}\delta C_z \triangleq\ & (\delta\rho + 2\,\delta\Omega)_y V_x - (\delta\rho + 2\,\delta\Omega)_x V_y \\ & + (\rho + 2\Omega)_y\,\delta V_x - (\rho + 2\Omega)_x\,\delta V_y.\end{aligned} \tag{65}$$

Owing to the dependence of the normal gravity γ on the elevation [3],

$$(\partial\gamma/\partial h) = -2\gamma J - 2\Omega^2, \tag{66}$$

where $J = 0.5[M^{-1} + N^{-1}]$ is the mean curvature of the ellipsoid and M and N are the meridional and normal radii of curvature, the error in system-computed elevation leads to divergence of the vertical axis errors (δh, δV_z). Because of this effect, the system elevation computation error is normally bounded in aircraft applications by the use of a reference source of elevation such as a barometric altimeter, which is also used in a servoloop arrangement to bound the vertical velocity error and bias the error in the vertical acceleration measurements. This is done even when the level-axes computations are uncorrected with other reference sensor data and are operating in the "free-inertial" mode.

Because conventional fixed-gain error-control mechanizations using reference elevation measurements have obtained adequate vertical axis performance in most applications, this channel is often ignored in the application of Kalman filtering to inertial systems.[2] Further, since there is little cross coupling from the vertical axis to the level axes, there is little need to model the vertical axis error states in obtaining good control over the level-axis error states. In this regard the elevation error does not affect at all the propagation of error for the level axes, whereas the vertical velocity

[2]*Exceptions to this rule can occur when very precise measurements of elevation are available, which, if their use is to be optimal, requires full modeling of the vertical axis error propagation. In some cases, corrections can be obtained for level-axis tilts due to their acceleration-dependent effect on vertical velocity error in Eq. (64).*

error affects level-axis error propagation only through error in computation of the level-axes Coriolis acceleration components, as discussed next.

B. LEVEL-AXES CORIOLIS ACCELERATION ELIMINATION

The errors in the system-computed level-axes Coriolis acceleration components are

$$\begin{aligned}\delta C_x &\triangleq (\delta\rho + 2\,\delta\Omega)_z V_y - (\delta\rho + 2\,\delta\Omega)_y V_z \\ &\quad + (\rho + 2\Omega)_z\,\delta V_y - (\rho + 2\Omega)_y\,\delta V_z, \\ \delta C_y &\triangleq (\delta\rho + 2\,\delta\Omega)_x V_z - (\delta\rho + 2\,\delta\Omega)_z V_x \\ &\quad + (\rho + 2\Omega)_x\,\delta V_z - (\rho + 2\Omega)_z\,\delta V_x.\end{aligned} \tag{67}$$

In most aircraft applications, the vertical velocity V_z is nominally zero, except at a few times during flight. Consequently, modeling of such an effect would only be considered if small transient effects were important. For example, even if the vertical velocity were 100 fps (feet per second), the system-computed latitude error were a large 10 nautical miles (nm), thereby inducing an error in the computed earth rate of 0.03 $\widehat{\text{sec}}$/sec at midlatitudes (45°)[3] and the system velocity error were a large 10 fps (0.1 $\widehat{\text{sec}}$/sec), the acceleration error for the Coriolis components associated with V_z would be less than 3 mgal.

Due to bounding of the vertical velocity error to a few feet per second via the vertical axis mechanization previously discussed, the magnitude of the acceleration-error term due to δV_z is substantially less than the uncertainty in the

[3] *Assumed as an average condition.*

gravity-model terms $\gamma_{x,y,z}$ present in the full velocity-error equations [Eq. (20)]. For example, for a 1-fps error and midlatitude operation of a vehicle traveling at 1000 fps in a direction reinforcing the level-axis earth-rate terms, the Coriolis acceleration error is less than 5 mgal, which is small compared to the gravity-model uncertainty of 40-50 mgal on a worldwide basis. These effects are a fortunate coincidence for the Kalman filter designer because he can normally eliminate these dynamical vertical axis dependencies from his design model, along with the vertical axis model as noted previously.

This type of magnitude-of-effect analysis can be extended to the Coriolis error components involving the vehicle level-velocity components $V_{x,y}$ and the error in their system-computed values. One finds again for midlatitude operation with vehicle-velocity components of 1000 fps, errors of 10 fps in the system-computed velocity components and 10-nm latitude error, the magnitude of the error in these system-computed Coriolis acceleration terms is less than 10 mgal.[4] Consequently, for most applications the error in the system-computed Coriolis acceleration components can be ignored on a magnitude basis relative to a more dominating source of "noise" that arises from the uncertainty in the gravity model. There are some instances, however, where the error in these latter system-computed Coriolis terms may be important on a dynamical basis. Inspection of free-inertial error-propagation curves reveals that the cross coupling of the level-axis velocity

[4] *Here, we have presumed use of nonsingular forms of the navigation equations where* ρ_z *is comparable to the earth-rate component about the vertical axis.*

errors between axes induces modulation of the Schuler-error oscillations with the long-term Foucault period obtained as

$$\tau_f = (2\pi/\Omega_z), \tag{68}$$

which is 24 hr at the pole, 33.85 hr at latitude 45°, and infinite at the equator. Normally, however, when a Kalman filter is employed, the corrections to the inertial system errors using other reference sensors are obtained at substantially higher frequencies than involved here that "quench" such long-term oscillations and make them irrelevant. All in all, then, in most cases, the Kalman filter designer discovers that the dynamical coupling of errors associated with the error in the system-computed Coriolis acceleration error components may be deleted from his filter design model.

C. USE OF THE ψ EQUATION

As noted previously, the ψ equation [Eq. (62)] provides an alternative way of representing attitude error that is simpler than the attitude error-propagation Eq. (59), provided that position error is propagated via Eq. (39) such that attitude can be recovered at any time instant. Hence in most Kalman filter design models for inertial systems, Eqs. (69) and (70) are employed prior to further simplification, which may be possible in some applications, to describe position and attitude error propagation:

$$\delta\dot{\theta} = \delta\rho + \delta\theta \times \rho, \tag{69}$$

$$\dot{\psi} = \psi \times \omega + \epsilon, \tag{70}$$

where attitude error can be computed at any time via

$$\phi = \psi + \delta\theta. \tag{71}$$

D. *ALTERNATIVE DEFINITIONS OF AZIMUTH ERROR*

The two attitude errors $\phi_{x,y}$ define the tilt of the platform frame relative to the reference frame with ϕ_z defining the azimuth misalignment. Because error in system-computed position is defined by the error in latitude $\delta\Phi$ and longitude $\delta\lambda$, it is clear by Eq. (4) that the two level-position-error variables $\delta\theta_{x,y}$ are sufficient to define position error with $\delta\theta_z$ as an error variable to define the azimuth misalignment of the system-computed geodetic frame owing to error in the computed wander angle $\delta\alpha$ and error in knowledge of the north direction owing to an error in knowledge of longitude. Consequently, there appears to be a form of redundance in the system azimuth-misalignment definition that, if properly exploited, might lead to simplification of the describing error-model equations by reducing by one the number of azimuth-error states to be considered. A review of the material presented earlier reveals that the behavior of the wander-angle of the reference frame α has not specifically been defined. The discussion up to this point has only assumed that whatever this behavior is, the resulting error variables

$$\phi_z \triangleq \alpha_p - \alpha, \qquad \delta\theta_z \triangleq \alpha_c - \alpha + \delta\lambda \sin \Phi \tag{72}$$

remain small such that second-order effects can be ignored, preserving the linearity of the error model.

In the following discussion we confine ourselves to nonsingular mechanizations of the local-level, wander-azimuth navigation mechanization equations as noted at Eqs. (A8) and (A9) of the Appendix. Without loss of generality and for ease of exposition, we consider the most common wander-azimuth mechanization wherein

$$\rho_{z_c} \triangleq 0, \tag{73}$$

which yields via Eq. (A13)

$$\dot{\alpha}_c = -\rho_{N_c} \tan \Phi_c, \tag{74}$$

and via the definition

$$\rho_z = -\delta\rho_z. \tag{75}$$

Note that a complete definition of all terms in the error equations (20), (39), and (62) now only requires specific definition of the terms ρ_z, $\delta\rho_z$ such that overall linearity is preserved. This specification is obtained by imposing two constraints: the first is Eq. (16), which by Eqs. (73) and (74) yields

$$\dot{\alpha} = -\rho_N \tan \Phi - \delta\rho_z; \tag{76}$$

the second results from the selection of azimuth behavior for the error model in accordance with one of the alternatives discussed later which then obtains the specification of $\delta\rho_z$.

1. The Case of the Eight-State Level-Axes Error Model

To what might be termed the "normal" error model we apply the constraint

$$\rho_z = 0, \tag{77}$$

which yields the result via Eq. (75) that

$$\delta\rho_z = 0. \tag{78}$$

Clearly, Eqs. (77) and (78) are small so that an eight-state linear model for the error propagation is obtained using Eqs. (20), (39), (62), (77), and (78). The full set of eight differential equations are summarized in Table I where the additional simplifying assumption of nominally constant altitude of flight

$$V_z = 0, \quad A_z = \gamma \tag{79}$$

has also been made. An additional property of this error model not fundamental to the error propagation itself is seen to be, via Eq. (76),

$$\dot{\alpha} = -\rho_N \tan \Phi. \tag{80}$$

Table I. A Comparison of Three-Level Axes Linear Error Models for the Local-Level, Wander-Azimuth ($\rho_{z_c} = 0$, $\omega_{z_c} = \Omega_{z_c}$) Navigation Equations for Nominally Constant Altitude ($V_z = 0$, $A_z = g$)[a,b]

"Normal" eight-state error model

$$\delta\dot{\theta}_x = \delta\rho_x - \rho_y\,\delta\theta_z$$

$$\delta\dot{\theta}_y = \delta\rho_y + \rho_x\,\delta\theta_z$$

$$\delta\dot{\theta}_z = \rho_y\,\delta\theta_x - \rho_x\,\delta\theta_y$$

$$\delta\dot{V}_x = (\psi + \delta\theta)_z A_y - (\psi + \delta\theta)_y \gamma + 2\Omega_z\,\delta V_y + 2V_y\,\delta\Omega_z + \delta\gamma_x + \nabla_x$$

$$\delta\dot{V}_y = -(\psi + \delta\theta)_z A_x + (\psi + \delta\theta)_x \gamma - 2\Omega_z\,\delta V_x - 2V_x\,\delta\Omega_z + \delta\gamma_y + \nabla_y$$

$$\delta\rho_z = -\rho_z = 0$$

$$\dot{\alpha} = -\rho_N \tan \Phi$$

(Table I continues)

(Table I continued)

Seven-state $\delta\theta_z \equiv 0$ error model

$$\delta\dot{\theta}_x = \delta\rho_x$$

$$\delta\dot{\theta}_y = \delta\rho_y$$

$$\delta\dot{V}_x = \psi_z A_y - (\psi + \delta\theta)_y \gamma + 2\Omega_z\,\delta V_y + \delta\gamma_x$$
$$+ V_y\{(\rho + 2\Omega_x\,\delta\theta_y - (\rho + 2\Omega)_y\,\delta\theta_x\} + \nabla_x$$

$$\delta\dot{V}_y = -\psi_z A_x + (\psi + \delta\theta)_x \gamma - 2\Omega_z\,\delta V_x + \delta\gamma_y$$
$$- V_x\{(\rho + 2\Omega)_x\,\delta\theta_y - (\rho + 2\Omega)_y\,\delta\theta_x\} + \nabla_y$$

$$\delta\rho_z = -\rho_z = \rho_x\,\delta\theta_y - \rho_y\,\delta\theta_x, \qquad \psi_z \equiv \phi_z$$

$$\dot{\alpha} = -\rho_N \tan\Phi + \rho_z, \qquad \delta\alpha = -\delta\lambda \sin\Phi$$

Seven-state $\phi_z \equiv 0$ error model

$$\delta\dot{\theta}_x = \delta\rho_x + \rho_y\psi_z$$

$$\delta\dot{\theta}_y = \delta\rho_y - \rho_x\psi_z$$

$$\delta\dot{V}_x = -(\psi + \delta\theta)_y \gamma + 2\Omega_z\,\delta V_y + \delta\gamma_x + \nabla_x$$
$$+ V_y\{(\rho + 2\Omega)_x\,\delta\theta_y - (\rho + 2\Omega)_y\,\delta\theta_x - \dot{\psi}_z\}$$

$$\delta\dot{V}_y = (\psi + \delta\theta)_x \gamma - 2\Omega_z\,\delta V_x + \delta\gamma_y + \nabla_y$$
$$- V_x\{(\rho + 2\Omega)_x\,\delta\theta_y - (\rho + 2\Omega)_y\,\delta\theta_x - \dot{\psi}_z\}$$

$$\delta\rho_z = -\rho_z = \rho_x\,\delta\theta_y - \rho_y\,\delta\theta_x - \dot{\psi}_z, \qquad \psi_z \equiv -\delta\theta_z$$

$$\dot{\alpha} = -\rho_N \tan\Phi + \rho_z, \qquad \delta\alpha = -\psi_z - \delta\lambda \sin\Phi$$

---

[a] *All three models employ the "ψ" equation for three of their states.*

[b] *The following equations apply to all three error models: vector equations (19), (20), (39), (49), (59), (60), (62); scalar equations (2), (3), (4), (16).*

2. The Case $\delta\theta_z \equiv 0$

In many applications it turns out as a practical matter that the "position" azimuth error term $\delta\theta_z$ of the "normal" error model is small relative to the platform azimuth misalignment ϕ_z and can simply be ignored in the Kalman filter design. This amounts to the presumption that the system-computed local-level geodetic frame obtains the same azimuth as the local-level reference frame even though it is angularly displaced from it.

Thus we have

$$\delta\theta_z \equiv 0, \tag{81}$$

yielding via Eq. (38), because

$$\delta\dot{\theta}_z = 0, \tag{82}$$

that

$$\delta\rho_z = \rho_x\,\delta\theta_y - \rho_y\,\delta\theta_x. \tag{83}$$

Hence from Eq. (75),

$$\rho_z = \rho_y\,\delta\theta_x - \rho_x\,\delta\theta_y. \tag{84}$$

Clearly again, because Eqs. (83) and (84) are small, a linear model for the error propagation is obtained from Eqs. (20), (39), (62), (83), and (84), except that in this case by Eq. (81) it has only seven instead of eight states. The seven differential equations for this model, ignoring second-order effects, are summarized in Table I. Additional properties of this error model by Eqs. (76), (60), and (4) are

$$\dot{\alpha} = -\rho_N \tan\Phi + \rho_y\,\delta\theta_x - \rho\,\delta\theta_y,$$

$$\psi_z \equiv \phi_z, \quad \delta\alpha = -\delta\lambda \sin\Phi. \tag{85}$$

3. The Case $\phi_z \equiv 0$

The natural alternative to the prior case is that where the azimuth of the platform frame coincides with that of the reference frame such that

$$\phi_z \equiv 0, \tag{86}$$

yielding via Eq. (59), because

$$\dot{\phi}_z = 0, \tag{87}$$

that

$$\delta\rho_z = -\delta\Omega_z + \phi_y\,\omega_x - \phi_x\,\omega_y - \epsilon_z, \tag{88}$$

which by Eqs. (7), (17), (60), and (62) can be expressed as

$$\delta\rho_z = \rho_x\,\delta\theta_y - \rho_y\,\delta\theta_x - \dot{\psi}_z. \tag{89}$$

Hence from Eq. (75),

$$\rho_z = \dot{\psi}_z + \rho_y\,\delta\theta_x - \rho_x\,\delta\theta_y. \tag{90}$$

Clearly again, because Eqs. (89) and (90) are small, a linear error model for the error propagation is obtained from Eqs. (20), (39), (62), (89), and (90), where in this case only seven states are present because the substitution

$$\delta\theta_z \equiv -\psi_z \tag{91}$$

is made. The seven differential equations for this model, ignoring second-order effects, are summarized in Table I. Additional properties of this model by Eqs. (76) and (4) are

$$\dot{\alpha} = -\rho_N \tan\Phi + \dot{\psi}_z + \rho_y\,\delta\theta_x - \rho_x\,\delta\theta_y,$$
$$\delta\alpha = -\psi_z - \delta\lambda \sin\Phi. \tag{92}$$

One advantage of this design model relative to the prior ap approximation can be appreciated by comparing the velocity- and position-error equations in the second and third columns of Table I. This comparison indicates that the effect of azimuth misalignment can be modeled at either the acceleration level ($\delta\theta_z \equiv 0$) or the velocity level ($\phi_z \equiv 0$). The latter model can often be exploited to reduce computer duty-cycle requirements in that the coefficient terms ($\rho_{x,y}$) are in effect integrals of the acceleration terms ($A_{x,y}$) and are smoother and easier to deal with in implementing the model in the digital computer.

E. A PARTICULAR KALMAN FILTER DESIGN MODEL

If we combine a number of the error-model simplifications discussed earlier (e.g., elimination of the vertical axis model and Coriolis acceleration, use of the ψ equation, and the azimuth-error definition $\phi_z \equiv 0$), the following relatively simple seven-state design model for a Kalman filter is obtained, which has proved useful in practice:

$$\delta\dot{\theta}_x = -\delta V_y R^{-1} + \rho_y \psi_z, \qquad \delta\dot{V}_x = -(\psi + \delta\theta)_y \gamma + (\delta\gamma_x + \nabla_x),$$

$$\delta\dot{\theta}_y = \delta V_x R^{-1} - \rho_x \psi_z, \qquad \delta\dot{V}_y = (\psi + \delta\theta)_x \gamma + (\delta\gamma_y + \nabla_y),$$

$$\dot{\psi}_x = \Omega_z \psi_y - \omega_y \psi_z + \epsilon_x, \qquad \dot{\psi}_y = -\Omega_z \psi_x + \omega_x \psi_z + \epsilon_y,$$

$$\dot{\psi}_z = \omega_y \psi_x - \omega_x \psi_y + \epsilon_z.$$

VII. CONCLUSION

This article has developed a full linear error model for the local-level, wander-azimuth navigation equations, describing error propagation for Schuler-tuned, space-stable, or strapdown inertial system instrumentations. From this model, alternative approximate linear models have been developed which in different operational applications have proved to be adequate as "design models" for the application of Kalman estimation theory.

APPENDIX. SUMMARY OF LOCAL-LEVEL NAVIGATION-MECHANIZATION EQUATIONS

The coordinate frame [x, y, z] referred to herein has two axes [x, y] in the level plane with the z axis normal to the earth's surface at the position of the inertial system. The rates of change of the inertial system velocity relative to the earth, taken relative to the rotating local-level coordinate frame and expressed along these axes, are

$$\dot{V} \triangleq \begin{bmatrix} \dot{V}_x \\ \dot{V}_y \\ \dot{V}_z \end{bmatrix} = A + C - \gamma, \tag{A1}$$

where

$$A \triangleq \begin{bmatrix} A_x \\ A_y \\ A_z \end{bmatrix}$$

is the specific force measured by the accelerometers due to the true system acceleration and modeled gravity components expressed along the local-level coordinate axes. These measurements can be obtained by direct instrumentation wherein the accelerometers are maintained coincident with the local-level coordinate system as in a Schuler-tuned mechanization, or transformed onto these coordinates as occurs with strapdown or space-stable inertial systems.

$$C \triangleq \begin{bmatrix} [(\rho + 2\Omega)_z V_y - (\rho + 2\Omega)_y V_z] \\ [(\rho + 2\Omega)_x V_z - (\rho + 2\Omega)_z V_x] \\ [(\rho + 2\Omega)_y V_x - (\rho + 2\Omega)_x V_y] \end{bmatrix} = [\rho + 2\Omega]V$$

are the Coriolis acceleration components which account for earth rotation Ω and local-level navigation frame rotation $\omega = \rho + \Omega$, relative to inertial space.

$$\rho \triangleq \begin{bmatrix} \rho_x \\ \rho_y \\ \rho_z \end{bmatrix}$$

are the angular rates of rotation of the local-level coordinates expressed about these axes which result as the system moves relative to the earth.

$$\Omega \triangleq \begin{bmatrix} \Omega_x \\ \Omega_y \\ \Omega_z \end{bmatrix}$$

are the angular rates of rotation of the earth relative to inertial space expressed about the local-level coordinate axes.

$$\gamma \triangleq \begin{bmatrix} \gamma_x \\ \gamma_y \\ \gamma_z \end{bmatrix}$$

are components of the modeled gravity vector of the earth. Usually, the normal gravity field is assumed, which corresponds to an ellipsoidal equipotential surface as the reference figure of the earth where $\gamma_x = \gamma_y = 0$, and the effect of the earth rotation rate is included in the gravity determination.

$$[\rho + 2\Omega] \triangleq \begin{bmatrix} 0 & (\rho + 2\Omega)_z & -(\rho + 2\Omega)_y \\ -(\rho + \Omega)_z & 0 & (\rho + 2\Omega)_x \\ (\rho + 2\Omega)_y & -(\rho + 2\Omega)_x & 0 \end{bmatrix}$$

is a skew-symmetric matrix expressing the sum of earth rate and local-level frame spatial rate with respect to inertial space.

The relative angular rates of rotation are computed after the accelerometer measurements are corrected for Coriolis accelerations and the normal gravity and integrated to obtain the computed-level velocity components $V_{x,y}$ as

$$\rho \triangleq \begin{bmatrix} \rho_x \\ \rho_y \\ \rho_z \end{bmatrix} = \begin{bmatrix} -V_y R_y^{-1} \\ V_x R_x^{-1} \\ \dot{\alpha} + \rho_N \tan \Phi \end{bmatrix}, \tag{A2}$$

where the $R_{x,y}$ terms are the radii of curvature of an ellipsoidal equipotential surface assumed as the figure of the earth. [Note that different datums (different ellipsoids of reference) are often used which fit better the geoid in the different local areas of system use.] The Φ, λ terms are the geodetic latitude and longitude of system position, respectively; α is the azimuth of the y axis in the level plane; $\rho_N = [\rho_x \sin \alpha + \rho_y \cos \alpha]$ is the relative angular rate about the north axis. [Note that $\dot{\alpha} \equiv 0$ in the expression for ρ_z above yields the north-slaved local-level mechanization if $\alpha(0) = 0$. The earth-rate components are computed as

$$\Omega \triangleq \begin{bmatrix} \Omega_x \\ \Omega_y \\ \Omega_z \end{bmatrix} = \begin{bmatrix} \Omega \cos \Phi \sin \alpha \\ \Omega \cos \Phi \cos \alpha \\ \Omega \sin \Phi \end{bmatrix}, \tag{A3}$$

The relative angular rates of change can be used to compute the change in inertial system geodetic position and the azimuth angle α of the local-level coordinate system. This is normally achieved by using a direction-cosine mechanization of the form

$$[\dot{D}] = [\rho][D], \qquad \begin{bmatrix} x \\ y \\ z \end{bmatrix} = [D]\begin{bmatrix} X \\ Y \\ Z \end{bmatrix}. \tag{A4}$$

The matrix [D] is the orthogonal direction-cosine transformation between a set of earth-fixed axes [X, Y, Z], usually with Y coincident with the terrestrial pole and X, Z in the equatorial plane, and the local-level coordinate system as illustrated in Fig. 1. In this case the local-level coordinate axes are realized from the earth-fixed coordinates by performing a counterclockwise rotation about the earth's polar axis λ, a clockwise rotation Φ about the displaced X axis in the equatorial plane, and a final counterclockwise rotation α about the then vertical axis z. More explicitly,

$$[D] \triangleq \begin{bmatrix} \langle X, x\rangle & \langle Y, x\rangle & \langle Z, x\rangle \\ \langle X, y\rangle & \langle Y, y\rangle & \langle Z, y\rangle \\ \langle X, z\rangle & \langle Y, z\rangle & \langle Z, z\rangle \end{bmatrix}, \tag{A5}$$

$$\langle X, x\rangle = \cos\alpha\cos\lambda - \sin\alpha\sin\Phi\sin\lambda,$$

$$\langle X, y\rangle = -\sin\alpha\cos\lambda - \cos\alpha\sin\Phi\sin\lambda,$$

$$\langle X, z\rangle = \cos\Phi\sin\lambda, \qquad \langle Y, x\rangle = \sin\alpha\cos\Phi,$$

$$\langle Y, y\rangle = \cos\alpha\cos\Phi, \qquad \langle Y, z\rangle = \sin\Phi,$$

$$\langle Z, x\rangle = -\cos\alpha\sin\lambda - \sin\alpha\sin\Phi\cos\lambda,$$

$$\langle Z, y\rangle = \sin\alpha\sin\lambda - \cos\alpha\sin\Phi\cos\lambda,$$

$$\langle Z, z\rangle = \cos\Phi\cos\lambda.$$

Further,

$$[\rho] \triangleq \begin{bmatrix} 0 & \rho_z & -\rho_y \\ -\rho_z & 0 & \rho_x \\ \rho_y & -\rho_x & 0 \end{bmatrix} \tag{A6}$$

is the antisymmetric matrix of relative angular rates of change of the navigation-coordinate axes relative to the earth-fixed frame expressed in the navigation-coordinate axes.[5] These rates result as the inertial system position changes relative to the earth. More explicitly, the geodetic position and wander-angle rates of change may be expressed as

$$\begin{aligned} &\dot{\Phi} = -\rho_E = [\rho_y \sin\alpha - \rho_x \cos\alpha], \\ &\dot{\lambda} = \rho_N \sec[\Phi], \qquad \dot{\alpha} = \rho_z - \rho_N \tan[\Phi], \end{aligned} \tag{A7}$$

where ρ_z varies depending on the type of azimuth mechanization selected. The direction cosine mechanization avoids the previous apparent singularities if the relative angular rates $\rho_{x,y,z}$ remain nonsingular. The level components are nonsingular functions of the system velocity relative to the earth by Eq. (A2). The azimuth relative-rotation rate ρ_z is usually selected to be a nonsingular function μ which can, but need

[5] *As a note of interest, only six elements of the direction cosine matrix need to be propagated in the mechanization of the navigation equations. Inspection of the propagation equation (A4) reveals that the elements of any column of the direction cosine matrix is propagated by using only the other two elements of the column and the appropriate relative angular rates. Any column (row) specifies an earth-fixed (local-level) coordinate axis relative to the local-level (earth-fixed) frame. Two such columns (rows) are sufficient to completely define the transformation, since the missing axis is simply the vector cross product of the other two axes, e.g.,* $Z = X \times Y$. *Further inspection of the direction cosines (A5) reveals that* $[\Phi, \alpha, \lambda]$ *can be determined fully from five of the direction cosine elements.*

not, be a function of the computed navigation variables

$$\rho_z = \mu . \tag{A8}$$

Note that for nonsingular behavior of ρ_z, the rate of azimuth wander-angle change is singular as

$$\dot{\alpha} = -\rho_N \tan \Phi + \mu . \tag{A9}$$

The final navigation equation is that used to compute the system-position change along the local vertical relative to the reference ellipsoid. The equation that is integrated to obtain elevation change is

$$\dot{h} = V_z . \tag{A10}$$

In words, the time rate of change of elevation is the system velocity relative to the earth projected along the vertical axis of the local-level reference frame.

Actual Representation of the Local-Level Navigation-Mechanization Equations

The correct representation of the rate of change of velocity relative to the earth with respect to the local-level coordinate frame that is actually mechanized in the system computer differs from Eq. (A1) and is written

$$\dot{V}_c \triangleq \begin{bmatrix} \dot{V}_x \\ \dot{V}_y \\ \dot{V}_z \end{bmatrix}_c = A_p + [\rho + 2\Omega]_c V_c - \gamma_c, \tag{A11}$$

where

$$A_p \triangleq \begin{bmatrix} A_x \\ A_y \\ A_z \end{bmatrix}_p = [I + \phi]A$$

are the accelerometer measurements as they are made along the platform coordinate axes as defined in this article. Note that since the accelerometers measure the sum of system acceleration and actual gravity (as opposed to modeled gravity), and further, make these measurements with error due to instrument imperfections, the vector A_p should implicitly include such effects. Here, however, we choose to represent the difference between actual and modeled gravity and instrument-measurement error both in the vector ∇ of the text and to let A_p represent the sum of system acceleration and modeled gravity as viewed from the platform coordinate axes.

$$\gamma_c \triangleq \begin{bmatrix} \gamma_x \\ \gamma_y \\ \gamma_z \end{bmatrix}_c$$

are the components of the modeled gravity that are computed by using system-computed values of position and wander angle $[\Phi, \lambda, \alpha]_c$.

$$\Omega_c \triangleq \begin{bmatrix} \Omega_x \\ \Omega_y \\ \Omega_z \end{bmatrix}_c$$

are components of the earth rotation rate that are computed using the system-computed values of position and wander angle $[\Phi, \alpha]_c$.

$$\rho_c \triangleq \begin{bmatrix} \rho_x \\ \rho_y \\ \rho_z \end{bmatrix}_c \triangleq \begin{bmatrix} -V_y R_y^{-1} \\ V_x R_x^{-1} \\ \dot{\alpha} + \rho_N \tan \Phi \end{bmatrix}_c \tag{A12}$$

are the system-computed values of the relative angular rate using the system-computed values of velocity V_c that result from the integration of Eq. (A11), the radii of curvature that are computed using system-computed values of position and wander angle $[\Phi, \alpha]_c$, and ρ_{z_c} is the azimuth relative rotation rate that is not explicitly specified at this point. Note, however, that the terms in this equation

$$\rho_{z_c} = \dot{\alpha}_c + \rho_{N_c} \tan \Phi_c, \qquad \rho_{N_c} = \rho_{x_c} \sin \alpha_c + \rho_{y_c} \cos \alpha_c \tag{A13}$$

are all obtained from values which are computed in the system computer. The reader is cautioned not to associate the velocity triplet V_c with the computer coordinate system introduced in the text of this article, but simply to consider it as the set of numbers that result from the integration of Eq. (A11).

The actual direction cosine matrix between the earth-fixed axes and system-computed geodetic frame is obtained using the system-computed relative angular rates between these two coordinate frames as

$$[\dot{D}]_c = [\rho]_c [D]_c, \tag{A14}$$

where

$$[\rho]_c \triangleq \begin{bmatrix} 0 & \rho_{z_c} & -\rho_{y_c} \\ -\rho_{z_c} & 0 & \rho_{x_c} \\ \rho_{y_c} & -\rho_{x_c} & 0 \end{bmatrix},$$

and $[D]_c$ is the computation of $[D]$ in Eq. (A5) using $[\Phi, \lambda, \alpha]_c$.

Finally, the actual representation of the equation that is integrated in the system computer to obtain elevation is

$$\dot{h}_c = V_{z_c} . \qquad \text{(A15)}$$

REFERENCES

1. J. R. HUDDLE, "Application of Kalman Filtering Theory to Augmented Inertial Navigation Systems," *NATO-AGARDograph 139*, Chapter 11, February 1970.

2. A. J. BROCKSTEIN and J. T. KOUBA, "Derivation of Free-Inertial, General Wander-Azimuth Mechanization Equations," Litton Systems Inc., Publication 15960, June 1969 (revised, June 1981).

3. W. A. HEISKANEN and H. MORITZ, "Physical Geodesy," Freeman, San Francisco, California, 1967.

4. J. C. PINSON, "Inertial Guidance for Cruise Vehicles," *in* Guidance and Control of Aerospace Vehicles" (C. T. Leondes, ed.), McGraw-Hill, New York, 1963.

Comparisons of Nonlinear Recursive Filters for Systems with Nonnegligible Nonlinearities

DAVID F. LIANG

Defence Research Establishment Ottawa
Department of National Defence
Shirley's Bay, Ottawa, Canada

I. GENERAL INTRODUCTION

Considerable attention has been devoted to the study of optimal estimation problems for dynamical systems embedded in noisy processes. For linear dynamical systems corrupted by additive white noise, the procedure for obtaining optimal

ISBN 0-12-012720-2

unbiased minimum variance estimates was first formulated by Kalman and Bucy [1], and it has been successfully applied to a variety of engineering and scientific problems.

However, in many practical applications, the system dynamics as well as the measurements are inherently nonlinear. The truly optimal nonlinear filter equations were given in Kushner [2]; however, their exact solutions require infinite dimensional systems, which are practically impossible to realize except in some simple cases. Therefore, considerable attention has been devoted to methods of approximating the a posteriori density functions based on perturbations relative to a prescribed reference. The majority of these techniques [3-5] employ the Taylor series expansions of the dynamic and measurement nonlinearities, neglecting second-order or higher terms.

The application of the first-order extended Kalman filter (EKF) has been found to yield valid and satisfactory results, as long as the second-order (and higher) terms in the perturbation equations are negligible. If nonlinearities are significant, however, first-order approximations of the system equations are inadequate, and the EKFs tend to be unstable and exhibit divergent behavior. In some of these cases, Kushner [6], Athans *et al.* [7], and Widnall [8] reported that filter performance can be substantially improved by local iterations or the inclusion of second-order effects. On the other hand, Schwartz and Stear [9] on the basis of their simulation study, concluded that the added complexity of several second-order filters may not provide useful improvements relative to the EKF. Unfortunately, this conclusion is biased because they used very large measurement noise in their simulations, so that measurement nonlinearities were effectively masked by the noise. In Kushner's simulation [6] of the Van der Pol equation, he reported that the implementation of a modified Gaussian second-order filter cannot prevent the filter from diverging. In his text, Jazwinski [10] stated that it is questionable whether higher order approximations would improve performance in cases where the extended Kalman filter does not work at all (diverges).

In an attempt to alleviate some of the difficulties of the Taylor series expansion approach, Sunahara [11] proposed to replace nonlinear dynamic functions by quasi-linear functions via statistically optimized approximation. His results and also those of Austin and Leondes [12] indicate that this approach may be more accurate than those of Taylor series expansions.

Liang and Christensen [13,14] applied the matrix minimum principal to derive nonlinear estimation algorithms for discrete-time nonlinear time-delayed systems with measurements corrupted by white- and non-white-noise processes. They also derived [15] realizable minimum-variance estimation algorithms for nonlinear continuous-time dynamical systems corrupted by white- and non-white-noise processes, using the matrix minimum principal together with the Kolmogorov and Kushner equations. Liang [16] noted that for systems with polynomial, product-type, exponential, and state-dependent sinusoidal nonlinearities, the proposed minimum-variance algorithms could be practically realized without the need of approximation under the assumption that the estimation errors are Gaussian.

It is difficult to theoretically assess the virtues of any one suboptimal nonlinear filter vis-à-vis the others, and it is not even possible to solve for the optimal solution against which suboptimal solutions can be compared. Therefore, it is necessary to conduct extensive numerical simulations and tests to provide meaningful comparisons between the performance characteristics of the filters. Simulations of various nonlinear filters not only could provide considerable insight into the stability behavior of some of these filters, but also provide ad hoc guidelines to establish situations in which specific nonlinear algorithms would have demonstrable advantages.

Section II deals with state-estimation problems of continuous-time nonlinear dynamic systems. Various structures of dynamic continuous-time finite-dimensional nonlinear filters are tabulated. Three types of dynamic systems with nonnegligible nonlinearities were selected and simulated on a digital computer. Extensive simulation results accompanied by discussion, are presented to compare the performance behavior of these filters. They clearly indicate the superiority of the Liang and Christensen minimum-variance estimator over those of other filters investigated.

Section III deals with state-estimation problems of discrete-time nonlinear systems. Section III.A presents a brief summary of an EKF and the Liang and Christensen nonlinear discrete-time filter [13]. Their discrete-time minimum-variance filtering (MVF) algorithm is applied to a general class of discrete-time state-estimation problems where the system model and/or measurement model contain(s) second-order nonlinearities. Simulation results accompanied by discussion are presented in Sections III.B and III.C to compare the performance behavior of the MVF and EKF.

II. COMPARISONS OF CONTINUOUS-TIME NONLINEAR RECURSIVE FILTERS

A. COMPARISON OF CONTINUOUS-TIME FILTER STRUCTURES

Consider a general class of nonlinear systems described by the stochastic differential equation [10]

$$dx(t)/dt = f[x(t), t] + G[x(t), t]w(t), \tag{1}$$

with measurement given by

$$z(t) = h[x(t), t] + v(t), \tag{2}$$

where x(t) and z(t) are the n-dimensional state and m-dimensional measurement vectors, respectively; f and h are, respectively, n- and m-dimensional nonlinear vector-valued functions; and G is a vector-valued matrix.

The random vectors w(t) and v(t) are statistically independent zero-mean white Gaussian noise processes such that for all $t, \tau \geq t_0$,

$$\begin{aligned} &\text{cov}\{w(t), w(\tau)\} = V_w(t)\,\delta(t - \tau), \\ &\text{cov}\{v(t), v(\tau)\} = V_v(t)\,\delta(t - \tau), \\ &\text{cov}\{w(t), v(\tau)\} = 0, \end{aligned} \tag{3}$$

where $\delta(\cdot)$ is the Dirac delta function, and the variances $V_w(t)$ and $V_v(t)$ are nonnegative definite and positive definite, respectively.

The initial state vector $x(t_0) = x_0$ is a zero-mean Gaussian random process, independent of $w(t)$ and $v(t)$ for $t \geq t_0$, with a positive-definite variance matrix $\mathrm{var}\{x(t_0), x(t_0)\} = V_x(t_0)$.

In the design of nonlinear filters, a number of different exact and approximate nonlinear state and error-variance equations have been proposed in the literature [4,9-11,15]. For comparative purposes, various structures of these nonlinear filters are tabulated in Tables I and II.

Comparing the structures of the truncated, the quasi-moment, and the modified MVFs, the only difference is the error-forcing term that appears in the error-variance equations. In the quasi-moment filter it enters with a plus sign; in the truncated filter that term enters with a minus sign and a factor of 1/2; and the modified MVF is a compromise between the truncated and the quasi-moment filters. In comparing the stochastic linearization filter with the minimum-variance nonlinear filter, the latter has obviously preserved the error-forcing term. On the other hand, comparing the first four linearized filters with the last two filters, the essential differences are due to approximations made of expectations of $f(x)$, $\tilde{x}h(x)$, and $h(x)$. It is also noteworthy to mention that when $h(x)$ is linear, the modified, the truncated, and the quasi-moment MVFs are identical, and the MVF is identical to the stochastic linearization filter.

In order to compare the performance characteristics of these nonlinear filters, two different types of dynamic systems with nonnegligible nonlinearities were selected, and the stochastic equations were transformed to Stratonovich forms [10]

Table I. Various Exact and Approximate Nonlinear Filter Equations: Part I

Extended Kalman filter:

$$\dot{\hat{x}} = f(\hat{x}, t) + V_{\tilde{x}} \frac{\partial h^T(\hat{x}, t)}{\partial \hat{x}} V_v^{-1}\{z - h(\hat{x}, t)\} \tag{4}$$

$$\begin{aligned} \dot{V}_{\tilde{x}} = {} & \frac{\partial f(\hat{x}, t)}{\partial \hat{x}} V_{\tilde{x}} + V_{\tilde{x}} \frac{\partial f^T(\hat{x}, t)}{\partial \hat{x}} + G[\hat{x}, t] V_w G^T[\hat{x}, t] \\ & - V_{\tilde{x}} \frac{\partial h^T(\hat{x}, t)}{\partial \hat{x}} V_v^{-1} \frac{\partial h(\hat{x}, t)}{\partial \hat{x}} V_{\tilde{x}} \end{aligned} \tag{5}$$

Modified minimum-variance filter:

$$\begin{aligned} \dot{\hat{x}} = {} & f(\hat{x}, t) + \frac{1}{2} \frac{\partial^2 f(\hat{x}, t)}{\partial \hat{x}^2} : V_{\tilde{x}} + V_{\tilde{x}} \frac{\partial h^T(\hat{x}, t)}{\partial \hat{x}} V_v^{-1} \\ & \times \left\{ z - h(\hat{x}, t) - \frac{1}{2} \frac{\partial^2 h(\hat{x}, t)}{\partial \hat{x}^2} : V_{\tilde{x}} \right\} \end{aligned} \tag{6}$$

$\dot{V}_{\tilde{x}}$ = Right-hand side of Eq. (5)

Truncated minimum-variance filter:

$\dot{\hat{x}}$ = same as Eq. (6)

$\dot{V}_x$ = Right-hand side of Eq. (5)

$$-\frac{1}{2} V_{\tilde{x}}^2 : \frac{\partial^2 h(\hat{x}, t)}{\partial \hat{x}^2} : V_v^{-1} \left\{ z - h(\hat{x}, t) - \frac{1}{2} \frac{\partial^2 h(\hat{x}, t)}{\partial \hat{x}^2} : V_{\tilde{x}} \right\}$$

Tensor computation:

$$\left\{ \frac{\partial^2 f(\hat{x}, t)}{\partial \hat{x}^2} : V_{\tilde{x}} \right\}_i = \sum_{j,k=1}^{n} V_{jk} \frac{\partial^2 f_i(\hat{x}, t)}{\partial \hat{x}_j \, \partial \hat{x}_k}.$$

Table II. Various Exact and Approximate Nonlinear Filter Equations: Part II

Quasi-moment minimum-variance filter:

$$\dot{\hat{x}} = \text{same as Eq. (6)}$$

$$\dot{V}_{\tilde{x}} = \text{Right-hand side of Eq. (5)}$$

$$+ V_{\tilde{x}}^2 : \frac{\partial^2 h(\hat{x}, t)}{\partial \hat{x}^2} : V_v^{-1}\left\{z - h(\hat{x}, t) - \frac{1}{2}\frac{\partial^2 h(\hat{x}, t)}{\partial \hat{x}^2} : V_{\tilde{x}}\right\}$$

Tensor computation:

$$\left[V_{\tilde{x}}^2 : \frac{\partial^2 h_k(\hat{x}, t)}{\partial \hat{x}^2}\right]_{ij} = \sum_{q, r=1}^{n} \frac{\partial^2 h_k(\hat{x}, t)}{\partial \hat{x}_q \, \partial \hat{x}_r}(V_{iq}V_{jr} + V_{ir}V_{jq})$$

$$\left[V_{\tilde{x}}^2 : \frac{\partial^2 h}{\partial \hat{x}^2}\right] : \xi = \left[\sum_{k=1}^{m}\left\{V_{\tilde{x}}^2 : \frac{\partial^2 h_k(\hat{x}, t)}{\partial \hat{x}^2}\right\}_{ij} \xi_k\right]$$

Stochastic linearization filter:

$$\dot{\hat{x}} = \hat{f}(\tilde{x} + \hat{x}, t) + E[\tilde{x}h^T(\hat{x} + \tilde{x}, t)]V_v^{-1}\{z - \hat{h}(\hat{x} + \tilde{x}, t)\} \quad (7)$$

$$\dot{V}_{\tilde{x}} = E\{\tilde{x}f^T(\tilde{x} + \hat{x}, t)\} + E\{f(\tilde{x} + \hat{x}, t)\tilde{x}^T\}$$
$$+ E\left\{G[\tilde{x} + \hat{x}, t]V_w G^T[\tilde{x} + \hat{x}, t]\right\} \quad (8)$$
$$- E\{\tilde{x}h^T(\tilde{x} + \hat{x}, t)\}V_v^{-1}E\{h(\tilde{x} + \hat{x}, t)\tilde{x}^T\}$$

Minimum-variance filter:

$$\dot{\hat{x}} = \text{same as Eq. (7)}$$

$$\dot{V}_x = \text{Right-hand side of Eq. (8)}$$
$$+ E\left\{\tilde{x}\tilde{x}^T h^T(\tilde{x} + \hat{x}, t) - V_{\tilde{x}} h^T(\tilde{x} + \hat{x}, t)\right\}$$
$$\times V_v^{-1}\{z - \hat{h}(\tilde{x} + \hat{x}, t)\}$$

and then simulated on a digital computer. The integration scheme was performed by the minimum-error-bound fourth-order Runge-Kutta method [17].

B. NONLINEAR FILTERS FOR PHASE DEMODULATOR DESIGN

Section II.B deals with the design of nonlinear filters for a two-dimensional phase-lock loop. This phase demodulation problem is of major technological importance and widely known in communication and control engineering problems. The dynamic model selected is represented as

$$\dot{x}_1 = x_2, \quad \dot{x}_2 = w,$$

and the measurements are given by $z_1 = \cos x_1 + v_1$ and $z_2 = \sin x_1 + v_2$, where w, v_1, and v_2 are zero-mean white Gaussian noise processes with variances V_w, V_{v_1} and V_{v_2}, respectively.

Both the EKF and stochastic linearization filter (SLF) are described by the following equations:

$$\dot{\hat{x}}_1 = \hat{x}_2 - V_{v_1}^{-1} V_{11} E \sin \hat{x}_1 (z_1 - E \cos \hat{x}_1)$$
$$+ V_{v_2}^{-1} V_{11} E \cos \hat{x}_1 (z_2 - H \sin \hat{x}_1),$$

$$\dot{\hat{x}}_2 = -V_{v_1}^{-1} V_{12} E \sin \hat{x}_1 (z_1 - E \cos \hat{x}_1)$$
$$+ V_{v_2}^{-1} V_{12} E \cos \hat{x}_1 (z_2 - E \sin \hat{x}_1),$$

$$\dot{V}_{11} = 2V_{12} - V_{11}^2 E^2 V_{v_1}^{-1} \sin^2 \hat{x}_1 - V_{11}^2 E^2 V_{v_2}^{-1} \cos^2 \hat{x}_1,$$

$$\dot{V}_{12} = V_{22} - V_{11} V_{12} E^2 V_{v_1}^{-1} \sin^2 \hat{x}_1 - V_{11} V_{12} E^2 V_{v_2}^{-1} \cos^2 \hat{x}_1,$$

$$\dot{V}_{22} = V_w - V_{12}^2 E^2 V_{v_1}^{-1} \sin^2 \hat{x}_1 - V_{12}^2 E^2 V_{v_2}^{-1} \cos^2 \hat{x}_1.$$

In the case of the SLF, E is equal to $\exp(-V_{11}/2)$, whereas for the EKF, E is equal to 1. Therefore, the major difference between the EKF and the SLF is due to the approximation made of $\exp(-V_{11}/2)$. The effect of this term is accentuated when the measurement residual is significant and the error variances V_{11}, V_{22}, and V_{12} are large. The measurement residual is significant when the a priori state estimates are significantly different from the true values. It is also affected by the level of noise inputs.

For the MVF, the equations for $\dot{\hat{x}}_1$ and $\dot{\hat{x}}_2$ are identical to those of the SLF, but the error-variance equations have the following terms in addition to those of the SLF: For

$\dot{V}_{11}$, $\dot{V}_{12}$, and $\dot{V}_{22}$,

add

$-V_{11}^2EF$, $-V_{11}V_{12}EF$, and $-V_{12}^2EF$,

respectively, where

$$E = \exp(-V_{11}/2),$$

$$F = V_{v_1}^{-1} \cos \hat{x}_1(z_1 - E \cos \hat{x}_1) + V_{v_2}^{-1} \sin \hat{x}_1(z_2 - E \sin \hat{x}_1).$$

The effect of this error-forcing term in proportion to all the other terms is accentuated when V_{11} is small and the measurement residual is significant, and also when both V_{11} and V_{12} are large.

To compare the performance characteristics of these three filters, their filtering equations were simulated on a digital computer. Each output response presented in Figs. 1 to 9 represents the average results of five simulation runs that are representative of many other simulation runs not presented in this article.

Figures 1 to 3 show the effects of initial state estimates for the following three sets of prior statistics: For

Fig. 1, $V_{11}(0) = V_{22}(0) = V_{12}(0) = 1.0$;

Fig. 2, $V_{11}(0) = V_{22}(0) = 1$, $V_{12}(0) = 0$;

Fig. 3, $V_{11}(0) = V_{22}(0) = 0.01$, $V_{12}(0) = 0$;

where $V_v = V_w = 0.01$ and $x_1(0) = x_2(0) = 2.0$. From Figs. 1 to 3, it is apparent that the performance of the EKF and SLF are almost identical to that of the MVF for small noise variances and for when a priori state estimates are close to the true values. However, when a priori state estimates are significantly different from the true values and initial error variances are overly optimistic, the performance characteristics of both the EKF and SLF are significantly inferior to those of the MVF. The same thing can be said when the knowledge of a priori estimates is poor and V_{11} and V_{12} are large. In this case, the difference between SLF and EKF also becomes quite significant. These experimental results agree well with what was theoretically expected.

When the noise variances are increased to 1.0 from 0.01, the output from these three filters is as presented in Figs. 4 and 5. It is interesting to observe that when the noise input levels are relatively high compared to the effects of nonlinearities, the EKF is as good as any nonlinear filter investigated, and no particular filter can be said to be

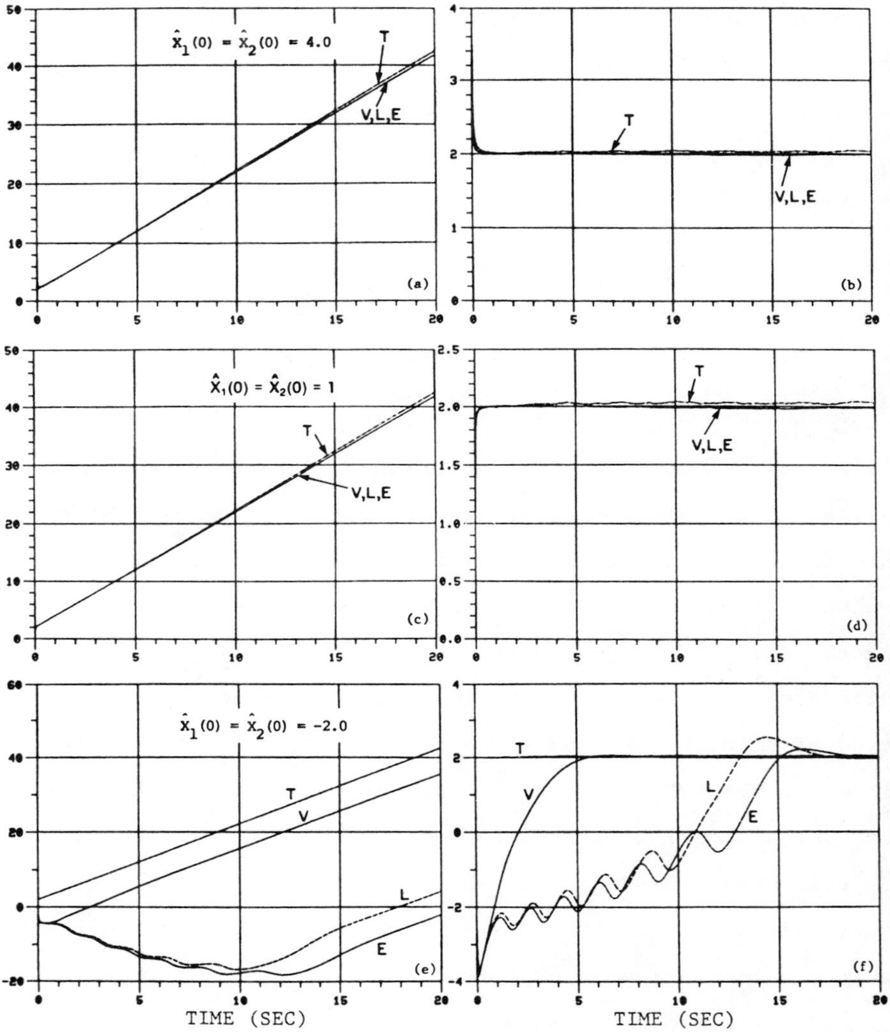

Fig. 1. Phase demodulator, effects of $\hat{X}(0)$ with small V_v and V_w and larger V: $V_{12}(0) = 1.0$; $V_{11}(0) = V_{22}(0) = 1.0$; $X_1(0) = X_2(0) = 2.0$; $V_v = V_w = 0.01$. The following abbreviations occur throughout the illustrations in this article: T, true state; V, minimum-variance filter; L, stochastic linearization filter; E, extended Kalman filter; S, second-order filter. (a), (c), and (e) filter estimates and true X_1 versus time; (b), (d), and (f) filter estimates and true X_2 versus time. (a,b) $\hat{X}_1(0) = \hat{X}_2(0) = 4.0$; (c,d) $\hat{X}_1(0) = \hat{X}_2(0) = 1.0$; (e,f) $\hat{X}_1(0) = \hat{X}_2(0) = -2.0$.

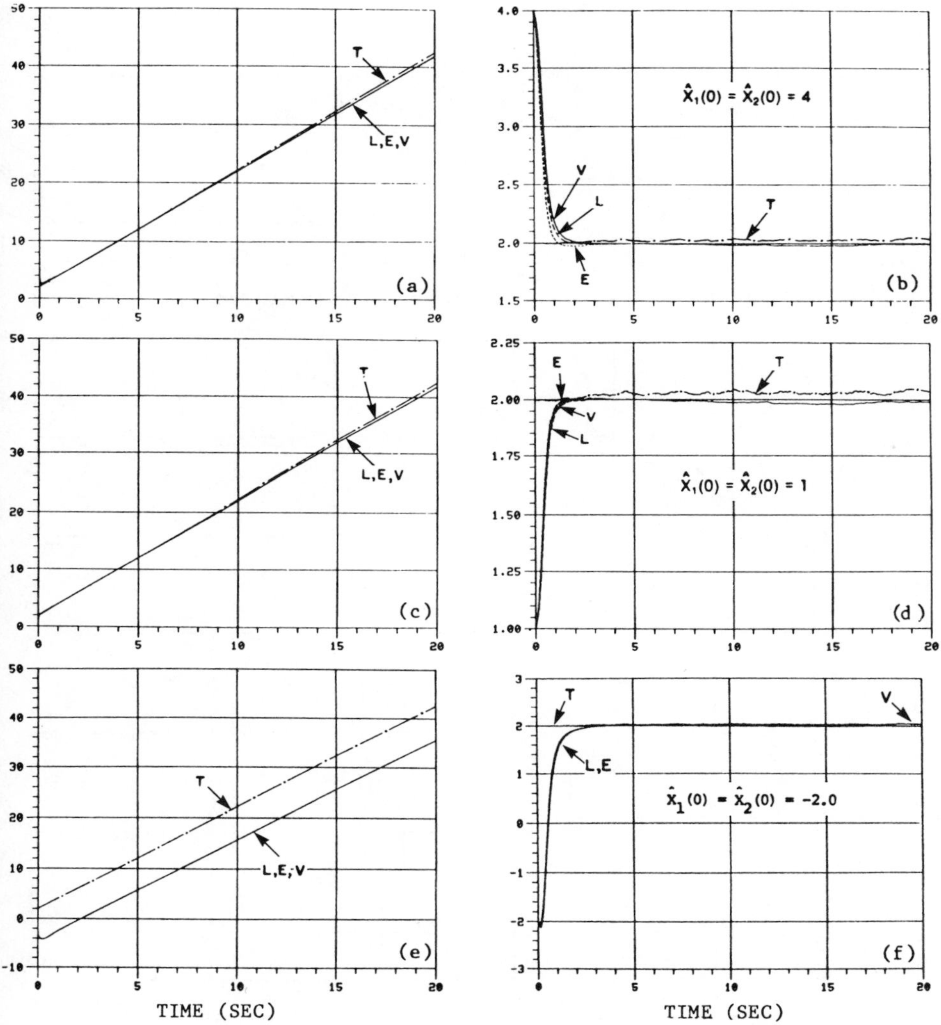

Fig. 2. Phase demodulator; effects of $\hat{X}(0)$ with small V_v and V_w larger V and $V_{12} = 0$: $V_{12}(0) = 0.0$; $V_{11}(0) = V_{22}(0) = 1.0$; $X_1(0) = X_2(0) = 2.0$; $V_v = V_w = 0.01$. (a), (c), and (e) filter estimates and true X_1 versus time; (b), (d), and (f) filter estimates and true X_2 versus time: $\hat{X}_1(0) = \hat{X}_2(0) = 4.0$ (a,b), 1.0 (c,d), and -2.0 (e,f).

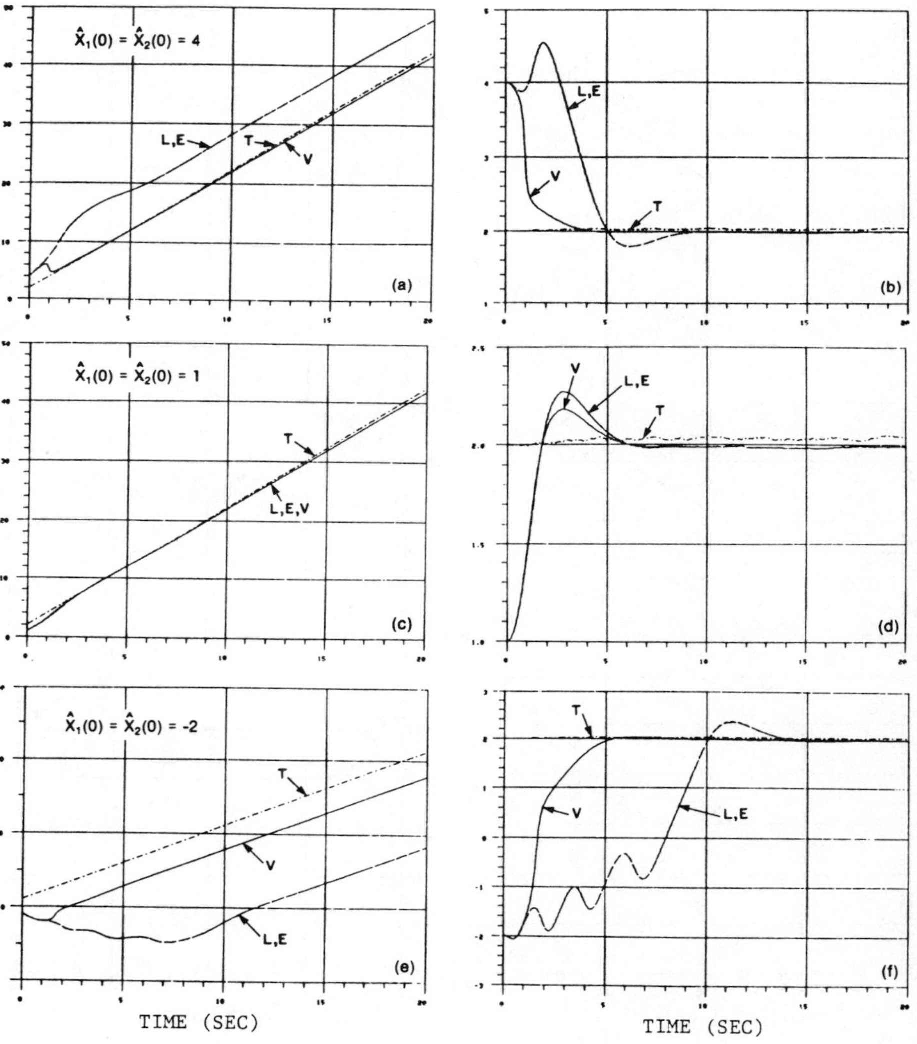

Fig. 3. Phase demodulator filters; effects of $\hat{X}(0)$ with small V_v and V_w and smaller V: $V_{11}(0) = V_{22}(0) = 0.01$; $V_{12}(0) = 0.0$; $X_1(0) = X_2(0) = 2.0$; $V_v = V_w = 0.01$. (a), (c), and (e) filter estimates and true X_1 versus time; (b), (d), and (f) filter estimates and true X_2 versus time: $\hat{X}_1(0) = \hat{X}_2(0) =$ 4.0 (a,b), 1.0 (c,d), and -2.0 (e,f).

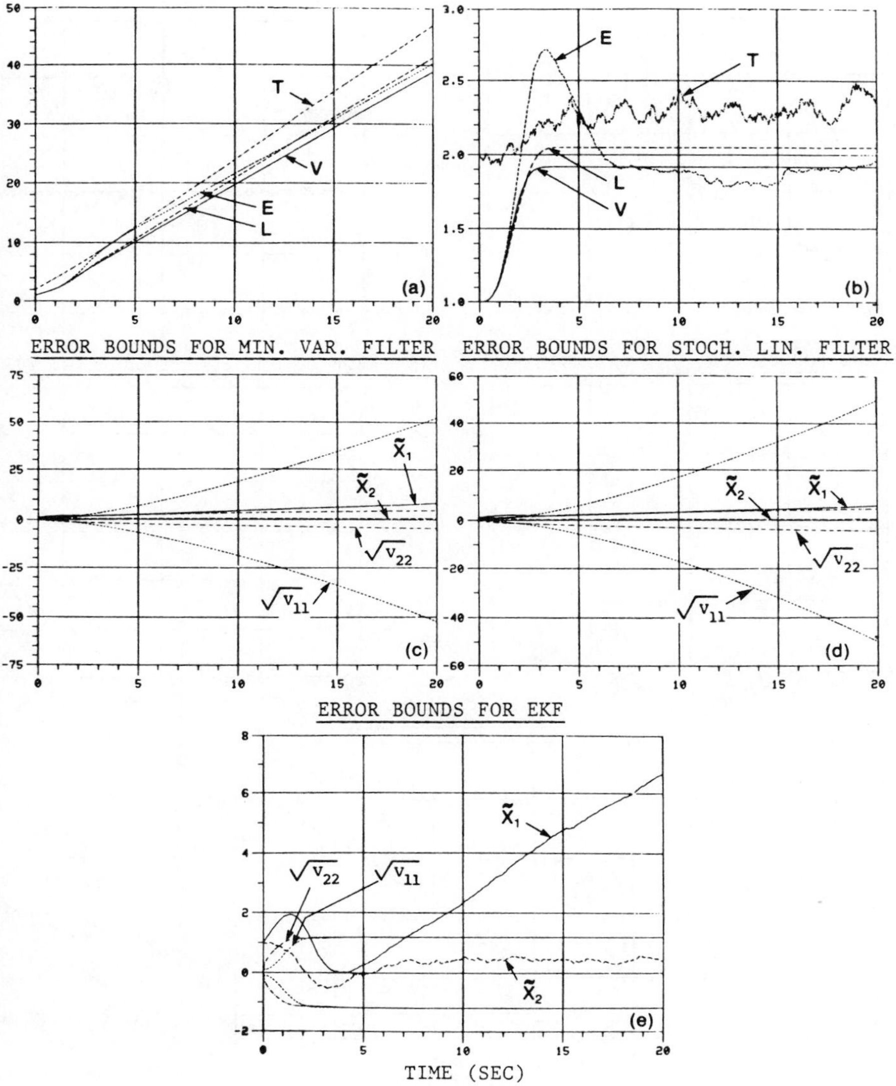

Fig. 4. Outputs of phase demodulator fitlers with larger V_v and V_w: $V_{11}(0) = V_{22}(0) = 0.01$; $V_{12}(0) = 0.0$; $X_1(0) = X_2(0) = 2$; $\hat{X}_1(0) = \hat{X}_2(0) = 1.0$; $V_v = V_w = 1.0$. (a) Actual filter output for X_1 and (b) for X_2; error bounds for (c) MVF, (d) SLF, and (e) EKF.

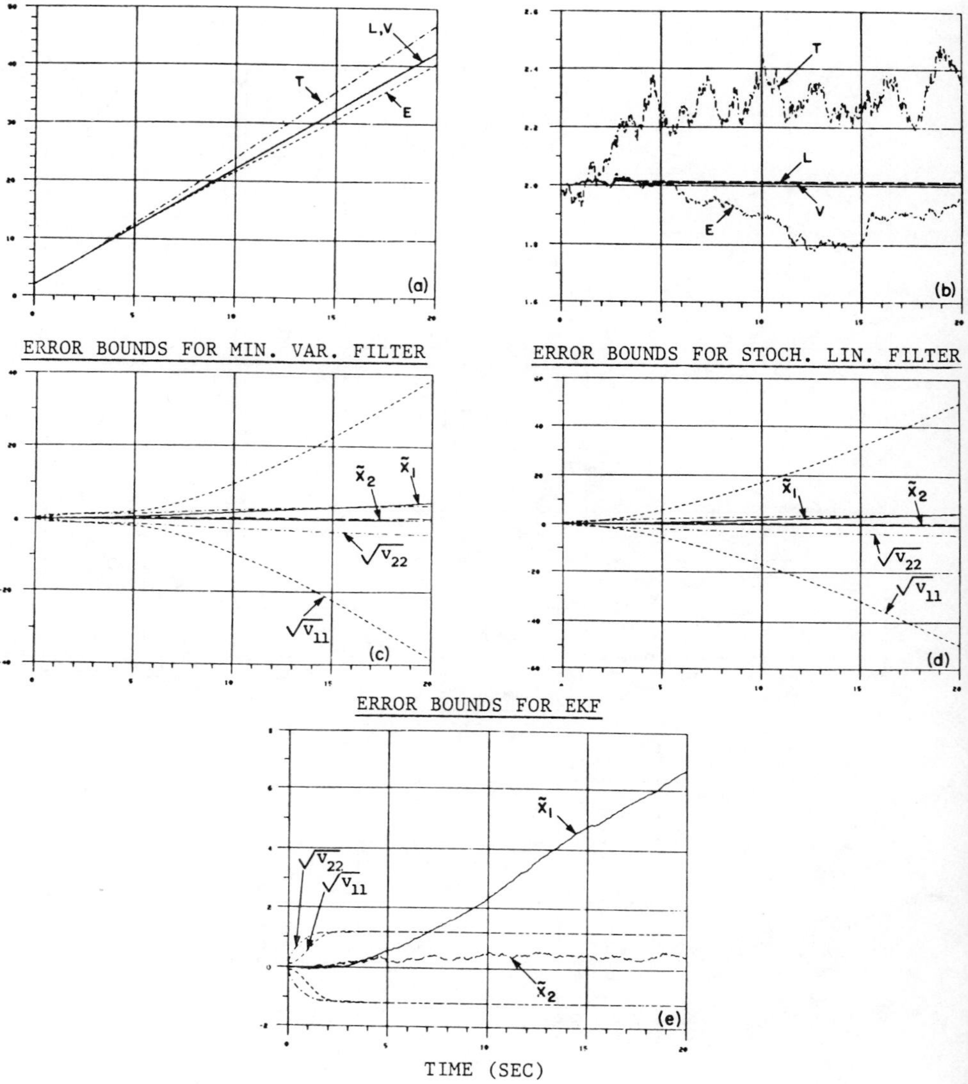

Fig. 5. Outputs of phase demodulator filters with larger V_v *and* V_w: $V_{11}(0) = V_{22}(0) = 0.01$; $V_{12}(0) = 0$; $X_1(0) = X_2(0) = 2.0$; $\hat{X}_1(0) = \hat{X}_2(0) = 2.0$; $V_v = V_w = 1.0$. *(a) Actual filter output for* X_1 *and (b)* X_2; *error bounds for (c) MVF, (d) SLF, and (e) EKF.*

consistently superior to any other nonlinear filter. This appears to be intuitively obvious because large noise inputs can effectively "cover" neglected nonlinearities.

On the other hand, when the noise variances are reduced to 0.001, and values of initial error-variances are set to 1, both the EKF and SLF diverged, whereas the MVF tracks the true values of the phase and phase rate amazingly well. Typical simulation results for some of these runs are presented in Fig. 6. It should be noted, however, that if the noise variances are further reduced to 0.0001, and when the initial state estimates are far from the true values of the system states, even the MVF would diverge as others had done so much sooner. But if one were to drastically reduce the initial variances, occasionally the MVF and also the EKF and SLF would all be stable again: One such example is illustrated in Fig. 7. For this case, the MVF is only slightly better than the others. This indicates that in some applications of nonlinear filters, the system designer must be careful not to select the initial variances too large; however, when values of the filter assumed V_v are increased to 0.05 from 0.001, which is a common measure to prevent the filter from diverging, the results are as presented in Fig. 8. They clearly show the superior performance of the MVF over that of the EKF and SLF, but, as in Fig. 9, when the initial error variances are increased to 1.0 from 0.01, all three filters are practically identical in performance. As a whole, our extensive simulation results show that the MVF is significantly more insensitive to the selection of a priori state estimates and initial error variances.

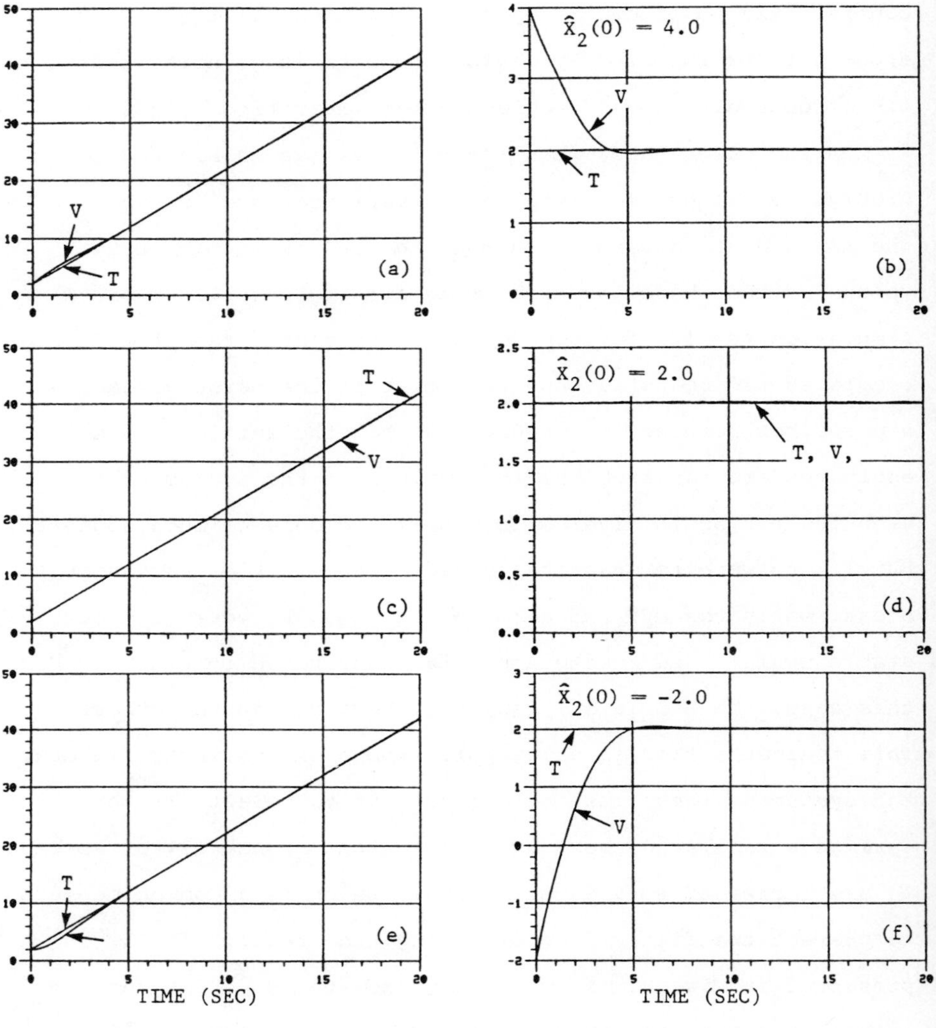

Fig. 6. Phase demodulator filters; outputs of MVF with very small V_v and V_w: $V_{11}(0) = V_{22}(0) = V_{12}(0) = 1.0$; $X_1(0) = X_2(0) = \hat{X}_1(0) = 2.0$; $V_v = V_w = 0.001$. Filter outputs and true X_1 versus time (a,c,e); filter outputs and true X_2 versus time (b,d,f): $\hat{X}_2(0) = 4.0$ (a,b), 2.0 (c,d), and -2.0 (e,f).

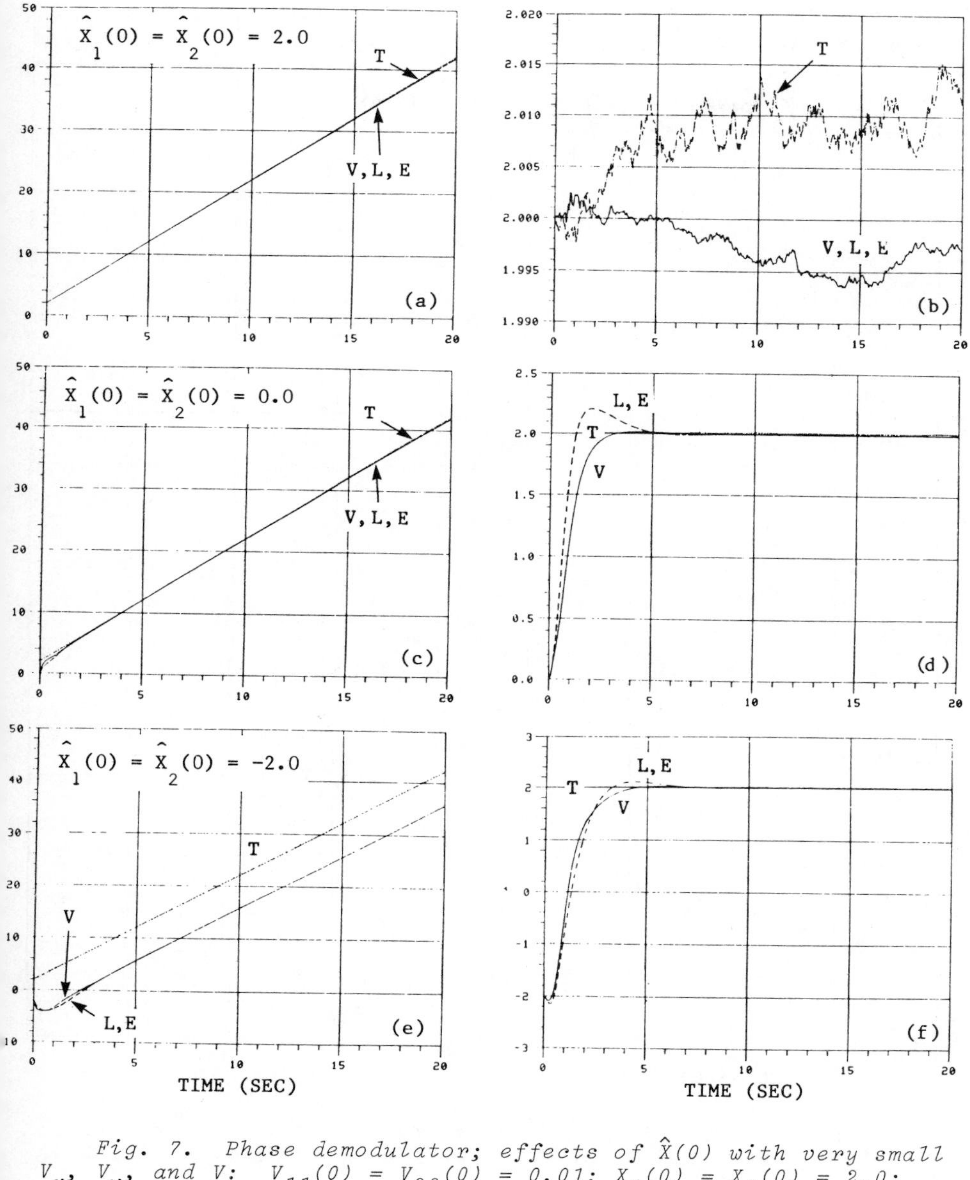

Fig. 7. Phase demodulator; effects of $\hat{X}(0)$ with very small V_v, V_w, and V: $V_{11}(0) = V_{22}(0) = 0.01$; $X_1(0) = X_2(0) = 2.0$; $V_v = V_w = 0.001$; $V_{12}(0) = 0$. Filter estimates and true X_1 versus time (a,c,e); filter estimates and true X_2 versus time (b,d,f): $\hat{X}_1(0) = \hat{X}_2(0) = 2.0$ (a,b), 0 (c,d), and -2.0 (e,f).

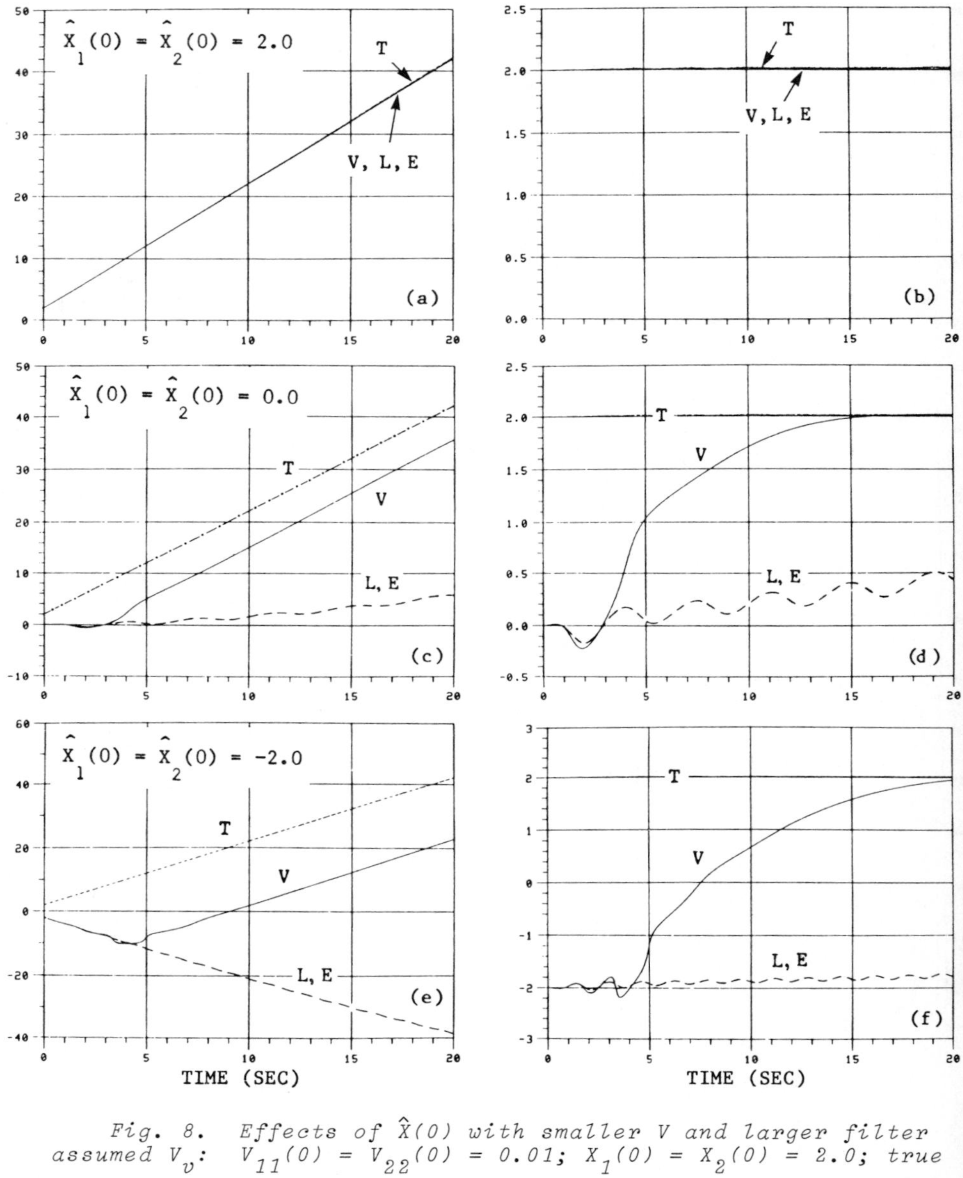

Fig. 8. Effects of $\hat{X}(0)$ with smaller V and larger filter assumed V_v: $V_{11}(0) = V_{22}(0) = 0.01$; $X_1(0) = X_2(0) = 2.0$; true $V_v = V_w = 0.001$; assumed $V_v = 0.05$; assumed $V_w = 0.001$. Filter estimates and true X_1 versus time (a,c,e); filter estimates and true X_2 versus time (b,d,f): $\hat{X}_1(0) = \hat{X}_2(0) = 2.0$ (a,b), 0 (c,d), and -2.0 (e,f).

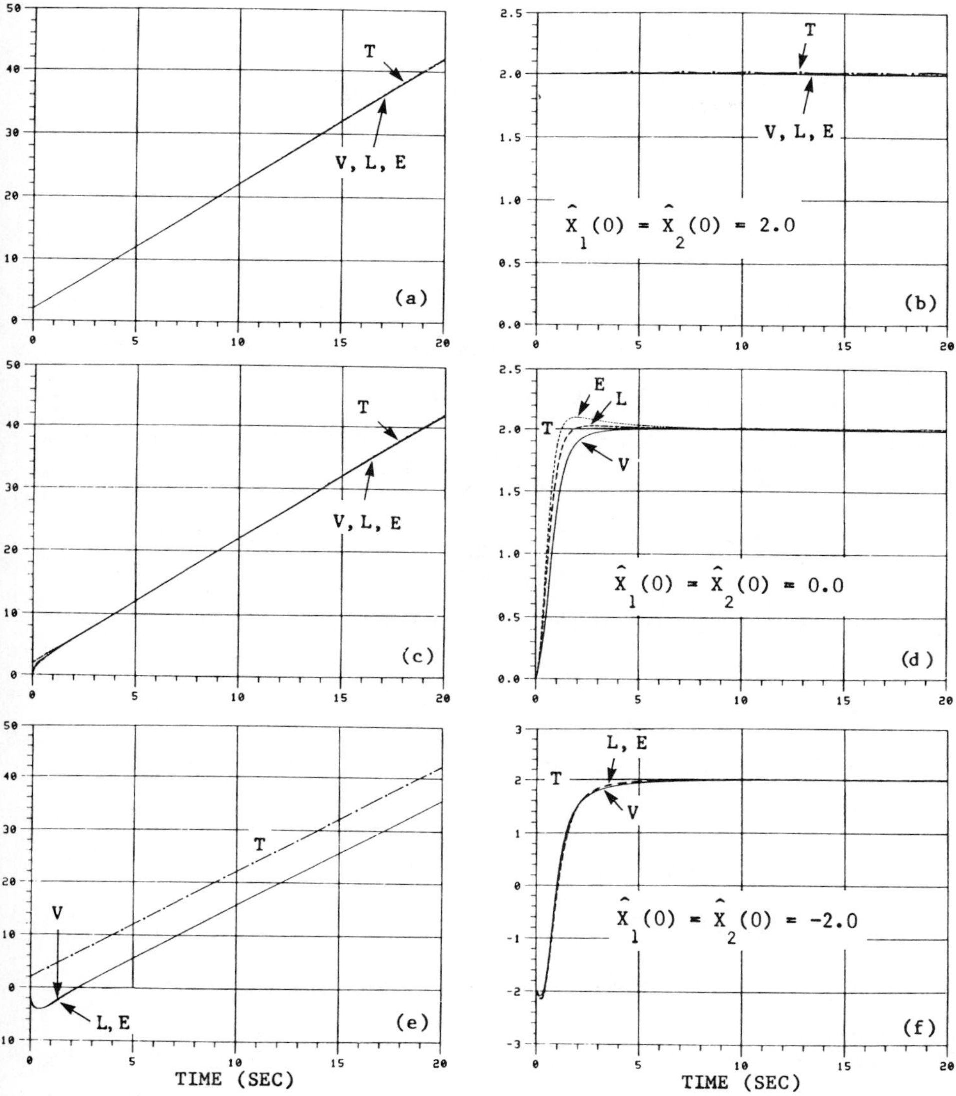

Fig. 9. Effects of $\hat{X}(0)$ with larger V and larger filter assumed V_v: $V_{11}(0) = V_{22}(0) = 1.0$; $X_1(0) = X_2(0) = 2.0$; true $V_v = V_w = 0.001$; assumed $V_v = 0.05$; assumed $V_w = 0.001$. Filter estimates and true X_1 versus time (a,c,e); filter estimates and true X_2 versus time (b,d,f): $\hat{X}_1(0) = \hat{X}_2(0) = 2.0$ (a,b), 0 (c,d), and -2.0 (e,f).

C. *NONLINEAR FILTERS FOR THE VAN DER POL OSCILLATOR*

Consider a state-estimation problem of the Van der Pol oscillator described by

$$\dot{x}_1 = x_2, \quad \dot{x}_1 = -x_1 + 3x_2\left(1 - x_1^2\right),$$

with measurement given by $z = x_1 - 0.1x_1^3 + v$.

This example was selected not only because of its third-order nonlinearities but also because Kushner [6] had previously shown that for this state-estimation problem, even with a linear measurement model the linearized filter was extremely unstable and was completely useless within a fraction of a time unit, and even the implementation of a Gaussian second-order filter proved to be unstable. Therefore, in this study we are only concerned with the comparison of an MVF with an SLF.

The structural difference between these two filters is mainly due to the preservation of error-forcing terms in the MVF, namely, for

$$\dot{V}_{11}, \quad \text{the additional term is} \quad -0.6V_{11}^2\hat{x}_1V_v^{-1}[z - \hat{z}],$$

$$\dot{V}_{22}, \quad \text{the additional term is} \quad -0.6V_{12}^2\hat{x}_1V_v^{-1}[z - \hat{z}],$$

$$\dot{V}_{12}, \quad \text{the additional term is} \quad -0.6V_{11}V_{12}\hat{x}_1V_v^{-1}[z - \hat{z}],$$

where $\hat{z} = \hat{x}_1 - 0.1\left(\hat{x}_1^3 + 3\hat{x}_1V_{11}\right)$. Therefore, it can be expected that the difference between the SLF and MVF will be accentuated wherever the values of initial error variances and $\hat{x}_1$ are increased and also when the measurement residual is significant.

To verify this, some typical results of extensive simulations are presented in Figs. 10 to 14. Here, we have

$$\hat{x}_1(0) = x_1(0) = 2.0, \quad \hat{x}_2(0) = x_2(0) = 0.0, \quad V_{12}(0) = 0.0.$$

Figures 10 to 12 illustrate the effects of noise variances and initial error variances on the performance of the SLF and MVF. From these, it is evident that when initial error variances are very small, and the a priori estimates are reasonably accurate, the performance characteristics of the SLF and MVF are almost identical, with the SLF having a slightly smaller phaseshift. However, as expected from theoretical considerations, for increasing values of initial error variances, the difference between the performance of the SLF and MVF becomes more significant. Here, quite consistently, the MVF is far more capable than the SLF in tracking the true values of the states, and the MLF is also much less sensitive to these selections of initial error variances.

To further illustrate the difference in filter responses, Fig. 13 presents the filter state estimates, the errors of state estimates, and their 1σ error bounds for the following statistics:

$$V_v = 0.1, \quad V_{11}(0) = V_{22} = 0.5, \quad V_{12}(0) = 0.$$

The poorer performance of the SLF is evidently due to its optimistic estimation of error bounds.

Figure 14 is presented to demonstrate the severe effects of initial state estimates and error variances on the performance of the SLF and MVF. It is quite evident that the system designer must be careful in his selections of appropriate initial error variances. The extensive simulation experience

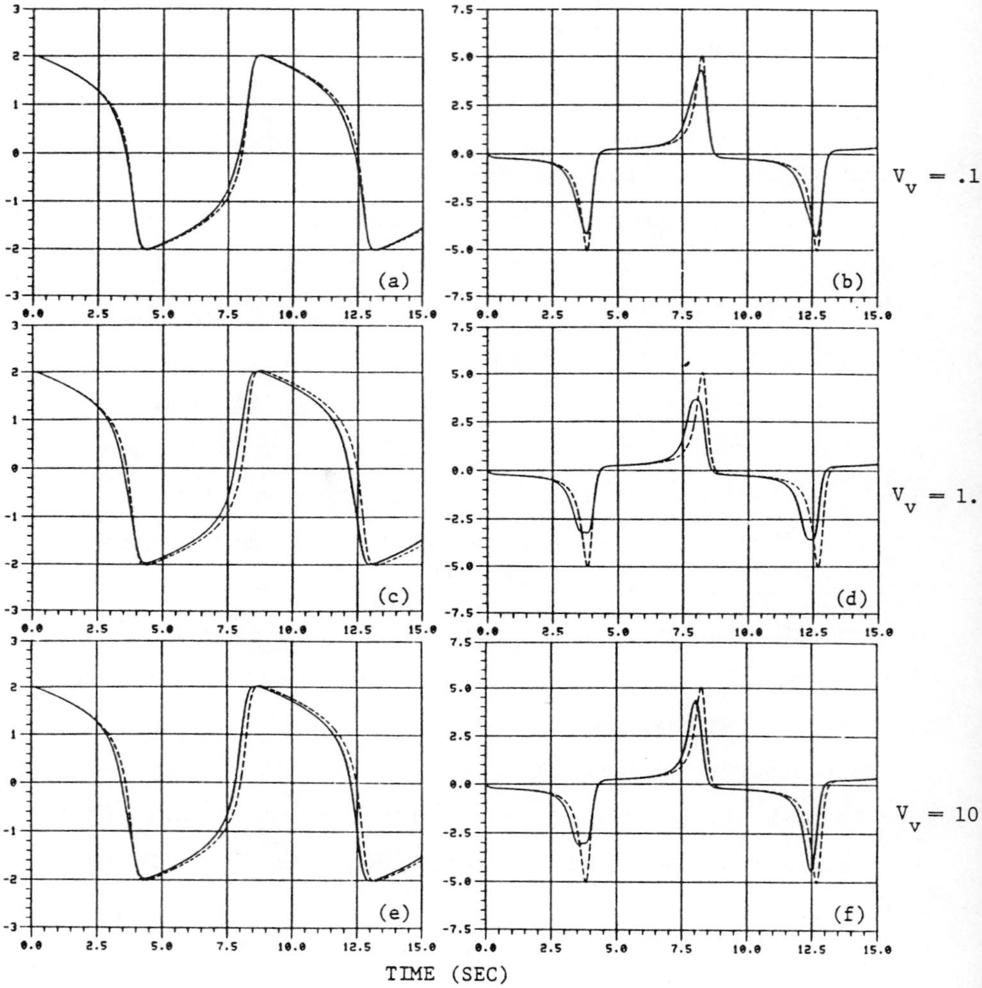

Fig. 10. The Van der Pol oscillator; effects of V_v with very small V: $V_{11}(0) = V_{22}(0) = 0.01$; $V_{12}(0) = 0$; $X_1(0) = \hat{X}_1(0) = 2.0$; $X_2(0) = \hat{X}_2(0) = 0$. Filter estimates and true X_1 versus time (a,c,e); filter estimates and true X_2 versus time (b,d,f): $V_v = 0.1$ (a,b); 1.0 (c,d); and 10 (e,f); (-) true state; (—) MVF; and (---) SLF.

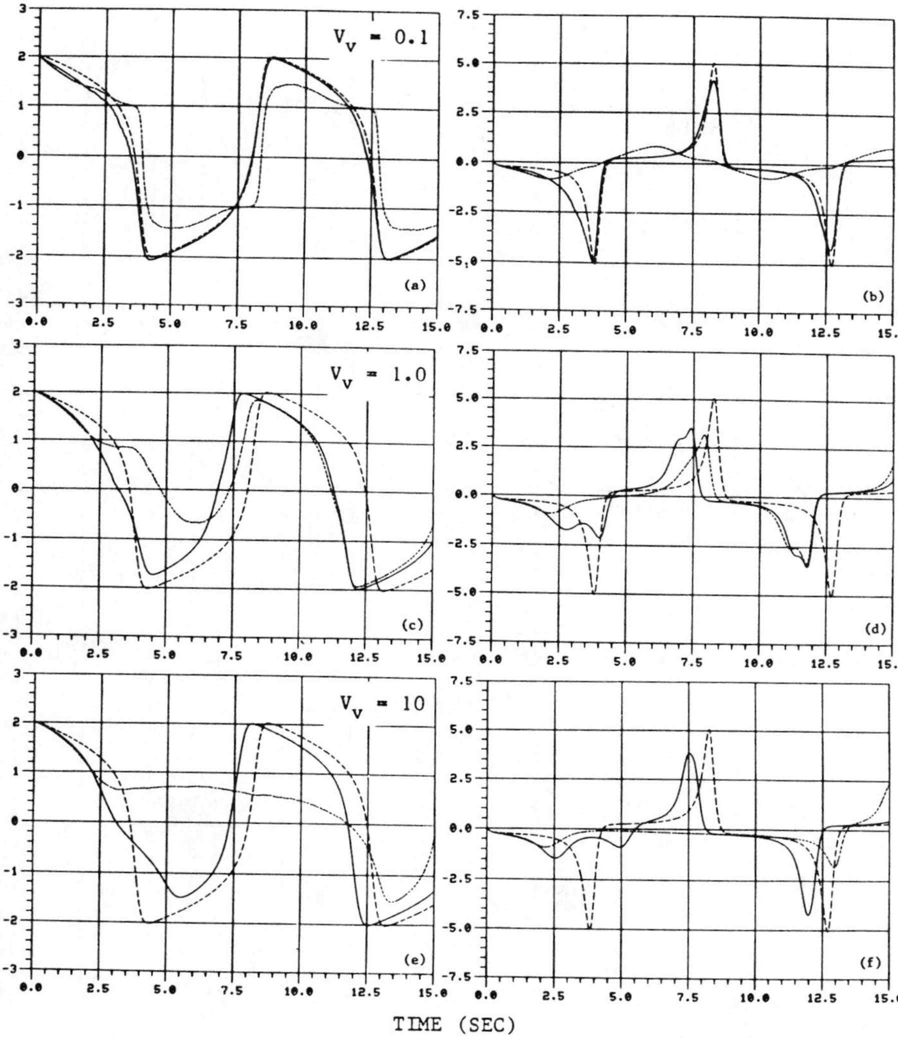

Fig. 11. The Van der Pol oscillator; effects of V_v with small V: $V_{11}(0) = V_{22}(0) = 0.5$; $V_{12} = 0$; $\hat{X}_1(0) = X_1(0) = 2.0$; $X_2(0) = \hat{X}_2(0) = 0$. Filter estimates and true X_1 versus time (a,c,e); filter estimates and true X_2 versus time (b,d,f): $V_v = 0.1$ (a,b); 1.0 (c,d); and 10 (e,f); (-) true state; (—) MVF; and (---) SLF.

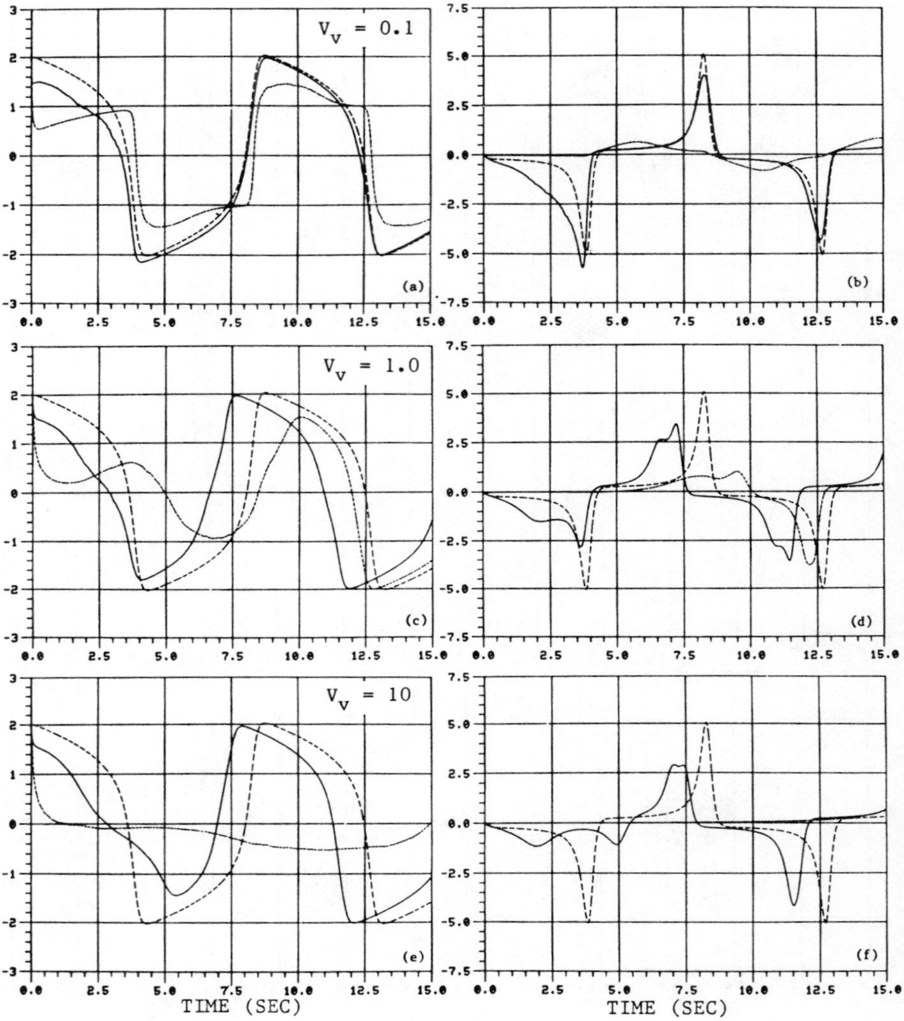

Fig. 12. The Van der Pol oscillator; effects of V_v with larger V: $V_{11}(0) = V_{22}(0) = 5.0$; $V_{12}(0) = 0$; $\hat{X}_1(0) = X_1(0) = 2.0$; $\hat{X}_2(0) = X_2(0) = 0$. Filter estimates and true X_1 versus time (a,c,e); filter estimates and true X_2 versus time (b,d,f): $V_v = 0.1$ (a,b); 1.0 (c,d); and 10 (e,f); (-) true state; (—) MVF; and (---) SLF.

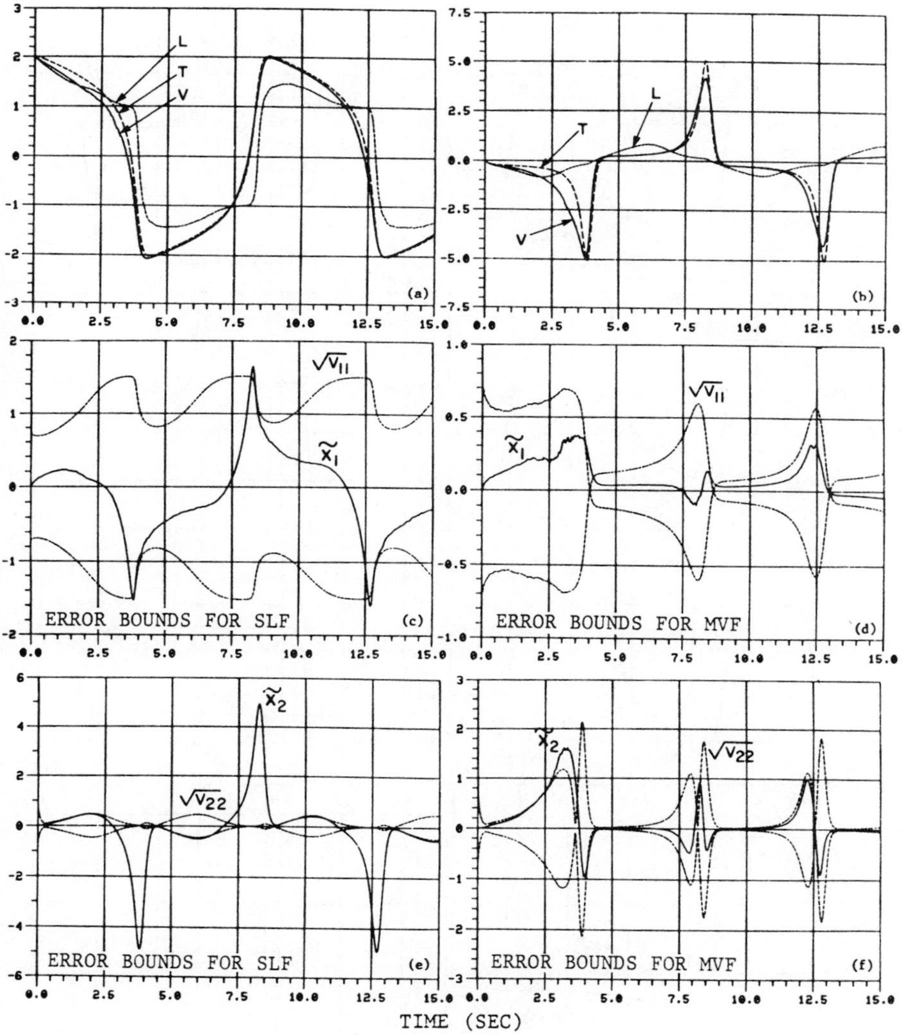

Fig. 13. Outputs of the Van der Pol oscillator with "reasonable" initial estimates and V_v: $V_{11}(0) = V_{22}(0) = 0.5$; $V_{12}(0) = 0$; $\hat{X}_1(0) = X_1(0) = 2.0$; $\hat{X}_2(0) = X_2(0) = 0$; $V_v = 0.1$. *(a) Filter estimates and true* X_1 *versus time; (b) filter estimates and true* X_2 *versus time; error bounds for SLF (c,e) and for MVF (d,f).*

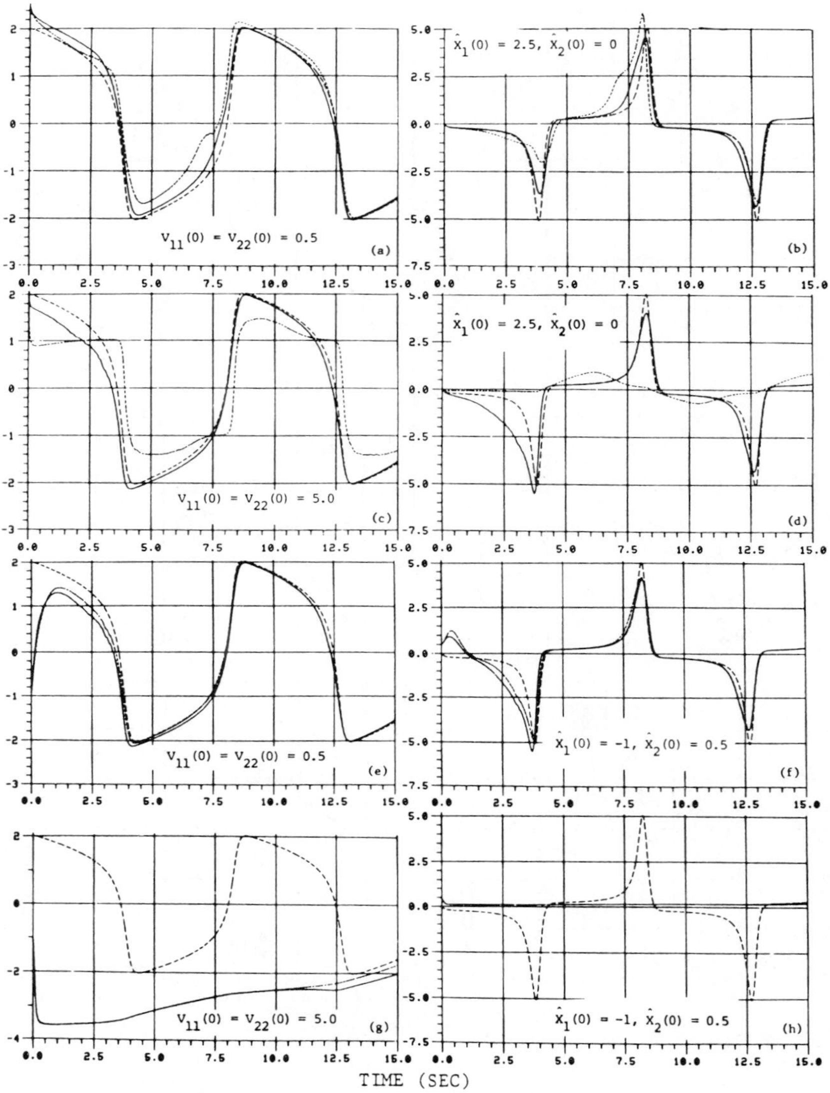

Fig. 14. The Van der Pol oscillator; effects of initial state and error variance: $X_1(0) = 2$; $X_2(0) = 0$; $V_{12}(0) = 0$; $V_v = 0.1$. *Filter estimates and true* X_1 *versus time (a,c,e,g); filter estimates and true* X_2 *versus time (b,d,f,h): (a,b)* $V_{11}(0) = V_{22}(0) = 0.5$, $\hat{X}_1(0) = 2.5$, $\hat{X}_2(0) = 0$; *(c,d)* $V_{11}(0) = V_{22}(0) = 5.0$, $\hat{X}_1(0) = 2.5$, $\hat{X}_2(0) = 0$; *(e,f)* $V_{11}(0) = V_{22}(0) = 0.5$, $\hat{X}_1(0) = -1$, $\hat{X}_2(0) = 0.5$; *(g,h)* $V_{11}(0) = V_{22}(0) = 5.0$, $\hat{X}_1(0) = -1$, $\hat{X}_2(0) = 0.5$.

of the author suggests that in the design of the SLF and MVF for dynamic systems with nonnegligible nonlinearities, it is important not to use overly pessimistic initial error variances, since error variances that were too large could excessively damp the system dynamics and Kalman gain matrix to reject some of the valuable measurement-data inputs.

D. NONLINEAR FILTERS FOR GROUND-BASED RADAR TRACKING

This section deals with the design of nonlinear filters for a ground-based radar-tracking problem involving third-order nonlinearity. Wagner [18] apparently pioneered the application of linear MVFs to the ground-based radar tracking of reentry vehicle. Athans *et al.* [7] and then Wishner *et al.* [19] compared several second-order filters as applied to this nonlinear ground-based tracking problem. The emphasis here is to compare the performances of the MVF, the second-order filter, and the EKF when the a priori knowledge is reliable as well as when it is unreliable.

The message model is described by

$$\dot{x}_1 = -K_0 x_2, \quad \dot{x}_2 = -K_1 \exp(-K_2 x_1) x_2^2 x_3, \quad \dot{x}_3 = 0,$$

where $K_0 = 0.1$, $K_1 = 10$, and $K_2 = 5$. The measurement model of Type I or Type II radar-tracking problem is described by

$$z_1 = x_1 + v \quad \text{or} \quad z_2 = x_2 + v,$$

respectively, where v is a zero-mean white Gaussian noise process with variance V_v.

The major difference between the EKF, MVF, and second-order filter is best illustrated by Figs. 15 to 20. In Figs. 15 and 16, the Type I measurement model was used, with the statistics

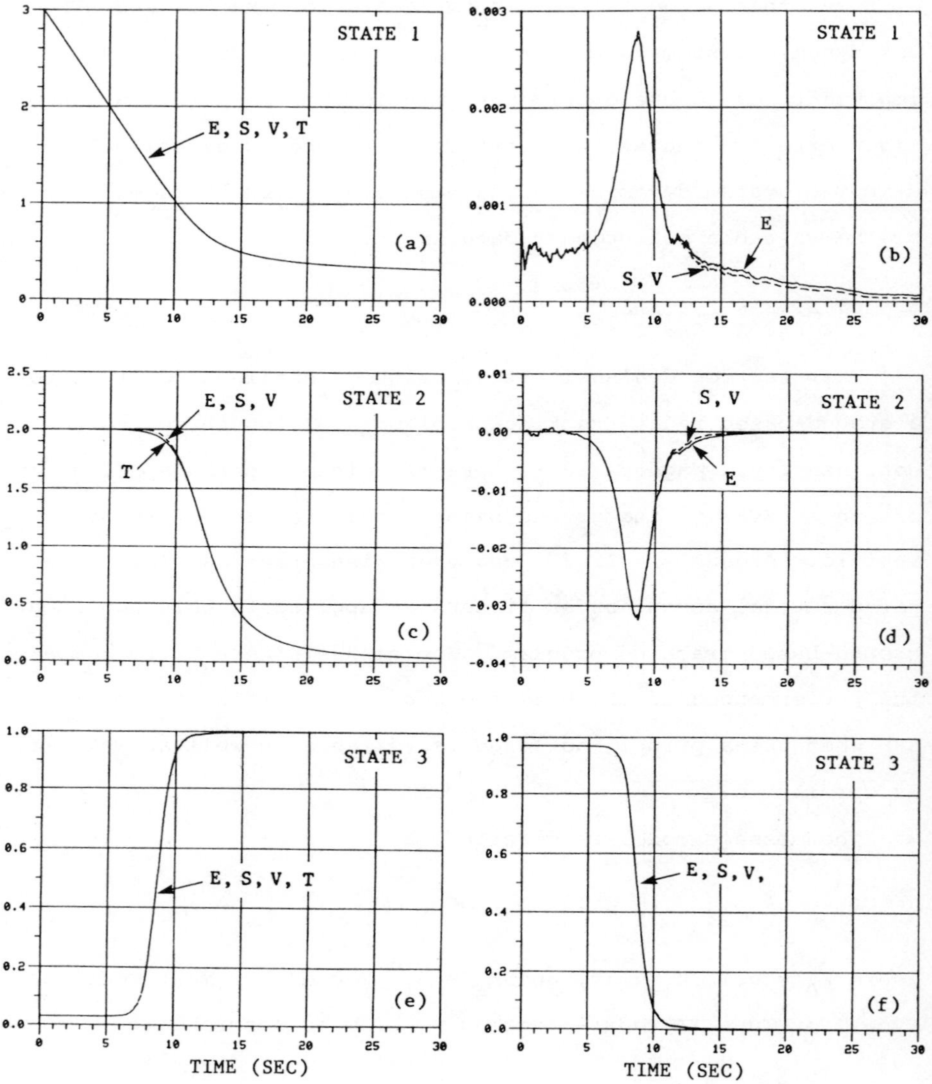

Fig. 15. Radar tracking with Type I measurement; simulation results with reasonable a priori information: $X_1(0) = \hat{X}_1(0) = 3.0$; $\hat{X}_3(0) = 0.03$; $X_2(0) = X_2(0) = 2.0$; $X_3(0) = 1.0$; $V_{11}(0) = 10^{-4}$; $V_{22}(0) = 4 \times 10^{-4}$; $V_{33}(0) = 0.1$. *Filter estimates and true states: (a) state 1, (c) state 2, (e) state 3. Estimator errors: (b) state 1, (d) state 2, (f) state 3.*

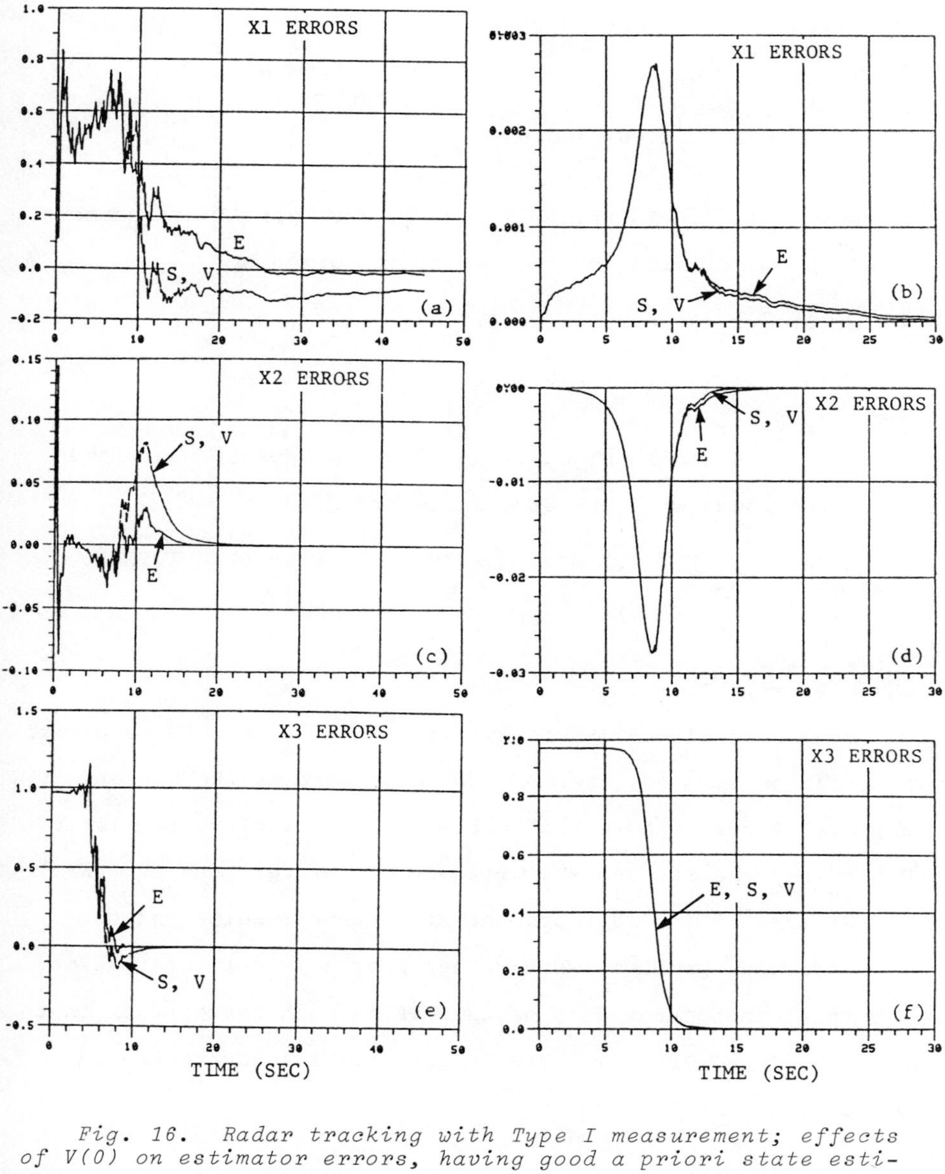

Fig. 16. Radar tracking with Type I measurement; effects of V(0) on estimator errors, having good a priori state estimates: $X_1(0) = \hat{X}_1(0) = 3.0$; $\hat{X}_3(0) = 0.03$; $X_2(0) = \hat{X}_2(0) = 2.0$; $X_3(0) = 1.0$. $V_{11}(0) = 10^{-4}$; $V_{22}(0) = 0.04$; $V_{33}(0) = 100$: *(a)* X_1 *errors, (c)* X_2 *errors, (e)* X_3 *errors.* $V_{11}(0) = 10^{-6}$; $V_{22}(0) = 4 \times 10^{-6}$; $V_{33}(0) = 0.1$: *(b)* X_1 *errors, (d)* X_2 *errors, (f)* X_3 *errors.*

are given by

$$x_1(0) = \hat{x}_1(0) = 3.0, \quad x_2(0) = \hat{x}_2(0) = 2.0,$$

$$x_3(0) = 1, \quad \hat{x}_3(0) = 0.03,$$

where $V_v = 10^{-6}$. In Figs. 17 and 18, the Type II measurement model was used, with the statistics are given by

$$x_1(0) = \hat{x}_1(0) = 3.0, \quad x_2(0) = 2, \quad \hat{x}_2(0) = 2.5,$$

$$x_3(0) = 1, \quad \hat{x}_3(0) = 0.6,$$

where $V_v = 10^{-3}$. In Figs. 19 and 20, the Type II measurement model was used, with the statistics are given by

$$x_1(0) = 3, \quad \hat{x}_1(0) = 4, \quad x_2(0) = 2, \quad \hat{x}_2(0) = 2.5,$$

$$x_3(0) = 1, \quad \hat{x}_3(0) = 0.6,$$

where $V_v = 10^{-3}$.

From Figs. 15 to 18, it is apparent that when the a priori information is good, the EKF can be as good as the SLF and MVF, especially when the initial variances are overly pessimistic. Otherwise, the SLF and MVF will perform better than the EKF.

Figures 19 and 20 represent simulation results for the same tracking problem, with rather poor a priori information. For this, the performance of the MVF is much better than that of the EKF and SLF. The EKF in particular tends to have more pronounced bias errors.

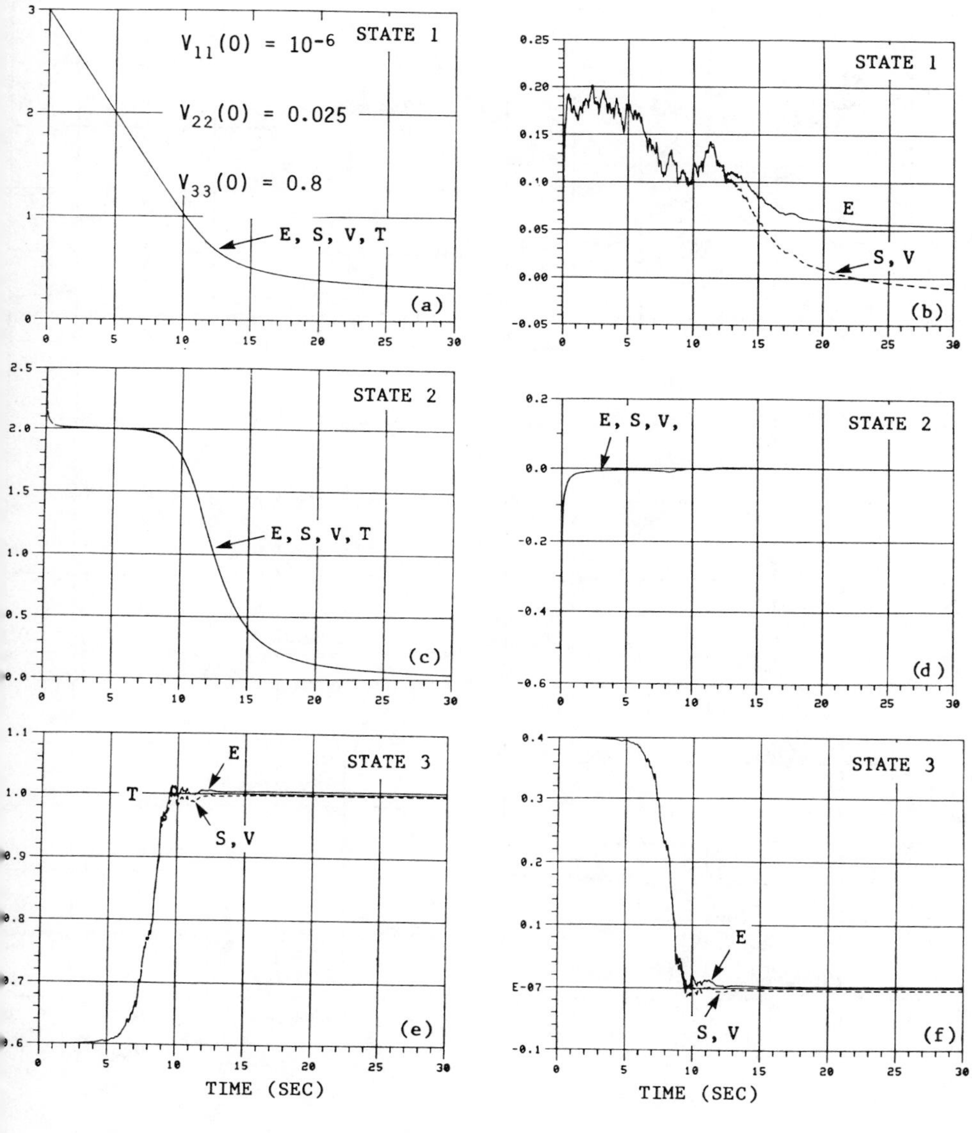

Fig. 17. Radar tracking with Type II measurement; simulation results with smaller error variances when $X_1(0) = \hat{X}_1(0)$: $X_1(0) = \hat{X}_1(0) = 3$; $V_v = 10^{-3}$; $X_2(0) = 2$; $\hat{X}_2(0) = 2.5$; $X_3(0) = 1.0$; $\hat{X}_3(0) = 0.6$; $V_{11}(0) = 10^{-6}$, $V_{22}(0) = 0.025$, $V_{33}(0) = 0.3$. *Filter output and true states: (a) state 1, (c) state 2; (e) state 3. Estimator errors: (b) state 1, (d) state 2, (f) state 3.*

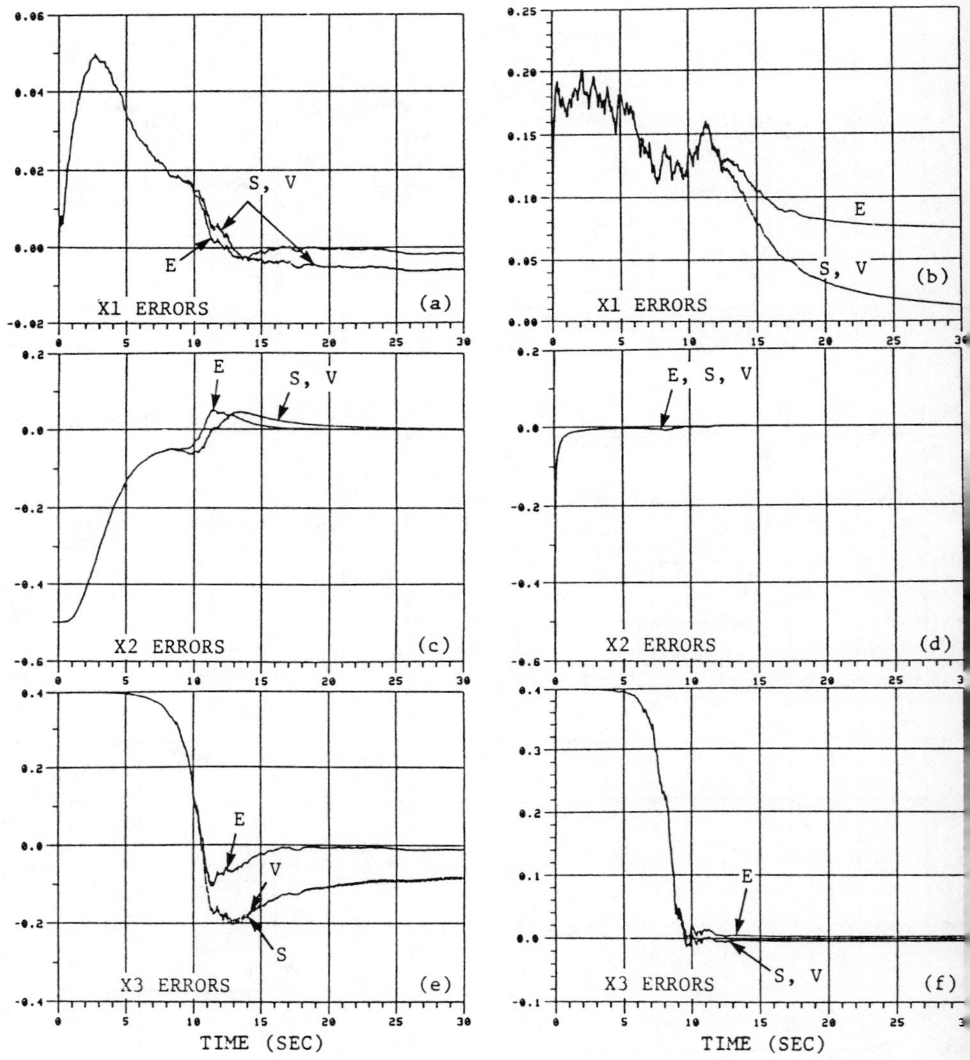

Fig. 18. Radar tracking with Type II measurement; effects of V(0) on estimator errors when $X_1(0) = \hat{X}_1(0)$: $X_1(0) = \hat{X}_1(0) = 3$; $V_v = 10^{-3}$; $X_2(0) = 2$; $\hat{X}_2(0) = 2.5$; $X_3 = 1.0$; $\hat{X}_3(0) = 0.6$. $V_{11}(0) = 10^{-2}$, $V_{22}(0) = 0.025$, $V_{33}(0) = 0.8$: *(a)* X_1 *errors, (c)* X_2 *errors, (e)* X_3 *errors.* $V_{11}(0) = 10^{-4}$, $V_{22}(0) = 0.025$, $V_{33}(0) = 0.8$: *(b)* X_1 *errors, (d)* X_2 *errors, (f)* X_3 *errors.*

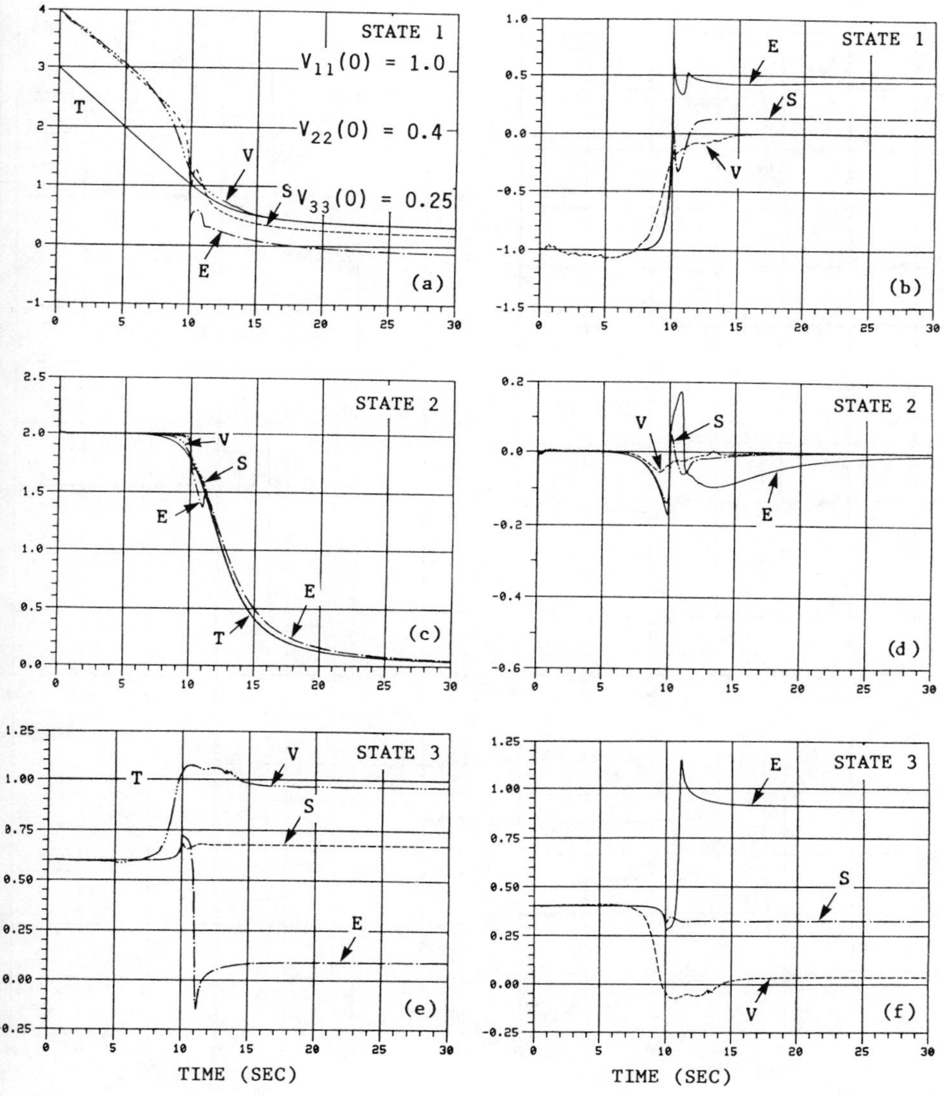

Fig. 19. Radar tracking with Type II measurement; simulation results with reasonably good a priori V(0) when $X_1(0) \neq \hat{X}_1(0)$: $X_1(0) = 3$; $\hat{X}_1(0) = 4$; $V_v = 10^{-3}$; $X_2(0) = 2$; $\hat{X}_2(0) = 2.5$; $X_3(0) = 1$; $\hat{X}_3(0) = 0.6$; $V_{11}(0) = 1.0$, $V_{22}(0) = 0.4$, $V_{33}(0) = 0.25$. *Filter output true states: (a) state 1; (c) state 2; (e) state 3. Estimator errors: (b) state 1; (d) state 1; (f) state 3.*

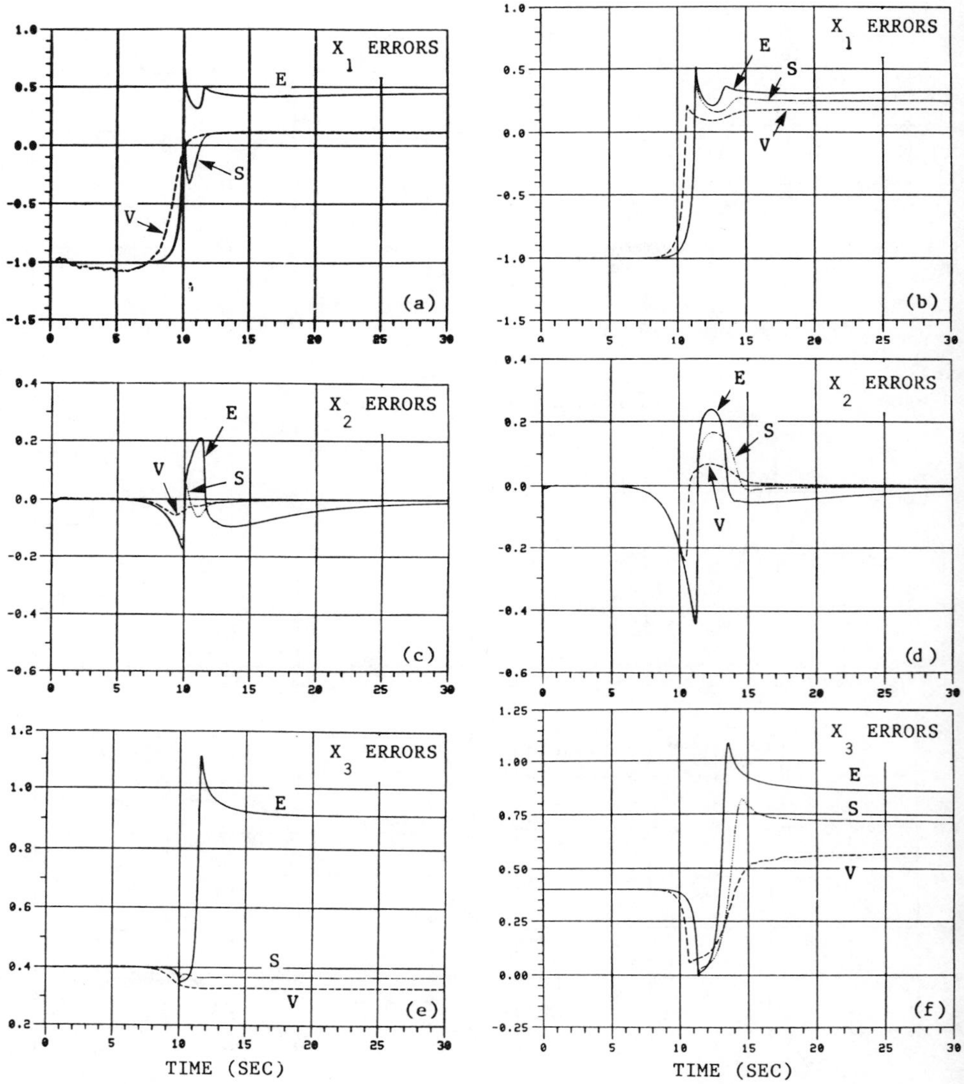

Fig. 20. Radar tracking with Type II measurement; effects of V(0) on estimator errors when $X_1(0) \neq \hat{X}_1(0)$*:* $X_1(0) = 3$*;* $\hat{X}_1(0) = 4$*;* $V_v = 10^{-3}$*;* $X_2(0) = 2$*;* $\hat{X}_2(0) = 2.5$*;* $X_3(0) = 1$*;* $\hat{X}_3(0) = 0.6$*.* $V_{11}(0) = 1$*,* $V_{22}(0) = 0.4$*,* $V_{33}(0) = 0.1$*: (a)* X_1 *errors, (c)* X_2 *errors, (e)* X_3 *errors.* $V_{11}(0) = 0.1$*,* $V_{22}(0) = 0.4$*,* $V_{33}(0) = 0.1$*: (b)* X_1 *errors, (d)* X_2 *errors, (f)* X_3 *errors.*

III. COMPARISONS OF DISCRETE-TIME NONLINEAR RECURSIVE FILTERS

A. COMPARISON OF SOME DISCRETE-TIME FILTER STRUCTURES

Consider a general class of discrete-time nonlinear systems described by

$$x(k + 1) = f[x(k), k] + G[x(k), k]w(k), \tag{9}$$

with measurements represented by

$$z(k) = h[x(k), k] + v(k), \tag{10}$$

where the state x is an n vector, the measurement z an m vector, the state noise sequence w an r vector, the measurement noise v an m vector; G is a nonlinear state-dependent $n \times r$ matrix, and f and h are, respectively, n and m dimensional.

The random vectors w(k) and v(k) are independent zero-mean white Gaussian noise sequences for which

$$E_k\{w(k)w^T(j)\} = \Psi_w(k)\delta_{kj}, \quad E_k\{v(k)v^T(j)\} = \Psi_v(k)\delta_{kj},$$

$$E_k\{w(k)v^T(j)\} = 0,$$

for all integers k and j, where $E_k\{\cdot\}$ denotes the expectation operation conditioned on $Z(k) = \{z(0), z(1), \ldots, z(k)\}$; Ψ_w and Ψ_v are $r \times r$ and $m \times m$ positive definite matrices, respectively.

For purposes of comparison, the structures of the EKF and a realizable minimum-variance discrete-time nonlinear filter are tabulated in Tables III and IV.

Table III. Extended Discrete Kalman Filter Algorithm

Message model:

$$x(k+1) = f[x(k), k] + G[x(k), k]w(k)$$

Measurement model:

$$z(k) = h[x(k), k] + v(k)$$

Prior moments:

$$\mathrm{cov}\{w(k), w(j)\} = \Psi_w(k)\delta_{kj}, \qquad \mathrm{cov}\{v(k), v(j)\} = \Psi_v(k)\delta_{kj}$$

$$\mathrm{cov}\{v(k), w(j)\} = 0$$

Filter equations:

$$\hat{x}(k+1/k+1) = \hat{x}(k+1/k) + K(k+1) \times \{z(k+1) - h[\hat{x}(k+1/k), k]\}$$

$$\hat{x}(k+1/k) = f[\hat{x}(k), k]$$

$$K(k+1) = V_{\tilde{x}}(k+1/k)H^T(k+1) \times \Big[H(k+1)V_{\tilde{x}}(k+1/k)H^T \times (k+1) + \Psi_v(k+1)\Big]^{-1}$$

$$V_{\tilde{x}}(k+1/k) = \frac{\partial f[\hat{x}(k), k]}{\partial \hat{x}(k)} V_{\tilde{x}}(k) \frac{\partial f^T[\hat{x}(k), k]}{\partial \hat{x}(k)} + G[\hat{x}(k), k]\Psi_w(k)G^T[\hat{x}(k), k]$$

$$V_{\tilde{x}}(k+1/k+1) = [I - K(k+1)H(k+1)]V_{\tilde{x}}(k+1/k)$$

where

$$H(k+1) = \left.\frac{\partial h[x(k+1), k+1]}{\partial x(k+1)}\right|_{x(k+1)=\hat{x}(k+1/k)}$$

Table IV. Minimum-Variance Discrete Nonlinear Filter Algorithm

---

Message model:

$$x(k+1) = f[x(k), k)] + G[x(k), k]w(k)$$

Measurement model:

$$z(k) = h[x(k), k] + v(k)$$

Prior moments:

Same as Table III

Filter equations:

$$\hat{x}(k+1/k+1) = \hat{x}(k+1/k) + K(k+1) \times \{z(k+1) - \hat{h}[x(k+1), k+1/k]\} \quad (11)$$

where

$$\hat{x}(k+1/k) = \hat{f}[x(k), k/k] = E_k\{f[x(k), k]\}$$

$$\hat{h}[x(k+1), k+1/k] = E_k\ h[x(k+1), k+1]\} \quad (12)$$

$$K(k+1) = E_k\{\tilde{x}(k+1/k)h^T[x(k+1), k+1]\} \times \left(\Psi_v(k+1) + E_k\{\tilde{h}[x(k+1)/k]\tilde{h}^T \times [x(k+1)/k]\}\right)^{-1} \quad (13)$$

where

$$\tilde{h}[x(k+1)/k] = h[x(k+1), k+1] - \hat{h}[x(k+1), k+1/k]$$

$$\tilde{x}(k+1/k) = x(k+1) - \hat{x}(k+1/k)$$

$$V_{\tilde{x}}(k+1/k) = E_k\{\tilde{f}[x(k), k/k]\tilde{f}^T[x(k), k/k]\} + E_k\{G[x(k), k]\Psi_w(k)G^T[x(k), k]\} \quad (14)$$

(Table IV continues)

(Table IV continued)

where

$$\tilde{f}[x(k),\ k/k] = f[x(k),\ k] - \hat{f}[x(k),\ k/k]$$

and, finally,

$$V_{\tilde{x}}(k+1/k+1) = V_{\tilde{x}}(k+1/k) - K(k+1)E_k \times \{\tilde{h}[x(k+1)/k]\tilde{x}^T(k+1/k)\} \quad (15)$$

Let us consider the special case where the measurements are represented by

$$z(k) = H_k x_k + \sum_{j=1}^{m} \phi_j x_k^T E_k^j x_k + v_k, \quad (16)$$

where E_k^j represents a set of m-symmetric $n \times n$ matrices. Now, $\phi_1, \phi_2, \ldots, \phi_m$ denote the natural basis vectors

$$\phi_1 = \begin{bmatrix} 1 \\ 0 \\ \vdots \\ 0 \end{bmatrix}, \quad \phi_2 = \begin{bmatrix} 0 \\ 1 \\ \vdots \\ 0 \end{bmatrix}, \quad \ldots, \quad \phi_m = \begin{bmatrix} 0 \\ 0 \\ \vdots \\ 1 \end{bmatrix}.$$

Then, the minimum-variance discrete-time filtering equations of Table IV can be rewritten as those represented in Table V. Notice that the error-variance equation presented is numerically stable.

Table V. Minimum-Variance Filter for Systems with Quadratic Measurement Nonlinearities

$$x(k+1) = f[x(k), k] + G[x(k), k]w(k)$$

$$z(h) = H_k x_k + \sum_{j=1}^{m} \phi_j x_k^T E_k^j x_k + v_k, \quad \phi_1 = \begin{bmatrix} 1 \\ 0 \\ \vdots \\ 0 \end{bmatrix}, \quad \ldots, \quad \phi_m = \begin{bmatrix} 0 \\ 0 \\ \vdots \\ 1 \end{bmatrix}$$

$$\hat{x}(k+1/k) = \hat{f}[x(k), k/k]$$

$$\hat{x}(k+1/k+1) = \hat{x}(k+1/k) + K_{k+1} \times \left[z(k+1) - \left\{ H_{k+1} + \sum_{j=1}^{m} \phi_j \hat{x}^T(k+1/k) E_{k+1}^j \right\} \times \hat{x}(k+1/k) - \sum_{j=1}^{m} \phi_j \, tr\left\{ E_{k+1}^j V_{\tilde{x}}(k+1/k) \right\} \right]$$

$$K_{k+1} = V_{\tilde{x}}(k+1/k) \left[H_{k+1} + 2 \sum_{j=1}^{m} \phi_j \hat{x}^T(k+1/k) E_{k+1}^j \right]^T \times \left[\Psi_v(k+1) + \left\{ H_{k+1} + 2 \sum_{j=1}^{m} \phi_j \hat{x}^T(k+1/k) E_{k+1}^j \right\} \times V_{\tilde{x}}(k+1/k) \left\{ H_{k+1} + 2 \sum_{\ell=1}^{m} \phi_\ell \hat{x}^T(k+1/k) E_{k+1}^\ell \right\}^T + \sum_{j,\ell=1}^{m} 2\phi_j \, tr\left\{ E_{k+1}^j V_{\tilde{x}}(k+1/k) E_{k+1}^\ell V_{\tilde{x}}(k+1/k) \right\} \phi_\ell^T \right]^{-1}$$

$$V_{\tilde{x}}(k+1/k) = E_k\{\tilde{f}[x(k), k/k] \tilde{f}^T[x(k), k/k]\} + E_k\left\{ G[x(k), k] \Psi_w(k) G^T[x(k), k] \right\}$$

(Table V continues)

(Table V continued)

$$V_{\tilde{x}}(k+1) = \left[I - K_{k+1}\left\{H_{k+1} + 2\sum_{j=1}^{m} \phi_j \hat{x}^T(k+1/k)E_{k+1}^j\right\}\right]$$

$$\times V_{\tilde{x}}(k+1/k)\left[I - K_{k+1}\right.$$

$$\left.\times\left\{H_{k+1} + 2\sum_{\ell=1}^{m} \phi_\ell \hat{x}(k+1/k)E_{k+1}^\ell\right\}\right]^T$$

$$+ K_{k+1}\left\{\Psi_v(k+1) + 2\sum_{j,\ell=1}^{m} \phi_j\, tr\left[E_{k+1}^j V_{\tilde{x}}(k+1/k)\right.\right.$$

$$\left.\left.\times E_{k+1}^\ell V_{\tilde{x}}(k+1/k)\right]\phi_\ell^T\right\}K_{k+1}^T$$

In the special case where the measurement model is represented by Eq. (16) and the message model is

$$x(k+1) = \Phi_k x_k + \sum_{i=1}^{s} \phi_i x_k^T G_k^i x_k + w_k,$$

where G_k^i represents a set of s-symmetric $n \times n$ matrices.

Then, Eqs. (12) and (14) are, respectively, further reduced to

$$\hat{x}(k+1/k) = \phi_k \hat{x}(k/k) + \sum_{i=1}^{s} \phi_i\left\{\hat{x}^T(k/k)G_k^i\hat{x}(k/k) + tr\left[G_k^i V_{\tilde{x}}(k/k)\right]\right\},$$

$$V_x(k+1/k) = \left[\Phi_k + 2\sum_{q=1}^{s} \phi_i \hat{x}^T(k/k) G_k^i\right] V_{\tilde{x}}(k/k)$$

$$\times \left[\Phi_k + 2\sum_{q=1}^{s} \phi_q \hat{x}^T(k/k) G_k^q\right]^T + \Psi_w(k)$$

$$+ \sum_{i,q=1}^{n} 2\phi_i \ \mathrm{tr}\left[G_k^i V_{\tilde{x}}(k/k) G_k^q V_x(k/k)\right] \phi_q^T.$$

For this particular case, the filtering equations presented are identical to those derived by H. W. Sorenson [20]. He noted that the structure of this filter has the effect of modifying the linear system matrices ϕ, H and the effective noise covariances.

B. STATE- AND PARAMETER-ESTIMATION PROBLEM: CASE I

To test and compare the performance characteristics of the minimum-variance discrete-time estimator with those of the EKF, three simple state- and parameter-estimation problems were selected. The first is represented by the following equations:

$$x_1(k+1) = x_1(k) - x_1(k)x_2(k) + w,$$

$$x_2(k+1) = x_2(k), \quad z(k) = x_1(k)x_2(k) + v,$$

where noise variances of v and w are, respectively, Ψ_v and Ψ_w. The dynamic structures of the MVF and EKF are represented in Table VI.

It is apparent that the major difference between the EKF and MVF is due to the terms $V_{12}^2 + V_{11}V_{22}$ and V_{12}. Therefore, it can be expected that the performance characteristics of these two filters will be reatly affected by the selections of

Table VI. Dynamic Structures of the EKF and MVF

Extended Kalman filter	Additional terms for MVF
$\hat{x}_1(k+1/k) = \hat{x}_1(k) - \hat{x}_1(k)\hat{x}_2(k)$	$-V_{12}(k)$
$\hat{x}_2(k+1/k) = \hat{x}_2(k)$	None
$V(k+1/k) = \Phi(k+1/k)V(k/k) \times \Phi^T(k+1/k) + Q$	$+JG_M$
where	where
$\phi(k+1/k) = \begin{bmatrix} 1 - \hat{x}_2(k) & -\hat{x}_1(k) \\ 0 & 1 \end{bmatrix}$	$G_M = \begin{bmatrix} 1 & 0 \\ 0 & 0 \end{bmatrix}$
$0 = \begin{bmatrix} \Psi_w & 0 \\ 0 & 0 \end{bmatrix}$	$J = V_{11}(k)V_{22}(k) + V_{12}^2(k)$
$K = V(k+1/k)H^T W^{-1}$	None
where	
$H = [\hat{x}_2(k+1/k)\hat{x}_1(k+1/k)]$	
$W = HV(k+1/k)H^T + \Psi_v$	$+V_{11}(k+1/k)V_{22}(k+1/k) + V_{12}^2(k+1/k)$
$V(k+1) = (I - KH)V(k+1/k) \times (I - KH)^T + K\Psi_v K^T$	$+K[V_{11}(k+1/k)V_{22}(k+1/k) + V_{12}^2(k+1/k)]K^T$
$\hat{z} = \hat{x}_1(k+1/k)\hat{x}_2(k+1/k)$	$+V_{12}(k+1/k)$
$\hat{x}(k+1) = \hat{x}(k+1/k) + K(z - \hat{z})$	None

initial variances, including the choice of $V_{12}(0)$. To compare the performance of these two filters, some typical results of extensive simulations are presented in Figs. 21 to 25. Here, each of the graphs presented represents the average results of 150 simulation runs.

Figure 21 shows the filter-output responses for perfect a priori initial state estimates, with small noise variances and initial error variances. For this particular case it is obvious that the MVF is only marginally better than the EKF.

Figure 22 shows the effects of initial state estimates on filter performance for

$$x_1(0) = x_2(0) = 2.0, \quad \Psi_v = \Psi_w = 0.01,$$

$$V_{11}(0) = V_{12}(0) = V_{22}(0) = 0.01.$$

When the initial error variances are increased to the value of 1.0, simulation results for similar conditions are shown in Fig. 23. When simulation results of Figs. 22 and 23 are compared with the outputs of the true states presented in Fig. 21a, it is evident that the MVF is much less sensitive to the choice of initial state estimates. It is further observed that when the appropriate values of state estimates are made available, the EKF is slightly better than the MVF. But when the a priori state estimates are far different from the true values of system states, the MVF is far superior than the EKF for both large and small initial variances; however, when the noise variances are increased, the gap between the MVF and EKF gradually diminished. For these cases, the EKF performs almost as well as the MVF. Moreover, it should be noted that when

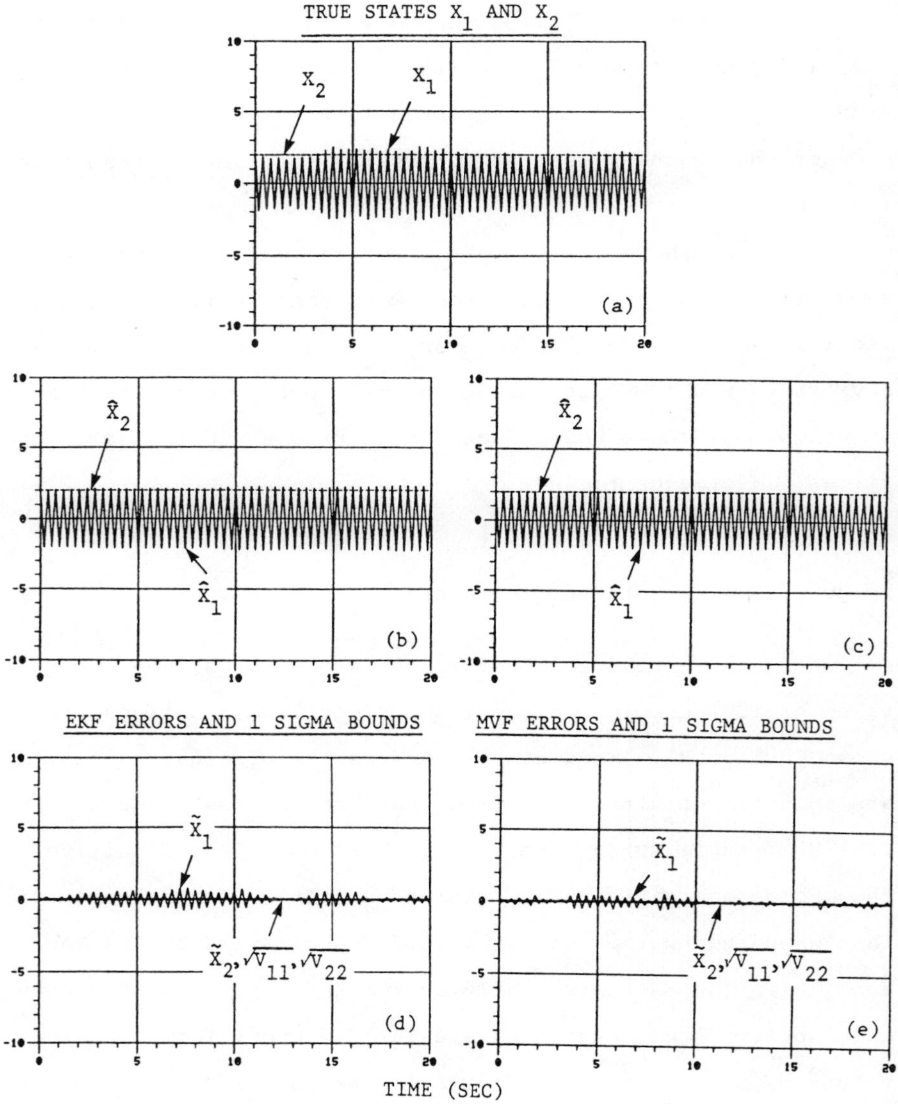

Fig. 21. Outputs of discrete case I; small Ψ *and V:* $\Psi_v = \Psi_w = 0.01$; $X_1(0) = X_2(0) = \hat{X}_1(0) = \hat{X}_2(0) = 2.0$; $V_{11}(0) = V_{22}(0) = V_{12}(0) = 0.01$; $X_1(k+1) = X_1(k) - X_1(k)X_2(k) + w$; $X_2(k+1) = X_2(k)$. *(a) True states* X_1 *and* X_2; *(b) EKF and (c) MVF outputs for states* X_1 *and* X_2; *(d) EKF and (e) MVF errors and* 1σ *bounds.*

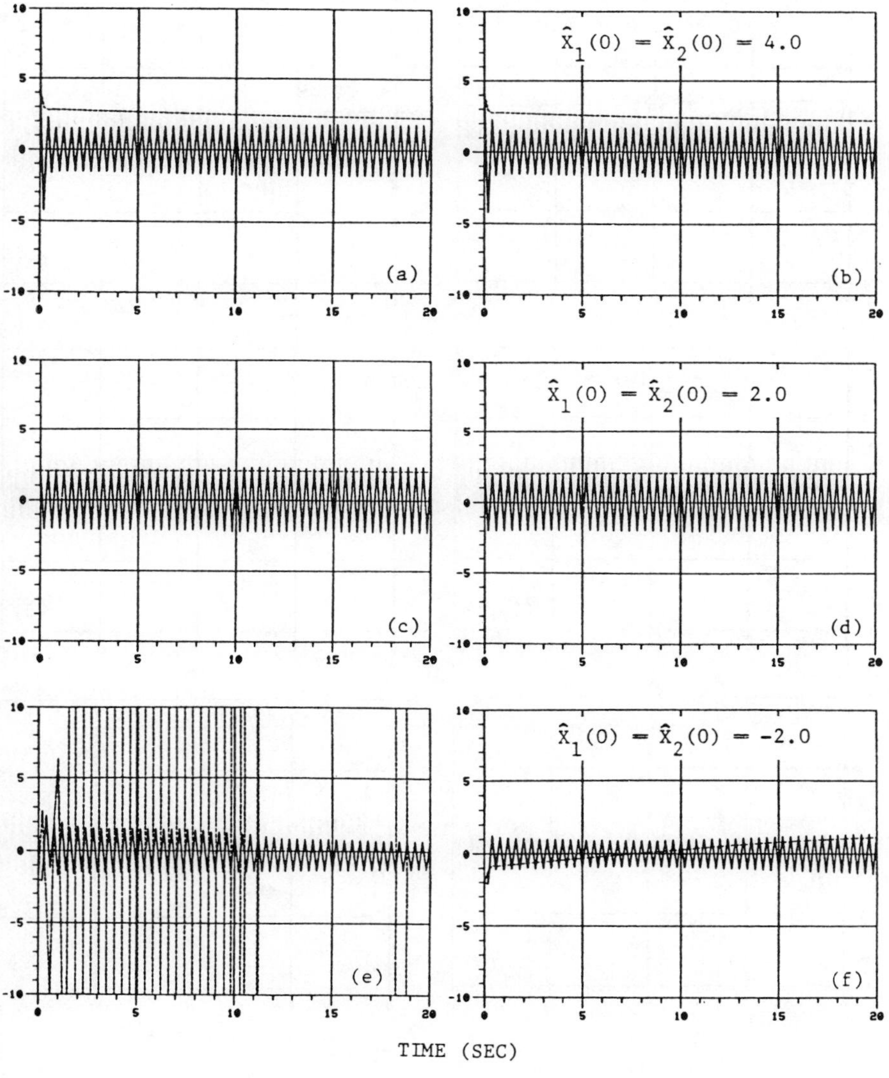

Fig. 22. Discrete case I; effects of $\hat{X}(0)$ with small Ψ and V: $\Psi_v = \Psi_w = 0.01$; $X_1(0) = X_2(0) = 2.0$; $V_{11}(0) = V_{22}(0) = V_{12}(0) = 0.01$: filter estimates $\hat{X}_1$ (solid curve) and $\hat{X}_2$ (dashed curve). EKF (a,c,e) and MVF (b,d,f) outputs for states X_1 and X_2. $\hat{X}_1(0) = \hat{X}_2(0) = 4.0$ (a,b), 2.0 (c,d), and -2.0 (e,f).

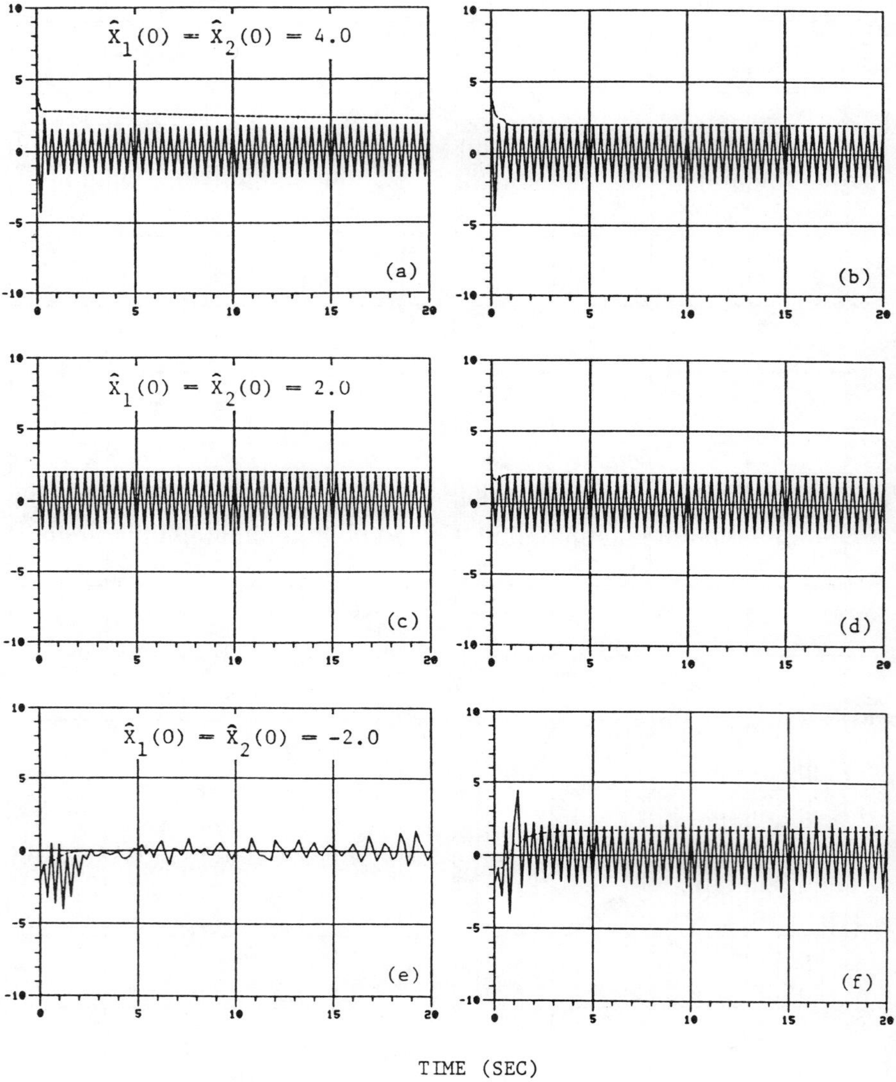

Fig. 23. Discrete case I; effects of $\hat{X}(0)$ with small Ψ and larger V: $\Psi_v = \Psi_w = 0.01$; $X_1(0) = X_2(0) = 2.0$; $V_{11}(0) = V_{22}(0) = V_{12}(0) = 1.0$: filter estimates $\hat{X}_1$ (solid curve) and $\hat{X}_2$ (dashed curve). EKF (a,c,e) and MVF (b,d,f) outputs for states X_1 and X_2. $\hat{X}_1(0) = \hat{X}_2(0) = 4.0$ (a,b), 2.0 (c,d), and -2.0 (e,f).

the initial error variances are increased, the difference between the EKF and MVF becomes much more pronounced. These experimental results agree well with what was theoretically expected.

Figures 24 and 25 further demonstrate the effects of initial variances V_{11}, V_{22}, and V_{12} on the performance of the filters. It is apparent that the selection of initial V_{12} is as important as the selection of V_{11} and V_{22}: It seems that the selection of an inappropriate $V_{12}(0)$ may have more significant effects on the stability and performance of both filters. From the author's simulation experinece it is noted that in the design of the EKF for systems with nonnegligible nonlinearities, the designer should be careful not to use overly optimistic initial error variances, and, as mentioned earlier, in the design of the MVF, the designer should be careful not to use overly pessimistic initial error variances, since error variances that were too large could excessively enlarge the added measurement variances. As a result, valuable measurement data could end up being rejected.

C. STATE AND PARAMETER ESTIMATION: CASES II AND III

Two more numerical examples that were investigated are described by the following equations: for Case II,

$$x_1(k+1) = x_1(k)x_2(k) + w, \quad x_2(k+1) = x_2(k),$$

$$z(k) = x_1(k)x_2(k) + v;$$

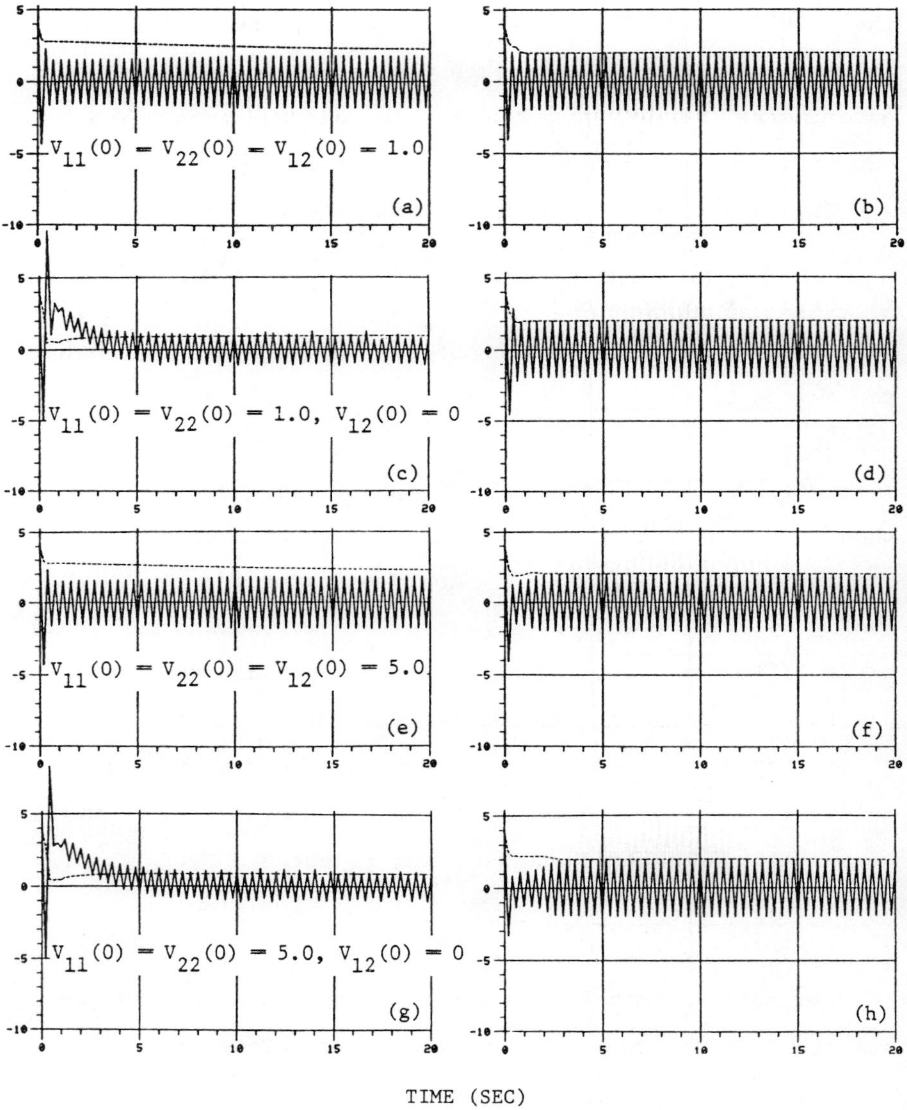

Fig. 24. Discrete case I; effects of initial V with small Ψ: $\Psi_v = \Psi_w = 0.01$; $X_1(0) = X_2(0) = 2.0$; $\hat{X}_1(0) = \hat{X}_2(0) = 4.0$. *Filter estimates* $\hat{X}_1$ *(solid curve) and* $\hat{X}_2$ *(dashed curve). EKF (a,c,e,g) and MVF (b,d,f,h) outputs for states* X_1 *and* X_2. *(a,b)* $V_{11}(0) = V_{22}(0) = V_{12}(0) = 1.0$; *(c,d)* $V_{11}(0) = V_{22}(0) = 1.0$, $V_{12}(0) = 0$; *(e,f)* $V_{11}(0) = V_{22}(0) = V_{12}(0) = 5.0$; *(g,h)* $V_{11}(0) = V_{22}(0) = 5.0$, $V_{12}(0) = 0$.

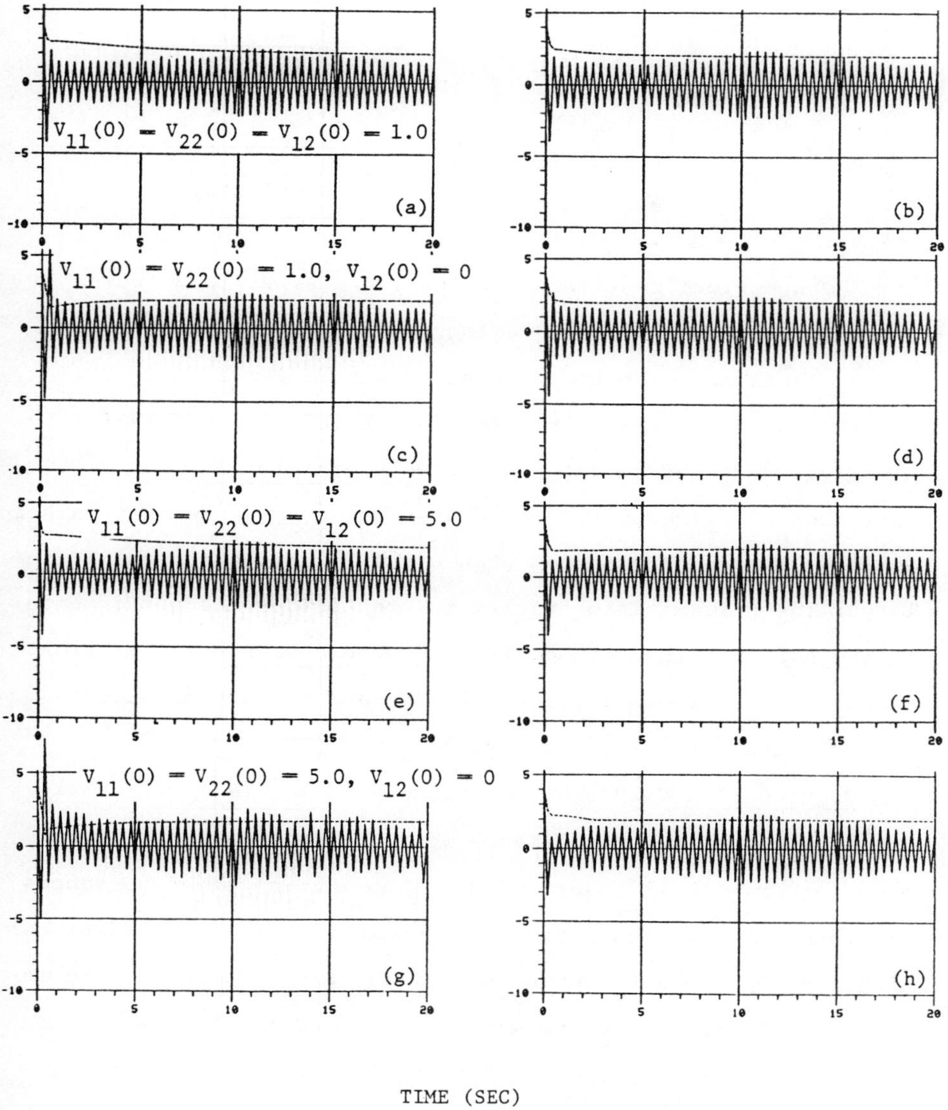

Fig. 25. Discrete case I; effects of initial V with larger Ψ: $\Psi_v = \Psi_w = 1.0$; $X_1(0) = X_2(0) = 2.0$; $\hat{X}_1(0) = \hat{X}_2(0) = 4.0$. *Filter estimates* $\hat{X}_1$ *(solid curve) and* $\hat{X}_2$ *(dashed curve). EKF (a,c,e,f) and MVF (b,d,f,h) outputs for states* X_1 *and* X_2. *(a,b)* $V_{11}(0) = V_{22}(0) = V_{12}(0) = 1.0$; *(c,d)* $V_{11}(0) = V_{22}(0) = 1.0$, $V_{12}(0) = 0$; *(e,f)* $V_{11}(0) = V_{22}(0) = V_{12}(0) = 5.0$; *(g,h)* $V_{11}(0) = V_{22}(0) = 5.0$, $V_{12}(0) = 0$.

for Case III,

$$x_1(k + 1) = -x_1(k)x_2(k) + w, \quad x_2(k + 1) = x_2(k),$$

$$z(k) = x_1(k)x_2(k) + v,$$

where the noise variances of v and w are, respectively, Ψ_v and Ψ_w.

The numerical results presented in Figs. 26 to 31 were all obtained from 25-run Monte Carlo simulations. Figures 26 to 29 were obtained from the discrete-time problem of Case II. Figures 30 and 31 were obtained from the example of Case III.

Figures 26 and 27 show the effects of initial error variances on filter performance when noise variances are rather small. It is apparent that when noise variances are small, the larger the initial error variances, the better the performance of the MVF over that of the EKF. However, when initial error variances are too small, both the MVF and the EKF can not properly track the true states.

Figures 28 and 29 show the effects of initial error variances on the filter performance when the noise variances are much larger. It is observed that when initial error variances are rather small, the performance of the EKF is still identical with that of the MVF. When the initial error variances are increased, the difference between the EKF and the MVF is accentuated. It is interesting to observe that when the a priori information is good, the EKF can sometimes be slightly better than the MVF, but in most cases, the MVF is far superior to the EKF.

For the discrete-time example of Case III, Figs. 30 and 31 show the effects of initial error variances with small noise variances. Again, various comments that were made earlier are equally applicable for this example.

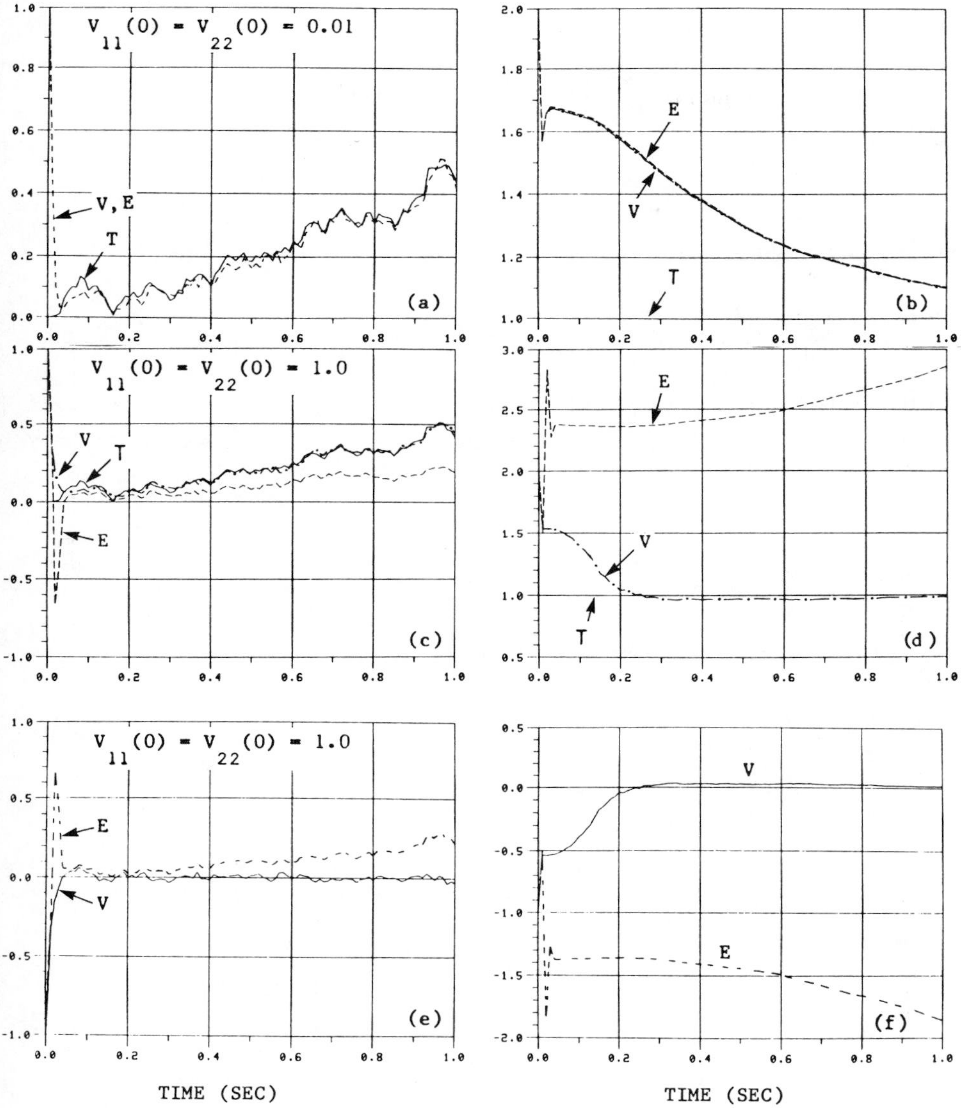

Fig. 26. Discrete case II; effects of V with small Ψ: $\hat{X}_1(0) = 1.0$; $\hat{X}_2(0) = 2.0$; $X_1(0) = 0$; $X_2(0) = 1.0$; $\Psi_v = \Psi_w = 0.01$. Filter estimates and true X_1 versus time (a,c); filter estimates and true X_2 versus time (b,d); estimator errors for X_1 (e) and X_2 (f). $V_{11}(0) = V_{22}(0) = 0.01$ (a,b) and 1.0 (c,d,e,f).

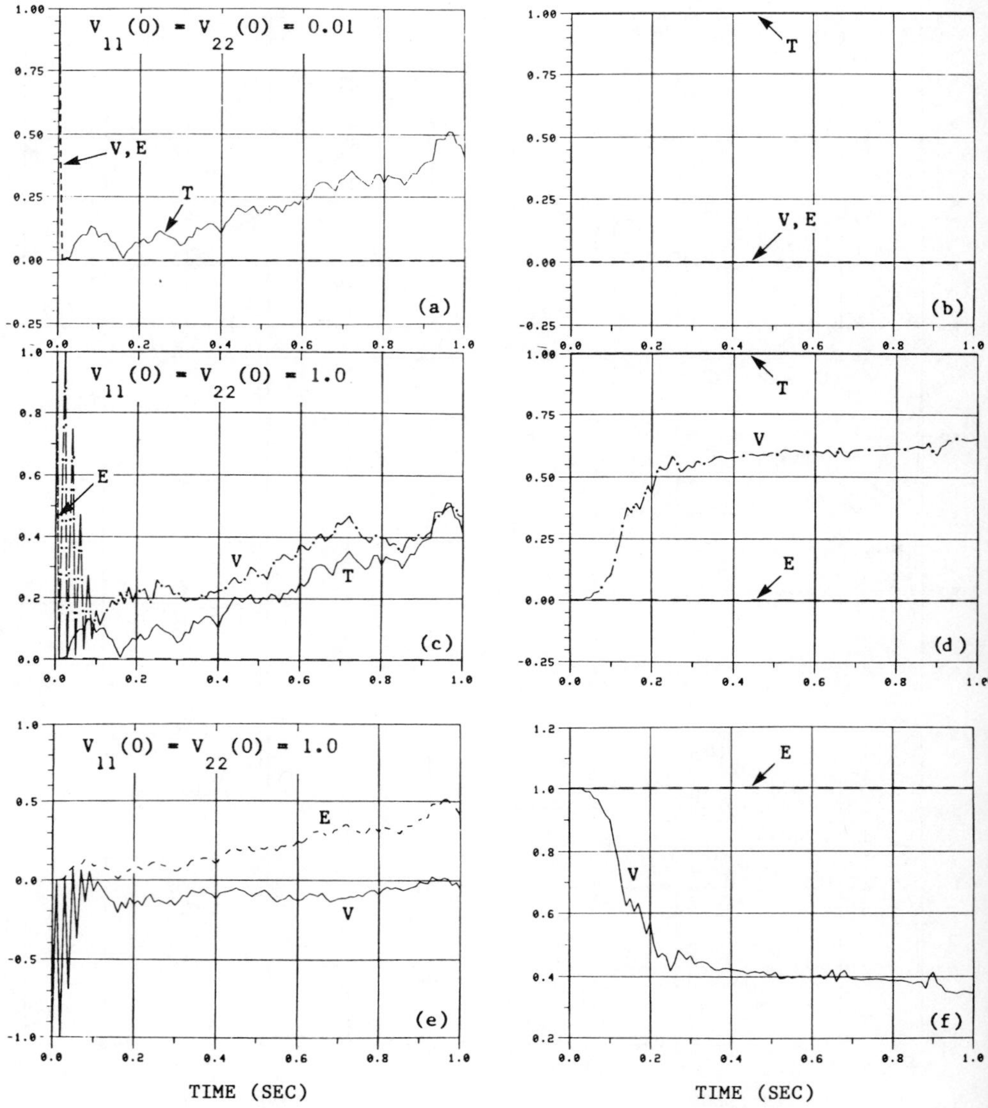

Fig. 27. Discrete case II; effects of V with small Ψ: $\hat{X}_1(0) = 1.0$; $\hat{X}_2(0) = 0$; $X_1(0) = 0$; $X_2(0) = 1.0$; $\Psi_v = \Psi_w = 0.01$. Filter estimates and true X_1 versus time (a,c); filter estimates and true X_2 versus time (b,d); estimator errors for X_1 (e) and X_2 (f). $V_{11}(0) = V_{22}(0) = 0.01$ (a,b) and 1.0 (c,d,e,f).

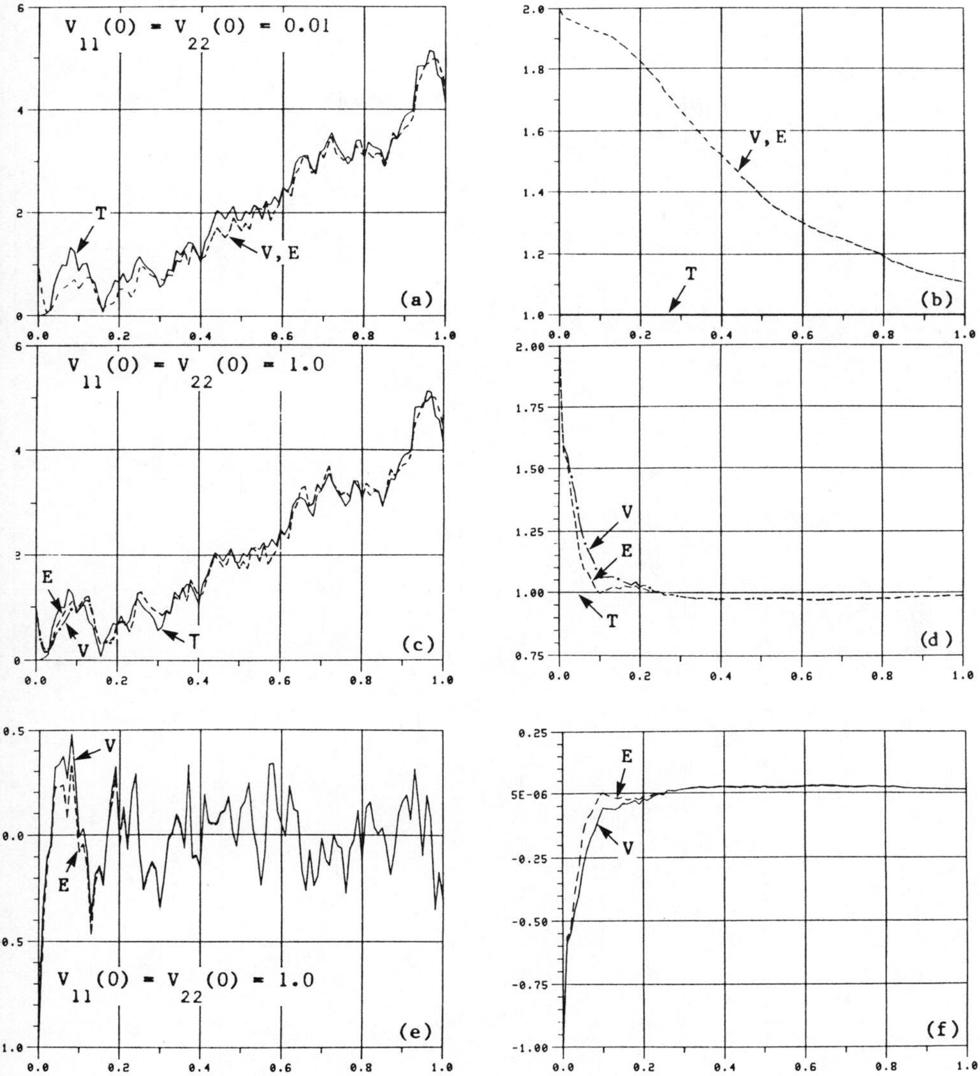

Fig. 28. Discrete case II; effects of V with larger Ψ: $\hat{X}_1(0) = 1.0$; $\hat{X}_2(0) = 2.0$; $X_1(0) = 0$; $X_2(0) = 1.0$; $\Psi_v = \Psi_w = 1.0$. Filter estimates and true X_1 versus time (a,c); filter estimates and true X_2 versus time (b,d); estimator errors for X_1 (e) and X_2 (f). $V_{11}(0) = V_{22}(0) = 0.01$ (a,b) and 1.0 (c,d,e,f).

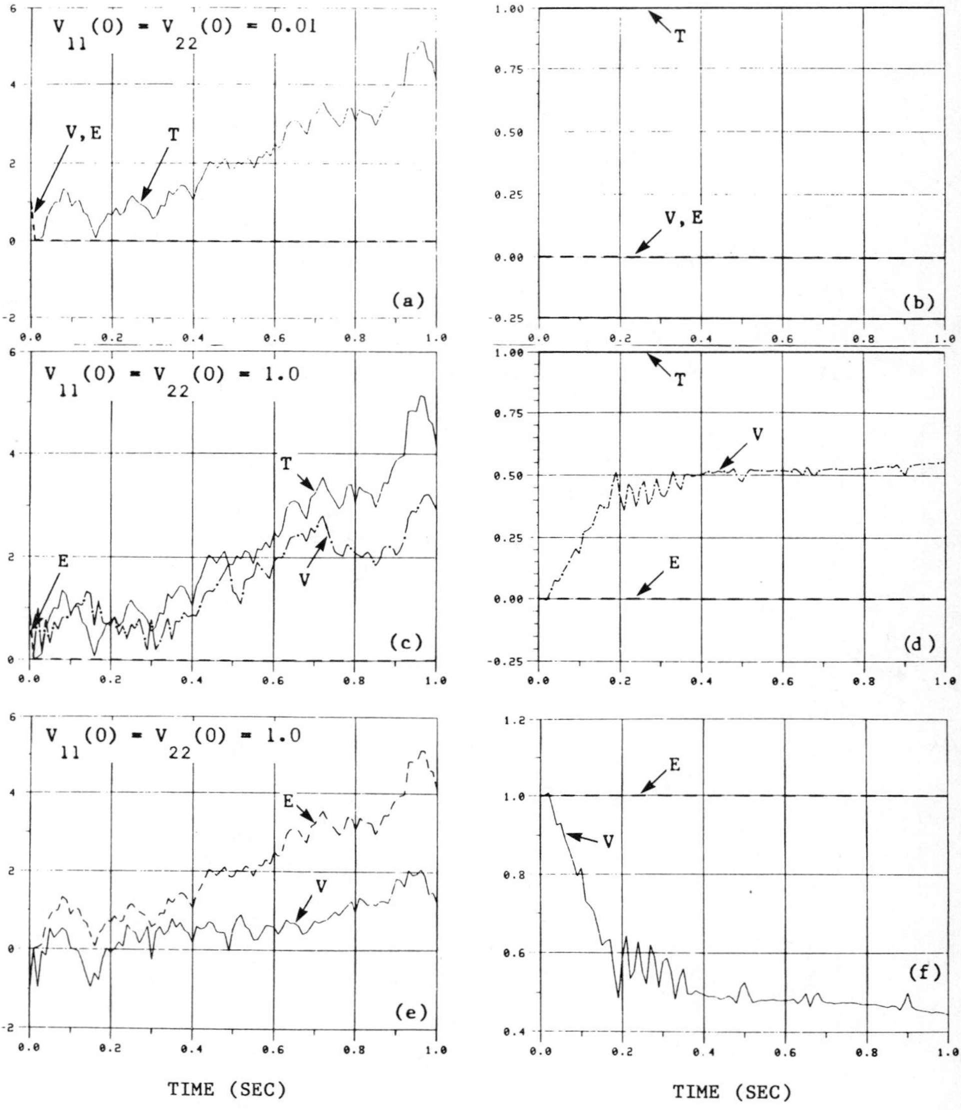

Fig. 29. Discrete case II; effects of V with larger Ψ: $\hat{X}_1(0) = 1.0$; $\hat{X}_2(0) = 0$; $X_1(0) = 0$; $X_2(0) = 1.0$; $\Psi_v = \Psi_w = 1.0$. Filter estimates and true X_1 versus time (a,c); filter estimates and true X_2 versus time (b,d); estimator errors for X_1 (e) and X_2 (f). $V_{11}(0) = V_{22}(0) = 0.01$ (a,b) and 1.0 (c,d,e,f).

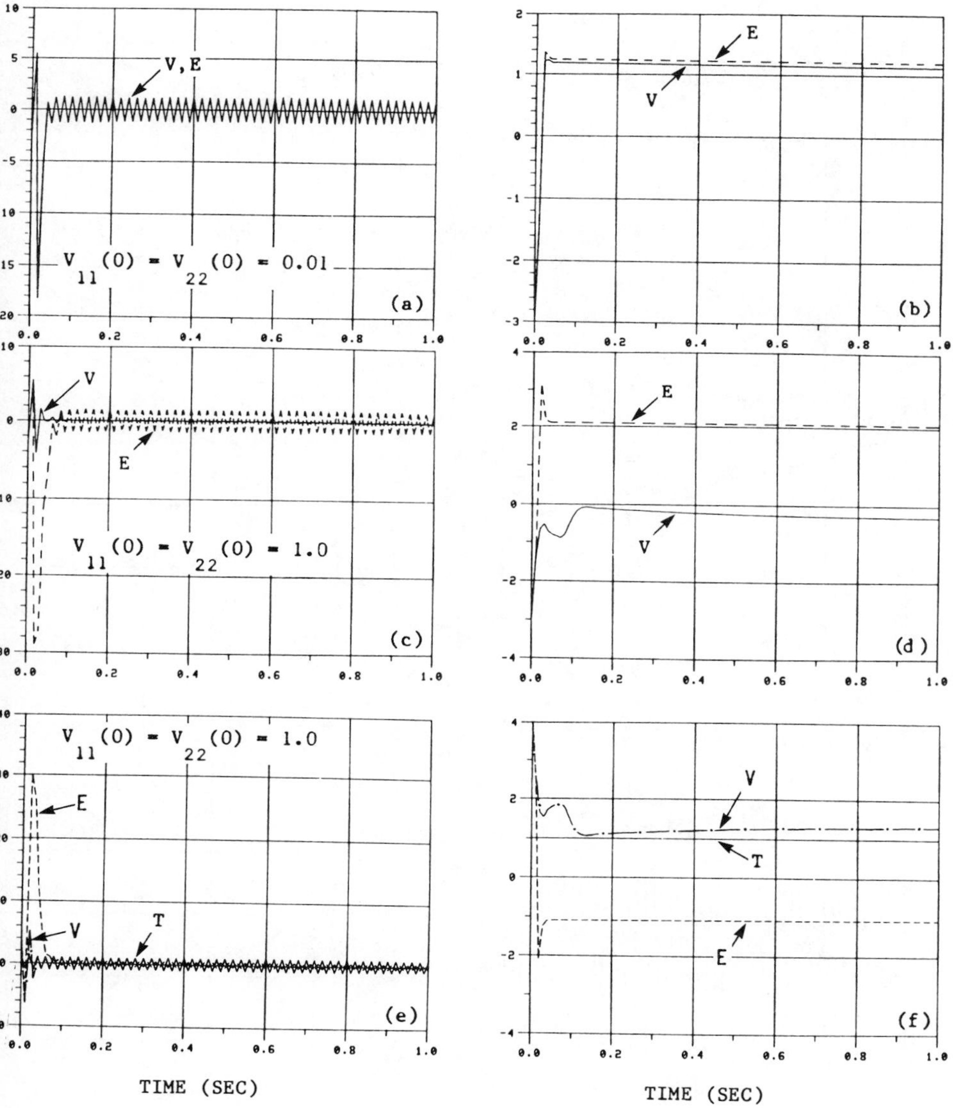

Fig. 30. Discrete case III; effects of V with small Ψ: $\hat{X}_1(0) = \hat{X}_2(0) = 4.0$; $X_1(0) = X_2(0) = 1.0$; $\Psi_v = \Psi_w = 0.01$. Estimator errors for X_1 versus time (a,c); estimator errors for X_2 versus time (b,d); filter estimates and true X_1 (e); filter estimates and true X_2 (f). $V_{11}(0) = V_{22}(0) = 0.01$ (a,b) and 1.0 (c,d,e,f).

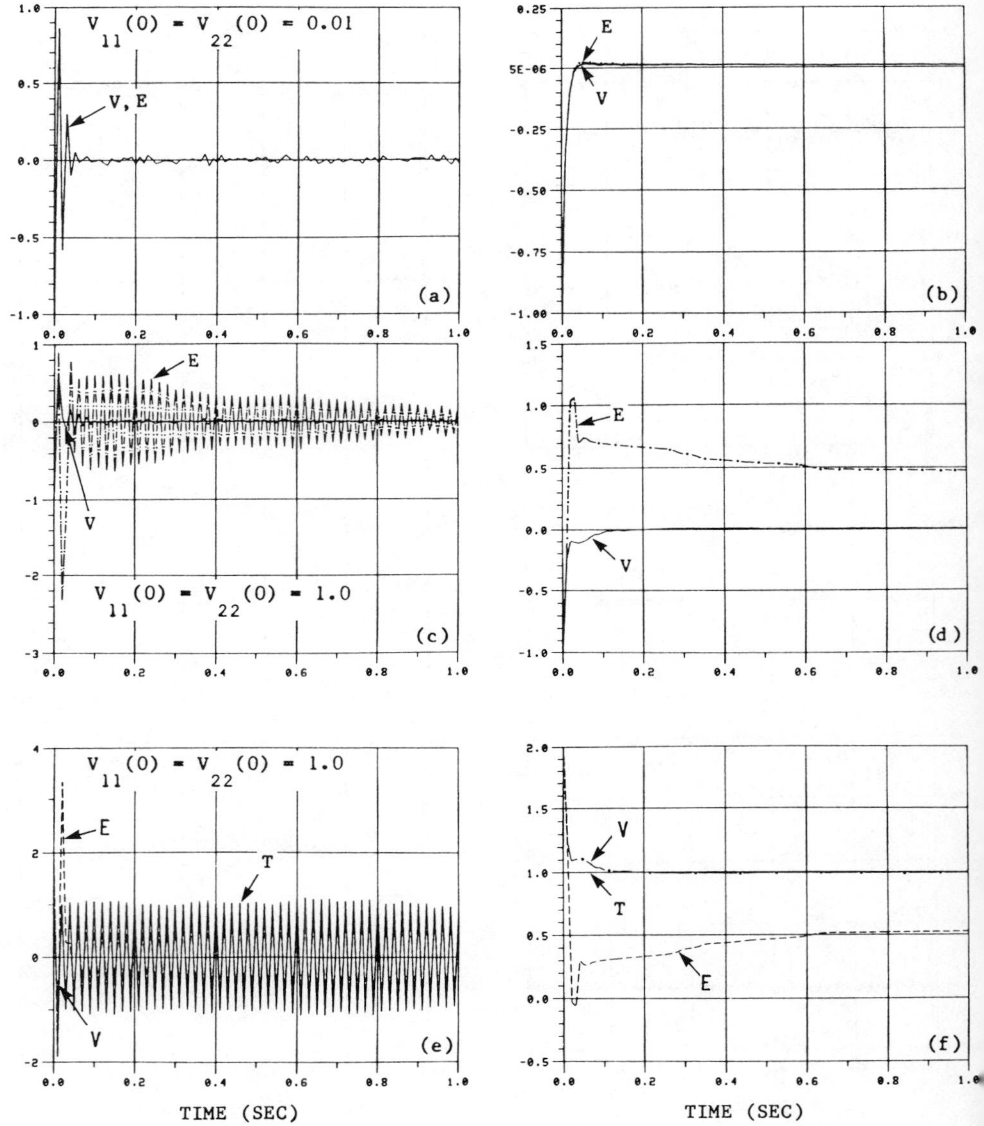

Fig. 31. Discrete case III; effects of V with small Ψ: $\hat{X}_1(0) = \hat{X}_2(0) = 2.0$; $X_1(0) = X_2(0) = 1.0$; $\Psi_v = \Psi_w = 0.01$. Estimator errors for X_1 versus time (a,c); estimator errors for X_2 versus time (b,d); filter estimates and true X_1 (e); filter estimates and true X_2 (f). $V_{11}(0) = V_{22}(0) = 0.01$ (a,b) and 1.0 (c,d,e,f).

IV. CONCLUSIONS

This article has presented a brief summary on the comparisons of dynamic structures for various continuous-time and discrete-time finite-dimensional filters. Extensive simulation results accompanied by discussions were presented to compare the performance behavior of some of these filters.

From the extensive numerical results obtained one can derive several conclusions, some of the most important are stated here.

(1) When the level of noise inputs is large enough to effectively cover the effects of nonlinearities, no particular filter can be said to be consistently superior to any other filter. In most cases, however, the MVF could outperform all other nonlinear filters considered.

(2) When the noise inputs are not "too small" (relative to the effects of nonlinearities), and as long as the a priori estimates are available, the EKF can be expected to perform as well as any other nonlinear filter.

(3) When nonlinear effects are nonnegligible and the a priori estimates are not accurate, the performance of the realizable MVF is far superior to any other filter investigated. It is also much less sensitive to the choice of a priori estimates.

(4) In general, in the design of the EKF for dynamic systems with nonnegligible nonlinearities, the designer should be careful not to select overly optimistic initial error variances; however, in the design of the MVF, the designer should be careful not to select overly pessimistic initial error variances.

It should also be noted that for nonlinear systems with polynomial, product-type, exponential and sinusoidal non-linearities, the derivation and implementation of the MVF would only be slightly more difficult than the EKF or the SLF, etc; however, the MVF could be much more accurate and stable than the other estimators investigated.

ACKNOWLEDGMENTS

This work was carried out with the generous support of the Defence Research Establishment Ottawa, Canada. The author wishes to thank Mr. C. R. Iverson, Chief, DREO for his encouragement. Thanks are also due to Mr. W. Royds for his contributions, especially in his software-programming support. and Miss B. L. Pershaw for her patience in typing the manuscript.

REFERENCES

1. R. E. KALMAN and R. S. BUCY, *J. Basic Engr. 83*, 95-107 (1961).
2. H. J. KUSHNER, *J. Diff. Equations 3*, 179-190 (1967).
3. D. M. DETCHMENDY and R. SRIDHAR, *J. Basic Engr. 88D*, 362-368 (1966).
4. R. W. BASS, V. D. NORUM, and L. SCHWARTZ, *J. Math Anal. Appl. 16*, 152-164 (1966).
5. H. COX, *IEEE Trans. Autom. Control AC-9*, 5-12 (1964).
6. H. J. KUSHNER, *IEEE Trans. Autom. Control AC-5*, 546-556 (1967).
7. M. ATHANS, R. P. WISHNER, and A. BERTOLINI, *IEEE Trans. Autom. Control AC-13*, 504-514 (1968).
8. W. S. WIDNALL, *AIAA J. 11*, 283-287 (1973).
9. L. SCHWARTZ and E. B. STEAR, *IEEE Trans. Autom. Control AC-13*, 83-86 (1968).

10. A. H. JAZWINSKI, "Stochastic Processes and Filtering Theory," Academic Press, New York, 1970.

11. Y. SUNAHARA, *J. Basic Engr. 92D*, 385-393 (1970).

12. J. W. Austin and C. T. Leondes, *IEEE Trans. Aerosp. Electron. Syst. AES-17*, 54-61 (1981).

13. D. F. LIANG and G. S. CHRISTENSEN, *Int. J. Control 23*, 613-625 (1976).

14. D. F. LIANG and G. S. CHRISTENSEN, *Int. J. Control 28*, 1-10 (1978).

15. D. F. LIANG and G. S. CHRISTENSEN, *Automatica 11*, 603-613 (1975).

16. D. F. LIANG, "Exact and Approximate State Estimation Techniques for Nonlinear Dynamic Systems," *in* "Control and Dynamic Systems," Vol. 19 (C. T. Leondes, ed.), Academic Press, New York, 1983.

17. A. RALSTON, "A First Course in Numerical Analysis," McGraw-Hill, New York, 1965.

18. W. E. WAGNER, *J. Spacecr. Rockets 3*, 1321-1327 (1966).

19. R. P. WISHNER, J. A. TABACZYNSKI, and M. ATHANS, *Automatica 5*, 487-496 (1969).

20. H. W. SORENSON, *IEEE Conf. on Decision and Control*, New Orleans, Louisiana 620-625 (1977).

INDEX

H

I

J

K

L

T